ONE YEAR
In
Proverbs

ONE YEAR *In* *Proverbs*

LONNY E. YOUNG

To know wisdom and instruction, to perceive the words of understanding, to receive the instruction of wisdom, justice, judgment, and equity; to give prudence to the simple, to the young man knowledge and discretion.

Proverbs 1:2-4

Library of Congress Control Number:	2019917750

HARDBACK:	978-1-951461-59-1
PAPERBACK:	978-1-951461-58-4
EBOOK:	978-1-951461-60-7

Ordering Information:

For orders and inquiries, please contact:
1-888-404-1388
www.goldtouchpress.com
book.orders@goldtouchpress.com

Printed in the United States of America

PREFACE

"It is not the size of the dog in the fight; it is the size of the fight in the dog." Our pastor quoted that proverb one Sunday morning. Here is my favorite: "It is folly to argue with a fool. Listeners can't tell which is which." I guess you could say these are the "proverbs" of today. You will probably find the same "principles" somewhere in the Bible. Can you think of any?

When I undertook this endeavor I didn't know where it would go. I had read Proverbs several times and was always frustrated that there was no "storyline." It is hard to follow something in this format.

It reminds me of a lot of taking daily vitamins. You may not realize the impact but they are necessary; they are a "daily" regiment to be followed. I hope this daily walk through the book of Proverbs will inspire a closer look at God's word and how it impacts our daily lives, even today.

This is my third book. In this volume, I want to thank the "ladies" who impacted my Christian walk. Encouraged me, supported me and guided me to a deeper relationship with God. In my second book, *David's Walk with God*, in the forward I listed the men who had made a difference in my Christian walk.

I will always be grateful to my wife, Mary, and our two daughters, Tammy and Shannon, for their love, encouragement, and support.

It is my prayer that this and the other books that God has laid on my heart will bless and encourages you to have a more intimate fellowship with God.

100 Questions: You have heard of the S.A.T. and the G.E.D. This is the B.K.T. (Bible Knowledge Test). Take the challenge! If you take it, that is between you and God. Your score is between you and God. What you do with it is between you and God! The answers are in the back of this book. May I share three verses?

All Scripture is given by God, and is profitable for doctrine, for reproof, for correction, for instruction in righteousness, that the man of God may be complete, thoroughly equipped for every good work. (2 Timothy 3:16-17)

Study to show yourself approved of God, a workman who need not be ashamed, rightly dividing the word of truth. (2 Timothy 2:15)

This book of the Law shall not depart from your mouth, but you shall meditate in it day and night, that you may observe to do according to all that is written in it. For then you will make your way prosperous, and then you will have good success. (Joshua 1:8)

All Scripture is taken from the New King James version.

Dedicated to the ladies
who have blessed me through the years:

Judy Anderson

Della Armstrong

Linda Arndt

Judy Bell

Kelcy Beyers

Rachel Boman

Ronnye Jo Bryant

Julie Buckallew

Opal Burrell

Dee Carrender

Elizabeth Coutu

Barbara Dancy

Sandy Dorrel

Doris Drago

Katie Dyer

Karen Favor

Margaret Gardner

Kim Geiger

Evora Glassford

Ruby Green

Patty Haskins

Shirley Henson

Betty Jo Hicks

Katie Hoppenstedt

Audrey Huff

Fontella Jamison

Lacy Jones

Kathy Jungeblut

Cathy Kennon

Kelly McConnell

Brenda McKinley

Claudia Molt

Sue Nichols

Mary O'Toole

Janetta Phillips

Stacy Reeder

Jody Sims

Fran Smith

Dona Starr

Barbara Tomaszewski

Courtney Trussler

Samantha Wade

Joyce Wolfe

Suzie Wolfe

Machele Wyatt

Lona Young

ANSWER SHEET:

1. a b c d	26. a b c d	51. a b c d	76. a b c d
2. a b c d	27. a b c d	52. a b c d	77. a b c d
3. a b c d	28. a b c d	53. a b c d	78. a b c d
4. a b c d	29. a b c d	54. a b c d	79. a b c d
5. a b c d	30. a b c d	55. a b c d	80. a b c d
6. a b c d	31. a b c d	56. a b c d	81. a b c d
7. a b c d	32. a b c d	57. a b c d	82. a b c d
8. a b c d	33. a b c d	58. a b c d	83. a b c d
9. a b c d	34. a b c d	59. a b c d	84. a b c d
10. a b c d	35. a b c d	60. a b c d	85. a b c d
11. a b c d	36. a b c d	61. a b c d	86. a b c d
12. a b c d	37. a b c d	62. a b c d	87. a b c d
13. a b c d	38. a b c d	63. a b c d	88. a b c d
14. a b c d	39. a b c d	64. a b c d	89. a b c d
15. a b c d	40. a b c d	65. a b c d	90. a b c d
16. a b c d	41. a b c d	66. a b c d	91. a b c d
17. a b c d	42. a b c d	67. a b c d	92. a b c d
18. a b c d	43. a b c d	68. a b c d	93. a b c d
19. a b c d	44. a b c d	69. a b c d	94. a b c d
20. a b c d	45. a b c d	70. a b c d	95. a b c d
21. a b c d	46. a b c d	71. a b c d	96. a b c d
22. a b c d	47. a b c d	72. a b c d	97. a b c d
23. a b c d	48. a b c d	73. a b c d	98. a b c d
24. a b c d	49. a b c d	74. a b c d	99. a b c d
25. a b c d	50. a b c d	75. a b c d	100. a b c d

January 1   1-364   Proverbs 1

The proverbs of Solomon the son of David, king of Israel.
(Proverbs 1:1)

For he was wiser than all men—than Ethan the Ezrahite, and Heman, Chaicol, and Darda, the sons of Mahol; and his fame was in all the surrounding nations. He spoke three thousand proverbs, and his songs were one thousand and five. (1 Kings 4:31-32)

Solomon the "wisest man who ever lived" is the title, Solomon, king of Israel is credited within the Bible. Let me share a prayer of Solomon's when he became king:

Therefore, give to Your servant an understanding heart to judge Your people, that I may discern between good and evil. For who is able to judge this great people of Yours?" (1 Kings 3:9)

When you seek for a source to help you arrive at a decision, how much of God's Word is in your heart to help you make the right decision?

Before Solomon began his reign as king, God asked him what God could give him. The verse above was his response. We should pray daily for God's wisdom, God's direction, on this path of life.

Notice what God says in the book of James:

If any of you lacks wisdom, let him ask of God, who gives to all liberally and without reproach, and it will given to him. (James 1:5)

One last thing about Solomon, you might want to read all of Solomon's prayer (1 Kings 3:3-9). Four times in these verses Solomon refers to himself as "servant". Much as his father David did in his prayer in 2 Samuel 7:18-29. In these verses, David referred to himself as "servant" ten times. That is the attitude we should bring to God!

Search with me through this awesome book. Let's find some nuggets of wisdom to incorporate into our daily lives, to make us better "servants" to our God. Let's work on our fellowship with our heavenly Father and our walk with God.

1.   Who was the captain of the Ark?
     a. Job   b. Noah   c. Jonah   d. Lot

> To know wisdom and instruction, to perceive the words of
> understanding. (Proverbs 1:2)

No, we are not going verse by verse through Proverbs. This is a one year walk. We will select twelve or more verses from each chapter and meditate on each and try to discern the Wisdom of Solomon, and God, and how it could impact our lives.

I have been a Sunday School Director in some capacity for over thirty years. I marvel at the dedication and faithfulness of these unsung servants, our teachers, who faithfully teach God's Word every Sunday.

Have you ever read through the Bible? There are great plans to help you read through it in a year. If that seems like a long time, you have never tried it. But, just don't "read" through it, meditate on it, absorb it, incorporate it into your life. You must "receive" the instruction to gain its benefits. Here is a favorite verse of mine:

This book of the Law shall not depart from your mouth, but you shall meditate in it day and night, that you may observe to do according to all that is written in it. For then you will make your way prosperous, and then you will have good success. (Joshua 1:8).

I'm not a big proponent of memorizing verses. I do think we can remember addresses. If you have trouble, in every Bible there are blank pages in the front or back, write down the addresses. I have over a hundred verses underlined or bracketed in my Bible. The wisdom of God!

Why do you suppose God went to so much trouble to provide for us the very Word of God? It is not to store valuable papers, record certain dates, adorn our coffee tables, or collect dust. He meant for us to "search the scriptures" (John 5:39).

The *words of understanding*; what does that mean to you? Did you know that it is practically impossible for a lost person (someone who doesn't know Jesus Christ) to understand the Bible? Once you become a child of God the Holy Spirit will open the Bible in ways you have never known before. You need the help of the Holy Spirit!

> To receive the instruction of wisdom, justice, judgment, and equity. (Proverbs 1:3)

The first few verses of Proverbs pertain to wisdom. So, let's look at a couple more examples; first, in Ecclesiastes, also written by Solomon. In Ecclesiastes, Solomon shares the results of his life-long quest for wisdom. He had the resources to try everything "under the sun." In the beginning, he says, "All is vanity". Now, look at the conclusion he came to...

Let us hear the conclusion of the whole matter: Fear God and keep His commandments, for this is man's all. (Ecclesiastes 12:13).

Remember that Solomon had over six hundred wives. WOW! Right, these same wives drew Solomon away from the God he had prayed to earlier. The wisdom of the head can be deceived by the contents of the heart. The heart that is focused on God will better respond to the things of God.

We have been extolling the virtues of wisdom, let's look at another verse in the New Testament:

But God has chosen the foolish things of the world to put to shame the wise, and God has chosen the weak things of the world to put to shame the things which are mighty. (1 Corinthians 1:27).

While we are here let's look at another companion verse in the same chapter:

For the message of the cross is foolishness to those who are perishing, but to us who are being saved it is the power of God. (1 Corinthians 1:18)

Are you a child of God? If not, these verses will be foolishness; you cannot grasp the power of God's Holy Word apart from a relationship with Jesus Christ.

> The fear of the Lord is the beginning of knowledge, but fools despise wisdom and instruction. (Proverbs 1:7)

The "fear of the Lord" will appear throughout God's Word. Just what does that mean? It DOESN'T mean what we might think it means. You might want to replace the word "reverence" for the word fear. "The reverence of the Lord is the beginning of knowledge". It works better.

The verse says, "It's the beginning of knowledge" don't let that confuse you. God cares a lot about knowledge. The problem comes when "knowledge" comes between us and God. It has been said that most people will miss heaven by eighteen inches: the distance between the head and the heart. Look at this verse:

*If you confess with your mouth the Lord Jesus and believe in your **heart** that God has raised Him from the dead, you will be saved.* (Romans 10:9)

You can be very "knowledgeable" of the facts of Jesus Christ. You may even have seen the "Passion of the Christ," but until the Person of Jesus has come into your heart, all you have is head knowledge, not heart knowledge. This is so important. Pray about it.

Did you notice the Proverbs verse says the "beginning" of knowledge? How much time do you spend in God's Word? How much of the Bible are you familiar with? Let me continue to challenge you to read through the Bible at least once in your life. Whatever schedule you desire but read through it. I am a big proponent of reading each book so that is given in the Bible. Never mind chronological. The same Spirit that put together these sixty-six books also led in the order they appear. Take the challenge; get to know the God of the Bible, both Old, and New Testament!

I think Solomon is clear how he feels about those who disdain the truths of Scripture. We will talk later about this but I also want you to take a trip through Psalm 119. The longest chapter in the Bible is all about the Bible! Look for yourself.

2. In Genesis 1, what day was man created?
    a. 2nd   b. 7th   c. 5th   d. 6th

          Lonny E. Young

> My son, hear the instruction of your father, and do not forsake the law of your mother. (Proverbs 1:8)

This is so contrary to the belief of today's generation, is it not? We must learn for ourselves. Our parents are from another generation, what do they know of my needs? Granted, they are from a different era but most principles are the same.

I distinctly remember one evening in our kitchen when my dad said, "There are three things to remember son: Don't lie, cheat or steal." Simple enough. You don't suppose he got those from the Ten Commandments? My parents never openly talked about God or Jesus. Much later, my mother was baptized and joined a church. This was long after I had left home. My parents did instill in me a "reverence" for the things of God.

My grandmother made a special effort to bring her grandchildren to church on Easter. Later, when I had surrendered to the ministry my grandmother supported me in encouragement and prayer. There are "basics" we can learn from our parents. God made a special point to include this relationship in His Ten Commandments:

Honor your father and your mother, that your days may be long upon the land which the Lord your God is giving you. (Exodus 20:12).

Someone once said that this is the only Commandment with promise. God will bless this relationship with our parents. Granted, in this falling world, there are some bad parents. It doesn't say "like," it says honor, respect. God used them to bring you into this world. God chose them to accomplish His will. Honor that!

Do you remember who Solomon's parents were? David and Bathsheba. Not exactly your perfect parents. In Solomon's household, David had over eight wives. Imagine the confusion. Two of David's sons rebelled against him and threatened to kill him to be king.

In this proverb, Solomon acknowledges both parents. Both contribute to the person we are. You might want to think about God's plan.

> My son, do not walk in the way with them, keep your foot from their path. (Proverbs 1:15)

I love this picture. I have been preaching in my previous two books, THE PATH, and DAVID'S WALK WITH GOD, the concept of a path of life. From the day, we were born God has put us on a path. We see in Jeremiah 29:11-13 that God has a perfect plan for us, a path if you will. I love the words to this verse in Psalms:

You will show me the path of life; in Your presence is fullness of joy; at Your right hand are pleasures forevermore. (Psalm 16:11).

I want you to keep this concept of a path in your thoughts. We are on a journey with God. He is walking right beside you if you are a child of God. Check out Romans 8:14-17.

In the verse in Proverbs, Solomon is warning us about getting off that path; taking our "own" path, that is so dangerous. Our peers, our co-workers, our friends will entice us to follow a different path. If you are on God's path, walking with God He has only the best in mind for you. There are many lessons to learn on this path; lessons that will strengthen our faith and increase God's willingness to use you in miraculous ways. First, you must learn to trust Him.

Solomon is warning those who are tempted to go astray; an interesting concept I have come to recognize. When you do stray from the path of God's choosing you will find out soon that you are out of fellowship with God. He is no longer walking with you. Then you must return to where you left God, return to walking with God, on His path.

It is so clear here from Solomon, "Don't Go There!" You come to many, many forks in this path. You will need to determine what is God's will, what is God's path. It begins with prayer. If you are not a child of God this makes no sense. Read Romans 8:14-17 again. Pay close attention to the relationship you have with your heavenly Father. Are you walking with God? Have you asked Jesus into your heart? If not, it just takes a simple prayer. It will change your life!

> So are the ways of everyone who is greedy for gain; it takes
> away the life of its owner. (Proverbs 1:19)

If you have spent any time in this first chapter you notice that Solomon has a couple of lengthy passages on three subjects: Wisdom and knowledge (1:2-9) and sinners (1: 10-19), - Three subjects to pay close attention to.

Look what David wrote in Psalm 14:

The fool has said in his heart, "there is no God." They are corrupt, they have done abominable works, there is none who does good. (Psalm 14:1).

Did you notice where this decision was made? In the heart! I get the picture from the first several verses in Proverbs that Solomon acknowledges the fact that "wisdom" begins with acknowledging the existence of God. If you are reading the Bible I hope you have come to that conclusion.

Let me share another principle I have noticed in the Bible. There is a difference between a "relationship" with God and "fellowship" with God. Bear with me a minute. A "relationship" occurs when we have asked Jesus into our heart. Then we become children of God. (Romans 8:14-17). That is an unbreakable bond if entered in faithfully! (1 John 5:13)

The next, the "fellowship" is our intimate walk with God our Father. That fellowship can be broken. NOT our relationship, that is permanent, because of Christ's death on the cross; that "adoption" is permanent (Romans 8:15). BUT, we can break our "fellowship" with God by indulging in sin; by disobeying God's direction. Sometimes it is referred to as grieving or quenching the Holy Spirit.

Speaking of the Holy Spirit, that is God's "presence" within us as children of God. A great promise that Jesus gave us in John 15:15-21. When we disobey the prompting of God through His Holy Spirit we break that "fellowship" with God. He essentially takes His hand off our lives and allows us to proceed on our own. That is illustrated in the Garden of Eden. Adam and Eve disobeyed God and were rejected from God's perfect environment. Think about this! Where are you in your relationship to God? - Also illustrated in the Prodigal Son in Luke 15:11-32.

3. How many books are in the Bible?
    a. 27   b. 76   c. 66   d. 39

> Turn at my rebuke; surely, I will pour out my spirit on you; I will make my words known to you. (Proverbs 1: 23)

This always fascinated me. Many believers understand that God's Spirit will call passages of the Bible to our mind when they are needed. Question: How can God call something to our mind that is not ALREADY in our mind? The point being, if the Word is not there, God can't bring it to our mind.

I have encouraged you to read through the Bible at least once. You need to get those words in your mind. It constantly amazes me, when I teach a class, how God will bring certain passages or examples in the Bible to my mind when I need them; because at some point, I have read that passage, especially in the Old Testament. I have come to believe that the "principles" taught in the New Testament are illustrated in the lives of the Old Testament characters. You must read about them to understand that.

Has God ever tried to get your attention? *"Turn at My rebuke"*. That is God getting your attention. When you head down that wrong road, God will warn you. It is up to you to heed that warning. The Holy Spirit can be so powerful in our lives. The problem is He can also be ignored. He won't force us to turn here or there. He may warn us; the response is up to us. OBEDIENCE is the key.

One of my biggest mistakes was trying to get ahead of God. I felt sure I knew God's plan but I couldn't wait. I wanted it now. I paid a dear price. It is that picture of walking with God, again. I wish I could encourage you to grasp this concept. The fellowship with our heavenly Father is so critical to living the kind of life God desires for us. When we ignore God's prompting from His Spirit we are headed for danger.

Storms in our life are great spiritual tools God uses to get us back on track. I love the way Dr. Charles Stanley puts it: Because God is Omniscient (all-knowing) He knows where we are at in the storm. Because God is Omnipresent (everywhere) He is with us in the storm. Because God is Omnipotent (all-powerful) He will bring us through the storm. Our response? - Okay, God what is the lesson for me, in this storm?

> Because you disdained all my counsel, and would have none
> of my rebuke. (Proverbs 1:25)

To continue with what we talked about yesterday.

Look at this verse in Hebrews:

And you have forgotten the exhortation which speaks to you as to sons: "My son, do not despise the chastening of the Lord, nor be discouraged when you are rebuked by Him; for whom the Lord loves He chastens, and scourges every son whom He receives." (Hebrews 12:5-6)

The author of Hebrews is quoting from Proverbs 3:11-12.

I am curious. Are you "blaming" God for a disappointment in your life? God didn't hurt someone, take someone from you, and hurt you in some way? Do you blame God? Is that the response of a child of God? I know you probably never said to your parents "I hate you!" Have you said that to God?

The next time you think God is trying to get your attention, ask Him, "God, what is it you are trying to teach me?" You see God only wants the best for His children. The same as any parent wants for their children. When we take the wrong road, God will try to get our attention and bring us back, out of harm's way. The question is, "Do you know more than God?"

Think about that! When you disobey God, you are saying to Him, "I know better than You what is right," are you not questioning God? You are questioning God's direction for your life. The one who created you, the one who has a perfect plan for your life, why are you questioning His wisdom. The Creator of the universe! - Really?

You disdained my counsel. Now, what counsel would that be? How about your approach to the Bible, the Word of God? Where does God's Word fit into your daily routine? I calculated that in my forty years since I started taking vitamins, I have probably taken 14,600 vitamins. I would be dead if my body didn't assimilate those pills, absorb those nutrients. The same is true with the Word of God! The benefits are amazing!

> When your terror comes like a storm, and your destruction comes like a whirlwind, when distress and anguish come upon you. (Proverbs 1:27)

Do you know what comes to my mind with a verse like this? A foundation, - One of my favorite passages (I will use this phrase a lot) is in 1 Corinthians:

For no other foundation can anyone lay than that which is laid which is Christ Jesus. (1 Corinthians 3:11).

Do you remember earlier, I said that principles taught in the New Testament were illustrated in the Old Testament? Here is a great example. In Genesis 37,

*This is the history of Jacob. Joseph, being **seventeen years old**, was feeding the flock with his brothers.* (Genesis 37:2a).

I hope you are familiar with the story of Joseph, all that he went through.

Now look at this verse:

*Joseph was **thirty years old** when he stood before Pharaoh king of Egypt.* (Genesis 41:46).

Look at all that Joseph went through for thirteen years. Don't you know he questioned God about the circumstances in his life? BUT, Joseph remained faithful to God. Even after the temptation of Potiphar's wife, being wrongly accused and sent to prison. Jacob had built a foundation in Joseph so that when he left home, his brothers tried to kill him, his treatment in Egypt, Joseph remained faithful to God. God rewarded Joseph's faithfulness. The point is the foundation that was laid by Jacob.

I can't go into detail here but think about King David. David was called from the shepherd's field to become God's chosen king of Israel. What kind of "foundation" might Jesse have laid in David's life?

4. What is the name of Adam's wife?
    a. Sarah   b. Mary   c. Eve   d. Tamar

> Then they will call on me, but I will not answer; they will seek
> me diligently, but they will not find me. (Proverbs 1:28)

This word has resounded in my mind. I know that word from somewhere. This time the concordance couldn't help me. I kept searching my memory. GOT IT!

Look at this verse:

*But without faith it is impossible to please Him, for he who comes to God must believe that He is, and that He is a rewarder of those who **diligently** seek Him.* (Hebrews 11:6)

That word "diligently" struck me when I first saw this verse in Hebrews. What definition would you give to diligent? I am thinking of a snapping turtle. My dad always told my brothers and me that once they clamped onto something you had to kill them to get them to let go. That is how we are to seek God!

But look at the verse in Proverbs, *Then, they will call on me, but I will not answer.* When a child of God refuses the counsel of God, at some point, God will no longer hear their pleas.

Look at this verse in Romans:

Therefore, God also gave them up to uncleaness, in the lusts of their hearts, to dishonor their bodies among themselves. (Romans 1:24).

You need to read the whole passage. (Romans 1:24-32). The point is that at some point God will leave us to our sin, and no longer convict us through His Spirit. What about a Christian? No, they will NOT lose their relationship with God. God, in order to preserve His name, will take them home early!

We see in John 15 that Jesus sent the Holy Spirit to convict the world of sin, righteousness, and judgment. The lost person may not realize that God's Spirit is working on them even now; making them curious about the things of God, convicting them of their lifestyle and the sin in their lives. At some point, hopefully, a Christian will come along and share the gospel with them. The work of God's Spirit!

> But whoever listens to me will dwell safely, and will be secure,
> without fear of evil. (Proverbs 1:33)

Do you have that peace, that assurance? If you died right now you would go into the presence of God? I found these verses while working on my last book. Check this out:

For as many as are led by the Spirit of God, these are sons of God. For you did not receive the spirit of bondage again to fear, but you received the Spirit of adoption by whom we cry out, "Abba, Father." The Spirit Himself bears witness with our spirit that we are children of God, and if children, then heirs—heirs of God and joint heirs with Christ, if indeed we suffer with Him, that we may also be glorified together. (Romans 8:14-17).

Do you see the relationship? We are "children" of God. The peace and assurance that comes when we recognize that fact when we have opened our heart and received Jesus Christ as our Savior is amazing!

Did you catch the first part? *Whoever listens to Me!* I mentioned yesterday that the Holy Spirit is working on the lost all the time. That is why it is so important to be praying before and during the witnessing encounter. If God's Spirit is not working in the experience, and the lost person, you won't get very far.

Many times, I have heard this discussion about what verses to use, how to approach a lost person. What do you say? I have one problem with quoting the Bible right off. The lost person has no respect or confidence in the Bible. They will say, "I don't believe the Bible." Then what do you do? The most powerful tool a Christian has is their testimony! What God has done in their lives? How God has changed their lives and turned them around. How God has blessed them daily, etc.

The greatest communication between God and us today is the Bible. But you must be a child of God to fully understand God's message in these sixty-six books. In a sense, you need to know God to understand the letter that He has given us. This letter tells us all we need to know about God and what God desires of us. From Genesis to Revelation!

        Lonny E. Young

> My son. if you receive my words, and treasure my commands within you, so that you incline your ear to wisdom, and apply your heart to understanding. (Proverbs 2:1-2)

Did you catch the most frustrating word in the English language? IF. Basically, it falls on you. There are always options. You can listen to your parents, but you don't have to obey. You can know the "laws" of the land, but you don't need to obey them. You can know what is right and true, but you don't have to follow them. It is all a choice.

I truly believe that is why God put that extra tree in the Garden of Eden. Man will always be confronted with choices, all the way back to the beginning. Many time's the "choices" we make will have little or no consequences. BUT! Sometimes those choices will have "eternal" consequences! Like where you will spend eternity.

In this verse, it is interesting to figure out who is speaking to whom. As a Christian, we need to think of it as God speaking to us. That may not have been Solomon's intention. Anyway, the command is still the same.

God gave us the Bible as another option. He provided us with truth, His truth, and His "options". He even gave us some Old Testament examples of those who obeyed and those who didn't. Again, it's our choice.

Did you notice that God mentions the "ear" and the "heart"; I looked again, no mention of the mind? Isn't that where our decisions are made? How about this advice, "follow your heart."? Have you heard that? God knows what motivates us, what guides us, it's the heart.
Your partner for life is determined by your heart, not your head!

Fellowship is of the heart; those who you feel comfortable around, a close bond with. The fellowship of God is the same way. Do you feel comfortable chatting with the God of the Universe? Do you have that "fellowship" with God? If you are a child of God you can have that fellowship. I love the term in Romans 8:15, "Abba, Father". I heard it is interpreted "Daddy". Can you image calling God "daddy"? To have that kind of fellowship with the Creator is an awesome thing. That is what the Bible says we have when we become children of God (Romans 8:14-17). Are you a child of God? Why not?

5. To what city was Jonah sent to by God?
    a. Jericho   b. Sodom   c. Jerusalem   d. Ninevah

> For the Lord gives wisdom; from His mouth come knowledge and understanding. (Proverbs 2:6)

So, how do we get this wisdom, knowledge, and understanding from the Lord? Let me offer two sources, both from the Bible. First, you might want to begin with the Sermon on the Mount, the words of Jesus. Matthew chapters 5-7, one hundred and eleven verses of wisdom from God!

For me, let me especially emphasize chapter 6. Jesus tells us three things, that if we do them in secret God promises to reward us openly. Check it out.

Next, the gospel of John; First, you need to meditate seriously on verses one and two of chapter one; then move down to verse fourteen to answer this riddle, - very powerful. It concerns the source of this wisdom. Next, John 13 through 18; these chapters take place in the Upper Room, just before Jesus is to go to the cross. His last opportunity to impact His disciples! The last words are always powerful! There is a lot to take in here!

I think every Bible today has the words of Jesus in red. Why should you pay special attention to these? Understand these are the words of God Himself; think about it for a minute.

In the Old Testament, we have this picture of God "judging" Israel. God is always trying to get Israel focused on Him, not on idols. It was a constant battle, even to the point of removing Israel from their land. He removed the northern ten tribes permanently, using Assyria. The southern tribes went into exile in Babylon and returned later.

Now think about the New Testament; understand this is the same God. God takes on the mantle of humanity and visits His creation, not a message of judgment that will come in the time of the Revelation. No, He visits to show us the intimate, loving, caring, passionate, compassionate side of God; never confuse the two! THEY ARE BOTH THE SAME GOD! God simply takes a different approach. In the Old Testament, His focus was on Israel; in the New Testament God comes to the whole world with one message! Believe on the Lord Jesus Christ and you will be saved!

He guards the paths of justice, and preserves the way of His
saints. (Proverbs 2:8)

This principle has fascinated me for a long time; the concept of a path. When I
was a child, my brothers and I were in the woods walking along this very narrow
path, along a creek. We had to walk single file, it was that narrow. I can picture
our Christian walk much like this path.

There are always forks in this path. You're in the woods so you can't know what is
ahead, no matter the fork you take. You need a guide; someone who knows what is
up ahead, someone to keep you on the right path. Enter God, through the person
of the Holy Spirit!

Don't miss the nuance of the verse above. He "guards" the path of justice. God is
always ready to protect His children. Not in the sense of "protecting" us from harm
but giving us guidance. Just because we are on this path doesn't mean nothing will
happen to us. But it does mean that God is right there to pick us up, encourage us,
and then put us back on track.

He preserves the way of His saints. Isn't it encouraging that God refers to us, children
of God, as saints? We have lifted that title to mean more than it really means in the
Bible. A "saint" is simply a child of God. A servant if you will.

When I became aware of this concept of a "path," I found this verse in the Psalms:

*You will show me the path of life; In Your presence is fullness of joy; at Your right hand
are pleasures forevermore.* (Psalm 16:11)

Did you catch the proximity of God? "At Your right hand" that is where it is the
safest! That is where we need to be on this walk with God. Oh, don't overlook that
word "walk" either, it is used throughout the Bible in reference to "walking with
God." The concept is all through the Bible, look at each of the individuals from
Genesis to Revelation; they are pictured or described in relation to their "walk"
with God.

> Then you will understand righteousness and justice, equity and every good path. (Proverbs 2:9)

This path we talked about yesterday is a learning process. We see that in the verse above, "understand" is the keyword. The more we concentrate on walking with God on this path of life, the more we can understand God's plan for our life. This means we must spend as much time as possible in the Word of God; that is God's communication with us, along with the Holy Spirit.

When we learn the heart of God, through reading His Word, the easier it is to follow Him and trust His leading in our life. After our former pastor led my wife and me to the Lord, as soon as he left, I went and opened my Bible. It opened a whole new world for me. I understood what God was trying to tell me. I am still learning and growing closer to God after forty years of studying.

The more we understand God's heart, how He feels about us, our fellowship with Him increases, our joy increases. The thing that excites me the most is being able to see God work all around me. As a child of God, I can now recognize His working in the world around me. I look forward every day to seeing what God is going to do today!

Let me give you some precious words in Proverbs that have helped me:

Trust in the Lord with all your heart, and lean not on your own understanding; in all your ways acknowledge Him, and He shall direct your path. (Proverbs 3:5-6)

There is that word "path" again. There is so much in these two verses. Write them down, meditate on them, and absorb them into your mind and heart. They are the key to walking with God.

I hope you will stay with me this year, as we walk through the book of Proverbs. I have just finished a study on David, the trip was amazing. Let's see what we can learn from Solomon and the wisdom God gave him. Like the vitamin analogy I used earlier, we can take a "daily dose" of God's wisdom that will help us stay on track, on this path of life that God has laid out before us.

6.   What is the name of the last book in the Old Testament?
     a. Malachi   b. Nahum   c. Haggai   d. James

> When wisdom enters your heart, and knowledge is pleasant
> to your soul, discretion will preserve you; understanding will
> keep you. (Proverbs 2:10-11)

I thought wisdom was in our knowledge. Isn't it interesting how much Solomon focuses on the heart? Of course, the heart is where our salvation begins:

*If you confess with your mouth the Lord Jesus and believe in your **heart** that God has raised Him from the dead, you will be saved. For with the **heart** one believes unto righteousness, and with the mouth confession is made unto salvation.* (Romans 10:9-10)

How would you describe "righteousness"? I have heard that righteousness is "right-living". By accepting Christ as our Savior, we have "imputed" righteousness; that is the righteousness of Jesus Christ is transferred to us. When we stand before God, our Creator does not see our sin but the righteousness of His Son Jesus. What an awesome picture to understand!

You see, in the verse in Proverbs Solomon, throughout the Proverbs, keeps referring to "understanding". What is our understanding of God's desire and plan for our life? The more we study God's Word, understand His reason for creating us in the first place, the better our whole outlook on life will be.

A great way to achieve this "understanding" is to study the individuals in the Old Testament. I just finished a study of David. I wanted to know why God referred to David as, "A man after God's own heart" (1 Samuel 13:14 and Acts 13:22). If David is an illustration of a man after God's heart, by studying David we may get a glimpse into God's heart.

I did a "word search" on the word heart. I put an asterisk in front of the word heart. It was amazing how many different descriptions of the heart are in the Bible. Throughout the Proverbs, Solomon will refer to the heart. Isn't it interesting that it was his heart that betrayed him, as king of Israel, with six hundred wives, who led him away from God? (1 Kings 11:3)

From those who leave the paths of uprightness to walk in the ways of darkness. (Proverbs 2:13)

If this was not so important, why would Solomon spend so much time on the subject of walking a path? Here Solomon uses the term uprightness, - uprightness, righteousness, it simply means doing the right thing. Now we ask how we know the right thing. Simple, - read God's Word; walk with me through this marvelous book.

Proverbs is unique to any other book in the Bible. The other books speak in "paragraphs", in thoughts. Proverbs is so hard to read that way, granted in the first chapter there are a couple of paragraphs, others throughout the book. For the most part, it consists of individual verses with a pro/con approach to a subject; do this, don't do that, approach.

I used the picture earlier of taking vitamins. One simple little pill each day is supposed to help keep us healthy. The Proverbs are our "spiritual" vitamins. Nutrients that will help keep us on this path and walking toward the ultimate goal that God has for our life. But, just like vitamins, it must be a daily routine.

Have you thought about something pertaining to "walk"? It is an "action" word. You can't walk standing still or sitting. You must be in motion.

Look at this verse:

But those who wait on the Lord shall renew their strength; they shall mount up with wings like eagles, they shall run and not be weary, they shall walk and not faint. (Isaiah 40:31)

Do you see sitting or standing in this verse? So, if we are "waiting" on God why should we keep moving? You're on a path, remember? You are headed somewhere. God has never intended for us to be idle!

Look at Genesis:

*Then the Lord God took the man and put him in the garden of Eden **to tend and keep** it.* (Genesis 2:15)

> Who rejoice in doing evil, and delight in the perversity of the wicked; those ways are crooked, and who are devious in their paths. (Proverbs 2:14-15)

There is that word "path" again. What path are you on? Are you where God wants you to be? Just ignore God, He won't care. You can't see or touch Him. He isn't in control of your life! I have my desires, my plans, I don't need God! Famous last words!
You can't fool God. You can wear your crosses, pray, walk the aisle in church, etc.

Look at this verse:

*But the Lord said to Samuel, "Do not look at his appearance or at his physical stature, because I have refused him (Eliab). **For the Lord does not see as man sees; for man looks at the outward appearance, but the Lord looks at the heart."** (1 Samuel 16:7).*

In God's calling of David to follow Him and eventually to become king of Israel, God saw something in David's heart that got God's attention. How about you? How is your relationship with God? Are you a child of God? How about your fellowship with God if you are saved?
Solomon is pointing out, in this verse in Proverbs that we can do all the "right" things but our hearts can be wicked! God knows. We are not fooling Him. We may have those around us fooled but God looks at the heart. Does He see darkness or light?

The heart is so critical throughout the Bible. I mentioned that I did a word search once. In the King James Version, I found the following numbers: The most used prefix is "your" (35) times. Next, is "whole" (13) times. #3 is "mans" (10) times. I must include the fourth most used prefix to the word "heart", that is "perfect" (9) times. - Interesting.

God is very much concerned with "your" heart. Take some time here, early in this New Year, examine your heart and your relationship with God. Where does He fit on your priority list? Oh, I ought to mention that another heart is mentioned 6 times. Solomon touches on it above, the word is "evil". How about a check-up here!

7.   On what mountain did Moses receive the Ten Commandments?
      a. Mt. Tabor   b. Mt. Sinai   c. Mt. Carmel   d. Mt of Olives

> To deliver you from the immoral woman, from the seductress
> who flatters with her words, who forsakes the companion
> of her youth, and forgets the covenant of her God.
> (Proverbs 2:16-17)

I don't think I have to go into detail about immoral women. You're not stupid. What is important, are the tricks the devil likes to play on us. Do you remember his first lie?

"For God knows that in the day you eat of it your eyes will be opened, and you will be like God, knowing good and evil." (Genesis 3:5)

Isn't that the lie today? We will be like God. Satan had the nerve to try that with God Himself in Isaiah 14. (14:12-15). He was going to take God's throne. If you want a refresher look at Job chapter one; Satan can do NOTHING but what God allows him.

Who does the delivering? God of course! But how does He do that? He reaches down and yanks us by our shirt collar out of harm's way? Not hardly. Wouldn't it be nice if He did? If you're a child of God you have the Holy Spirit within you to warn you. If you are not His child, God helps you.

I found some interesting verses in my study of David. I think these verses will work here. Two sets of four words that may shed some light here:

And the woman conceived; so, she sent and told David, and said, ***I am with child."***
(2 Samuel 11:5)

We know this was Bathsheba, after David had summoned her from her home. The power of the king! An innocent woman; now look at these four words:

Then Nathan said to David, ***"You are the man."*** *Thus, says the Lord God of Israel.*
(2 Samuel 12:7)

This, after at least nine months; caught and confronted! Guilty!

> For her house leads down to death, and her paths to the dead; none who go to her return, nor do they regain the paths of life. (Proverbs 2:18-19)

Have you noticed in these last few verses that Solomon refers to them as "paths" plural? There are always choices! Even Adam and Eve had a choice in the Garden of Eden. Listen to the counsel of a serpent or the Word of God. Don't miss the tactic Satan used, a "half-truth". (Genesis 3:4-5)

How do you discern the right choice, the right "path" to follow? Again, there are two options, besides listening to the devil. First, you can know God's will by reading His Word. The more time you spend there the less opportunity to take the wrong path; second, the prompting of God's Spirit. That is assuming you are a child of God. If you're lost you do not have the option of the Holy Spirit. For the most part, if you are lost, you will not glean much from the Bible either.

If you're lost you are not on God's path anyway. There are many paths in life. Look what Jesus says:

"Enter by the narrow gate; for wide is the gate and broad is the way that leads to destruction, and there are many who go by it. Because narrow is the gate and difficult is the way which leads to life and there are few who find it. (Matthew 7:13-14).

This passage is in the Sermon on the Mount, I mentioned it earlier. Matthew 5-7 must-read Scripture! You get the picture. What is implied is that it is your choice which road you take. Don't miss the picture. The path with God, walking in His will, is not an easy path. God has much to teach you along the way. Always be assured that God is right there with you, encouraging, lifting you, pushing you to be the best child of God you can be.

Solomon is using the illustration of a woman but the results are the same. The devil will use any means to drag you down, to trip you up, to draw you away from God. He has a wide assortment of tricks in his bag. You need the guidance of God's Spirit to avoid these pitfalls!

> So, you may walk in the way of goodness, and keep to the
> paths of righteousness. (Proverbs 2:20)

Let me clarify something about "righteousness". There is no way you will attain righteousness. The Bible says, "All our righteousness is as filthy rags." (Isaiah 64:6) There is nothing we can do to obtain an audience with All Mighty God! One of the most profound illustrations to open my eyes is found in Exodus:

*Now the blood shall be a sign for you on the houses where you are. And **when I see the blood, I will pass over you**; and the plague shall not be on you to destroy you when I strike the land.* (Exodus 12:13).

That is the only "righteousness" we can claim as a child of God; the righteousness in the blood of Jesus Christ who died on the cross of Calvary for our sins. Only this blood allows us entrance into the presence of God.

The interesting thing to me about this passage in Exodus is if an Egyptian believed these words and put the blood on his doorposts and lintel he would have been spared! If a Jew refused to apply the blood he would have died. It is the application, by faith, of the blood that leads to salvation!

For a long time, I just accepted that Jesus had to die for my sins. I didn't grasp the message until I understood this passage in Exodus. It finally made it all clear. When I stand before God in the judgment I will have "applied" the righteousness of Christ through His shed blood on the cross!

So, you may walk. Again, this walking toward a destination; the destination is heaven of course. For me, I have one desire when I stand before God. It is found in Matthew:

His Lord said to him, "Well done, good and faithful servant; you were faithful over a few things, I will make you ruler over many things. Enter into the joy of your Lord. (Matthew 25:21).

8. What are the first four books of the New Testament called?
    a. Pentateuch   b. Biographies   c. Epistles   d. Gospels

For the upright will dwell in the land, and the blameless remain in it. (Proverbs 2:21)

A little history lesson, I guess. The thing that fascinated me the most about this "Promised Land" thing is this: Israel had a "readymade" environment just waiting for them to take possession; much like the Garden of Eden. They didn't have to plant vineyards, build houses or cities, or plant crops. Everything was there for the taking. God provided above and beyond their wildest dreams.

God demonstrated His power first with crossing the Jordan, then with the defeat of Jericho. YET, they refused to obey God. Beginning with Ai, they failed to listen to God. God eventually gave them the land. Do you remember Joshua's parting words to Israel?

And if it seems evil to you to serve the Lord, ***choose for yourselves this day whom you will serve,*** *whether the gods which your fathers served that were on the other side of the River, or the gods of the Amorites, in whose land you dwell.* ***But as for me and my house, we will serve the Lord.*** (Joshua 24:15)

Choices! We talked about that before. Joshua gave them options. How quickly they forgot all that God had given them. Do you know what book follows Joshua? - The book of Judges. If you want to get depressed read Judges. The same cycle, over and over. Into bondage—pray for deliverance—a deliverer is sent—then back into bondage and the process continues. Much like we are today.

God will bless us, provide for our needs and soon we turn our backs on God, we even blame God when something goes wrong, much like Israel did. God simply asks for "consistent faith", not here today, gone tomorrow; with faith comes obedience. We believe God and obey Him because our faith says God is always there, good or bad, to walk through this storm with us. A good question we might ask is: What is the lesson God is trying to teach me through this experience? Think about that one a minute!

How is your walk with God so far, this year?

But the wicked will be cut off from the earth, and the unfaithful will be uprooted from it. (Proverbs 2:22)

How are things going? I know you noticed that this verse is the opposite of the verse we saw yesterday. I gave you the negative yesterday, today I want to think about some positives; beginning with this principle in 1 Corinthians:

For no other foundation can anyone lay than that which is laid, which is Jesus Christ. (1 Corinthians 3:11)

You can't be "uprooted" if you have a firm foundation. Israel never learned this in the Promised Land. They kept looking to themselves, what they wanted, what they were lacking, etc.

Let me encourage you to spend some quality time in 1 Corinthians 3. There is some great stuff there.

Look at verse 6:

I planted, Apollos watered, but God gave the increase! (1 Corinthians 3:6)

We are put here as stewards of what God has blessed us with; nothing is ours, it all belongs to God. Paul is telling the church at Corinth that whatever fruit is obtained is the work of many people, each passing on to the next, till God gives the increase. We each have a role to play, - a purpose! Has God lain on your heart to do something? Are you doing it?

It is early in the year, January is almost over. What have you done for God this New Year? Did you plant some seed last year but haven't seen a crop? Remember the verse above. I knew a fellow once who was disappointed in his ministry because he wasn't seeing the fruit he expected. He doesn't produce, God does. He is simply called to plant, water, or whatever, it is God who gives the increase. The neat thing is we may never see the fruit. Just keep planting and watering!

Take note of the contrast in these two verses (21-22). Many of the verses Solomon includes in his Proverbs use this approach; plus/minus. The question is, which are you?

Lonny E. Young

> My son, do not forget my law, but let your heart keep my
> commands; for length of days and long life and peace they
> will add to you. (Proverbs 3:1-2)

What a guarantee from God! Is that what you think He means? If you keep all God's commands, He will give you a long life? When you were conceived in the womb, God had a plan for your life. If He meant for you to die at thirty-two, you will die at thirty-two. Your actions will not deter His plans.

There is an interesting promise here though; it is that "peace" part. How long do we struggle to look for peace? If we just had this. . . If we just had that . . . really? Things and people will not bring us peace, as much as we would like that.

I have said this before as well as others when God created us, He created us with a piece missing, - that piece is God! We can spend our whole life trying to fill that void. Take a minute and read Ecclesiastes. Solomon had all of God's resources at his disposal. He tried, in his words, "everything under the sun." And his conclusion:

Let us hear the conclusion of the whole matter: Fear God and keep His commandments, for this is man's all. (Ecclesiastes 12:13)

This is the same man who wrote over three thousand proverbs.

Look at these words:

And God gave Solomon wisdom and exceedingly great understanding and largeness of heart like the sand of the seashore. Thus, Solomon's wisdom excelled the wisdom of all the men of the East and all the wisdom of Egypt. (1 Kings 4:29-30)

I refer you back to 12:13. The lesson at the end of his quest, fear God! We can look at all the promises of a long life in the verse in Proverbs. If God is not part of that life it is empty. So many people don't realize that until most of their life is used up. The sooner you connect with God, the greater your quality of life. - Length? That is up to God!

9.   What was the Apostle Paul's name before it was changed?
     a. Saul   b. Naman   c. Tarsus   d. Stephen

> Let not mercy and truth forsake you; bind them around your neck, write them on the tablet of your heart, and so find favor and high esteem in the sight of God and man. (Proverbs 3:3-4)

Another reference to the heart; in both passages, it is the heart God is dealing with, isn't it?

Here is some homework: In all of Paul's letters he begins, in salutation, pretty much the same way:

Grace *to you and* **peace** *from God the Father and our Lord Jesus Christ.* (Galatians 1:3)

He uses pretty much the same greeting. Paul also wrote what is known as the "pastoral epistles" (1 & 2 Timothy, Titus). These books are written primarily to pastors, by way of Timothy. Notice the addition of a word in his greetings in these three books.

Mercy and truth, - an interesting combination; things that seem to be lacking in our culture today, maybe you could include trust with mercy. We are missing a lot of traits God has given us as children of God. The world has seemed to have drowned them out.

"The tablet of your heart" Solomon uses an interesting term here, doesn't he? I wonder if we are to write them in pencil so they could be erased. If that were true, I wonder if our names written in "Lambs Book of Life" (Revelation 17:8) would be in pencil as well. Not hardly! Once we are entered into God's Book it is permanent (Romans 8:15-16). We are adopted into God's family!

Mercy and truth, - both traits are held in high regard by God (Proverbs 3:3); I wonder what God is thinking about "truth" today? It seems to be a lost art, a lost concept.

I wonder what Solomon means by *"write them on the tablet of your heart."* Does he mean the words themselves or the concept and practice of these words? Do we just "honor" the words or practice the meaning of the words? It is easy to write the "words" but quite another to practice the use of the words. Truth? Mercy? What do these words mean to you? Are they written on your heart?

                Lonny E. Young

> Trust in the Lord with all your heart, and lean not on your
> own understanding; in all your ways acknowledge Him, and
> He will direct your paths. (Proverbs 3:5-6)

If you ever committed any Scripture to memory these are the ones. I am sure you have noticed in the verses and chapters we have covered that Proverbs is a book of "contrasts", dos and don'ts right and wrong, etc. Life is made up of choices! When you have those dilemmas in your life bring this verse to your mind. There is so much wisdom in these two verses.

Let me draw your attention to the last few words: *He will direct your paths.* Isn't that what we have been talking about? The paths in life that we CHOOSE to walk; make no mistake it is all about choices.

Here, Solomon says that God will direct our paths; IF we let Him. Then it reverts to the beginning of these verses, "Trust" in the Lord. You will not follow someone you don't trust. What has God done in your life so far? Can you list them? I don't know where you are in your Christian walk. I don't know if you're a Christian. That must be the first step.

If you're not a child of God these verses are meaningless. The promise is to His children, even as children we tend to be rebellious, defiant, and self-righteous. God cannot use someone in rebellion. Don't miss these words: *In all your ways acknowledge Him.* Until you are willing to trust God and do it His way, you will wander down paths you wish you hadn't!

I could dissect these verses for days. Look at these words: *Lean not on your own understanding.* God will lead us down a path that just seems wrong. You question God; you want to back-track, you, of course, know better than God. Trust these words. Many times God will test our faith, our obedience by putting things in a path we don't understand; you must trust His plan, His wisdom, He is teaching you something you will need on your journey.

Again, by using the word "paths" we have the picture of a journey. Are you walking with God? Have you rebelled against God's plan, God's path? Think about it! Meditate on these two verses!

> Do not be wise in your own eyes; fear the Lord and depart from evil. It will be health to your flesh, and strength to your bones. (Proverbs 3:7-8)

Do you know what is going to happen on Tuesday of next week? How about on May 16th of this year? Of course, you don't. God does. Isn't it foolish to question the direction that God is leading you? We touched on this yesterday. The closer we follow God and His direction, the more blessed we will be.

Of course, God will not traffic with evil. He will not walk the same path with evil. When you flirt with the things that turn God away, you are flirting with disaster! If you are a child of God, you have the Holy Spirit to warn you, heed the warning. If you are not a child of God, you only have your conscience, which we seldom listen to anyway.

These first few words always remind me of people who put God in a box. What does that mean? It means that God cannot do anything we cannot conceive of in our minds. God is "restricted" by our faith. We cannot trust God to do anything that we cannot comprehend. When it comes to measuring faith, I love this verse in Matthew:

Then He touched their eyes, saying, **according to your faith let it be to you.** (Matthew 9:29).

The "amount" of our faith will determine how much God can work in our lives; how much we are willing to trust Him. Of course, with these verses I must quote this verse in Hebrews:

But without faith it is impossible to please Him, for he who comes to God must believe that He is, and that He is a rewarder of those who diligently seek Him. (Hebrews 11:6).

Don't miss that critical word "diligently", it is paramount that we continually seek God's plan and purpose for our life. The path He has chosen for us to travel. Don't try to figure it out, just trust Him and His wisdom, not yours!

10. Name the book that follows the Gospels.
  a. Romans   b. Joshua   c. Acts   d. Judges

> Honor the Lord with your possessions, and with the first fruits
> of all your increase; so, your barns will be filled with plenty,
> and your vats will overflow with new wine. (Proverbs 3:9-10)

Are your vats overflowing with new wine? Now, what do you suppose Solomon is talking about? How are you doing this month? Has God blessed you in any way? I want to challenge you to write those blessings in a journal of some kind. It will help to remind where your blessings come from, and most importantly, to be on the lookout for them.

Honor the Lord with your possessions. You do realize that you own "nothing"? Everything belongs to God. You are simply the "custodian" or steward of all that God blesses you with. I hope you are a faithful steward. Now, how do you suppose we honor God with our "first fruits"? You know where I am going!

*"Bring all the tithes into the storehouse, that there may be food in My house, **and try Me now in this**", says the Lord of hosts, "If I will not open for you the windows of heaven and pour out for you such blessing that there will not be room enough to receive it."* (Malachi 3:10)

Do you want to prove God wrong? Prove His Word is not true? Take His challenge. I like how Dr. Stanley puts it, "If you can count to ten you can tithe!"

But I don't trust the church; I don't think they will handle it right. Let me be clear, do you see the "church" mentioned anywhere here? When you "tithe" you are giving the money to God NOT the church. You are being obedient to this challenge from God.

Keep a journal, write it down; one thing I would ask, don't measure your blessings in dollars and cents. God can bless in too many other ways, - peace, direction, guidance, bigger barns, etc. You see that picture in the verses in Proverbs; the blessing is in material goods. Never measure God with money!

Remember the first words in verse 5, *"trust in the Lord"* try it!

> My son, do not despise the chastening of the Lord, nor detest
> His correction; for whom the Lord loves He corrects, just as a
> father the son in whom he delights. (Proverbs 3:11-12)

Have you ever been spanked? Of course, it is "politically incorrect" today; the child calls 9-1-1.

I remember when I was spanked; my mother had me place my hands on the top of our dryer and there she spanked me, but "what for"? I was fighting with my brothers; I was the eldest so I was responsible!

The author of Hebrews quotes this verse in Hebrews 12:5-6. A biblical principle is so important for today! Have you had a "spanking" from the Lord? I have. It cost me dearly. I got ahead of God, I thought I knew what God wanted and I didn't want to wait. I tried knocking down the doors instead of waiting for God to open them. It didn't work!

How do you respond to spanking? If you're a parent I'm sure you have heard this phrase at least once: "I hate you!" Right? Have you ever said that to God? I hope not. Let me give you a dear verse I have come to love. It is in Romans 8:

For you did not receive the spirit of bondage again to fear, but you received the Spirit of adoption by whom we cry out, "Abba, Father." (Romans 8:15).

That is about as personal as you get. I have heard the word "Abba" means "daddy" in Greek. Do you have that fellowship with God that you can call Him "Daddy"? Understand, this verse is written to His children. When we become a child of God we can approach His presence as His child. After we have accepted Christ as our Savior we are "adopted" into God's family. When we are disobedient we will be "corrected" by our loving Father. God will restore that fellowship between His children and Himself when we seek it!

We are almost through with January. What kind of month has it been? Trying? Dull? If you're like me you are usually glad when the "holidays" are over. Don't take your eyes off God. Watch Him!

> Happy is the man who finds wisdom, and the man who gains understanding; for her proceeds are better than the profits of silver, and her gain than fine gold. (Proverbs 3:13-14)

Isn't it interesting that Solomon equates wisdom and understanding with a woman? I guess with six hundred wives you might think that.

Do those words, wisdom, and understanding, sound familiar? You will see them frequently throughout Proverbs. They also appear early in the first few verses of chapter one. Why are they so important?

You know the proverb about the difference between giving a person some food and teaching him to fish. It works the same way in God's family. God has given us His Holy Word, but, until we apply these principles to our everyday life, they are just words in a book.

I don't know if Solomon uses this proverb, maybe you have heard it? "A fool and his money are soon parted". I think that might clarify the proverb above.

There is a catch to having riches. First, you need to recognize the source, not your work, but God's grace. Next, you need to use it for God's glory. I think it is interesting how a person has no problem giving one dollar out of ten but scoffs at 100 dollars out of a thousand. It is still the same. Have you heard the retort? "Now we are talking real money". Money means nothing to God; it is what we do with it, and how much control it has over us, our priority!

I would think, if anyone knows the difference it would be Solomon. Solomon had all the riches we could ever imagine. Yet, look at his open in Ecclesiastes:

The words of the Preacher, the son of David, king of Jerusalem. "Vanity of vanities" says the Preacher; "Vanity of Vanities, all is vanity." (Ecclesiastes 1:1-2)

Solomon recognized the truth; wealth is not in our wisdom and knowledge and understanding, but in godly wisdom, knowledge and understanding. Look at Solomon's prayer in 1 Kings 3:6-9.

11. What is the last word in the Old Testament? (King James Version)
    a. end   b. amen   c. curse   d. God

> The Lord by wisdom founded the earth; by understanding He established the heavens; by His knowledge the depths were broken up, and clouds drop down the dew. (Proverbs 3:19-20)

Have you ever wondered about "creation"? Think about it. God could just as easily have spoken everything into existence with four words, "let it be done". He didn't! Instead, he broke it down into six daily exercises. Why was that? Have you ever tried to tackle an enormous job and get it all done in one day? God teaches us in the very beginning: "How do you eat an elephant? One bite at a time." My Sunday school teacher taught me that truth; Lonny's translation of Genesis 1 and 2.

Did you notice Solomon didn't say, "By His spoken Word God founded the earth?" I heard someone say, "God didn't check with His advisers before beginning His creation process." - Really? What would it be like to have the wisdom of God? - The "understanding" and knowledge of God. We do!

God, in His Word, has given us "everything" we need. But I have so many questions. Of course, you do; have you ever sat in a Sunday school class and heard the questions? We have so many "unanswered" questions. Think about it. If God revealed everything we wanted to know, we could not be able to carry that book!

God has given us everything we need to establish a "relationship" with our Creator; to have fellowship with our heavenly Father. To live the life that God has planned for us. He has even given us the option to say, "No". It is our choice!

One of my favorite verses is in 1 Corinthians:

But God has chosen the foolish things of the world to put to shame the wise, and God has chosen the weak things of the world to put to shame the things that are mighty. (1 Corinthians 1:27).

Just about the time we think we have it all figured out, pops up something we never thought of. That is God exercising His wisdom over our great "minds". Never underestimate God's working in your life; His wisdom is far beyond our comprehension!

> My son, let them not depart from your eyes— keep sound wisdom and discretion; so, they will be life to your soul and grace to your neck. (Proverbs 3:21-22)

If you wake up this morning and asked yourself, what is he talking about? It is important to keep in mind the "context," as it is important in meditating on any passage of scripture! Of course, Solomon is talking about wisdom and knowledge.

Do you know what I see? You need to keep these elements "close" to you. In that, I mean a "close" walk with God, the source of wisdom and knowledge. I love this illustration our pastor gave this morning about the church.

A lot of Christians are like "corn" to the body of Christ (the church). I suspected, and he confirmed it, our bodies do not "digest" corn. It simply passes through our bodies. Much like some Christians who walk down the aisle, they are baptized, and then you rarely see them again; unless it is Christmas or Easter. I guess you could call them "corny" Christians. I love the illustration!

In the verses from Solomon, I can see this relation. Solomon is admonishing us to walk close to God. *"And grace to your neck."* Do you know anyone who wears a cross around their neck? It is that picture. God should be as near as that cross, better still He should be in our hearts at all times.

If you are (really) a Christian that goes without saying; how often do you "listen" to this God who is supposed to be in our hearts? The problem is He is so easily ignored! The Holy Spirit keeps trying to get our attention and we have learned to "turn Him off!" That is not the picture in these two verses.

We have the "mind of God" right in our hands (Bible). How much time and effort do we spend trying to discern God's will for our life? Most Bible reading schedules ask for about three chapters a day. Fifteen to twenty minutes. Can you spare that? Would that not be, *grace to your neck?*

How are you coming this year? We are into a new month and half-way through the third chapter of Proverbs. Are you bored yet? Why might that be? Are you "meditating" on these verses, or just reading them?

> Then you will walk safely in your way, and your foot will not stumble. When you lie down you will not be afraid; yes, you will lie down and your sleep will be sweet. (Proverbs 3:23-24)

When was the last time you had a "good" night's sleep? Is it hard to go to sleep at night?

I used to drive over-the-road for United Parcel Service, most of the time it was at night. I would come home in the morning, try to sleep before going to work that night. I knew I needed to sleep so I would not fall asleep while on the road. I would try to "force" myself to go to sleep, it isn't happening. The harder I tried the harder to cross that threshold into sleep.

I found an interesting method that works sometimes. Try memorizing Proverbs 3:5-6. Instead of "counting sheep" try running these two verses over and over in your mind; beginning with *"Trust in the Lord."* That can be the kicker!

I have been watching some "dude ranch" type shows lately; watching people riding horses off into the forest, or rocky terrain. Do you know if or how a horse watches his feet? I don't see it. How do they know where to walk?

Look at these words: *"Then you will walk safely in your way, and your foot will not stumble."* Is that a promise from God? How would you apply that to your life? There is that principle of God knowing what is up ahead, God knows the "stumbling blocks" if your following close behind God you will miss those dangerous areas. BUT, you must be following God, not the world, not your plans or pathway. It must be the path God is leading in.

We were talking about sleep earlier. When you have that special peace that comes from a right fellowship with our heavenly Father, you will be surprised how easily we can cross that threshold into sleep. When we accept that God is in control, tomorrow is in His hands, God will guide us through each day, each storm, each trial; we can have that peace that will allow us to move right into His presence with the calm assurance, as a child of God, He is in control of our tomorrows through eternity! Do you have that peace?

12. How many books are in the New Testament?
    a. 38   b. 16   c. 27   d. 39

> Do not withhold good from those to whom it is due, when
> it is in the power of your hand to do so. Do not say to your
> neighbor, "Go and come back, and tomorrow I will give it."
> When you have it with you. (Proverbs 3:27-28)

I heard this story once, a group of people was in a prayer meeting; someone shared that their car broke down, they needed another one temporarily. The group began to pray. The one leading the prayer realized he had a car they could use, so he stopped the prayer. He said, "I have a car you can borrow." So, they ceased to pray. Would you do that? Or would you take some time and "think" about offering your car?

I guess the question is, "are you willing to give, as God prompts you?" Do you argue with God or debate the logic of it, etc.? Matthew six gives us a great promise:

"But when you do a charitable deed, do not let your left hand know what your right hand is doing, that your charitable deed may be in secret; and your Father who sees in secret will Himself reward you openly." (Matthew 6:3-4).

What do you suppose Jesus meant by *"do not let your left hand know what your right hand is doing."*? I think it means it should become second-nature. We don't have to "think" about it, we just naturally give. That is where God wants our heart!

You see, in verse Proverbs 28 he tells his neighbor to come back tomorrow. He must think about it, ponder the consequences, and decide whether he should give or not. That is not what God wants. If we are able, we should give. I like the way it is worded in Matthew: *"charitable deed"* It doesn't refer to money specifically, does it? It could be an act of kindness, something you have around the house, anything that will aid another in need.

In verse Proverbs 27 it simply says: *Do not withhold good from those to whom it is due.* That could mean anything. I think, sometimes, we are so caught up in our world we don't see the need!

> Do not devise evil against your neighbor, for he dwells by you
> for safety's sake. Do not strive with a man without cause, if
> he has done you no harm. (Proverbs 3: 29-30)

I heard this story about the early settlers in our country, when they would receive, say, forty acres where they would build their homes in the "middle" of the acreage. It didn't take them long to realize by doing that, they isolated themselves from their neighbors, so they would build their homes on the corner of their property and their neighbors would do the same. Even today we have "Neighborhood Watch" programs to watch out for our neighbors. You didn't know that was Biblical, did you?

It is so different today, most of us just have a casual acquaintance with those living around us; we are just not as open as we once were.

Years ago my wife and I would sit in the same pews in a church (of course). It wasn't long before we became close friends with those around us in the pews in front and back of us. I called them "Pew Pals". We have since changed pews but are still close to those we met there. We form bonds with those we associate with regularly.

How is your bond with Jesus? Do you talk with Him much? Do you spend much time in His Word? That is one way that our heavenly Father speaks with us, through His Word. Do you have a "casual" relationship with Him or is it deeper? How much of your life, your desires, your dreams, do you share with Him? Have you asked Him if there was anything you could do for Him? Why not?

I think we can get the idea that God is this person WAY off in heaven somewhere and He isn't interested in the things in our daily life. - Really? If you're a child of God, God is as close as your heart, in the person of the Holy Spirit. He is there any time, night or day if you are willing to talk to Him. He is open, willing to commune and fellowship with you whenever you have a spare minute to give Him. That's the case, isn't it? You just don't have time. - Really? Think about that a minute!

When was the last time you shut "everything" off, sat quietly, and talked to God? Try it. You might be surprised!

> Hear, my children, the instruction of a father, and give attention to know understanding; for I give you good doctrine: do not forsake my law. (Proverbs 4:1-2)

Doctrine: a belief or set of beliefs held and taught by a church, political party, or other groups. That is the definition given by Google. *"Do not forsake my law."* I know, in the context, Solomon is talking father to son. We really need to take this as our heavenly Father talks to us. Human understanding falls far short of God's understanding!

Let me refresh your memory of what Solomon prayed when he became king of Israel:

At Gibeon, the Lord appeared to Solomon in a dream by night; and God said, "Ask! What shall I give you?" "Therefore, give to Your servant an understanding heart to judge Your people, that I may discern between good and evil. For who is able to judge this great people of Yours?" (1 Kings 3:5, 9)

Would that not be the prayer of any father? ; That their children would have an understanding of good, versus evil. They would have an understanding of what it meant to have both a relationship AND fellowship with their heavenly Father. That is my prayer and God's prayer for His children.

Look at this verse in First John 3:

Behold what manner of love the Father has bestowed on us, that we should be called children of God! Therefore, the world does not know us, because it did not know Him. (1 John 3:1).

I invite you to read through the book of First John. All through this book, we are given the picture of our "fellowship" with our heavenly Father! We are referred to constantly, by John, as children of God. God uses that term through the New Testament. Just a reminder to check out Romans 8:15!

Just as fathers here, we desire our children to be obedient, not out of fear, but out of love and respect. That is God's desire as well!

13. What was the occupation of the first disciples?
    a. priests   b. scribes   c. farmers   d. fishermen

> When I was my father's son, tender and the only one in the sight of my mother, he also taught me, and said to me: "Let your heart retain my words; keep my commands and live." (Proverbs 4:3-4)

The verses above are expounded on in 1 Chronicles 28:

As for you, my son Solomon, know the God of your father, and serve Him with a loyal heart and with a willing mind; for the Lord searches all hearts and understands all the intent of the thoughts. If you seek Him, He will be found by you; but if you forsake Him, He will cast you off forever. (1 Chronicles 28:9)

Isn't it interesting the difference between the Old Testament and the New Testament? That last part: *He will cast you off forever.* If you are a child of God after Christ's resurrection, it is a "permanent" condition. (Romans 8:15). You are adopted into God's family forever. It is a permanent relationship! You may break the "fellowship" but your relationship is permanent.

Wouldn't David's charge to his son Solomon be the prayer of every parent? *"a loyal heart" "a willing mind"* I noticed that David also uses a phrase that Jeremiah uses in Jeremiah 29:

And you will seek Me and find Me, when you search for Me with all your heart. (Jeremiah 29:13)

That is the key, isn't it? You must want to have that relationship with God. He might knock on your heart's door (Revelation 3:20) but you must respond. He will not force you; it must be your desire! God's Spirit will work on your heart, to lure you away from the tricks and lies of the devil, but in the end, it is your choice. Which will you listen to, and which will you obey?

Here we notice again:

*Let your **heart** retain my words!* (v. 4) the heart not the head!

        Lonny E. Young

> Get wisdom! Get understanding do not forget, nor turn away from the words of my mouth. Do not forsake her, and she will preserve you; love her, and she will keep you.
> (Proverbs 4:5-6)

Have you ever said, "If I knew then, what I know now."? The older you get, of course, you have! We can look back over our lives and ask, "Why did I do those stupid things?" because you were ignorant of the path they would lead you down. I love this concept of a "path" of life. I know you have figured that out.

At one point in my life, I had to make a choice. My mother told me, "Do you want to go back to school (eleventh grade) or go into the military." I chose the military. I got my G.E.D. in the United States Air Force but I have always regretted not finishing school; one of those forks in the road that can change your whole life.

That is just one example. The person you marry, the college you attend, and the major you choose, etc.; Decisions in life that will have eternal consequences. Which path do I take? I love the way this verse begins:

Get wisdom! Get understanding. (4:5)

So, how do we know which path to take? Look at those words again! Where do you *get wisdom* where do you get *understanding*? Let me give you another verse:

If any of you lacks wisdom, let him ask of God, who gives to all liberally and without reproach, and it will be given to him. (James 1:5)

You knew I would quote the Bible. You're laughing and scoffing is exactly the fork in the road you need to seriously consider! If you have asked Jesus into your heart you know "exactly" what this verse means. If you're not a child of God you can laugh. Go ahead and take that broad road that leads to destruction (Matthew 7:13). The wisdom of God can only come from knowing God personally and walking with Him regularly. It is that simple. I will close with this question: "Do you know what is going to happen next month"? God does!

> Wisdom is the principle thing; therefore, get wisdom. And in all your getting, get understanding. Exalt her, and she will promote you; she will bring you honor, when you embrace her. (Proverbs 4:7-8)

Does it seem like Solomon won't get off this subject? Why do you think he is spending so much time on these two words?

I was just thinking, one of the characteristics of wisdom knows when to keep your mouth shut. Not how to respond, but whether to respond. That is a great sign of wisdom. Let me explain.

Our Sunday school was growing. We needed to switch some classes around to make room. I approach our Trustees about using our gym for a class. They turned me down. I didn't argue, fuss, or get mad. I simply put it in God's hands, and in a year, we had remodeled some rooms and had almost doubled our space. God took care of it. I just put it in HIS hands!

That is wisdom from God. I guess the best sign of wisdom is when we are willing to turn something over to God. Take our hands-off, trust God for the results. I love the way Dr. Charles Stanley puts it: "Obey God, leave all the consequences to Him." That is godly wisdom!
Another trait, which I have yet to master, is to "wait" on God's timing. God has been working on me, about this, for a long time. Here is another verse from James:

My brethren, count it all joy when you fall into various trials, knowing that the testing of your faith produces patience. (James 1:2-3)

God is always stretching His children, stretching their faith, to trust Him more. It is almost like a mother bird pushing their chick out of the nest. She knows they are ready they just don't know it yet. God is pushing us to fly and accomplish things we never thought we could. It isn't until we trust (totally) Him and put the circumstance in His hands. Then we can (really) see God work, which in turn strengthens our faith and trust in His guidance and providence! When was the last time you turned a difficult situation over to God?

14. What was the name of the first city conquered by Joshua?
    a. Bethlehem   b. Jericho   c. Bethel   d. Ai

> Hear, my son, and receive my sayings, and the years of your
> life will be many. I have taught you in the way of wisdom; I
> have led you in right paths. (Proverbs 4:10-11)

Take a minute, if you will. Do you remember the early days of school? Just learning the basics; addition, subtraction, multiplication, etc. I remember the first time I learned to spell "arithmetic", I was so proud I could spell such a large word, ten letters, WOW! I thought I was something.

By the time you left grade school and moved into high school, you had learned so much. I remember thinking what more could they teach me? I shared earlier that I did not finish high school, the biggest mistake ever! My mother had to work as well as my dad. My mother bought me a typewriter; she asked if I would prepare a typed report every day on our favorite soap opera, "The Edge of Night". So, I did.

I got into country music and started keeping a notebook of the various songs played on the radio. I would have to re-write the pages and keep listing them in alphabetical order, great practice. When I got bored I would take a piece of paper and start adding 1 + 1=2, 2 + 2=4, 4 + 4=8, 8 + 8, and so on, till I was in the millions, I learned simple math.

The point I want to make is that our learning process never stops. Through life experiences lessons learned, through failure, lessons learned from God's Word put into practice, we are constantly learning. In learning, we should be learning what God wants for our life. What is God's plan for our life (Jeremiah 29:11).

I love that Solomon, again, mentions the "path" we are traveling on. Are you just strolling along, admiring the scenery or are you learning along the way? Are picking up wisdom that can help you along the way? Many times, I would be led off in some strange direction. Later I would realize that the wisdom I picked up came in VERY handy when the Lord led me down a certain path. When I "reflect" back I see the wisdom of God in the path He led me to follow.

I am seventy-two; I never thought I would ever attempt to write a book, this will be my third book. I am scared to death to stand before a crowd; God has chosen this means to get my message out!

> When you walk, your steps will not be hindered, and when
> you run, you will not stumble. Take firm hold of instruction,
> do not let go; keep her, for she is your life. (Proverbs 4:12-13)

I used to love running; there might be several blocks from school to home, I would run all the way. I guess I was around eight years old or so, I contracted Hepatitis. It took the energy right out of me, I was in the hospital for several weeks, and I never had the strength again; I don't know how I survived Basic Training in the Air Force.

I was thirty-five when God came into my life and Jesus into my heart. I discovered a whole new world in the Word of God. I couldn't get enough. With my limited education, it was tough sometimes to grasp the lessons. I started teaching Sunday school. I became a Director, my main weapon was my enthusiasm; I never lost my passion for sharing the truths of the Bible.

When God called me into the ministry, of course, my first thought was a pastor. I prayed and God opened some doors, God truly blessed me in those days; my passion was still the Sunday school ministry, it has been an interesting path. My passion is teaching and sharing the Word of God.

That is the path God has chosen for me; I pray daily that God will keep me on the path of His choosing, not mine. When I discover a verse that speaks to me, at this point in my walk, I get excited and want to share it with others.

How is your walk? Is God leading you, or are you "suggesting" to God the right path. Are you leading or is God? Have you asked Him lately? I seem to remember a verse in Psalms:

Delight yourself also in the Lord, and He shall give you the desires of your heart. (Psalm 37:4)

Psalm 37 is my favorite psalm, there is so much there. Don't miss the catch to this promise; you first must delight yourself in the Lord. If you are clinging to that leadership position, you have put your desires above God, - that will never work; FIRST, you delight in the Lord, you obey Him, THEN He will bless you!

                    Lonny E. Young

> Do not enter the path of the wicked, and do not walk in the
> way of evil. Avoid it, do not travel on it; turn away from it and
> pass on. (Proverbs 4:14-15)

Here is the analogy of a "path" again. Have you ever "tempted" fate? I can handle it, I'm smarter than that. - Really? Would you recognize it if you saw it? Let's be reminded of one of the tricks of Satan:

Then the serpent said to the woman, "You will not surely die. For God knows that in the day you eat of it your eyes will opened, and you will be like God, knowing good and evil." (Genesis 3:4-5)

Satan uses the same three weapons he used on Jesus in the wilderness:

For all that is in the world—the lust of the flesh, the lust of the eyes, and the pride of life—is not of the Father but is of the world. And the world is passing away, and the lust of it; but he who does the will of God abides forever. (1 John 2:16-17)

Do you see these three "temptations" in Jesus trip to the wilderness? (Matthew 4). God shows us clearly here the temptations we face in this world. Flesh, eyes, pride. Don't go down those roads! The tough part is, there are no signs that say "Beware".

Sometimes we might travel down this path for a while before we realize it is the wrong path. What do you do? Ask God's forgiveness and go back to where you left God at the fork. He is waiting there for your return, much like the Prodigal son; the father was waiting at home for his son to realize his mistake and return to God. (Luke 15:11-32).

In Ecclesiastes, I think Solomon dealt with all three; a good book to spend some time meditating in. When I was doing my study of David, I often wondered about the household Solomon grew up in; his father, the king, had several wives, two sons in rebellion, etc.

15. What happened to Lot's wife after leaving Sodom and Gomorrah?
    a. got saved   b. healed   c. turned to salt   d. killed

> For they do not sleep unless they have done evil; and their
> sleep is taken away unless they make someone fall. For they
> eat the bread of wickedness, and drink the wine of violence.
> (Proverbs 4:16-17)

This has always fascinated me. Evil is not content! They must drag others down with them. Have you ever noticed in movies how gangs always have this leader that is never satisfied unless he can demonstrate his authority?

I made this observation before. Have you ever known a thief to say, "Okay, I have enough, I'll quit stealing now?" They MUST continue until they are caught. They are never satisfied; the same is true with gangs. They must continue to disrupt, commit chaos, and break the law until they are stopped. They are never content.

Notice the first words here? *For they do not sleep unless they have done evil.* There is no contentment. Evil does not lead to any sort of contentment. I like the picture in these verses, eating, and drinking, thirst and hunger for evil. Evil is never satisfied!

Solomon is very clear about evil.

Now, look at these verses:

Now godliness with contentment is great gain. For we brought nothing into this world, and it is certain we can carry nothing out. And having food and clothing, with these we shall be content. (1 Timothy 6:6-8)

Are you content? Then you are on the right path! If you are not satisfied with what God has given you, you are headed down the wrong path. God is not walking with you. Your priorities are wrong. When we are content with what God has blessed us with. God will continue to bless; it is when we travel down that road marked "MORE" that we run into the verses above in Proverbs.

Evil separates us from God. Just like the lie, the devil told Eve. "You will be like God." If that is your desire you have travel way too far down the wrong path. You have taken directions from Satan, and not from God!

There is a bench. Sit down and check to see if God is with you!

        Lonny E. Young

> But the path of the just is like the shinning sun, that shines
> ever brighter into the perfect day. The way of the wicked is
> like darkness; they do not know what makes them stumble.
> (Proverbs 4:18-19)

Did you ever hear something so simple, yet so profound? Our pastor made the statement on Sunday morning, preaching through the gospel of John. He said, "Darkness and light cannot occupy the same space." The same is true as Christians. You cannot be "half" saved, almost saved, and nearly saved. Either you have light or darkness; it is that simple.

Do you see the contrast in Solomon's proverb? It is the same principle. I am sure you have had those days two or three in a row where it just seemed like it will never stop raining. You don't want to do anything, you don't want to get out of bed; you're just depressed.

Then the sun comes out, just looking out the window lifts your spirits; you want to do something, you're excited again you look forward to the day! - Light versus darkness.

Here goes that word "path" again. I have a special liking for that word. It was the title of my first book, "The Path." I think that word, that concept, captures our walk in this life. We are all on a path. Where it leads we have no idea. God does. What will happen? Only God knows; until we realize that fact, until we are willing to trust God's guidance on this path, we are lost!

Today is Valentine's Day. I hope you have remembered to tell that "significant other" that you love them. Have you told God today that you love Him? If you want your Valentine from God, just turn to John 3:16. Every time I buy a new Bible I turn to John 3:16 and cross out "world" and write my name, "Lonny" in its place. It's personal between God and me. I know how much He loves me! Do you know how much God loves you?

The just and the wicked, light and darkness, perfect or stumble. Proverbs is a book of contrasts. It can be hard to read. You could almost meditate on each contrast. How does this apply to me? Just like the illustration I used above about the rainy days.

I think God is a God of contrasts - lost or saved, heaven or hell, the Spirit or the flesh, fellowship or estranged. Which of these are you?

> My son, give attention to my words; incline your ear to my sayings. Do not let them depart from your eyes; keep them in the midst of your heart; for they are life to those who find them. And health to all their flesh. (Proverbs 4:20-22)

Do you know where to find the words of life? That seems like a dumb question but, when was the last time you opened your Bible? I am serious! Was it last Sunday? I hope not! Do you have a plan to read your Bible? Have you ever read Leviticus? These words, right off, made me think of Joshua:

This book of the Law shall not depart from your mouth, but you shall meditate in it day and night, that you may observe to do according to all that is written in it. For then you will make your way prosperous, and then you will have good success. (Joshua 1:8)

Before God sends Joshua into the Promised Land, He gives him this challenge, this mandate. I love the promise here as well.

I could give so many verses in the Bible. How about Revelation 1:3? Or Hebrews 4:12. Don't overlook the fact that the Bible is God's letter to us. Solomon is giving us "principles" to live by. The whole Bible was given to us from God so that we might have that "relationship" and "fellowship" with our heavenly Father (Romans 8:15).

Don't misunderstand Solomon here. He doesn't "memorize" them. Where does Solomon say to keep them? *"In the midst of your heart."* Yesterday was Valentine's Day. You have that special "someone" in your heart. How about including some special scriptures?

You ought to use the blank pages in the front of my Bible. A word and then the verse; verses I want to remember where they are at. I have become great friends with my concordance in the back of my Bible. I did a deep study of David. Now I am very familiar with passages from 1 Samuel 16 to 1 Kings 2, David's life. He is also in 1 Chronicles but I focused on the Samuel passages. I have gotten to know David a lot better through that study. There is a promised blessing for spending "quality" time here!

16. Who wrote the book of Revelation?
    a. Jeremiah   b. John   c. Joshua   d. James

     Lonny E. Young

> Keep your heart with all diligence, for out of it spring the issues of life. Put away from you a deceitful mouth, and put perverse lips far from you. Let your eyes look straight ahead, and your eyelids look right before you. (Proverbs 4:23-25)

Being in my seventies, I have been doing a lot of "reflecting" and looking back. A lot of things I wish I had done differently, things I cannot change. Solomon tells us here to keep our eyes looking ahead, which can be dangerous as well. The only thing we need to see when we look straight ahead is the back of God, walking ahead of us. He must be in the lead.

I wonder what Solomon means by *"keep your heart with all diligence."* Does he mean not to have it broken? We can't help it sometimes. I hope you have noticed the importance Solomon has put on the heart through these verses. We make most of our decisions based on our head and not our heart. We must keep our heart true!

That brings to my mind a crucial verse in Romans:

*If you confess with your mouth the Lord Jesus and believe in your **heart** that God has raised Him from the dead, you will be saved. For with the **heart** one believes unto righteousness, and with the mouth confession is made unto salvation.* (Romans 10:9-10)

Do you see the significance of the heart? The mouth is confirmation of what has taken place in the heart. The sad part is we can profess something that is NOT in our heart. Basically, "words are cheap." If there hasn't been a heart transplant it matters not what the mouth says.

Can the heart be fooled? Ask anyone who has received a "Dear John" letter. A heart that has accepted Jesus as Savior and received the indwelling power of the Holy Spirit will not easily be deceived. God's Spirit will convict us of making wrong choices; assuming we are listening, that is the key.

Solomon mentions that in these verses, *a deceitful mouth.* We can say anything, it is what is in the heart that God looks at, God knows.

Take a minute and look at this verse: 1 Samuel 16:7. Interesting!

> Ponder the path of your feet, and let all your ways be established. Do not turn to the right or the left; remove your foot from evil. (Proverbs 4:26-27)

Now, if we don't know what is going to happen in the next hour, how can we ponder the path of our feet? I think it depends on the foundation we have laid in our life. If we have a solid foundation, we have our salvation in Jesus Christ; we are reading our Bible and praying, - we have that foundation. One of my favorite verses:

For no other foundation can anyone lay than that which is laid which is Jesus Christ. (1 Corinthians 3:11)

A great illustration is the life of Joseph in Genesis.

*This is the history of Jacob. Joseph, **being seventeen years old**, was feeding the flock with his brothers.* (Genesis 37:2a)

What kind of foundation did Jacob build in Joseph? Another note:

*Joseph was **thirty years old** when he stood before Pharaoh king of Egypt.* (Genesis 41:46)

Joseph had spent thirteen years, in prison, as a slave. I wonder how many times Joseph "questioned" God about his life? One more verse if you will:

But as for you, you meant evil against me; but God meant it for good, in order to bring it about as it is this day, to save many people. (Genesis 50:20)

Jacob had laid a foundation of trusting in God in the heart of Joseph. Joseph was able to travel the path he traveled, because of that foundation. You are on a path. Solomon has established that. What kind of foundation do you have, to help you walk by faith the path God has for you?

February 18   49-316   Proverbs 5

> My son, pay attention to my wisdom; lend your ear to my
> understanding. That you may preserve discretion, and your
> lips may keep knowledge. (Proverbs 5:1-2)

Have your parents ever said to you, "Pay attention"? Your teacher says, "Pay attention to what I am telling you". Why do you suppose they must say that? Does it do any good? I thought not. If we must ask for "attention" we have lost it. Here is an interesting question. How do you get someone's attention?

God is "always" trying to get your attention, especially if you are headed down the wrong path. He will try to get your attention and turn you around. Someone once said, "Sometimes God has to put us on our back to get us to look up." I hope it doesn't have to go that far.

Now if you're not a child of God, all God is interested in is getting you to the cross. Getting you to recognize that the path you are on leads to destruction! That is priority one!

Wisdom, understanding, knowledge is all keywords throughout Proverbs. There is another word here: discretion. Where to know what to say, and when? - That is Lonny's definition; a lesson that took me years to learn, and many embarrassing moments. It is a tough lesson to learn to not disconnect your mouth from your brain or your heart. They must be connected at all times. Sometimes a moment's pause and reflection on what you're going to say will save a lot of problems later! Verse two could be saying that very thing. Solomon has such a way with words. I hope these daily meditations in the Wisdom of Solomon are helping in your daily walk with God.

I am sure you have heard skeptics say, "If Solomon was so smart why he had six hundred wives?" It is not like he was falling in love every day, and marrying a new bride. Most of his wives were "political" overtures, a way of diplomacy with other countries; an interesting way to do it, but not very practical. Where Solomon made his mistake was being lured away from God into pagan gods; the gods of his various wives (1 Kings 11:3). A lesson for us today: Pay attention to which you associate with. You don't have to marry them, although that can be dangerous as well

17. Who arranged for Samson's haircut?
    a. Delilah   b. Jezebel   c. Rebekah   d. Deborah

> For the lips of an immoral woman drip honey, and her mouth is smoother than oil; but in the end, she is bitter as wormwood, sharp as a two-edged sword. (Proverbs 5:3-4)

We have talked about the lure of the flesh. I have already mentioned Solomon's six hundred wives; not sure if that is what Solomon is talking about here, but the deception is just as real. Whether man or woman, Solomon can be cautioning us about the power of words. Do you believe everything you hear or see?

A great principle to keep in mind in acquiring knowledge and wisdom is to "consider the source". What are the credentials of the one you are listening to? What is their "authority" to say what they are saying? Can they back it up? Maybe you need some "fact-checkers" in your life. I can suggest one, the Bible.

Oh, that again. I don't believe the Bible. Why should I trust it? It doesn't matter whether you "believe" it or not. It has been proven for centuries to be true. Even today they are uncovering artifacts that continue to prove the authenticity of Scripture. Here is another, - the pure persistence of the Bible; the devil has been trying to destroy God's word since the Garden of Eden when he said to Eve, "Hath God said?"

If you want a fascinating study, read the history of the Bible. Not just the King James but the Geneva and even earlier! There was even politics in the writing of the King James but God prevailed. Read the story. There is your authority. Check it out.

We are nearing the mid-term elections. I wonder how many people will decide their vote (if they vote) on how the candidate "looks" that he or she is eloquent, etc. Paying no mind to what they actually stand for, that is pretty much what Solomon is saying in verse 3.

Finally, where do you get your "facts" to make crucial decisions in your life? What is your source of wisdom, or who? How do you determine which path to go down? What "signs" do you look for? If you're a child of God, right away, you have the Holy Spirit to guide you; the Word of God, godly friends, and a pastor. There are several options. If you are lost you might as well flip a coin. Leave it to luck, really?

        Lonny E. Young

> Her feet go down to death, her steps lay hold of Hades. Lest
> you ponder her path of life—Her ways are unstable; you do
> not know them. (Proverbs 5:5-6)

Maybe you do know them. What path are you walking today? How much is God in your life today? Of course, I don't mean you must constantly think of God. Where do you turn to make decisions? Do you have a "special" peace that only God can bring?

Do you struggle each day, just trying to make it through the day? Are their fears, each day that just drain you of all your energy? Why is that? Do you think you must face this all alone? You don't! Let me remind you of this precious passage:

Trust in the Lord with all your heart. Lean not upon your own understanding; in all your ways acknowledge Him, and He will direct your paths. (Proverbs 3:5-6)

There is so much there. Which of these two paths are you walking? The lady mentioned above, or God's perfect plan for your life? (Jeremiah 29:11-13). Another precious passage to chew on! - Either passages, Proverbs, or Jeremiah are rich with God's wisdom, not the worlds. The hardest part is, trusting God and walking His path, not yours.

All through the Bible, we see the results of those who choose their path. They refused to walk God's path. Just follow the history of Israel in the Old Testament. If you want to see what I'm talking about, read the book of Judges. It can be depressing but look at their plan:

In those days, there was no king in Israel; everyone did what was right in his own eyes. (Judges 21:25)

They chose their path away from God. When you choose to walk with God it requires faith, trusting in God's provision, trusting in God's desire to provide and protect His children. Are you a child of God? Take a minute and read Romans 8:15. Is that you?

> Therefore, hear me now, my children, and do not depart
> from the words of my mouth. (Proverbs 5:7)

"My children" don't you love that term. The apostle John uses it a lot in First John. I mentioned this verse yesterday, take a minute and meditate on these words:

For as many as are led by the Spirit of God, these are sons of God. For you did not receive the spirit of bondage again to fear; but you received the Spirit of adoption by whom we cry out, "Abba, Father." The Spirit Himself bears witness with our spirit that we are **children of God***.* (Romans 8:14-16)

If you are a child of God, it was not by your choosing. Notice *"For as many as are led by the Spirit of God."* You see? It was God's Spirit working on you as a lost person that spoke to your heart; you were missing a piece in your heart. That piece is Jesus Christ.

"And do not depart from the words of my mouth." Solomon is urging us to stay true to the truth we have heard, read, learned. Why is it, when we know the truth we still must stray from that truth? It is a word that is slowly disappearing from our culture. It is called "commitment". Marriage is disappearing. Contracts with each other are only as valid as the number of lawyers you possess. The worst, to me, is the commitment to God's church. To worship regularly the God of this Universe!

Did you notice a special word in the Romans passage (8:14-16)? - The word "adoption". In biblical day's this was a very special word. It had much more "permanence" than it has today. Even though, I have heard it is very difficult to break an adoption. When you ask Jesus into your heart, you become a child of God, through adoption into God's family. Ponder that relationship a minute. God becomes your heavenly Father.

Just like any father, He desires only the best for His children. He is also in charge of our spiritual upbringing, lessons that we must learn in growing up as a Christian. How do you take to discipline? Not well, I suppose. Most of us don't. It is God's love that teaches us!

18. Who was the Apostle Paul's first traveling companion?
    a. Silas   b. Peter   c. Luke   d. Barnabas

      Lonny E. Young

> Remove your way far from her, and do not go near the door of her house, lest you give your honor to others, and your years to the cruel one. (Proverbs 5:8-9)

I am sure you have said, at one point or another, "If I knew then what I know now." We all wish there were some things in our past we could change. You can't. So, what do we do? We continue, on this path toward God's purpose for our life.

Do you think you are "over-the-hill"? It doesn't matter what age you are. A friend of mine approached me at church last night and said. "Well, hello old man." I replied, "I'm not old, I will ALWAYS be Young". My last name is Young. He didn't appreciate the humor.

I know you have heard "You're only as old as you feel." That depends on what time of day you ask. We get older as the days pass.

Age is irrelevant. Today is what matters. None of us know how many days, weeks, months, years we have left. Only God knows. My mother-in-law was diagnosed with cancer and was given six months to live. She lived over six years longer. Only God knows how many days we have. That is not important. What are you doing with each new day God has given you?

We are almost through the month of February. Do you remember when you started this journey in January? I hope you have been challenged, and growing in your walk with God. Have you learned anything about God, or yourself? Life is a "growing" process. God expects us to grow as Christians, and as His children!

Solomon is warning us again, in these verses to pay attention to the path we are walking. If you do not sense God's presence each day, you need to ask why. Have I strayed onto another path that God is not on? Check on your daily "fellowship" with your heavenly Father. Have you talked to Him recently? Why not? Is there sin in your life?

I like the analogy of those last words:

And your years to the cruel one.

You know who the "cruel one" is! How much have you given him?

> Lest aliens be filled with your wealth, and your labors go to the house of a foreigner; and you mourn at last, when your flesh and your body are consumed. (Proverbs 5:10-11)

I don't know your age, obviously, up until now what has your life been meaning? By that, have you laid any foundations? When people look at you what do they see? Have you made any impact on someone else's life? Have you passed down any "truth" that might help the next generation to have a closer walk with God? Are you "making a difference"?

The picture I get from Solomon's verses is: To what have you invested the previous days of your life?

Look at these verses in 1 Corinthians:

For no other foundation can anyone lay than that which is laid, which is Jesus Christ. Now if anyone builds on this foundation with gold, silver, precious stones, wood hay straw, each one's work will become clear; for the Day will declare it, because it will be revealed by fire; and the fire will test each one's work, of what sort it is. If anyone's work which he has built on endures, he will receive a reward. (1 Corinthians 3:11-14)

This is a good argument for "works" based religion. I have not found throughout the Bible a list of what counts (gold, silver, precious stones) or what does NOT count (wood, hay, straw). You notice that the wood, hay, and straw are burnt up by the fire. So, what do we build on that foundation that will last? You might start with the Word of God.

If God put such an effort into writing and preserving His desires for His children, do you not think it would be worthy of your attention, your study, your commitment to follow? Just how familiar are you with God's precious word?

I hope you noticed the wording in the 1 Corinthians passage. What is the foundation that we are to build on? How about the gospel of John?

In the beginning was the Word, and the Word was with God, and the Word was God. (John 1:1)

> And say: "How I have hated instruction, and my heart despised correction! I have not observed the advice of my teachers, nor inclined my ear to those who instructed me! (Proverbs 5:12-13)

Did you have a favorite teacher? My favorite teacher was a seventh grade "Common Learnings" teacher named, Mrs. Stenson. I don't recall anything specific she taught me. She made me "excited" about learning. She was one of those teachers, if you asked them a question, off the subject, you could get them to talk away the hour. BUT, she gave me a fascination for American History that persists today.

Solomon, of course, is talking about teachers in the text above. It doesn't have to be "school" teachers. There is a big interest in "vocational" teaching today; passing on a "trade" to the younger generation. I wonder how you pass on the desire to teach God's Word.

Of course, Solomon is talking about "hating" instruction and correction, - high school especially; by the time you reach high school you already know all there is to know and you're ready to get out into the world and conquer civilization! Right?

I remember a chart once in High School that showed the difference in income between a college education, a high school diploma, and failing grade school. They tried to impress the importance of education, which is what Solomon is cautioning about. A senior in high school is more focused on "social" activities than what they might glean from a class. Why is that?

When, at what point, do we lose our desire to learn? Maybe it is that "I know it all" mindset. I hope not.

I think I have read through the Bible ten times at least, I am still amazed at what I don't know. This past Wednesday night our pastor was teaching on Mark chapter 6; Jesus walking on the water to meet His disciples in a storm. I know the story frontwards and backward. Yet, I still gleaned a new perspective, - that is the miracle of Scripture.

I can't begin to count the worship services, the evening services, and the Sunday school classes I have sat in; still, I hunger to learn more about God's word. That is totally opposite of what Solomon is talking about. How is your appetite for the Bible? Do you hunger and thirst?

19. Which of the twelve disciples betrayed Jesus?
    a. Simon   b. Judas   c. Thaddeaus   d. Thomas

"I was on the verge of total ruin, in the midst of the assembly and congregation." (Proverbs 5:14)

Have you ever been at the end of your rope? Seriously! - You saw no hope, no way out, no more answers. I can remember a time when I was working with United Parcel Service; I had a package delivery route in Grandview, Missouri. I was standing on the dock, exhausted one evening, saying, "Is this my life will be?" A month later, I was training to be an over-the-road driver and left that situation.

Just when we think "I am stuck," God has a way of picking us up, and putting us back on track. The funny part about Grandview is that I wasn't a Christian at the time; yet, I can look back and see God's hand in certain events that brought me to His throne of grace.

Solomon gives us this picture of our "failures" being before the congregation. I think the picture should be before the throne of God. Have you ever stood before God's throne and shook your fist and said, "Why me?" Does that help? I love the words to Kris Kristofferson's song, "Why me, Lord." Not sure if he includes the word, Lord. Anyone that has been used of God will ask that question.

I mentioned earlier about being at the end of your rope. What do you do when things have changed, and you have recovered? I know, it's like the high school senior, "I know it all". Now, you said, "Look what I did". That's sad; you think God had no part in that?

Why do you suppose, Jesus has not returned as He said He would in the Bible? Have you ever pondered the book of Revelation? It can be (really) scary, total destruction, millions dying, it is the end. Let me give you a thought. It is God's grace.

If Jesus returned right now, would you go to heaven? If not, then do you want Him to return now? You see, God's grace is willing to wait for as long as it takes for you to find God. He will wait—only so long. At one point, He will determine that all who will have turned to Him, thus, He will return and complete the prophecy in Revelation. No one knows when that might be. If you're not a child of God it is not too late. It is your choice. It has always been your choice. God is waiting . . . but not for long! Do you know when your last day on earth is?

> Drink water from your own cistern, and running water from
> your own well. Should your fountains be dispersed abroad,
> streams of water in the streets? (Proverbs 5:15-16)

My study Bible titles this chapter *Immorality rebuked.* Solomon has an interesting approach to getting his message across. To me, the message may be that YOU are responsible for keeping your own "water". Your life is your responsibility. A big problem today is that we feel we can blame everyone else but ourselves for our dilemma; our parents, our upbringing, our circumstances, our environment, our teachers, our government, etc. No personal responsibility.

Granted, parents do have the biblical responsibility to bring their children up in the Lord.

Look at this verse:

And these words which I command you today shall be in your heart. You shall teach them diligently to your children, and shall talk of them when you sit in your house, when you walk by the way, when you lie down, and when you rise up. (Deuteronomy 6:6-7)

Even in Proverbs we are instructed to teach our children:

Train up a child in the way he should go, and when he is old he will not depart from it. (Proverbs 22:6)

There comes a time when the child is responsible for his or her actions. You, as parents, hopefully, have done your part, and then the consequences are in the adult's hands; that is the point, I think, that Solomon is making. When we stand before our Judge we will give an account of what we have taught our children, how we raised them. They will give account for what they did with what they were taught.

I think this is what makes Proverbs hard to read and understand. Here is where the Holy Spirit takes over. As you continue in this chapter, let God's Spirit speak to your own needs and instruction. That is the fascinating thing about the Bible. It speaks to every "individual" need for instruction; instruction that is from God!

Let them be only your own, and not for strangers with you.
Let your fountain be blessed, and rejoice with the wife of your
youth. (Proverbs 5:17-18)

I know, many today, can't make that statement. Divorce is so common today; blended families are almost the norm. Imagine Solomon's household with over six hundred wives. And he is giving us advice?

It is like when I grew up, where both my parents were smokers, both died of cancer. Some of my brothers and sisters smoke, some don't, why is that? We each make our own decisions. We are each, as well, accountable for those decisions.

Is Solomon teaching that we should not "share"? I think not. He, as I said yesterday, is emphasizing the personal accountability of each person. The things that are "only your own" are those things that God has blessed you with. What you do with them, is between you and God.

I love the example of our men's group. We sought once a motto, something that described our group of Christian men who gathered once a month for breakfast. I suggested "Rivermen" in the context that as God has blessed us, we are to turn around and bless others. Even Solomon, speaking of water, can use that picture.

Look at this verse:

And whoever gives one of these little ones only a cup of cold water in the name of a disciple, assuredly, I say to you, he shall by no means lose his reward. (Matthew 10:42)

Jesus speaking in this passage of the simple act of giving; God has blessed His children in so many ways, not just money. He also, through His Holy Spirit, puts within us the desire, and the ability, to share what God has blessed us with.

This may be a good example of looking at the culture of the day. You might want to spend a few minutes and read the book of Ecclesiastes. This book, also by Solomon tells of his endeavors to find the answers to life. I would be curious to know when Solomon wrote Proverbs, a collection of sayings, versus Ecclesiastes. In Ecclesiastes, he is searching for the "perfect" life. Look at 12:13.

20. Name the place where Jesus was crucified.
    a. Bethel   b. Babylon   c. Golgatha   d. Samaria

> For the ways of man are before the eyes of the Lord, and He ponders all his paths. (Proverbs 5:21)

Why do we think we can hide anything from God? I don't know if you thought about it. Let me use David as an example (I just finished an in-depth study of David).

We know about David's sin with Bathsheba. Maybe you didn't think about this. From the time Bathsheba said to David, "I am with child." (2 Samuel 11:5), till the time David was confronted by Nathan, when he said, "You are the man" (2 Samuel 12:7) was approximately nine months. During this time David had arranged for Uriah's death (2 Samuel 11:15). Nine months. I wonder if David thought he had gotten away with his sin.

I love the Old Testament for just this reason. The principles taught in the New Testament are illustrated in the Old Testament. There are so many "lessons" to learn just from King David's life. A great lesson can be, "how to restore your fellowship with God"; how to return to God after you have broken His heart with your sin.

It is God's fondest desire that we walk the "path" that He has set out before us. No detours, no side paths, just His path! When we think we know more than God and decide to wander off on some path other than God's will, we will fail. Like the story of David, God is not in any hurry to spank us. It's like our mother used to say, "Wait till your father gets home." God will deal with us in His time and in His way!

A hiker, worth his salt, never goes hiking without his compass. He may be expert in the area he is hiking. He may know all the paths and terrain, but a "smart" hiker will always have his compass with him.

God is our compass in life. To think we could navigate daily through the tricks and deceits of the devil is foolish. "I am just going to work and back", nothing extraordinary today; I don't need my compass, that is asking for disaster. When we think we have it all figured out, we know just where God is going, we think we can run ahead of Him. We are looking for "major" trouble. It must be in God's time, in God's way. Anything else is T.R.O.U.B.L.E!

Trust His guidance and direction! A great warning from Solomon!

His own iniquities entrap the wicked man, and he is caught in the cords of sin. He shall die for lack of instruction, and in the greatness of his folly he shall go astray. (Proverbs 5:22-23)

The day we begin to think it is all about "us", we begin a downward spiral that leads to destruction.

I can picture this: A smart lawyer, great prestige, recognized in his profession. He is standing in front of God and presenting his case for entry into heaven. He lists all his great accomplishments. He lists all the "pro-bono" work for the poor he has done. He may even quote some Bible verses. God will look at him and send him to Hades. Why? He has all these credentials. When God looked at him, He did not see the blood of His Son, Jesus; nothing else matters but the blood of Christ.

Did you catch these words? *"He shall die for lack of instruction"*

I had been saved for some time. I had, by faith, asked Jesus into my heart. One day, I don't know why, I asked myself, "Why did Jesus have to die on the cross?" I accepted the fact that He paid for my sins, etc., but WHY the cross? The Lord led me to this passage in the Old Testament:

*Now the blood shall be a sign for you on the houses where you are. **And when I see the blood, I will pass over you**, and the plague shall not be on you to destroy you when I strike the land of Egypt.* (Exodus 12:13)

It didn't matter if he was Hebrew or an Egyptian. If God saw the blood of the sacrificed lamb, God would pass over the house and it would not suffer the judgment. To make my point, one more verse in the Gospel of John:

The next day John saw Jesus coming toward him, and said, "Behold! The Lamb of God who takes away the sin of the world!" (John 1:29)

Have you applied the blood of Christ to your heart? Why not?

> My son, if you become surety for your friend, if you have shaken hands in pledge for a stranger. You are snared by the words of your mouth; you are taken by the words of your mouth. (Proverbs 6:1-2)

Do you know what this is? It is plain and simple "trust". Is it not? When you pledge on the word of someone else you have put your trust in their word. When Solomon uses the word "surety" today that is the same as "co-signing", for whatever reason, on the word of another.

Solomon warns against it, Dave Ramsey, in his book Total Money Makeover, warns against it. Why is this so dangerous? You are pledging for another person. You don't know the future. You don't know what God is doing in their life, what God has planned for their life. Most of us don't know what God has planned for "our" life. It is a "gamble!"

Did you notice the "contract" in Solomon's day? *If you have shaken hands*, of course, that is null and void today. Your word is as trustworthy as the number of lawyers you can secure. That is so sad today. Even worse "lying" has become an art form. Rumor, innuendo, half-truths, just plain lying is almost "accepted" and when you're caught there are no consequences. Where have we come to?

I had a youth class once. I challenged them to find the word "blessed" in the Bible. We had been studying Be-attitudes. I told them there were a lot more than the ones listed in Matthew 5. All they had to do was use their concordance. I offered a "Snickers" bar to any participant. I got just a few. "Blessed" can be a promise from God. If they found one I would then ask: "What is the promise"? Then I would ask, "What is the condition to that promise"? They had to think. It didn't last long.

God's Word is full of promises from God. Most of them come with conditions. Even our salvation is determined by our faith in Jesus Christ. (Romans 10:9-10). If you really want to get serious, take the promise in Malachi 3:10. I dare you!

How good is your word? That can be dangerous. We don't know what the future holds; it is tough to make "promises" in the future. BUT, we know who holds the future. Do you?

21. How many people escaped the flood on the ark in the book of Genesis?
    a. 5   b. 7   c. 8   d. 12

> So, do this, my son, and deliver yourself; for you have come
> into the hand of your friend: go and humble yourself, plead
> with your friend. Give no sleep to your eyes, nor slumber to
> your eyelids. Deliver yourself like a gazelle from the hand
> of the hunter; and like a bird from the hand of the fowler.
> (Proverbs 6:3-5)

How can I make this up to you? What can I do to make it right? Can you have that attitude? Or, do you just make excuses for not keeping your word? - That is the easy way out; we can ALWAYS find an excuse, except the truth.

Did you notice this? Solomon is talking like he knows you will break the contract from your handshake. It is a foregone conclusion. So, Solomon offers a repentant attitude. Besides keeping your word today, which is fast disappearing, the ability to say, "I'm sorry" is also disappearing. Like I said before, it is easier to make excuses.

Solomon says; do not rest until you have made it right! Have you noticed that the longer you put something like this off, the less likely you are to apologize? Solomon says, deal with it right now! Don't go to bed until you have made things right!

Have you noticed how hard it is to admit your failures? - That is what we are talking about here. The book of Proverbs is about wisdom and knowledge, it is also about humility and our relationship with each other, and it is a priority with God as well. If you look at the Ten Commandments, the first FOUR pertain to our relationship with God; the next SIX pertain to our relationship with each other. I believe it is the ninth Commandment that talks about lying or "bearing false witness". (Exodus 20:16).

Yesterday Solomon admonished us not to make commitments we can't keep. Today, in the same chapter he is helping us to remedy the situation when we have made those commitments and then fail to keep them. Does Solomon know us, or what?

Look at this verse:

No temptation has overtaken you except such is common to man; but God is faithful, who will not allow you be tempted beyond what you are able, but with the temptation will also make the way to escape, that you may be able to bear it. (1 Corinthians 10:13)

> Go to the ant, you sluggard! Consider her ways and be wise,
> which having no captain, overseer or ruler, provides her
> supplies in the summer, and gathers her food in the harvest.
> (Proverbs 6:6-8)

I was eating a banana the other day and I had this thought; I wondered what the first person to discover a banana thought when he tasted it? Do you ever have weird thoughts like that? As I was writing these verses I wondered how Solomon knew the ant was a "she". Don't miss the point!

We all have natural instincts that were given to us by our Creator; instincts for food, for shelter, for purpose in life. God has created us for a specific purpose. Here is another "wonder". Why didn't we discover penicillin in the 1600s? We were not "ready" for that discovery. Would we have known what to do with it then?

When I look back over history I ask myself why God didn't reveal certain "truths" earlier. God has a purpose and a plan for every great invention, every great thought, and every great discovery in His time. A great example is the coming of Jesus Christ. Look what Paul writes in Galatians:

*But when the **fullness of time** had come, God sent forth His Son, born of a woman, born under the law.* (Galatians 4:4)

God waited over four-hundred years after the prophet Malachi to visit us in the person of His Son Jesus. The time had to be perfect, as God is perfect. Roman culture was such, as to be a perfect time, roads, language, persecution, etc. God's timing is always perfect!

The same is true in your life. Are you waiting for something to happen? Can you wait on God? Take it from someone who knows. You don't want to get ahead of God; that's what I like about the passage in Jeremiah 29:11, God has a plan for our lives, your life. It is up to us whether we are willing to follow His plan or ours.

That is the picture that Solomon is painting in the verses above. Even the ant is following a set plan that God had created her to follow. A purpose that God has created them for! How about you?

> How long will you slumber, O sluggard? When will you
> rise from your sleep? A little sleep, a little slumber, a little
> folding of the hands to sleep—So shall your poverty come
> on you like a prowler, and your need like an armed man.
> (Proverbs 6:9-11)

Okay, Solomon, what are you getting at? I kind of feel sorry for those who are asleep. Those who feel they don't have any need for God. I doubt that is what Solomon is talking about. I get the picture that he might be talking about those who have no "clue" about the world around them. What God is doing is unknown to those around us.

God is working miracles daily, most don't even realize it. I am so thankful for the series of movies that have been produced, The "God Is Not Dead" series. Have you noticed the theme? So many things that God is doing around us, but we are asleep.

I remember, as a baby Christian, what my pastor quoted me once; I think it was from D.L. Moody. He said, "The world has yet to see what God can do with a life fully committed to Him." To me, I guess the closest would be the Rev. Billy Graham. There are countless others throughout the world making a difference. Are you changing YOUR world? Are you making a difference?

After thirty years of Sunday school work I felt it was time to pass it on to the younger generation. I didn't know what God was going to do, I was in neutral. One day, through a series of circumstances, He lay on my heart to write a devotional. Different things had come together, I felt inadequate. I didn't even finish High School, but, I sat down and started writing. I am seventy-two, this is my third book. I think God has one more after this. It is all His plan and His leading. It may not do anything but I must be obedient.

Too many people think that once they have retired then you can just set back and "let it happen." It doesn't work that way. God's plan and purpose don't end at "retirement"! Now you have more free time for "ministry!" Wake up. Look around you!

I don't know where this is going, - that's not important; what is important is doing what God has laid on my heart to do. - If it blesses someone else, Praise God. It is all in God's hands to use as He sees fit!

22. The birthplace of Jesus was in what city?
    a. Nazareth   b. Bethlehem   c. Capernaum   d. Bethel

> A worthless person, a wicked man, walks with a perverse mouth; he winks with his eyes, he shuffles his feet, he points with his fingers. (Proverbs 6:12-13)

Okay, what signs do you look for? How do you "size up a person"? Don't tell me you don't judge a person when you first meet them. We all do. How about this "proverb," you don't get a second chance to make a first impression. See, we even have "proverbs" today. If you stopped and thought about it, we have several "proverbs" today. I'll bet most could be traced back to the Bible. We may run into some in our journey.

Do you know a key way to "size up" someone you just met? Listen to the Holy Spirit. As a Christian we have, dwelling within us, a key power that can help us. Have you ever had an "uneasy" feeling about someone? If you're a Christian, of course, you have. God is warning us. The Holy Spirit of God, dwelling within us.

It is the same principle espoused in Romans:

The Spirit Himself bears witness with our spirit that we are children of God. (Romans 8:16).

Of course, the verse is referring to our connection with God. It also applies to people we meet. I have heard stories of Christians who walk into a crowded room and will quickly move toward other Christians, led by God's Spirit. We just need to learn to listen to and trust the leading of God!

When I was driving over-the-road with United Parcel Service I started running a CB. It didn't last very long. I got so fed up with the language, one night, I said, "Did you know that profanity is ignorance made audible." Someone on the radio offered to meet me and discuss the comment. I got rid of my CB. Profanity is disgusting to me. Look again at what Solomon said, *Walks with a perverse mouth.* I won't go any further!

Who is in your circle of friends? Hopefully, they don't fall into any of the descriptions above. You need to pray about this!

> Perversity is in the heart, he devises evil continually, he sows
> discord. Therefore, his calamity shall come suddenly; suddenly
> he shall be broken without remedy. (Proverbs 6:14-15)

You know what "fall out" is, don't you? Do you see the promise in these verses? God will judge this person; you don't want to be around when He does.

Have you ever tried to be their judge? I hope not. That is not your province, God is the judge. You may voice your displeasure, but the judging belongs to God.

Look at these verses in Matthew:

So, Jesus said, "Are you still without understanding? Do you not yet understand that whatever enters the mouth goes into the stomach and is eliminated? But those things which proceed out of the mouth come from the heart, and they defile a man. For out of the heart proceed evil thoughts, murders, adulteries, fornications, thefts, false witness, blasphemies. These are the things which defile a man, but to eat with unwashed hands does not defile a man. (Matthew 15:16-20).

Just as Jesus said, it begins in the heart, - the language, the evil, the perversity, etc. I loved to point to this verse when I am told to wash my hands before eating. They don't think it is funny. The point being the things that defile us comes from what is in our hearts, not on our minds.

I am not surprised that Jesus uses the same idea as Solomon; the same Holy Spirit wrote both truths. Never forget that it is God's Spirit that authored the Bible. God just used their hands, guided by His Spirit, to convey God's message. It will be consistent throughout the Bible.

Jesus was chastising the Pharisees about their "ritual" hand washing, yet their hearts were black as sin. We can have perfectly clean hands and have perverse and wicked hearts.

Solomon begins this paragraph describing a "worthless person" (v. 12). They are worthless without the presence of God in their heart. God would love to come in and "clean up" that worthless heart.

> These six things the Lord hates, yes, seven are an abomination
> to Him: A proud look, a lying tongue, hands that shed
> innocent blood. (Proverbs 6:16-17)

We have been brought up not use the word "hate," haven't we? Yet, God uses the word to describe how He feels about these seven things.

A "proud look", what do you suppose that means? I heard someone refer to a person with "smirk". That, to me, would be that proud look, "I know more than you" look. Pride is also mentioned in the three things that God says are "of the world."

For all that is in the world—the lust of the flesh, the lust of the eyes, and the pride of life—is not of the Father but is of the world. And the world is passing away, and the lust of it; but he who does the will of God abides forever. (1 John 2:16-17)

I could use the rest of this space talking about lying. It is so prevalent today it almost goes without notice. The problem is it is never addressed or corrected.

Isaiah has a great verse about innocent blood:

When you spread out your hands, I will hide My eyes from you; even though you make many prayers, I will not hear. Your hands are full of blood. (Isaiah 1:15)

We will be held accountable for the deeds we have done! Is there any hope? Of course, there is! God has made a provision to be rid of that innocent blood. He sent His very own Son, Jesus Christ, the epitome of "innocent blood" to die on the cross of Calvary that you might be able to enter into God's presence. *I will hide my eyes from you.* Until we have cleansed ourselves in the blood of Christ, God will not look upon us, or even consider our prayers! The only prayer God wants to hear from a child of the world is, "Lord, save me!"

Don't think you can fool God either. God knows our heart. In your heart, you must truly desire to be forgiven and cleansed, and saved.

23. Who followed King David on the throne of Israel?
    a. Isaac   b. Judah   c. Solomon   d. John

> A heart that devises wicked plans, feet that are swift in running to evil, a false witness who speaks lies, and one who sows discord among brethren. (Proverbs 6:18-19)

This completes the seven things God hates. Isn't it interesting that Solomon mentions lying twice? Verse 17, *a lying tongue*, and here *a false witness;* different but the same.

It is also interesting that he describes the "origin" of these "wicked plans". They originate in the heart. The first mention of the heart in these four verses; the thing that God is most concerned about . . . our heart!

Don't overlook that it says, "God hates" these things. He doesn't just frown on them, detests them, HE HATES THEM! Now, where do these seven things fit in "your" priority of things to hate? Are you serious about not doing these seven things?

What kind of person are we describing in these seven traits? Of course, he or she is someone with no connection to God. Oh, we live in a wicked world, so many evil people all around us. They are not hard to spot. Look at something else in the last verse: *brethren.* Those are close acquaintances, maybe even fellow "Christians". Do you think "Christians" would do any of these seven things?

The term Christian is a "title"! Anyone can claim to be a Christian. Of course, I mentioned before, God knows their heart. We, on the other hand, may not be so discerning.

As a "child of God" we would not even consider doing any of these things, right? Read that list again. Is there something in there that you may have done? Is God dealing with you about any of these seven? You need to get right with God. Have you seen any of these seven in other "Christians"? You need to be praying for them.

Solomon, in his wisdom, has listed these seven things for our meditation. God, through His Holy Spirit, gave Solomon this list of seven things God hates. They are not here for us to read over and move on to the next passage. They are here for us to remember, to be aware of, and to watch for. They are a warning from God Himself that these seven things are important to God, - a warning not to be overlooked.

My son, keep your father's command, and do not forsake the
law of your mother. Bind them continually upon your heart;
tie them around your neck. (Proverbs 6:20-21)

Do you know what comes to mind here? Check these verses out:

*And these words which I command you today shall be in your heart. You shall teach
them diligently to your children, and shall talk of them when you sit in your house,
when you walk by the way, when you lie down, and when you rise up. You shall
bind them as a sign on your hand, and they shall be as frontlets between your eyes.*
(Deuteronomy 6:6-8)

Such a crucial passage, both in Proverbs and here in Deuteronomy; Moses, in
Deuteronomy, is giving his final instructions to Israel before Joshua leads Israel into
the Promised Land. Solomon, maybe, remembering the struggles he went through
as David's son reflects on David's wisdom, learned the hard way, passed down to
him. Above all, this book you hold in your hand (the Bible) is God's message, His
instructions for us.

The question, above all else, is: What are you going to do with these instructions?
I had the strangest thought. Do you remember a TV series early in 2000? The title
was, "The Early Edition". In this series, this investment broker has a newspaper
delivered to his front door every day. No big deal, except the paper, was from the
NEXT DAY. The first few episodes are his struggle in knowing what to do with
the information he has been given. He struggles with such a gift. He finally realizes
that this gift was given to him to help people. To save lives.

That is the struggle we have today. God has given us this wonderful gift of His Holy
Word. It has all the secrets of life for anyone who will read, learn, and apply these
God-given truths! We have all this, right in our hands, yet we choose to ignore it;
Too much trouble. Why should I believe God? He is only the one who created you,
the one who promises that He has a plan for your life (Jeremiah 29:11).

> When you roam, they will lead you; when you sleep, they will keep you; and when you awake, they will speak with you. For the commandment is a lamp, and the law a light; reproofs of instruction are the way of life. (Proverbs 6:22-23)

Of course, Solomon is referring to the admonition in the previous verses, both in verse 20 and verse 23 Solomon calls them "commands". Would that we thought of them that way, we think they are "suggestions" from God. God doesn't make "suggestions".

I hope you noticed the attention they are to be given. Both here and in the Deuteronomy passage from yesterday. It is a "constant" thing! Daily, walking, sitting when you lie down or get up. Constantly!

How much of God's presence occupy your daily thinking? How many "one sentence" prayers do you pray each day? How many times, during the day, do you thank God for a simple blessing during the day? I hope you know what I am talking about!

I like this line: *Reproofs of instruction are the way of life!* I love that. Have you ever noticed just how many different "truths" you learn in a day? Most of them, of course, come from the mistakes we make. We learn what "not" to do. That is a part of life. From a toddler learning what fire is, to an elderly person learning their "limitations!" Life is a process of learning. The challenge is learning and putting that wisdom to use.

What is your first response when someone tells you, you are wrong? Rebellion! Denial! Argument! Instead, take a minute, think about the rebuke then ask yourself, "Can I be a better person if I just listen?" I love the fact that God gave us two ears and only one mouth for a reason!

That might be a good meditation exercise. Begin in chapter 1 verse 1 and underline how many times Solomon uses the word "instruction". Maybe we think we don't need any. We know all we need to know. I am seventy-two and still haven't learned when to keep my mouth shut! It's a long story!

I don't think it was an accident that God would put a book like Proverbs right after the book of Psalms. After praising, we need to learn!

24. Who wrote the first five books of the Bible?
     a. David   b. Joshua   c. Luke   d. Moses

> People do not despise a thief if he steals to satisfy himself when he is starving. Yet when he is found, he must restore sevenfold. (Proverbs 6:30-31)

Interesting concept; if I remember correctly our country once practice a variation of this principle. Some judges have tried a similar concept, "Community Service." Notice that it is not determined by the "motive" even if he is starving he still must restore sevenfold. There must be consequences.

I have asked this several times, it goes with the verses above. Have you ever heard of a thief, at some point say, "I have enough, I think I will quit now?" No. Hardly! The only thing that will discourage stealing is consequences.

God deals with us in the same way. If we were permitted to "avoid" consequences for our sin do you think we would stop? Not hardly. I have always wanted to ask God, later, why He doesn't bring the consequences immediately? "Just wait till your dad gets home!" I am sure we have heard that at some point growing up. Well, we used to anyway.

Let me give you an example from David's life:

And the woman conceived; so, she sent and told David, and said, **"I am with child."** (2 Samuel 11:5)

David saw Bathsheba bathing. He ASKED for her. About nine months later, while David arranged for her husband to be killed, we see this verse:

Then Nathan said to David, **"You are the man!"** *Thus, says the Lord God of Israel, and I delivered you from the hand of Saul.* (2 Samuel 12:7)

At least nine months from the sin until God brought judgment on David. David's response?

So, David said to Nathan, **"I have sinned against the Lord."** (2 Samuel 12:13)

> Whoever commits adultery with a woman lacks understanding; he who does so destroys his own soul. Wounds and dishonor, he will get, and his reproach will not be wiped away. (Proverbs 6:32-33)

Let's continue the storyline with David. When David was NOT where he was supposed to be, he was at home walking on his balcony. David spies Bathsheba. Now he has two options. We ALWAYS have options. He chose to pursue his desires. Even so today, and always: WE HAVE OPTIONS!

David paid dearly for his choice of options; both in the baby that was conceived and in his fellowship with God. His relationship, thank God, was not broken. David retained the Holy Spirit which he received at his first anointing by Samuel:

*Then Samuel took the horn of oil and anointed him in the midst of his brothers; and the **Spirit of the Lord came upon David from that day forward**. So, Samuel arose and went to Ramah.* (1 Samuel 16:13)

Why is that significant?

Look at some verses that followed:

*But the **Spirit of the Lord departed from Saul**, and a distressing spirit from the Lord troubled him.* (1 Samuel 16:14).

David committed a grave sin. Not only with Bathsheba but in having Uriah killed. If you read further God could have had David killed, but God spared his life; the grace of God.

It took a long time before David was able to repair his fellowship with God. David had some growing up to do. He was faced with "options" later. This time he chose to rely on God and make some right choices.

We are always confronted with choices. Here's a "proverb" from the past: "The grass is always greener on the other side of the fence." Does that sound like David? According to my study Bible at the time David sent for Bathsheba he had eight wives, it is all about choices; some can have eternal consequences!

            Lonny E. Young

> My son, keep my words, and treasure my commands within you. Keep my commands and live, and my law as the apple of your eye. (Proverbs 7:1-2)

Just curious, do you know who Solomon's "son" is?

Then Solomon rested with his fathers, and was buried in the City of David his father. And Rehoboam his son reigned in his place. (1 Kings 11:43)

David returned to God. Solomon slowly drifted from God. Where are you today?

And he had seven hundred wives, princesses, and three-hundred concubines; and his wives turned away his heart. (1 Kings 11:3).

In David, Solomon's father, we saw the grave mistakes he made. He repented and gradually restored his fellowship with God, not so with Solomon. He started great; asking God for understanding to lead His people. Slowly, slowly his many wives drew Solomon away from God and into idol worship. I can see that happening to our nation today. A slow process, but just as sure!

We have removed all evidence of God's Law from our public square. Why? It is too convicting, it brings us face to face with right and wrong. We can't allow that. Just as Solomon cautions his son to stay true to God's word, our generation has cautioned this next generation. Will they listen? The jury is out!

Again, the admonishment to keep God's Law, God's will and purpose always before you (Apple of his eye). God's plan and purpose should always be our goal and focus. If that is the case, how familiar are you with God's Word? How much time is spent reading and learning what God took such pains to provide for His children? - That is what I like about regular church attendance. Sometimes my feeble efforts in getting into God's Word leave much to be desired. I look forward to church to supplement my growth in God's Word!

25. How many were crucified with Jesus?
     a. none   b. one   c. four   d. two

> Bind them on your fingers; write them on the tablets of your heart. Say to wisdom, "You are my sister," and call understanding your nearest kin. (Proverbs 7:3-4)

I love the picture! Our pastor has been stressing, as well as our previous pastor, the importance of our "church family". That is what it is! We are all brothers and sisters of God, as children of God. (Romans 8:15).

Our Sunday school class has a tradition. After every lesson, after we close the class in prayer, we sing:
"I'm so glad I'm a part of the family of God.
I've been washed in the fountain, cleansed by His blood.
Joint heirs with Jesus as we travel this sod.
For I'm a part of the family, the family of God."

That is awesome! We need to be reminded every day of our relationship with God.

Do you see the earnestness in Solomon's words?

Bind them, write them on the tablets of our hearts! (7:3)

Short version; Do you realize all that is written on the tablets of your heart? You don't until you sit down and meditate on your life. Let's take your conversion: Where were you? What happened? Who led you to salvation in Jesus? If I may, let me ask you one more question. How did your reading of the Bible change?

The night I was saved I went into our living room and found a Bible I had been taking to church (just carrying it). I opened it and read Third John, (all fourteen verses). I was so excited I had read a whole book in the Bible; I have been hungry ever since. The exciting thing is that the Holy Spirit, which I received at conversion, helped me to understand, more fully, what I was reading. I couldn't get enough.

I have heard several stories of the same thing. Let me give you this verse to ponder:

For the message of the cross is foolishness to those who are perishing, but to us who are being saved it is the power of God! (1 Corinthians 1:18)

March 16   75-290   Proverbs 7

> That they may keep you from the immoral woman.
> (Proverbs 7:5)

How can the Bible, the Law, the commandments, God's Word keep you from an immoral woman? - That's the context of what Solomon is talking about. Do you remember yesterday's comments? It was Solomon's wives and concubines that drew him away from God and into worshipping idols.

Speaking of idols, look at these verses:

*Their idols are silver and gold, the work of men's hands. They have mouths, but they do not speak; Eyes they have, but they do not see; they have ears, but they do not hear; noses they have but they do not smell; they have hands, but they do not handle; feet they have but they do not walk; nor do they mutter through their throat. **Those who make them are like them; so is everyone who trusts in them.*** (Psalm 115:4-8)

What do idols have to do with an immoral woman? - It is whatever draws you away from God and His precepts! Like the case of Solomon.

Interesting question: Exactly what was it that made Israel create the "Golden Calf" at the base of Mt. Sinai (Exodus)? Think about it. It was impatience. They couldn't wait for Moses to return from the mountain. So, a few convinced the others they needed an "idol" to lead them back to Egypt. It is so easy to set up your idol, isn't it? It all depends on WHO you trust!

Solomon, in all his wisdom, was led away from God by his wives and concubines, into trusting idols who had never done any of the things God had done for him. - Really? Of course, you wouldn't do that. What is it in your life that stands between you and God? What keeps you from worshipping God on the Lord's Day? What keeps you from reading your Bible? What keeps you from praying daily?

Here is a tough one, "You just don't have the time". Is time your idol? You better think about that one, because God can eliminate that idol right now. He can just call you home right now. Think about that one thing that keeps you from a fellowship or a relationship with God.

> For at the window of my house I looked through my lattice,
> and saw among the simple, I perceived among the youths, a
> young man devoid of understanding. (Proverbs 7:6-7)

Okay, the logical question would be, "What do I do about it?" You see someone who is about to make a terrible mistake, what do you do? Do you warn them? Do you try to stop them? Do you say, "It's none of my business"? What do you do?

Does it seem Solomon is picking on "youths"? Only in the context of not living long enough to have obtained wisdom. Wisdom comes from experience.

Now suppose he warns the youth. Do you think that a young person will listen? Not really! A wise youth might, but most don't.

I am so excited to see our youth group in our church growing as big as it is. Of course, when they graduate High School most will drift away from the church, which is sad; maybe a few might stay faithful, but not many.

Maybe that is some of what Solomon is talking about here. Now how do you suppose Solomon thought that youth was "devoid" of understanding? Maybe he was smoking something, drinking something, cursing, fighting; there must have been an outward sign of his ignorance, - interesting. We will see in the next two verses.

I go back to my original question, "What do you do?" I am a grandparent; I have seen both our children and our grandchildren make mistakes. What do I do? The problem, usually, is that they know what is right and wrong, yet, they do foolish things anyway. I guess what they don't understand is how much that ignorance or rebellion hurts those who love them; you must want to be helped.

Don't misunderstand me; I am not picking on the youth. There are far too many adults the same way. It keeps coming back to "what do I do?" You keep warning, you keep praying, you keep being the example that God has called you to be. Pray that God's Spirit will reach their hearts, get their attention, and turn them in the right direction. Only God, sometimes, knows just what to do. He may need to do something in their life to get their attention, - who knows?

26. How many churches are mentioned in Revelation 1-3?
    a. 12   b. 3   c. 40   d. 7

> Passing along the street near her corner; and he took the
> path to her house. In the twilight, in the evening, in the black
> and dark night. (Proverbs 7:8-9)

Does this sound like a murder mystery, a Hallmark movie? Why does Solomon or God for that matter think it is important to include this narrative? There must be a lesson here for us. Of course, it is hard to diagnose apart from the whole context.

He is talking about the wiles of women, we see that, but he is also talking about the deceitfulness of sin. The tricks the devil uses to trick us into sin. The devil cannot "make" us sin. No more than God can "make" us accept His Son as our Savior.

Do you see the overall picture? Demonstrating the necessity of wise choices; the criteria we use for making those wise choices, the results of bad choices!

I have used David as a great example. There are many throughout the Bible; even Abraham, how Sarah persuaded him to have a child by Hagar. Noah, getting drunk after the ark landed, and of course, Adam and Eve. How about Judas Iscariot? On and on throughout the Bible; life is about choices, it is also about seeing the danger ahead, being warned, and responding to those warnings.

I guess if anyone knew about the tricks of the "ladies," it might be Solomon. Let's not lay it all on the women now. There are so many temptations out there. We need to listen to the warnings of God's Spirit if you are a child of God.

Look at this verse:

Therefore, let him who thinks he stands take heed lest he fall. No temptation has overtaken you except such as is common to man; but God is faithful, who will not allow you to be tempted beyond what you are able, but with the temptation will also make the way to escape, that you may be able to bear it. (1 Corinthians 10:12-13)

There are always choices. God will provide a way out if you choose it. As I said, the devil can't make you sin, God can't make you saved, it is ALL your choice!

> And there a woman met him, with the attire of a harlot, and
> a crafty heart. She was loud and rebellious, her feet would
> not stay at home. (Proverbs 7:10-11)

One of the things I used to say to myself when I saw a woman dressed provocatively was "It pays to advertise". - Misjudgment? Maybe so, but, what is the message being sent from her? Do you see how Solomon puts it? *"And a crafty heart."* She desires to attract you. It is your choice not to follow.

Now it is interesting in the story of David and Bathsheba. I have heard several say, "She should not have been bathing out on the roof." Don't neglect the culture of the day. We don't know the circumstances. It may have been hot. This may have been her daily custom. There are many options, as with David, he already had several wives. There was no reason for him to do what he did; he had a choice at that point.

I think the problem today is that we don't think there will be consequences. It is a "one-night stand," a one-time affair. It doesn't work that way. The danger?

And do not grieve the Holy Spirit of God, by whom you were sealed for the day of redemption. Let all bitterness, wrath, anger, clamor, and evil speaking be put away from you, with all malice. And be kind one to another, tenderhearted, forgiving one another, even as God in Christ forgave you. (Ephesians 4:30-32).

When you make the wrong choice, you grieve God's Holy Spirit within you. The way I describe it is, "God takes His hand off your life". He is no longer directing you. You are still a child of God! But, you have chosen not to listen to Him or obey Him. So, God just "backs off" and allows you to make your choices, and pay the consequences. He warns you, of course, through that same Holy Spirit. You decide whether to listen and obey, or not!

Solomon chooses this scenario to make this point. The attractions of a woman to a man; there are right ways and wrong ways, - your choice!

> At times she was outside, at times in the open square, lurking at every corner. So, she caught him and kissed him; with an impudent face, she said to him: "I have peace offerings with me; today I have paid my vows." (Proverbs 7:12-14)

That is the description of temptation: *Lurking at every corner.* If we are looking it is not hard to find "opportunities". They are all around us. The "choices" are staggering. I guess the question might be, "How grounded are you?" Grounded in the principles and truths of God's Word!

I think there is something else here; maybe I might be "stretching" it a bit. I get the impression she is trying to come across as "Christian".

Look at verse 14:

"I have peace offerings with me, I have paid my vows."

Peace offerings can be traced to Leviticus 3, which deals with "peace offerings." Whether that is her reference or not, I don't know. I think it is an interesting remarks to someone she is trying to lead astray.

I think it is interesting the amount of time and the tactic that Solomon is using to warn us of the wiles of Satan.

Do you realize that God created (within us) these desires, these attractions? The problem is that these are godly instincts that can be used for ungodly purposes. If God gave us these feelings I guess we can blame God for the results. - Really? God has blessed us with so many great things; it is what we do with them.

I remember thinking before I was saved, that if God created the "hops, rice and best barley malt" (commercial). Then God thinks it is okay to drink beer. It is what man has done with what God created. God has nothing to do with liquor. The same is true with our "attraction" to the opposite sex. It is not the attraction; it is what we do with that God-given emotion.

I keep harping on decisions and consequences but isn't that what the Bible is all about? That is the message God is trying to tell us.

27. In what book of the Bible contains the longest chapter in the Bible?
    a. Jeremiah   b. Psalms   c. John   d. Leviticus

> So, I came out to meet you, diligently to seek your face, and
> I have found you. (Proverbs 7:15)

We can usually find what we are seeking, be it good or bad; it all comes down to what is in our heart. Here is a familiar verse, I hope:

But seek first the kingdom of God and His righteousness, and all these things shall be added to you. Therefore, do not worry about tomorrow, for tomorrow will worry about its own things. Sufficient for the day is its own trouble. (Matthew 6:33-34)

Here is my take: "You don't need to go looking for trouble, you will find it soon enough." We are given God's priority in Matthew. This guy in Proverbs is looking for trouble. Notice the promise in Matthew? If we are seeking the things of God, God will give us the right person to commit our lives to. The problem is we can't wait on God; we want what we want when we want it.

How familiar are you with Solomon's life? Let me give you some verses:

*You shall surely set a king over you whom the Lord your God chooses; one from among your brethren you shall set as king over you; you may not set a foreigner over you, who is not your brother. But he shall **not multiply horses** for himself, nor cause the people to return to Egypt to multiply horses, for the Lord has said to you, 'You shall not return that way again. Neither shall he **multiply wives** for himself, lest his heart turn away; nor shall he **greatly multiply silver and gold** for himself.* (Deuteronomy 17:16-17)

I guess Solomon missed that lesson in Sunday school (look at 1 Kings 10 and 11). Solomon acquired all three, against the directions of God in Deuteronomy. Solomon paid the price for his disobedience in chapter 11. There are consequences for ignoring the Word of God. So, how familiar are you with God's Word? I hope this devotional will encourage a more committed effort to spend more time in God's Word.

          Lonny E. Young

> I have spread my bed with tapestry, colored coverings of
> Egyptian linen. I have perfumed my bed with myrrh, aloes,
> and cinnamon. (Proverbs 7:16-17)

Okay, time for a refresher course:

*So, when the woman saw that the tree was good for food, that **it was pleasant to the eyes**, and a tree desirable to make one wise, she took of the fruit and ate. She also gave to her husband with her, and he ate.* (Genesis 3:6)

Of course, we just reviewed that David SAW Bathsheba bathing and desired her. Satan has so many tricks up his sleeve, the lust of the eye (1 John 2:16) is a very useful trick.

Have you noticed the new CGI techniques used today? That is how Spiderman and others can do all these tricks; it's an animation that looks so real. I was watching this movie about the 300 soldiers that defended Israel or something like that. There are two versions, the one with actors, and then there is one with animation (CGI). It is hard to tell the difference; our eyes are deceived.

Satan does the same thing. Do you notice the lengths this woman goes through to "entice" her prey? Satan does not only dress it up but then whispers in our ear, "it's okay!" I'm sure you have been fooled more than once by "packaging". The question is, how do we prevent it?

I love the story of the U.S. Treasury agents detecting counterfeit money. They become so "familiar" with the REAL THING that when they see a phony they can recognize it. Again, that's where the Word of God comes in. If you are ignorant of God's best, God's plan and purpose, you will fall for any trick the devil throws in your path.

I mentioned before that one of his tricks is "impatience". It is the "right now" syndrome. Satan is more than willing to provide whatever you want right now . . . at a cost! The greatest cost is being out of God's will. What is Satan promising you today? Will you fall for his lies or trust God to give what you want when you need it?

> Come, let us take our fill of love until morning; let us delight ourselves with love. For my husband is not at home; he has gone on a long journey. He has taken a bag of money with him, and will come home on the appointed day. (Proverbs 7:18-19)

Famous last words! No one knows what will happen in the next hour, let alone a week from now; when you begin counting on "your" timetable, you are headed for disaster!

Again, deception, deceit, lying, adultery, sin! The trap has been set. The surroundings perfect, "Come into my parlor", said the spider to the fly. Nothing has changed. The only difference today is, the decor, the extreme methods used, the enticing message, - it is still the same lie! You don't have to follow God's principles. You will be okay, don't worry.

I once got to spend the weekend with some friends who ran a motel in California. They told me the biggest difficulty was detecting a "bad" situation. Sometimes it boils down to instinct.

Why would God go to such lengths to include these examples in His Word? It is a warning, a graphic picture of the obstacles we face in this world; the tricks that Satan is "allowed" to play. We are tested in this world to see what kind of "relationship" we have with our heavenly Father. Sure, God allows these tests. How can He know if He can use us for greater things? If we fail, God continues to put "lessons" in our path, hoping, to grow us up as His children.

I mentioned that my favorite teacher in school was Mrs. Stenson; I had another teacher that I was reminded of the other day. One year, in grade school, I had missed almost six months because of Hepatitis. I did some homework, but not enough. I was sure she would fail me and have me take the fifth grade over. She didn't, she had let me pass me. Mrs. Mullins was not liked by the class. She even, at one point, smacked my hands with a ruler for being disruptive. I will never forget her as well.

God puts people in our path to teach us things. If we are walking with the Lord, on the path He has chosen, we will learn and grow. Grow our faith by trusting in God through these tests. When a test (trial) comes, we ask God, "Lord, what are you trying to teach me?"

28. Where was Paul going when he saw the resurrected Christ?
    a. Ninevah   b. Galilee   c. Damascus   d. Sodom

          Lonny E. Young

> Now therefore, listen to me, my children; pay attention to the
> words of my mouth; do not let your heart turn aside to her
> ways, do not stray into her paths. (Proverbs 7:24-25)

Do not let your heart turn aside to her ways. What a key statement. Where is your "heart" concerning God the Father? If you are a child of God, you have a "relationship" with God. (Romans 8:15). If you are a child of God you can never break that "relationship!" Also, if you are a child of God you CAN break your "fellowship" with God the Father. The same way a rebellious child breaks fellowship with his parents. Your sin can break that fellowship!

Let's back up a minute. How do you become a "child of God?" It is really simple.

Let's look at a verse in Romans:

*If you confess with your mouth the Lord Jesus Christ and believe in your **heart** that God raised Him from the dead, you will be saved.* (Romans 10:9).

Did you notice that it must begin in the heart? Let's finish the thought.

*For with the **heart** one believes unto righteousness, and with the mouth confession is made unto salvation.* (Romans 10:10).

These are all well and good. Can the heart be deceived? Of course, it can. Can you deceive God? Take a look:

But the Lord said to Samuel, "Do not look at his appearance or his physical stature, because I have refused him (Eliab). For the Lord does not see as man sees, for man looks on the outward appearance, but the Lord looks at the heart. (1 Samuel 16:7).

When you have opened your heart (Revelation 3:20) and received Jesus Christ as your Lord and Savior you become a child of God. Nothing after that will ever change that relationship!

> For she has cast down many wounded, and all who were slain by her were strong men. Her house is the way to Hades, descending to the chambers of death. (Proverbs 7: 26-27)

We learned yesterday how to become a child of God through faith in Jesus Christ. Let me give you my favorite verse on faith:

But without faith it is impossible to please Him, for he who comes to God must believe that He is, and that He is a rewarder of those who diligently seek Him. (Hebrews 11:6)

The picture that Solomon paints in these two verses is the result of rejecting the offer God has made. We have talked a lot about choices recently. Here is the most critical choice you will ever make in your life! It is not a decision based on "facts" or "knowledge" there are millions who know "who" Jesus is, that will not get them to heaven. It is faith in Christ's atonement for our sins on the cross of Calvary that gets you to access to the Kingdom of God.

I believe that God created every one of us with a piece missing. Many will spend a whole lifetime searching for that piece. Just read the book of Ecclesiastes and Solomon's search for that missing piece. Solomon had the where-with-all to try everything "under the sun." Look at his conclusion:

Let us hear the conclusion of the whole matter: Fear God and keep His commandments, for this is man's all. (Ecclesiastes 12:13).

I found a list of topics covered in Proverbs, there are 18 words listed; I think it is interesting that the "heart" is not listed, yet it is mentioned throughout Proverbs. I think that is why it is so important to have a "relationship" not a "religion" with God. He desires, of course, our praise and worship, but I think most of all, He would desire our obedience. It is so important to Him that He chose 40+ prophets throughout history to record His story and His desire for a relationship with His creation. He desired it so much He sent His son to die for us on the cross to pay for our sins.

Does not wisdom cry out, and understanding lift up her voice? She takes her stand on the top of the high hill, beside the way, where the paths meet. (Proverbs 8:1-2)

I love this picture! It is so relevant today. Where do you go for truth today? We are "consumed" with "Social Media". We have a world of knowledge in our hands. I don't know how many times I have "Googled" something to find an answer; instead of sleepless nights trying to remember an obscure fact, I just "Google" it.

I wonder what "Google" would say if I asked it how to get to heaven. No, I'm not going to. I think I can guess. It will give all the "learned" opinions of this "religion" and that philosopher, etc. Just consider the source! My source is the VERY Word of God!

There are those two words again - wisdom and understanding. Just a note here; Do you remember what Solomon prayed for, when he was made king, and God came to him and said?

At Gibeon the Lord appeared to Solomon in a dream by night; and God said, "Ask! What shall I give you?" (1 Kings 3:5)

*"Therefore, give to your servant an **understanding** heart to judge Your people. that I may discern between good and evil. For who is able to judge this great people of Yours?"* (1 Kings 3:9)

Have you ever asked God for an "understanding" heart? Not wisdom, not knowledge, but simple understanding, - quite a request.

Here is another reference to paths. If you are walking the path WITH God wisdom and knowledge are walking right there with you. Solomon asked God for the ability to discern good and evil. Interesting? That was the name of the tree that God forbid Adam and Eve from eating of (Genesis 2:17). That knowledge must come from God, not a tree. Satan encouraged them to disobey God and seek it for themselves. It is a great picture of today. We seek the knowledge of good and evil from every source but God. It is clear in God's Word what is good and what is evil. But we would rather "Google" it, instead of searching the Scriptures from a source that REALLY knows!

29. What unit of measurement was used to measure the ark in Genesis?
    a. feet   b. yards   c. denari   d. cubits

> She cries out by the gates, at the entry of the city, at the entrance of the doors: "To you, O men, I call, and my voice is to the sons of men. O you, simple ones, understand prudence, and you fool's, be of an understanding heart. (Proverbs 8:3-5)

I love that phrase, "understanding heart." It must start with the heart, that is where God's Spirit comes to dwell, and that is where God begins to work in our lives, to draw us closer to Him. Both Romans 10:9 and 10:10 refer to the heart, not the head. I have said before you can know everything there is to know about Jesus, historically. If you haven't accepted Him as Savior you will miss heaven

This is such a "cultural" thing here, "At the gates". I remember in my study of King David that two of his sons (Absalom, Adonijah) began their rebellion by standing at the gates and gradually pulling the people away from David. It is where the message is proclaimed.

Okay, let's use the same picture. Who or what is standing at the "gates" of your heart and calling out to you? If it is not the Word of God you are in trouble! That, to me, is the miracle of the Bible. You can read the same passage ten times. On that eleventh time, God will grab your heart and turn on a light that will blind your eyes! It speaks to you when God chooses to speak to you. The problem is you must read it to see the miracle!

We have "she's" at our gate in hundreds of ways proclaiming "truth" in our ears. How do you know who or what to listen to? I referred earlier to "Google". I pray that is not your source of knowledge. Is that the "she" that is proclaiming in your ear. "Google" is just a by-word for the internet. Now we are finding out that they can control the content of the web. So, the "world" has influence, if that is our source.

What is the warning of Solomon in this proverb? "Consider the source". Who or what are you listening to? Where do you go for "answers"? Here is a tougher question. What do you have for a foundation to base your decisions on? Grade school, high school, college all have contributed to your foundation. Your parents and peers have contributed to your foundation. Where does God fit in your foundation?

          Lonny E. Young

> Listen, for I speak of excellent things, and from the opening of my lips will come right things; for my mouth will speak truth; wickedness is an abomination to my lips. All the words of my mouth are with righteousness; nothing crooked or perverse is in them. (Proverbs 8:6-8)

Have you ever said something you wish you could take back? Of course, you have, we all have.

In our church once, as the Sunday School Director, I scheduled "Teachers Meetings" on Wednesday night before the Prayer Service. One night, after the meetings, a teacher walked in for the evening service. I remarked to her, "You're an hour late". In which case, she did an about-face and left the church. After the prayer service, I drove to her house and apologized. I will never forget that episode. Have I been perfect ever since? Not by a long shot. Why is there such a gap between our mouth and our brain?

One of the most frequently studied books in the New Testament is the book of James. Here is what James says:

My brethren, let not many of you become teachers, knowing that we shall receive a stricter judgment. For we all stumble in many things. If anyone does not stumble in word, he is a perfect man, able also to bridle the whole body. Indeed, we put bits in horses' mouths that they may obey us, and we turn their whole body. Look also at ships although they are so large and driven by fierce winds, they are turned by a very small rudder wherever the pilot desires. Even so the tongue is a little member and boasts great things. See how great a forest a little fire kindles! (James 3:1-5)

Great verses, great lesson. I mentioned before, we cannot retrieve words spoken. We can apologize, yes! Just like my memory, most of the time these "hurtful" words remain. It doesn't take but a split second to run those words you are about to say, through your mind, even better, through your heart! Are they necessary? Are they beneficial to the hearer? Can they edify the hearer? -Important questions to ponder before offering your two-cents worth; sometimes that's all their worth.

> They are all plain to him who understands, and right to those who find knowledge. Receive my instruction, and not silver, and knowledge rather than choice gold; for wisdom is better than rubies, and all the things one may desire cannot be compared with her. (Proverbs 8:9-11)

Have you ever given someone counsel that changed their life? Told someone a bit of wisdom that encouraged or uplifted someone? It is such an awesome feeling. Of course, we need to have that wisdom to pass along.

I got a call one evening from a friend who was struggling with something. Right away the Lord brought 2 Corinthians 1 to my mind. I shared these verses with them:

Blessed be the God and Father of our Lord Jesus Christ, the Father of all mercies and God of all comfort, who comforts us in all our tribulation, that we may be able to comfort those who are in trouble, with the comfort with which we ourselves are comforted by God. (2 Corinthians 1:3-4)

For a long time, I thought that these verses meant that if we have gone through a similar trial we can then comfort those who are going through the same trial. Then, I realized that the comfort Paul is talking about is not our shared trial, but the comfort of Jesus Christ. He comforts us just as He wants to comfort others. That is the point.

They are plain to him who understands! (8:9a). When we understand that God is working in our lives to, not only, teach us but to bless others. The "wisdom" from the Word is that blessing we pass on to others. One of my very favorite illustrations comes from Dr. Charles Stanley:

Because God is Omniscient He knows where we are in the (storm) trial. Because He is Omni-present He is with us in the (storm) trial. Because He is Omnipotent He will bring us through the storm (trial). Chew on these words a bit. Let them sink in. You are not alone in whatever you are going through. He brought you to it; He will bring you through it!

30. Who was thrown in the lion's den?
    a. Daniel   b. Joshua   c. Jonah   d. Matthew

> I, wisdom, dwell with prudence, and find out knowledge and discretion. The fear of the Lord is to hate evil; pride and arrogance and the evil way and the perverse mouth I Hate. Counsel is mine, and sound wisdom; I am understanding, I have strength. (Proverbs 8:12-14)

Great words! Solomon has such a way with words; wisdom, knowledge, understanding. What does this mean to me? This has been a struggle for me as well. It is so clear to me, but I am on this side of the glass. The glass?

It's hard to explain sometimes. It's like when you are witnessing to a lost person. You know where you are. But, they are on the other side of this wall or glass. You try to explain to them what it is like here. You might try to draw a "word picture" but unless they see it for themselves they can't begin to grasp the significance of your words; the difference between heaven and Hades.

Solomon uses these words like, understanding, wisdom, knowledge, etc., but unless you have asked Jesus into your heart, unless you have become a child of God; you can't fully understand what we are talking about.

We have been where you are. We know what it is like to be lost. I guess that's part of the frustration. You see, once you have taken that step, by faith, you will then remark, "Now I understand." You cannot say that until you have the Holy Spirit living within you. It is the presence of the Holy Spirit that opens the heart of God to you.

The Holy Spirit is working on you right now. If you're not a child of God the Holy Spirit is dealing with you, convicting you of your estrangement from God the Father. Your sin has separated you from any relationship with God. Until, by faith, you ask Jesus to come into your heart (Revelation 3:20) you cannot know the blessings of being on this side of the glass.

All of these big words that Solomon uses? They simply describe the joys of being a child of God. You have a much better understanding of God's Word. You relate to people differently. You realize that God has a very special plan for your life. (Jeremiah 29:11-13)

> By me kings reign, and rulers decree justice. By the prince's rule, and nobles, all the judges of the earth. I love those who seek me diligently and find me. (Proverbs 8:15-17)

Okay, I can't help it, there is too much similarity in these verses and my favorite verses:

*For I know the thoughts (plans) that I think toward you, says the Lord, thoughts (plans) of peace and not of evil, to give you a future and a hope. Then you will call upon Me and go and pray to Me, and I will listen to you. And you will seek Me and find Me, when you search for Me with all your **heart.** (Jeremiah 29:11-13)*

Don't overlook that word in Solomon's verse 8:17 "diligently". It must be something you have set your heart to do. Seeking God can be the most rewarding endeavor you have ever done in your life!

Do you see this? God is in charge. I'm sure you have "debated" those who have come along and have been elevated to "leadership" status? No doubt. Can you say that God raised them or set them down? If not, then you "limited" the power of God. That brings up an interesting point; if God raises and sets down those in leadership, what about King Saul? - God picked him, a bad king to rule His people, he didn't start that way. Don't forget it was the "peoples" request!

Samuel even told them they were making a mistake. They wanted it THEIR way, in their time! God gave them what they wanted. I personally, think David was God's plan all along. Israel just got ahead of God's plan. It's a long story!

The point is God is in control. Nothing surprises God, nothing catches Him off guard; there is one thing we can do to God, we can break His heart. I think that night that David sent for Bathsheba broke God's heart. David was called, "A man after Gods own heart." That night he broke God's heart. Was God surprised? Not really. I'm sure He had hoped for a different outcome, - surprised? No!

The same is true in our life. Just like Jeremiah 29, God has a plan to bless us. It is our choice what we do with that option!

> Riches and honor are with me, enduring riches and
> righteousness. My fruit is better than gold, yes, than fine
> gold, and my revenue than choice silver. I traverse the
> way of righteousness, in the midst of the paths of justice.
> (Proverbs 8:18-20)

I have to share this. An atheist once complained that there were no holidays for them. Then someone replied, "Sure there is, April 1st."

The fool has said in his heart, "There is no God." (Psalm 14:1)

Verse twelve begins this paragraph, *"I, wisdom."* So, the person, if you will, speaking is wisdom. So, everything the "world" offers is no match for wisdom; Gold, silver, riches, etc. How precious is wisdom? If it is so valuable, how do we get "wisdom?" This is one of the prominent words in the book of Proverbs.
This is the same author who wrote in Ecclesiastes:

I communed with my heart, saying, "Look, I have attained greatness, and have gained more wisdom than all who were before me in Jerusalem. My heart has understood great wisdom and knowledge." And I set my heart to know wisdom and to know madness and folly. I perceived that this also is grasping for the wind. For in much wisdom is much grief, and he who increases knowledge increases sorrow. (Ecclesiastes 1:16-18).

The same author wrote both quotes. Don't you wish we could get a "definite" definition of "wisdom"? What is your definition of wisdom? Does it mean we are so wise we don't make mistakes? Does it mean we have all the answers? Does it mean we are perfect? I don't think so; there was only one perfect person. So, what does wisdom mean?

For me, - I noticed a word that is frequently in the book of Proverbs and throughout the Bible; the word "path". To me, wisdom would mean being smart enough to find God's path for your life and then to walk in it, daily, one day at a time, one step at a time.

31. Who did Jesus raise from the tomb?
    a. Lydia   b. Lazarus   c. Luke   d. Jacob

> That I may cause those who love me to inherit wealth, that I may fill their treasures. The Lord possessed me at the beginning of His way, before His works of old. I have been established from everlasting. From the beginning, before there was ever an earth. (Proverbs 8:21-23)

Allow me to lay a couple of verses that came to mind here:

In the beginning was the Word, and the Word was with God, and the Word was God. He was in the beginning with God. (John 1:1-2)

And the Word became flesh and dwelt among us, and we beheld His glory as of the only begotten of the Father, full of grace and truth. (John 1:14)

*This book of the Law shall not depart from your mouth, but you shall meditate in it day and night, that you may observe to do according to all that is written in it. For **then** you will make your way prosperous, and then you will have good success.* (Joshua 1:8)

If you're looking for a definition of wisdom, meditate on these four verses; recognize that Jesus Christ is the Word of God in the flesh, then take Joshua's challenge and begin a regular time of meditation in the Word of God. Wisdom is the ability to recognize God working in your life; the ability to listen to AND obey the prompting of God's Holy Spirit, the ability to trust God by faith for the direction and path of your life, - THAT is wisdom!

Then there is the alternative, the "world", - the wisdom of the world. There is no god but you, you are in complete control of your destiny, you will determine what happens and how prosperous you will become; if that is your attitude you might want to read Isaiah 14:12-15.

There is only one God; that is the "beginning" of wisdom! The day you begin thinking you know more than God does, that you have complete control of your life. You might want to ask yourself, "Who determines my next breath?" God can take you home anytime according to His choosing, NOT yours!

          Lonny E. Young

April 3   93-272   Proverbs 8

> When there were no depths I was brought forth, when there were no fountains abounding with water. Before the mountains were settled, before the hills, I was brought forth; while as yet He had not made the earth or the fields, or the primal dust of the world. (Proverbs 8:24-26)

The older I get the more I seem to be doing this, - "Reflecting". Now, of course, I don't "live" in the past. That is not healthy; I don't know how many times I think back and wish I had done some things differently. God doesn't have that problem!

Do you think He wishes He had done things differently in the Garden? No! God knew the price He would pay for allowing His creation to have "free will"; He knew what man would do. Don't you think it pained Him to include this episode in His Word?

As a "baby" Christian I used to ask, "When God saw Adam and Eve in the Garden, did He see Jesus on the cross?" Of course, He did. When God sees His creation make such terrible decisions in their life it hurts Him terribly! When He saw David send for Bathsheba it broke His heart. That is the price for our "free will." The extent of how much God loves us is demonstrated, on the cross of Calvary. Throughout the Bible, if you read all of it, you can get this picture of God's ultimate plan; the final battle in Revelation, all the events that lead to that final victory. We are simply a small paragraph in that enormous victory.

I know that doesn't seem that important right now. The point, God knows what is going to happen in your life. There is a loving desire for your success and growth. THEN. There are the choices you make. It is in your hands. The steps you take, the course you chart, and the path you follow is YOUR choice.

Of course, God desires you follow in His footsteps, His path. The choice has always been and always will be yours! From the Garden of Eden to David and Bathsheba to the decisions you make today. It is God's will versus your will. Never forget that!

God even provided His constant presence in your life; if you are a child of God, in the person of His Holy Spirit living in your heart to help you make the right decisions, you simply must listen!

When He prepared the heavens, I was there, when He drew a circle on the face of the deep, when He established the clouds above, when He strengthened the fountains of the deep. (Proverbs 8:27-28)

Why do you suppose God took the time to include the first two chapters in Genesis? God goes into detail about the creation of man in the third chapter. So, why the first two? Several reasons. To demonstrate His awesome power of His spoken word! I think He wanted to show us that not everything can be completed immediately. To create something worthwhile takes take! We are in a "hurry-up" generation. Relax, take your time, do it right!

Later in Genesis, God also demonstrates that He can destroy His creation as well. The grace of God demonstrated, by choosing Noah and his family to restart His creation, - just a note. God was ready to destroy the nation Israel at Mt. Sinai as well. Then Moses interceded for them. (Exodus 32:10-14)

In the creation scenario, we can see the power of God. That same God wants to work in your life. The catch is you must trust Him. You must allow Him to work in your life!

I remember so vividly one night in our church; it was a "Watch-Night" service. They showed a film of the martyr Hess. Halfway through the film, I had to get up and leave. God was so real to me that night. He confirmed His call in my life, I will never forget that night. The miracles He performed in my life from then on are amazing. Maybe not to someone else, but I know what God has done. He can do miracles in your life as well if you trust Him!

Look at this verse:

But without faith it is impossible to please Him, for he who comes to God must believe that He is, and that He is rewarder of those who diligently seek Him. (Hebrews 11:6)

Don't miss those last parts, who diligently seek *Him*. It is your choice, as it has been from the first days of creation. When God created man, He gave him the ability to choose! It is your choice!

32. Who had to work fourteen years for his wife?
　　　a. Jacob　　　b. Isaac　　　c. Daniel　　　d. Joseph

When He assigned to the sea its limit, so that the waters would not transgress His command, when He marked out the foundations of the earth, then I was beside Him as a master craftsman; and I was daily His delight, rejoicing always before Him, rejoicing in His inhabited world, and my delight was with the sons of men. (Proverbs 8:29-31)

I heard a theory once to explain the Creation process; God is the owner, He determined to build the world and all its creation. His Son Jesus is the architect, He designed it all, and He drew up the plans. Finally, the Holy Spirit was the contractor.

Look at this verse:

*The earth was without form, and void; and darkness was on the face of the deep. And the **Spirit of God** was hovering over the face of the waters.* (Genesis 1:2).

Interesting thought, I like the analogy. All three of the God-head were involved in creation!

I love the reference to a foundation; that is such an important concept in the Christians life. Many times, when I think about Joseph's life (Genesis 37-50) I often ask myself what kind of "foundation" Jacob instilled in his son. Joseph was seventeen (37:2) when his brothers decided to sell him to slave traders in the wilderness. He went into bondage in Potiphar's home; he was falsely accused and sent to prison. Not exactly a promising life. Then after many years in prison, forgotten by friends he met in prison, Joseph becomes, next to the Pharaoh, the second most powerful man in Egypt. Joseph was thirty years old (41:46) when he became the second in charge of Egypt. My question is what kind of foundation did he have to remain true to God throughout thirteen years of slavery and bondage?

How does this apply to us today? "Foundation" is the keyword; a foundation that begins early in Sunday school and worship, a foundation in the Word of God. I love this verse:

For no other foundation can anyone lay than that which is laid which is Christ Jesus. (1 Corinthians 3:11)

> Now therefore, listen to me, my children, for blessed are those who keep my ways. Hear instruction and be wise, and do not disdain it. Blessed is the man who listens to me, watching daily at my gates, waiting at the posts of my doors. For whoever finds me finds life, and obtains favor from the Lord. (Proverbs 8: 32-35)

That phrase reminds me of Dr. Charles Stanley. He is always saying, "Are you listening, say amen." It is so hard to focus today. You have so many messages coming from so many different sources. It is hard to tell who to listen to or believe today. How is one to know? My favorite saying is "consider the source." Can you trust the source of your guidance?

"My children", the Apostle John uses that phrase so many times in First through Third John.

Look at this verse:

Behold what manner of love the Father has bestowed on us, that we should be called children of God! Therefore, the world does not know us, because it did not know Him. (1 John 3:1)

As for being "children of God" check out Romans 8:15, I love it!

There's a Be-attitude! Do you see it? *Blessed is the man who listens to me.* (v. 34), - A promised blessing. What is the "condition of the blessing? You must listen to the Word of God, hence, Solomon's writings here in Proverbs. Check this out for yourselves. You might need to use the concordance in the back of your Bible. Look up all references to the word "Blessed". Matthew 5 lists the "Be-attitudes". There are many, many more throughout the Bible; a promised blessing. Next, see if there is a "condition" to that blessing. Something in that verse that YOU must do to receive that blessing. Let me give you one more:

Blessed *is he who reads and those who hear the words of this prophecy, and keep those things which are written in it; for the time is near.* (Revelation 1:3)

          Lonny E. Young

> Wisdom has built her house, she has hewn out her seven pillars. (Proverbs 9:1)

Okay, do you have any idea what the "seven pillars of wisdom" might be? Solomon doesn't give any details. I guess, first, we can assume that wisdom is based on a foundation; there are seven tenets to this foundation. You can make your list; I think I will give it a try.

One: Our parents. Our parents begin very early in life to lay a foundation for the rest of our life; they teach us basic principles. Obedience for authority should be at the top!

Two: Our teachers. Today there is a priority on "Day Care" or preschool. We are finding out that children begin learning at a VERY early age; our teachers are critical in the early foundational truths.

Third: The church. The same is true with the church as it is with teaching; Sunday school, learning the basics of a relationship with God the Father. Learning about God's role in our life!

Fourth: Our peers. This can be good or bad; it is so important that a parent be aware of who their children hang out with. They can have a lifetime effect.

Five: Experience. We need to encourage our children to get out of their "comfort zone", try new things, NOT harmful things but things that will round them out as a person like sports, exploring, Scouts, etc.

Six: Relatives. These individuals can have a profound effect on a person growing up. Many times, children will confide in a grandparent or uncle before they will their parents; you must be aware of their counsel.

Seven: Read. Encourage reading, beginning with the Bible. Sunday school will help greatly here. Watch the books your children read, they can pick up ideas and habits that will not add to their lives; encourage the regular reading of books that will add to who they are.

That's my guess, maybe you have some to add or change. The point is to stir some thought into what kind of foundation is being built in your children, just because they have grown and left home doesn't mean your job is over; you can still contribute to their learning process. Point them to a relationship with God; If Christian, how is their fellowship with God?

33. Who was the first person to reach heaven?
    a. Adam   b. Enoch   c. Able   d. Seth

> She has slaughtered her meat, she has mixed her wine, she
> has also furnished her table. (Proverbs 9:2)

Preparation, - is that what you see here? Of course, we can go every which way in analogies with this picture. Again, Solomon doesn't bother to explain. After reading ahead a bit I think he is talking about the "sin" trap.

Of course, Satan is working overtime to "dress up" sin. He makes it look so inviting. Much of the proverbs we have read so far are in that vein; the "attractiveness" of sin, disobeying God. It is interesting how Solomon derides those who fall for these traps. Yet, his seven hundred wives and three hundred concubines did just that! They slowly drew Solomon away from the very God who blessed him with this wisdom.

Interestingly, Solomon uses food, the "dinner" table if you will. I am so thankful that I married a wife who can cook. She is fantastic because it is so important, Satan works overtime to dress up his "tricks" to deceive us. Satan can make sin look so enticing!

The trap is set, - could you recognize a "trap" if you saw one? How would you know? First, if you're a child of God you have the Holy Spirit getting your attention. Of course, if you're lost, assuming your conscience is not seared, you may be warned that way; it depends on how far you have fallen.

Look at this verse:

No temptation has overtaken you except such as is common to man; but God is faithful, who will not allow you to be tempted beyond what you are able, but with the temptation will also make a way of escape, that you may be able to bear it. (1 Corinthians 10:13)

That is if you have God's Spirit working within you; if you have broken fellowship with God, that Spirit may be so faint you can hardly hear Him. In which case, it will be easy to ignore Him. If you are walking with God that Spirit will be like a neon sign flashing "Beware!" It is your choice. I want God "active" in my life!

                    Lonny E. Young

> She has sent out her maidens, she cries out from the highest
> places of the city. (Proverbs 9:3)

Spring is just around the corner. I hope you are growing through this walk through the book of Proverbs; any study of the Word of God should draw you closer to God, encourage you in your daily walk, and challenge you to have a closer fellowship with God our Father!
It is all around us. The Bible calls it "the world".

Look at this verse:

"These things I have written to you, that in Me, you may have peace. In the world you will have tribulation, but be of good cheer, I have overcome the world. (John 16:33)

Jesus is telling us that we don't have to succumb to these tricks of the world. That is who this gal represents; the tricks of Satan, and the world. We have looked at these before. It bears repeating. The three, most, powerful tools Satan uses:

For all that is in the world—the lust of the flesh, the lust of the eyes, and the pride of life—is not of the Father but is of the world. and the world is passing away, and the lust of it; but he who does the will of God abides forever. (1 John 2:16-17)

The tricks of Satan can be boiled down to these three. Satan even tried to use them against our Lord in the wilderness (Matthew 4). His response? The Word of God, verses from Deuteronomy.

The message from Solomon in using this "temptress" is that Satan will use any means possible to draw us away from God. Is Satan tempting you right now? Another lie he likes to use is time. You don't have "time" to give to God. Sometimes "time" is ALL you must give to God. It comes down to a serious word: Priority!

Take a minute today before the day ends. Go over in your mind. What are the top five priorities in your life? Spouse, family, job, salary, home, whatever it might be. Then ask yourself, "Where does God fit into this list?" Think about it!

> "Whoever is simple, let him turn in here!" As for him who lacks understanding, she says to him, "Come, eat of my bread and drink of the wine I have mixed. (Proverbs 9:4-5)

Before I was saved I spent a year in Vietnam in the United States Air Force; I can boast that I have gotten drunk on about any mixture you can think of, I have also seen the effects on a buddy of mine. He had gotten a "Dear John" letter. We found him passed out between two buildings, we took him to the medics; when he came to, and it took four huge guys to hold him down. It was terrible.

After I was married I drank a little. After I was saved, I realized that my drinking took control of my mind and body OUT OF MY HANDS. I was no longer in control of what I thought or what I did. That was the end of my drinking; I get teased sometimes at parties when I ask for a cup of coffee, but that's all right. At least I can drive home.

I never want anything controlling me but the Spirit of God. Okay, that sounds hoaky, so be it.
This is the second mention of wine in this chapter. I have no problem with a glass of wine now and then. It's in the Bible. As it is with anything, it depends on the amount. It is said a little wine is good for you; emphasis on a "little." A lot of people like to quote this verse:

No longer drink only water, but use a little wine for the stomach's sake and your frequent infirmities. (1 Timothy 5:23).

I'll bet most people don't know where the verse is, yet they quote so often. Notice Paul also says a "little". You need to consider the culture as well. They like to quote the "Wedding at Cana" as well, where Jesus turns water into wine.

I am not here to debate the use of wine; when you lose control of your mental functions it is an open invitation for Satan to use you to say things you wouldn't normally say nor do things you wouldn't do, - that is not glorifying God!

That is Solomon's warning here: Beware of the tricks of Satan. Sometimes the consequences can last a lifetime!

34. How many disciples were in the upper room when Jesus first appeared after His resurrection?

    a. 12   b. 9   c. 11   d. 10

April 11   101-264   Proverbs 9

Forsake foolishness and live, and go in the way of understanding. (Proverbs 9:6)

Just as I thought!

Christians are not supposed to have any fun, Solomon says so. - Really? Can you look back over your life and see some "dumb" things you did and wish you could have a "Re-do"? Of course, you do.

I remember when I first started driving; I learned the hard way to pay attention to what I was doing, it was when I made a left turn in front of a police officer, - I woke up! The ticket also got my attention, I remember "noticing" how much money I was throwing away on bounced checks because I just didn't pay attention; lessons we learn as we grow older. That is what Solomon is talking about.

Of course, I could have avoided much of that with proper instruction; but then again I would need to heed the instruction. That is the whole point of Proverbs, the instruction is there. What you do with it is up to you.

"Go in the way of understanding." I got in trouble with my boss once. She asked me to do something and I asked her, "Why?" I told her that if I understood why I would do a much better job. She explained it to me; I understood and proceeded to do the job. Sometimes supervisors might get upset when you question them; you NEED to understand why you need to do something. THE BIBLE!

You see when you get a grasp on God's Word, you "understand" God and what He wants for your life; what your salvation cost God, your relationship with Him. When you begin to understand that your walk in this life will be so much more productive and enjoyable! It all boils down to understanding.

You can't understand anyone or anything until you become familiar with it, - that is the whole point of the Bible. If you have never read through the Bible, you can't really know God. There is a great book out; it's called "THE PATH". It will take you book by book through the Bible in one year. Sorry for the shameless plug, I wrote that book. The premise is true; a one year journey through the entire Bible, it is quite a journey. You will then understand God better!

> He who corrects a scoffer gets shame for himself, and he who rebukes a wicked man only harms himself. (Proverbs 9:7)

So, we should not correct someone? - If you think it will profit them. It has been my experience that it usually doesn't work. Want to know my approach? Just tell them, and then walk away. They are the ones who need to decide. It is the same as sharing the Gospel message. If the Holy Spirit isn't dealing with them, it won't work. You can share the message; plant the seed, then let God do the rest.

I saw this show the other day. It was about teaching "Dudes" on a dude ranch to corral steers. He said, "You push the steer as close to the gate as you can. Then you stop, let them think about it, then they usually will go into the corral." That is so true. You share the message. Allow them to choose from. You may need to come back later. DON'T PUSH IT!

Most people, you know this; don't take kindly to "instruction" or someone "correcting" them. Their first response is rebellion. Just state your case, and then back off. Let them "digest" what you have said. God's Holy Spirit can do a much better job than your "persuasive" words.
If they are lost how does the Holy Spirit work on them? They don't have the Holy Spirit within them.

Look at this verse:

And when He (Holy Spirit) has come, He will convict the world of sin, and of righteousness, and of judgment: of sin, because they do not believe in Me; of righteousness, because I go to My Father and you see Me no more; of judgment, because the ruler of this world is judged. (John 16:8-11)

Like the parable in Matthew 13. Your job is to sow the seed (Word of God) it is God's job to produce the crop! Don't take on more than your part. Let God do His part.
It would be easy to use Solomon's words and say that we should not say "anything". That is not the point. Have you heard this?

It is not wise to argue with a fool. Listeners can't tell which is which. My paraphrase; you get the point.

      Lonny E. Young

> Do not correct a scoffer, lest he hate you; rebuke a wise man,
> and he will love you. (Proverbs 9:9)

How would you describe a "scoffer"? This might help; it seems I knew this concept long before I read Proverbs. When I was in the United States Air Force I had this friend, his name was Smith (not real name), and we went through Basic Training together.

After Basic, we were transferred to Travis AFB in California, Smith was from St. Louis. This was in the mid-'60s. St. Louis had won the World Series and the Royals were the Athletics at this point. Anyway, Smith was always putting down Kansas City vs. St. Louis. It was constant; there was nothing good in Kansas City compared to St. Louis.

One day I got tired of it, we were at lunch in the Dining Hall. He started his tirade; I agreed with everything he said. I wouldn't argue or disagree, I agreed with everything. He got so mad he got up and left the table. Sometimes that is all they want, to argue!

Some have made up their minds and nothing will change it; that is who Solomon is talking about. No amount of experience, knowledge, proof or anything will convince them otherwise. Now, God can change their minds. He has a special way of reaching the "stubborn". All we can do is pray. Invoke the power of God to persuade them.

I don't claim to be a "wise" man by any stretch. I did learn early on, EVERYONE has something to teach us. Everyone who passes through our lives is for a reason. God sent them into your life for a reason.

The interesting thing about rebuke is if you refuse it or denies it; eventually, those with wisdom will not offer that critical advice that could solve some problem. You refuse counsel, your counsel will disappear. That has always been my goal early on. There IS always something you can learn from others if you are willing to listen and think about that counsel. Here is some counsel from the Psalms 1:1

*Blessed is the man who walks **not** in the counsel of the ungodly, nor stands in the path of sinners, nor sits in the seat of the scornful.*

35. What city did the apostle Paul come from?
    a. Ninevah   b. Tarsus   c. Bethel   d. Damascus

> The fear of the Lord is the beginning of wisdom, and the knowledge of the Holy One is understanding. For by me your days will be multiplied, and years of life will be added to you. (Proverbs 9:10-11)

Neither of my parents was "church-going" parents. The only effort to get us in the church was from our grandmother who would take us usually on Easter. My parents did instill in me one thing, a "reverence" for God; a "respect" for the things of God. No Bible, no prayer, nothing like that. I think they taught me the "existence" of God early on.

The "fear" of God is that reverence. It is not the traditional definition of fear as we know it; it is a "reverence". Of course, that is only the first step toward a real "relationship" with God. It's like Hebrews says:

But without faith it is impossible to please Him, for he who comes to God must believe that He is, and that He is a rewarder of those who diligently seek Him. (Hebrews 11:6).

If you don't have that "reverence," that faith that God exists, you are not going to search Him out. When God begins dealing in your life, you will have a million questions; the first thing you need to do is, by faith, ask Jesus to come into your heart. God will send His Holy Spirit into your heart and He will open the Bible to you, - through prayer, Bible study, going to church, you will begin to create a fellowship with the God of the Bible. Your understanding of your relationship with God will continually grow, and then God will "stretch" your faith. He will lay on your heart challenges that will test your faith in Him. Read about Abraham and Isaac.

The closer you learn to walk with God, the more you are willing to trust Him and step out of your comfort zone. Then the more God will use you in greater and greater ways; He must see the extent of your faith in Him. How much can He use you? Once you solely trust God's direction and leadership, you will be amazed at what God can and will do in your life. Trust me, I know!

April 15   105-260   Proverbs 9

> If you are wise, you are wise for yourself, and if you scoff, you will bear it alone. (Proverbs 9:12)

Have you heard this: "Keep your opinions to yourself?" I wonder if this is what Solomon is getting at. I can't count the number of times I have gotten into trouble by sharing what was on my mind, without thinking. People are not, usually, interested in "your" opinion. You would think at 72 years of age I would know better, - I don't! It is a tough lesson to learn.

I was teaching a Sunday school class once. This individual offered his opinion that was totally off the subject, I said to him, "That is irrelevant." He never came back to class; I was right of course, but it didn't need to be said. That's not the first time, you don't need the details.
How do you learn to run what you are going to say, through your brain, better still, your heart? I do have one good trait that Solomon is talking about. I don't ridicule or make fun of someone. I am nowhere near perfect; I have no right to talk down to anyone else.

Okay, let's look at what James says:

For we all stumble in many things. If anyone does not stumble in word, he is a perfect man, able also to bridle the whole body. Indeed, we put bits in horse's mouths that they may obey us, and we turn their whole body. Look also at ships: although they are so large and are driven by fierce winds, they are turned by a very small rudder wherever the pilot desires. Even so the tongue is a little member and boasts great things. See how great a forest a little fire kindles! (James 3:2-5)

I don't want to neglect to mention "Tax Day", - the day when we reimburse the government for "services rendered." Think on these things. Value for money spent is between you and the ballot box.

This might go along with the verse in Proverbs. How much complaining do you hear around this time of the year? Yet they wouldn't be caught dead in the voting booth; gripe and complain yet to do something is too much trouble. Interesting!

> A foolish woman is clamorous; she is simple, and knows nothing. For she sits at the door of her house, on a seat by the highest places of the city. (Proverbs 9:13-14)

I have been trying to chronicle my early life, leading up to when I met my wife. So, I went back and remembered four "girlfriends" who passed through my life. I can thank God that I never married any of them. God blessed me there! Of course, we never know, "what if". Just be thankful for the one God put in your life.

I am so thankful that my wife and I found the Lord at the same time. We had been married for fourteen years before we came to know Jesus as our Savior. In fact, it was just after our fourteenth anniversary; so, we can verify the tremendous difference God can make in a marriage. If you are not a child of God, you ought to be.

God thinks so much of the wife in a marriage that He included several verses at the end of Proverbs (31:10-31) about a virtuous wife.

Until you have found the one that God has joined you to, you will be miserable! Don't misunderstand; it is not all a bed of roses. The thing is that you "grow" in the Lord together. One may be saved longer than the other but you still learn together, if God is the center of your marriage.

I used to perform marriage ceremonies. During the sermon, I would give the illustration of two people joined together by a string. If you lift the center of the string you naturally draw the two parties together; that is the picture of Christ in marriage. If God is raised in marriage He will draw the man and woman together.

Of course, today, marriage is becoming extinct. Why bother, let's just live together. The thing about that is there is no "commitment" to each other; either one can walk out for any reason at any time. There is no "bond". When couples pledge to each other in marriage it is a "commitment" to each other that when the storms come they hold on to each other, not run away!

My wife and I have been married for fifty-one years. There are others in our church married much longer. They understand the meaning of marriage. It is a commitment!

36. Who was King Solomon's mother?
    a. Jezebel　　　b. Esther　　　c. Bathsheba　　　d. Tamar

> To call to those who pass by, who go straight on their way: whoever is simple, let him turn in here. As for him who lacks understanding she says to him. (Proverbs 9:15-16)

I have talked about those individuals who have passed through our lives and have impacted us in some way. How about you? Of course, it is hard sometimes to know if you have left your "mark" on someone; most of the time we don't know if anyone even notices what we do.

Years ago, I was the Sunday School Director, deacon, and I prepared the church bulletin each week and finally, I was the church clerk. The point is I was "involved" in our church. One day, I received a note in the mail; it was from a church member that said, "We are aware of all you are doing in our church. We appreciate your hard work and faithfulness." It blew me away. I have been noticed and appreciated.

Have you ever sent something like that? Once I prepared a "special" thank you note for the pianist and organist in our church and put them on their bench. They usually go unnoticed but are a vital part of our worship experience. Have you ever made a "special" effort to thank someone who works behind the scenes?

So, what does that have to do with the verses above? *"To call to those who pass by."* Many people pass through our lives. Some may be for only a day; they can leave a lasting impact. Especially if they teach you something that will benefit you the rest of your life. Do you notice them? Do you pay them any attention? Think about it.

Okay, I must share this verse from Hebrews:

Let brotherly love continue. Do not forget to entertain strangers, for by doing some have unwittingly entertained angels. (Hebrews 13:1-2)

I really believe this; God can and does send certain people into our lives for a purpose. Maybe to put us back on the right track, maybe to encourage us when we need it the most; any number of reasons. Don't let them go unnoticed. They may be in the form of "Pew Pals" you set with every Sunday, who knows?

> Stolen water is sweet, and bread eaten in secret is pleasant.
> But he does not know that the dead are there, that her guests
> are in the depths of Hades. (Proverbs 9:17-18)

All around us, people are dying and not going to heaven. One of my saddest moments, when I look back, has to do with my dad. I told my parents that I had surrendered to the ministry. Right away, my dad set about making me a portable "pulpit". It was fantastic! I still use it today if I am going to teach for any length of time.

When I went to pick it up, my dad said, "Let's hear a sermon." I had just surrendered and knew little or nothing about preaching. I hummed and hawed my way out of it. I could have at least talked about John 3:16. Something, - I never got another chance. To this day I don't know if I will see my dad in heaven. I am hoping he made a profession of faith during the war or something, I just don't know; a missed opportunity.

Are there any in your circle that you might share Jesus with? Are you praying for any lost souls? I have a list of names in my Bible that I pray for every morning. Are you praying?
You see, that is what I see in this verse above. *"But he does not know that the dead are there."* Do you remember what God warned Adam and Eve of, in the Garden?

But of the tree of the knowledge of good and evil you shall not eat, for in the day you eat of it you shall surely die. (Genesis 2:17)

We all know they ate of the fruit but they didn't die. Was God lying? Of course not; they died "spiritually", they broke that special fellowship they had with God. They died in their hearts! Just a note, - God told this to Adam before Eve was created! It was Adam's responsibility to teach or tell Eve.

The point is there are all kinds of "death". Dead people are walking all around us. NO, I'm not talking about a TV fantasy. I am talking "spiritually" dead who are condemned to an eternity in Hades if someone doesn't share with them the price that Almighty God paid so that they may spend eternity in heaven.

                         Lonny E. Young

> The proverbs of Solomon: A wise man makes a glad father, but a foolish son is the grief of his mother. Treasures of wickedness profit nothing, but righteousness delivers from death. The Lord will not allow the righteous soul to famish, but He casts away the desire of the wicked. (Proverbs 10:1-3)

I am seventy; both my parents have passed away. I would love to talk to them right now; I guess I would start by saying, "I'm sorry." I can look at back at so many mistakes, times I should have said, "I love you, and didn't", times I neglected them, and times I could have spent more time with them. You know the drill, I'm sure you would love the same opportunity. Are they still alive? Well?

Simple basic truths from Solomon; the righteous prevail the lost fail. If you have spent any time in the Bible you recognize that truth. So, what do you do about it? Because you know the truth and don't act on it, really makes you a fool. That is like seeing a stop sign but just driving right through it. Someday it will be fatal. Just because you made it once, doesn't mean the averages won't catch up with you.

Do you see the promise here? *The Lord will not allow the righteous soul to famish.* An interesting way to put it; you know as well as I, God never promises prosperity all the time to every Christian. God uses many different ways to "get our attention". He wants us to be mature, grown-up, Christians; to do that He will use various means to stretch us, mold us, shape us into the child He wishes us to be.

Here's a good challenge. What might the *"treasures of wickedness"* be; ill-gotten gains? Profiting from someone else's misery? There is no profit in that. *"Righteousness delivers from death."* Okay, if we are righteous we won't die. Come on. Our righteousness before God is as filthy rags (Isaiah 64:6). So how will that save us from death? Remember, we talked earlier about "spiritual" death. Some have used "right standing before God" as a definition for righteousness.

When we can stand before God, clothed in the blood of God's Son's by faith, we will be spared that "spiritual" death. We have the promise of God. When you have asked Jesus into your heart, we claim the power of Jesus atonement on the cross, and we will not die!

37. How many books of the Bible start with the letter "J" (not counting 1-2-3 John)
    a. 7   b. 10   c. 3   d. 9

> He who has a slack hand becomes poor, but the hand of
> the diligent makes rich. He who gathers in summer is a wise
> son; he who sleeps in harvest is a son who causes shame.
> (Proverbs 10:4-5)

We all know those in our life that worked hard all their life; many with little or nothing to show for it. Sometimes it is the next generation or later that reap the benefits of our labors. Here is a great promise:

Therefore, my beloved brethren, be steadfast, immovable, always abounding the work of the Lord, knowing that your labor is not in vain in the Lord. (1 Corinthians 15:58)

Now, if you read that verse you could almost make the argument that he is talking about "ministry". Is that what Solomon is talking about? Not really. There is that word "diligent" again. It is the "quality" of the work we do that glorifies our Lord. You could get the same impression from this next verse:

For God is not unjust to forget your work and labor of love which you have shown toward His name, in that you have ministered to the saints, and do minister. (Hebrews 6:10)

I think it is the "faithful" diligence to the work God has called us to, that Solomon is extolling. One more verse if I may:

His Lord said to him, "Well done, good and faithful servant; you have been faithful over a few things, I will make you ruler over many things. Enter into the joy of your lord." (Matthew 25:23)

The words of Jesus, - the greatest reward we possibly receive when we stand before our Lord would be these words: *"Well done, good and faithful servant."* A faithful "servant" is what God desires for our lives. No matter the "vocation" it is our faithfulness to God that will be rewarded!

> Blessings are on the head of the righteous, but violence covers the mouth of the wicked. The memory of the righteous is blessed, but the name of the wicked will rot. (Proverbs 10:6-7)

This is a typical Solomon proverb. Good versus bad, plus versus minus, do it, don't do. This, to me, is what makes proverbs hard to read as a whole. It is almost better to meditate on each segment. Example: *Blessings are on the head of the righteous, but violence covers the mouth of the wicked.* Two contrasts - The righteous and the wicked; plus and minus. Catch this promise?

Blessing on the head of the righteous. So, exactly what or who is "the righteous?" We could assume they are children of God. But, in Solomon's time, Jesus had not died on the cross. Then we might believe they are "believers" in God, - Just believers? I think not. The "righteous" are those who not only "know" God, but obey Him! That is a big difference.

Look at the promise: *Blessings.* Now, look at the results of the wicked: *Violence;* that is the "fruit" of disobedience, the fruit of the wicked. In violence, there is no peace, no "relationship" with God. The wicked are estranged from God, they have no peace.

I have used two such contrasts here. *The memory of the righteous is blessed.* Again, the contrast; this is a good place to encourage a separate notebook. Proverbs is meant for an in-depth study.

Take a 3-ring binder full of notebook paper. You could start with "righteous" or "righteousness". As you go through Proverbs note the verses and the promises associated with "righteous".

In my study Bible, it says there are 18 topics in Proverbs. Lying, laziness, wisdom, and fools seem to be the most used. There are some words for your notebook; a separate page for each. As you discover verses using any of these words note what is said. Soon you get a handle on what God is trying to teach us about each subject. It helps to gather together the various verses on one topic and glean the message God has for us.

Just a note: The same can be done with Psalm 119 which focuses on the Word of God. There are eight words consistent throughout Psalm 119; they are - Law, testimonies, precepts, statutes, commandments, judgments, ordinances, words.

> The wise heart will receive commands, but the prating fool
> will fall. He who walks with integrity walks securely, but he
> who perverts his ways will become known. (Proverbs 10:8-9)

I noticed in the list I sighted yesterday that the "heart" is not mentioned. Add that to your list. On that page about the heart, you might note the different "kinds" of hearts that are described. In this verse, it is a "wise" heart.

Let me caution you. NEVER tell someone to do something. There is something in our nature that automatically "bristles" at a "command". You ask or suggest, but never TELL someone to do something. That is the devil that whispers in your ear, "You don't have to do what they tell you." Notice what Solomon says above!

See the contrasts, the "wise heart" and the one who "walks with integrity", the pluses, versus the "prating fool" or the "perverts". And you thought that word was a recent word.

Have you ever thought of "correcting" anyone with these serious character flaws? The fool or the pervert. Solomon, to me, is warning us that God will deal with these character flaws. It is not up to you to point out the flaws of others. If I remember, God's counsel is to avoid them. Stay away from them. Don't associate with them. God has His methods of dealing with them

I wonder what Solomon means hereby: *"walks with integrity"*. It is a confident walk; a walk if you will with God. God is at his side in confidence that brings peace to the one with that integrity, "walks securely". There is a peace that comes in our walk when we know we are walking with God. We are on His game plan, His path that He has chosen for us. We can take each day with confidence and assurance that God is in control and He will take care of each step.

There is something along those lines with the "wise heart". Taking commands is not only from those around us but also commands from God. Has God ever asked you to do something that you thought was totally out of your "comfort zone."? Did you do it? That is part of what Solomon is getting at here. Not just the commands of those over us, but the "commands" of God in our walk with Him.

38. How many books of the Bible start with the letter "Z"?
     a. 2   b. 3   c. 1   d. none

> He who winks with the eye causes trouble, but a prating fool will fall. The mouth of the righteous is a well of life, but violence covers the mouth of the wicked. (Proverbs 10:10-11)

Have you ever been "misunderstood"? That is the trouble a "wink" can get you into. Gestures or comments not taken the way they were meant. Today in "Social Media" it is even worse. In Matthew 5:37 Jesus says,

"But let your 'Yes' be 'Yes', and your 'No, be 'No'. For whatever is more than these is from the evil one.

This is the second time Solomon has used "the prating fool will fall." Most of us understand what a "fool" is. A "prating fool"? My interpretation is one who rattles on and on. That is the picture I get. Have you ever talked to someone who has done everything you have done but better? That kind? That is the picture I get.

I made a mistake once when I visited a friend in the hospital; they said they were having "minor surgery". I came across as not that concerned, someone corrected me! If YOU are having a surgery it is NOT minor! - My mistake; that might be a "prating fool."

There is a neat statement: *The mouth of the righteous is a well of life.* Why is that? Contrary to my previous remark, we can say things that will inspire and lift. That is the mouth that Solomon is referring to; one that encourages even makes someone laugh.

Our pastor must employ some joke writers; each sermon has one of those jokes you wish you could remember to repeat. I am not good at telling jokes. The thing about his jokes is that they illustrate the point of his message; they point right to the heart of his message. There is a profitable joke!

Then some are the opposite; they spew hatred, vulgar language that insights crime and violence. It is sad the power that those "wicked" words have over people. The problem is that they don't listen, or think about the power of these words. They cause damage or death, words have consequences; that is the point, I think, Solomon may be trying to make here.

> Hatred stirs up strife, but love covers all sins. Wisdom is found on the lips of him who has understanding, but a rod is for the back of him who is devoid of understanding. (Proverbs 10:12-13)

There is so much in just one verse; if I did it one verse at a time I would not cover nearly as many verses.

Have you noticed the degree of hatred in our world today? Common sense has long since disappeared. You can't just be in favor of something; you must "hate" the alternative.
I remember growing up, and not too long ago, that parents chastised their children for using the word "hate". Now they are taught to hate anything they disagree with. The devil is truly in charge!
Now look: *But love covers all sins.* That immediately takes me to the cross.

*"For God so **loved** the world that He gave His only begotten Son, that whoever believes in Him should not perish but have everlasting life."* (John 3:16)

That is the love that covers our sins; because of that demonstrated love we have the right to stand before God cleansed of our sins; IF you have accepted Christ into your heart, and have become a child of God. That is the ONLY way your sins will be covered!

Do you remember what happened in the Garden of Eden? When Adam and Eve disobeyed God, they sinned; because they had sinned they could not remain in the presence of God. God "expelled" them from the garden; before He sent them away He replaced their man-made fig leaf clothing with animal skins (Genesis 3:21). Animals that had to die to provide them suitable covering.

That is a perfect illustration of what Jesus did on the cross of Calvary. Jesus became our sacrifice, our blood payment, to cover our sins. Only by the power of that sacrifice can we even approach the throne of God; because of that blood, we are no longer condemned to Hades but are now children of God. (Romans 8:15).

I see this picture, in the movie The Ten Commandments when pharaoh's son runs to the throne because he is his son, he has that right. That's us!

  Lonny E. Young

> Wise people store up knowledge, but the mouth of the foolish
> is near destruction. The rich man's wealth is his strong city; the
> destruction of the poor is their poverty. (Proverbs 10:14-15)

Have you learned all there is to learn? I am sure you have met people like that. Every day is fascinating to me. I am over seventy, I have read through my Bible over ten times. In Sunday school, I found a verse I had never seen before. I love the words in Romans 8:15, *"Abba, Father."* I keep quoting that verse. I found out Sunday that the same phrase is also used in Galatians 4:6. I never noticed it there before.

EVERY day is a learning experience. When you have shut your mind to new things, you are as good as dead. The dreaded "Comfort Zone" term we have come to fear. You learn new things when you dare to get out of that dreaded zone!

I think it is interesting that Solomon equates the "mouth" with destruction. Probably the biggest lesson a "wise" person learns is to keep their mouth shut. That is why God gave us two ears and one mouth. It is surprising how much you can learn when your mouth is not in use!
The beginning of verse 15 is an interesting quote. *The rich man's wealth is his strong city.* Jesus cautioned about wealth in Matthew:

*Then Jesus said to His disciples, "Assuredly, I say to you that it is **hard** for a rich man to enter the kingdom of heaven.* (Matthew 19:23)

Now, why would that be? Of course, the rich man begins to put his "faith" in his money instead of God. That would be called an idol. God hates idols! (Psalm 115:4-8). It was so important that the psalmist repeats it in Psalm 135:15-18. You see, Solomon points out that the "rich" take their refuge, their "security," in their wealth (strong city).

Be careful that knowledge doesn't become an "idol" as well. When you begin to think you have it all figured out. You know all there is to know, even about God; He has a way of bringing you to your knees, humbly before the God of the universe!

Our wisdom must be in the wisdom of God, - His direction, His provision, His plan for our lives. That is faith!

39. What is the first word in the Bible?
    a. It   b. Is   c. In   d. An

> The labor of the righteous leads to life, the wages of the wicked to sin. He who keeps instruction is in the way of life, but he who refuses correction goes astray. (Proverbs 10:16-17)

Do you see a theme here? Solomon is all about "instruction" isn't he? Of course, I talked about this before. We "receive" instruction from the first year of our birth. Two things: Do we make an effort to retain that instruction, and, do we use that instruction?; both important elements of instruction.

Have you noticed how much Solomon talks about "life" recently? That could go all kinds of directions. That "life" is the path that we were put on at birth. Look at this picture in Jeremiah:

Before I formed you in the womb I knew you; before you were born I sanctified you; I ordained you a prophet to the nations. (Jeremiah 1:5)

That is a message to every one of God's creation. We were created for a purpose. The problem is that God also gave us a "free will" to determine whether we will accept God's plan and purpose, or will we go our own way. How foolish not to seek God's plan. (Jeremiah 29:11).

April is almost over, soon we will be into the summer months, -vacations and many other things will battle for our time. Let me encourage you to maintain this walk through Proverbs; a daily time of reading and reflection. When we begin thinking we don't have time for God, we will more and more, begin trusting in our resources and wisdom and will drift further and further from God's influence. Don't let that happen during these busy summer months.

It is interesting how easily we can get distracted and confused about certain priorities in our life. How easy is it to distract you from God? I have begun being very aware of this. I will start the day with a certain plan unless God tells me otherwise; I must make myself stick to that plan. Now God may put detours, but that's fine! But sometimes it's just me, and I must say: "Stick to the plan!"

          Lonny E. Young

> Whoever hides hatred has lying lips, and whoever spreads
> slander is a fool. In the multitude of words sin is not lacking,
> but who restrains his lips is wise. (Proverbs 10:18-19)

Have you seen it? It is so prevalent today; unverified statements that seem to become facts yet are not. It is sad where our culture has come to; you know as well as I do, it must come to an end. What has happened to integrity anymore? Okay off my soapbox.

So, what does this have to do with me? It begins with you; take a minute, inventory your integrity. If you told someone something would they believe you? Do you know the definition of slander? It is simply lying about someone else. "Gossip" could fall in there somewhere.
Solomon doesn't mince words. It is flat-out wrong; even if you "think" something about someone else. Keep it to yourself. I love the second part (v. 19a):

In the multitude of words sin is not lacking.

Do you remember your grandmother's proverb? "If you can't say something nice, don't say anything at all." It is interesting how much "grandma's" sayings can be traced to the Bible; that doesn't change the truth of the saying, - be it, Solomon or grandma, the truth is the same. The problem is, no one is practicing it today.

Do you know what term they use today? "Drama", there is too much "drama" here; same difference. *He who **restrains** his lips is wise.* There is not a lot of variety in Solomon's truths; basic truths that he seems to express in different ways. That doesn't make them any less important. Maybe one of the "versions" will catch your attention and make a difference in your speech patterns.

One of my favorite sayings, before I became a Christian, was "I don't get mad, I get even." I'm sure you have never thought that. Look at 18a "*Whoever hides hatred has lying lips*" The Solomon translation of my statement. Hatred will eat you alive if you dwell on it. You must turn that over to God!

> The tongue of the righteous is choice silver; the heart of the wicked is worth little. The lips of the righteous feed many, but fools die for lack of wisdom. (Proverbs 10:20-21)

Let me share a verse concerning righteousness:

But we are all like an unclean thing, and all our righteousness are like filthy rags; we all fade as a leaf, and our iniquities, like the wind, have taken us away. (Isaiah 64:6)

Solomon has talked a lot about "righteous," and righteousness. My definition of that word is simply, "right standing before God." Who among us can claim enough righteousness to stand before Almighty God? None!

But now the righteousness of God apart from the law is revealed, being witnessed by the Law and the Prophets, even the righteousness of God, through faith in Jesus Christ, to all and on all who believe. For there is no difference. (Romans 3:21-22)

The only "righteousness" we can claim, in standing before God, is the righteousness given to us by faith in Jesus Christ. Until we have asked Jesus into our hearts and become children of God we have NO standing before God. All our "deeds" are as filthy rags.

Paul is arguing that many Jews claimed their "righteousness" through Abraham, through the Law of Moses. Paul says that the righteousness that God recognizes is through His Son Jesus. The Law simply pointed out our inadequacies in "self-righteousness."

Twice in the two verses above Solomon uses the term "righteous"; simply referring to those who walk in obedience to God. The Old Testament "saints" claimed "righteousness" from obedience to the Law. When they obeyed God, they were righteous. That would be where the sacrifices came in. Once Jesus died on the cross there was no more need for sacrifices. The ultimate sacrifice had been made. Our righteousness is now in faith in Jesus Christ!

40. What did God call the day following His finished creation?
    a. Sunday   b. Sabbath   c. Sanctified   d. Service

> The fear of the Lord prolongs days, but the years of the wicked will be shortened. The hope of the righteous will be gladness, but the expectation of the wicked will perish. The way of the Lord is strength for the upright, but destruction will come to workers of iniquity. (Proverbs 10:27-29)

How many ways can you say, the righteous versus the wicked? That is the message. - Solomon's simple contrasts. Ho hums, really? Is this not important? It doesn't matter how many "different" ways you say it, the message is the same.

From the Garden of Eden to the Revelation; those who follow God obey His commands, will prosper and eventually go to heaven. Those who don't won't. Wait a minute! Are you saying if you're good you go to heaven? Not in a long shot. I said, "Obey God." Do you think God sent His Son to die on a cross so we could have a nice Christmas story? Not hardly.

Without accepting Jesus Christ as your Savior; asking Jesus to come into your heart (Romans 10:9) you're not going to heaven. It is that simple. That is obeying God's commands. Without the blood of Christ, you are condemned to Hades!

Solomon is trying every expression he can imagine, to make one simple point. He settled that in the twelfth chapter of Ecclesiastes:

Let us hear the conclusion of the whole matter: Fear God and keep His commandments, for this is man's all. (Ecclesiastes 12:13)

Why were Adam and Eve expelled from the Garden? They disobeyed God's command. Why are the twenty-one plagues brought on the world in Revelation? To convince mankind that this is their LAST chance to turn to God. God is consistent throughout the Bible. Disobedience brings judgment, obedience brings salvation.

You must admit Solomon is very creative in bringing that simple message to our attention, and hopefully, to our hearts! It would be interesting to find out how many times the term "fear of the Lord" is used in the Old Testament, even more curious, the New Testament.

> The righteous will never be removed, but the wicked will not inhabit the earth. The mouth of the righteous brings forth wisdom, but the perverse tongue will be cut out. (Proverbs 10: 30-31)

The righteous and the wicked; the eternal battle, the eternal conflict, the eternal conclusion - Do you see that? *But the wicked will not inhabit the earth.* Even Solomon, in his day, knew that God would win in the end. He never even heard of the book of Revelation. Was it revealed by God? I think not. I think Solomon knows the power of God. Solomon talked to God. And God talked to him in a dream. Look in First Kings and further.

There he goes talking about the "mouth" of the wicked. If you listen to the lost very long you can know where they are headed. Usually, they have a filthy mouth; especially about God. No respect, no reverence. Their mouth betrays them.

The mouth of the righteous brings forth wisdom. The problem is when you talk of God too much you get turned off, tuned out, ignored! Why is that?

I remember when I was first saved it was hard for me to say "God." Jesus was okay; we talked about Him at Christmas. The name "God "was uncomfortable. It is interesting because the more I got to know God the more comfortable I became talking about Him. That was long before I found Romans 8:15, "Abba, Father." The term of endearment God's children used toward their heavenly Father.

Now there is another promise kept in the book of Revelation. *The righteous will never be removed.* Wait a minute. Doesn't the "Rapture" occur before the Tribulation? Yes, we may be temporarily taken to heaven but we will soon return with our Lord and inhabit "a new heaven and a new earth."

This earth belongs to God. Satan thinks he will win that battle and be the ruler of the earth. Satan must have forgotten who created it in the first place. God is "sovereign" over His creation. He is simply giving Satan free reign for a time. To give us the same choice He gave Adam and Eve. Follow Satan's lies, or trust God. Check out the first couple of chapters of Job you will get the picture!

Dishonest scales are an abomination to the Lord, but a just weight is His delight. When pride comes, then comes shame; but with the humble is wisdom. (Proverbs 11:1-2)

When was the last time you saw the word "abomination" used? It is a rhetorical question. It is not used that much, so it must be serious. God abhors dishonesty! Whether it is lying with crooked scales or trying to deceive your neighbor, or God Himself. Truth is the key word!

It is so hard today. Anyone can say anything with no proof, nothing, and demand to be believed, why? - The "truth or our "word" has come to mean little or nothing anymore. How did that happen? You used to be able to shake hands and it was considered an unbreakable contract. I would love to blame lawyers, but it isn't the lawyers, it is sin in our hearts. Sadly!

Do you remember the details of Christ's temptation in the wilderness in Matthew 4? Satan attempted to destroy Jesus' testimony with three attacks. He was hungry so Satan attacked the flesh. Satan offered Him all the kingdoms of world, the temptation of the eye. Finally, Satan offered Him to world to rule, the pride of life. You recognize these, don't you?

For all that is in the world—the lust of the flesh, the lust of the eyes, and the pride of life—is not of the Father but is of the world. And the world is passing away, and the lust of it; but he who does the will of God abides forever. (1 John 2:16-17)

This battle continues today. Think about the influence of these three temptations in your life. You are battling at least one right now. So, what is the answer? The same weapon Jesus used in the wilderness: The Word of God!

School will be out soon; more time on your children's hands. My mother was faced with this one year. At seventy-two I can still remember those days. She set out to teach us to name the fifty states in our country. To this day, I can name all fifty states. Why? - Because my mother was determined to teach them one summer. How about you?

41. Name one of Joseph's two sons.
    a. Naman   b. Manassah   c.Malachi   d. Ephraim

> The integrity of the upright will guide them, but the perversity
> of the unfaithful will destroy them. Riches do not profit in
> the day of wrath, but righteousness delivers from death.
> (Proverbs 11:3-4)

It is a growing process. For the most part, becoming a Christian is a growing process. When you get saved you have put your faith in the hands of God. You have asked Jesus to come into your heart and save you. Now what? Let me give you a hint. Get in the Word of God.

The integrity of the upright will guide you. So how do you get this *integrity of the upright.* By growing in the grace and **knowledge** of the Lord Jesus Christ! As you "grow" as a Christian, making the right decisions, they become more and more a part of your life.

When you ask Jesus into your heart (Revelation 3:20), you will automatically receive the power of the Holy Spirit. The Holy Spirit is so powerful; He will begin the process of cleaning house. He can work on your language, your bad habits (the hardest to change) and He will change your heart, to focus more toward God.

At first it will be awkward! You will begin to see things differently; your "priorities" will change. You will "gravitate" toward the things of God and away from the world. It may mean changing some of your friends. That won't be a problem, as you change, they will slowly find other friends. Don't worry you are NOT of the world, any longer.

It is interesting that as your "integrity" grows your outlook on life and your circle of friends will change. There must be a commitment to begin walking the path that God has chosen for you. (Jeremiah 1:5). God also has a plan for your life (Jeremiah 29:11). God wants only the best for you.

As we move into the summer months you may have more free time, or you may be busier than ever. Make it a "priority" to spend some time each day with God; both, in prayer and Bible reading. THE PATH has a great Bible reading schedule and some encouragement that can help you maintain this new-found fellowship, with the Creator of the universe.

The challenge is to not be distracted in these summer months. Stay focused in growing your fellowship with God the Father!

          Lonny E. Young

> The righteousness of the blameless will direct his way aright, but the wicked will fall by his own wickedness. The righteousness of the upright will deliver them, but the unfaithful will be caught by their lust. (Proverbs 11:5-6)

Righteousness, - Exactly what does that mean? I have shared that verse in Isaiah that says our righteousness is as "filthy rags". (Isaiah 64:6). So, how might we define "righteousness?" I have heard many different definitions. My favorite is "right living"; right living according to whom? - God, of course.

I hope this walk through the book of Proverbs might help in that definition. Just in that first line: *Righteousness of the blameless will direct his way aright.* We see that the closer we can walk with God, the easier to walk upright; to make the right choices. By contrast, *the wicked will fall.* They will stumble, they will be caught, and they will pay a price.

We look at the world today and we say, "Why don't they get caught and punished?" If you notice God doesn't give a timeline. He simply assures us they will. Can you trust that? Of course, you can. Just think about the number of times God says "wait" in His Word.

David is a great example; when David committed his sin with Bathsheba. Did God confront him right then? No, actually He waited over nine months. During that time David had Uriah killed; still no response from God. After the child is born God confronts David through the prophet Nathan. He could have confronted David as soon as Bathsheba said, "I am with child." (2 Samuel 11:5). No, maybe God was hoping David would confess and make things right. He didn't!

God deals with the wicked in His own way, in His own time. When we try to get involved, we cause all kinds of problems. Unless God specifically enlists your participation, you must allow God to be God!

I think what I am curious about in verse 6 is the word unfaithful. Unfaithful to what or whom, that can mean several things. Since they are caught in their lust, it doesn't describe their "spiritual" position. Are they saved? What does Solomon mean by "unfaithful"? Unfaithful to God's precepts? Unfaithful in following God. You decide!

> When a wicked man dies, his expectation will perish, and the hope of the unjust perishes. The righteous is delivered from trouble, and it comes to the wicked instead. (Proverbs 11:7-8)

I was thinking about the gospel message once; I came to this conclusion. Are you a gambling man? How much of the Bible do you know? Here is the point! Are you willing to bet eternity in Hades that the Bible may not be true? That is what you are doing. "Oh, I don't believe that book. It is all a fairytale". So, what will be your response when you stand before God? "Now I believe". - Really? I am afraid then it is too late.

One of my favorite stories is the "Passover" in Exodus 12.

Look at this verse:

For the Lord will pass through to strike the Egyptians; and when He sees the blood on the lintel and doorposts, the Lord will pass over the door and not allow the destroyer to come into your houses to strike you. (Exodus 12:23)

The "instructions" for applying this blood are given in verse 13. It is interesting that when God gave these instructions He didn't tell Israel WHEN the death angel would pass over. The interesting thing is that if an Egyptian believed this prophecy and applied the blood he would have been passed over as well. Likewise, if a Jew denied the prophecy his firstborn would have died. It was all a matter of faith in the prophecy.

If you can read the Gospels, the story of Jesus, and deny it, you are making the same gamble that the Egyptians made that night. "God wouldn't do that". - Really? You may want to spend some time in the book of Revelation as well. God waits, and waits, and waits until all have heard the message. One night He will pass through this earth with twenty-one plagues. Those who have not applied the "blood" will perish. It is that simple. One more verse in Revelation you might want to look at. Revelation 3:20. God is allowing you to apply that blood to your heart. It is up to you!

42. What were Adam and Eve wearing when they left the Garden of Eden?
    a. fig leaves   b. nothing   c. animal skins   d. robes

The hypocrite with his mouth destroys his neighbor, but through knowledge the righteous will be delivered. When it goes well with the righteous, the city rejoices; and when the wicked perish, there is jubilation. (Proverbs 11:9-10)

This is tough. I need to take issue with Solomon's last words here. As a Christian, it gives us no pleasure to see the "wicked" perish. It is sad. Granted, there is a part in us that "rejoices" when we see "justice." But the joy is quickly replaced with sadness because a lost soul is going to Hades. We never rejoice over someone, anyone, spending eternity in a place separated from God.
I understand Solomon's point. "Just rewards". They made their choice. Still, it hurts. Especially if it's someone you know. Why couldn't they see the truth? Why did they make the wrong decision? We don't know. God's plan from the creation in the Garden was that we would be held accountable for the choices we make, Adam and Eve were. It is nothing to rejoice in.

I wonder how many times Solomon mentions the "hypocrite"? You know what a hypocrite is. Says one thing, believes or does something else. Of course, there are no hypocrites in the church. Sorry, couldn't resist. We all know there are. There are hypocrites everywhere. The saddest are those who "profess" a relationship with God but show NO outward signs. There must be signs!

I am thinking Solomon's definition of the "righteous" maybe those who follow God; those who live godly lives. Christians for lack of a better term, it is hard to say in Solomon's day. Faithful to God?; Obedient to God's laws? Not sure. He uses the contrast throughout the Proverbs; the "righteous" versus the "wicked".

Do you think the lines are as clear cut today? Can you spot a "Christian"? The hardest part is trying to determine who is saved and who are not. We shy away from making that determination because then we would become "judges". We sure don't want to do that! By not questioning, we could very well be condemning someone to an eternity apart from God. Maybe they need to be confronted. At least both you and they will know what needs to be done!

> By the blessing of the upright the city is exalted, but it is overthrown by the mouth of the wicked. He who is devoid of wisdom despises his neighbor, but a man of understanding holds his peace. (Proverbs 11:11-12)

You know the "great commission" doesn't you? It is in Matthew:

Go, therefore and make disciples of all nations, baptizing them in the name of the Father and of the Son and of the Holy Spirit, teaching them to observe all things that I have commanded you; and lo, I am with you always, even to the end of the age. Amen. (Matthew 28:19-20)

I don't want to be a missionary! I can't go to some foreign land and witness to them. Let me ask you a question: Where does your world begin? The moment you step out of your door! Your "neighbor" is the beginning of your world. That person you work with every day, they are your world. What have you done to bring the Gospel to your "world"?

There is another "word" question. How many times does Solomon refer to his "neighbor"? Jesus was clear in His commission. I love it because of these words: *teaching them to observe all things.* I was called to be a teacher/pastor. That is my spiritual gift. Anything that reminds me to teach others, I get excited!

"Teaching them to observe all things", Observe "what" things. What things? Let's start with the Word of God. Observe what is written. Look what Luke wrote in Acts:

*These were more fair-minded than those in Thessalonica, in that they received the word with all readiness, and **searched the Scriptures** daily to find out whether these things were so.* (Acts 17:11)

I don't know what version they used, King James or NIV. They didn't have Bibles; they had the five books of Moses and some prophets. Probably Psalms and Proverbs; they searched them "daily!"

        Lonny E. Young

> A talebearer reveals secrets, but he who is of a faithful spirit conceals a matter. Where there is no counsel, the people fall; but in the multitude of counselors there is safety. (Proverbs 11:13-14)

A principle I have learned early on in my ministry. I will very rarely volunteer to speak. I will let God's Spirit lay it on someone's heart, to ask me. I have learned the hard way not to "knock" down doors, or try to force them open. That is the easiest way to head down the wrong path, apart from God's direction.

The same goes for "secrets". It seems the more I share the more trouble in getting into. I have increasingly learned to "shut up" and listen. You would be surprised how much you can learn. Especially about human personality! Don't miss the second part of verse 13!

Do you realize that the wisdom of verse 14 is demonstrated in the miracle of our Founding Fathers establishment of our government? I'm not sure of the exact breakdown. The U.S. House of Representatives selects congressman based on the population of each state. Then the Senate has two representatives from each state. The Executive Branch, the President is elected by the people. There is a multitude of counselors! Even the Electoral College, which many argue against, only when they lose, is based on the size of a state by population, not landmass.

The point being "a multitude of counselors"; Southern Baptist is often ridiculed for having so many committees. I am a firm believer in a multitude of counselors; with one exception. The twelve spies who were sent into the Promised Land, in the beginning. Interesting that Jesus had twelve disciples. I don't believe they "counseled" the Lord!

The godlier people who have in your circle of influence the easier it is to find God's will. Of course, it begins with your relationship with God. Are you listening to Him? Do you seek His counsel FIRST? You may be that "spiritual" influence on someone else seeking counsel. You need to maintain your fellowship with God; Walking in His Word, His wisdom, His direction.

Wise words from Solomon! I continually marvel at the wisdom of our Founding Fathers. Our system of government is like nothing else!

43. Who was the third child born to Adam and Eve?
    a. Cain   b. Able   c. Seth   d. Noah

> He who is surety for a stranger will suffer, but one who hates being surety is secure. A gracious woman retains honor, but ruthless men retain riches. (Proverbs 11: 15-16)

Sometimes, I have to let the Holy Spirit lead you in whatever you glean from certain verses.

This "surety" thing is interesting. I was dating a girl in Kansas City; I was stationed in Topeka, Kansas. I needed a car, I had no credit. My mother was gracious enough to co-sign for me. I don't think that is the same as the verse above. One more thing; that was the first and last co-signer I had.

The verse above says, "*for a stranger*" there is a big difference. There is a bit of wisdom I tried to pass on to my daughters once. The concept of trust is so fragile. You can spend years building trust between two people. It only takes one incident to destroy that trust; then the long process of rebuilding it. Trust is a fragile thing!

Have you been hurt by someone you trusted? I am sure you have heard the phrase, "Forgive and forget". We can forgive but we just can't seem to forget. It is in our minds permanently. The question then becomes, what do you do with it when it surfaces? Are you hurt again, or do you ignore it and move on. That is the "forgetting" part. What you do with it when it surfaces?

When you are surety for someone, that means you put your name behind theirs. You put your reputation, your word, on them. It is a very serious thing! Something that, one, is contrary to the Bible, two, must be seriously prayed about. I know there are "circumstances," but it must be prayed about.

I am writing this during the Supreme Court hearings; a woman's word versus a man's testimony. Integrity. This hearing could affect our culture for centuries to come. Our culture of "innocent until proven guilty" is in the balance, - unique to our culture and country; back to the Founding Fathers. Our country is unique! There is a constant battle to maintain the "rule of law". That is sad. You may want to spend a little extra time in this book of Proverbs; these are not just sayings from Solomon, these are truths inspired by God.

> The merciful man does good for his own soul, but he who is
> cruel troubles his own flesh. The wicked man does deceptive
> work, but he who sows righteousness will have a sure reward.
> (Proverbs 11:17-18)

Right off the bat, two verses in Galatians come to mind:

Do not be deceived, God is not mocked; for whatever a man sows, that will he also reap. For he who sows to his flesh will of the flesh reap corruption, but he who sows to the Spirit will of the Spirit reap everlasting life. (Galatians 6:7-8)

I love this concept of Dr. Charles Stanley based on this passage from Galatians. The Law of the Harvest: You will reap *what you sow, more than you sow, and later than you sow.* A biblical principle to meditate on. What you sow, more than you sow, and later than you sow!

The merciful man does good for his own soul. I have found this to be an interesting, subconscious change. When Jesus comes into our heart, He changes our heart. Things that didn't matter become important, caring becomes multiplied, and compassion is magnified; changes you might not realize at first. You look at people differently. If you have not asked Jesus into your heart, please consider thinking about it. The only "prayer" God hears from a lost soul is "Lord, save me." After that, the power of prayer becomes significant in your life!

I struggled with whether I should try this tonight. After witnessing the Senate hearings today, I saw real evil on display. I didn't want to bring those emotions here. But Solomon has been addressing evil and wicked people. To actually see it on display is scary.

My wife and I went to see "The Exorcist" when it came out. Even worse, we saw it in the theatre. My nervous system was out of whack for days. Granted, it was meant to be a horror film. I am not big on horror movies. There was something "evil" about this film that stirred us for weeks. I don't recommend it!

Solomon spends these many chapters and verses contrasting good and evil, righteousness and the wicked. For your edification!

The generous soul will be made rich, and he who waters will also be watered himself. The people will curse him who withholds grain, but blessing will be on the head of him who sells it. (Proverbs 11:25-26)

Generosity, giving, sowing if you will, all godly traits. I had to learn this the hard way. As a young Christian, I struggled with tithing. I knew I needed to. I wanted to. One year I got ahold of a book by Dave Ramsey, *Total Money Makeover*. It was simple, I could do this. Then I realized that an "unspoken" part of this plan was tithing. You needed God on your side.

One day I was looking at my bills. As an illustration: I would send a $100 payment to Capitol One. In a week, I would get the balance and then spend the remainder. Once I was a couple of days late. When I got the bill, after sending the $100, I owed more than I did before the payment. This must stop.

One Day, I asked the Lord: "Lord, if you will tell me who NOT to pay this month I will tithe." (It was that tight) God went to work. In two months, I had rearranged my bills, moved from the trailer we were trying to sell. Long story. Let me put it this way, in two months, I had enough "extra" each month, that it amounted to my "tithe". Go figure! I still didn't have any "extra" but I could now tithe.

In six months, I was on my way home; running this month's bills through my head. Guess what? I had a surplus this month. You guessed it "exactly" the amount of my tithe! I am a believer! In 2009, I had 69,000 dollars of debt. In March of 2016, I am completely debt-free. It took seven years of commitment, and Dave Ramsey's plan and God's grace, but God did it all!

When we are obedient to God's plan and God's principles God will lead us out of bondage! Check this verse in Proverbs:

The rich rules over the poor, **and the borrower is servant to the lender!** (Proverbs 22:7)

You are a "slave" to your creditors, make no mistake. You no longer control where your resources go. Think about it!

44. How long was Noah on the ark before it began to rain?
    a. a month   b. 7 days   c. 3 days   d. immediately

He who earnestly seeks good finds favor, but trouble will
come to him who seeks evil. He who trusts in his riches will fail,
but the righteous will flourish like foliage. (Proverbs 11:27-28)

Do you notice a theme in Solomon's remarks? It seems Solomon is saying that if you walk with God (righteous) everything will work out fine; you will be blessed, and no problems will occur. Do you see that?

Anyone who has been a Christian very long knows that is not true. We still get taken advantage of, ridiculed, and our path is by no means an easy one. We are living in a falling world. I used the word falling instead of fallen because it just seems to be getting worse all the time.

Let me give you a "what if." What if all God's children were blessed and nothing bad happened to them? The churches would be full and there would be professions galore! ; But what about their heart, their motive? Did you notice that word in verse 27? "Earnestly" seeks good. The motivation and desire must be from the heart.

A great example: I was told once that we could pray and ask God for an "amen". Some special blessing that day; something that would help us know that God was watching over us. I tried it once, it worked! I really saw a blessing that day. The thing is that I began doing it every day. It would be the same if God blessed us every day; we would either become accustomed to it, or expect it, or would do better to get more. It is human nature.

I have found through personal experience that it is when everything seems to go against us, our world seems to be falling apart, and it is then, that God wants us focused on Him. It is those who blame God and turn their back on God that misses the blessing. I think sometimes God may test our faithfulness. See if we are willing to go that extra mile WITH Him, not blame Him.

It is easy to blame God when things don't work out. Let me offer an alternative: Ask God what He is up to; Ask Him what is the "lesson" He is trying to teach us. Ask in prayer, and God may reply, He may not. It will be shown in some fashion, learn it, live it!

> The fruit of the righteous is a tree of life, and he who wins souls is wise. If the righteous will be recompensed on the earth, how much more the ungodly and the sinner. (Proverbs 11:30-31)

The last first, - We talked yesterday about the walk of the Christian; at least the Christian has someone to blame. I'm sorry, could not resist. Really, think about it. Who or what does the lost have to blame when their life falls apart. Actually, that should turn them to God, but sadly, it usually turns them to drugs or alcohol. At least, as a Christian, you have someone to turn to.

Solomon mentions, in verse 30, the "tree of life." Do you know why Adam and Eve were expelled from the Garden of Eden? Of course, in their sin, they could not be in God's presence. There is another reason:

Then the Lord God said, "Behold, the man has become like one of Us, to know good and evil. And now, lest he put out his hand and take also of the tree of life, and eat and live forever"- Therefore the Lord God sent him out of the garden of Eden to till the ground from which he was taken. (Genesis 3:22-23)

Did you know this tree appears again? Look:

Blessed are those who do His commandments, that they may have the right to the tree of life, and may enter through the gates into the city. (Revelation 22:14)

Isn't it interesting that "obedience" is the theme of both these passages? Because of Adam and Eve's "disobedience" they were expelled from the Garden; because of our "obedience" in Revelation, we now have access to that same tree, - a lesson to ponder.

I had a thought while I was reading this. When Adam and Eve were expelled it was just a garden. Here in Revelation that garden has become a city. God has been busy in the interim. Just a thought.

God blesses His children all the time; most of the time we don't even recognize it. We accept it as routine. That is sad! Thank you, God!

        Lonny E. Young

> Whoever loves instruction loves knowledge, but he who hates correction is stupid. A good man obtains favor from the Lord, but a man of wicked intentions He will condemn. (Proverbs 12:1-2)

I hate confrontation; there is something in my makeup that abhors confrontation. I would just as soon walk away, then to "argue" a point. I know that is frustrating to some who wish to argue. I just will not. My attitude is: "I will be proven right, or not, in the long run." I don't need to argue.

I heard this story once: Jesus was asked, in heaven, after His resurrection and ascension to heaven, "Do you have a plan 'B' if the disciples fail?" His response was: "No. They are My only hope." Time has proven the Lord correct. Think about what those twelve men (including Paul) have accomplished since then.

"Actions speak louder than words." Have you heard that "proverb"?
It is so true. What is the point of arguing with someone who is not listening anyway? You simply allow the results to speak for themselves.

Just like Solomon's proverbs. Great words, but if you ignore them, refuse to apply them, what is the point?

The more you read God's Word, apply the principles written therein, then God has an opportunity to work in your life. If you refuse to listen, to learn, to use what God has said, how can you expect God to work in your life?

There is another word our parents said was "not allowed". "Stupid" was a no-no. You can't call someone stupid, that's just not nice. Look how Solomon uses it in verse one.

But he who hates instruction is stupid.

I have pointed out before that our "first response" to correction is rebellion. The whole Bible is a book of correction; correction from the lies of Satan in the Garden of Eden. All through the Bible, especially the Old Testament, we see the consequences of rejecting God's wisdom, God's instructions, and God's correction. It is rebellion plain and simple. What is God telling you today?

45. What Book comes before the book of Revelation?
     a. James   b. Hebrews   c. John   d. Jude

> A man is not established by wickedness, but the root of the
> righteous cannot be moved. An excellent wife is the crown
> of her husband, but she who causes shame is like rottenness
> in his bones. (Proverbs 12:3-4)

I sat down once, while I could still remember, and wrote a couple of paragraphs about all the "girls" who, I had a crush on, in my school days. There were four that came to mind. Later, in the United States Air Force I became engaged to a gal in Ohio. We broke up while I was in Vietnam. Just before my discharge I met a gal from Topeka, Kansas. We have been married for 51 years right now. She was God's choice long before I met God. I firmly believe that God brought her into my life at just the right time.

If you have a godly wife, hold on to her! I love the way Solomon illustrates this:

An excellent wife is the crown of her husband. (12:4)

What does a king do with his crown? He wears it proudly; it is the "symbol" of his authority, is it not? A godly wife is that, and much more. We will cover this in greater detail in Proverbs 31.

When I was a teenager, before I knew about Jesus, my parents taught me there is a God; a "reverence" for God if you will. I remember praying, just before I left home, "God, I pray you would give me a wife who I can love, who will love me, and a family to love and support." Something close to those words!

God has answered that prayer, multiplied a thousand-fold.

A perfect life? Hardly! Bumps and detours along the way, faithful to my wife and our Lord, most definitely! Blessed? - Beyond measure; looking forward to thanking God in person one day.

If you are young and have not found that "excellent" wife yet, you need to pray earnestly that God would put that special someone in your path, and that you would recognize her! If you are sincere, and patient, God will answer that prayer. You need to be willing to wait. God is working on the other person as well!

     Lonny E. Young

> The thoughts of the righteous are right, but the counsels of the wicked are deceitful. The words of the wicked are, "Lie in wait for blood," but the mouth of the upright will deliver them. (Proverbs 12:5-6)

Have you noticed anything about the Bible? It is amazing how much pertains to blood. When I was teaching a high school boys class I challenged them to memorize some verses. One of my favorite verses was in Genesis:

Whosoever sheds man's blood, by man his blood shall be shed; for in the image of God He made man. (Genesis 9:6).

What does that say to you? ; To me, the argument for capital punishment. What do you think? This is just one example, as far as I am concerned, of the relevance of the biblical teachings.
Do you want to talk about blood? Read the book of Leviticus, all of the offerings, etc. Sometimes, in my imagination, I try to picture this altar in the tabernacle after a day of sacrifices. Yuk!

Let me encourage you to read an interesting chapter if you haven't run across it by now. It is Numbers chapter 7. I would guess that, apart from Psalm 119, it is probably the longest chapter in the Old Testament. It is the dedication of the tabernacle. All twelve tribes bring the same offering day by day. In that offering, we see 1 bull, 1 ram, 1 male lamb of the first year. One kid of the goats, two oxen, and five rams, five male goats, five male lambs. Let's see that makes 21 animals, right? Now multiply that by twelve tribes: 252 animals in twelve days. That is a lot of blood.

What is the point? God went into great detail, in the Old Testament, to stress the importance of the sacrifice, the blood. Don't miss Exodus twelve, the Passover ceremony that kept the death angel away from Israel's door; the importance of the blood. That message stressed over and over in the Old Testament. Why? So, you would understand the reason Christ needed to die on the cross of Calvary; the final blood sacrifice to pay for our sins for eternity. He died for you!

> The wicked are overthrown and are no more, but the house of the righteous will stand. A man will be commended according to his wisdom, but he who is of a perverse heart will be despised. (Proverbs 12:7-8)

You read this and you think Solomon is out of his mind. If Solomon could see our world today; you would think the wicked have a free reign. I think someone once said that the cycle of "good" versus "evil" goes in seven-year cycles. I disagree; he thinks that the pendulum swings far to one side, then swings back, far to the other side. I think we missed seven years. But who is counting if it is happening to you?

I think we have always had the perception that evil is prevailing. Haven't we? , especially if it is happening to you; you wonder, "When will this "bad luck" end. First of all, as a Christian, there is no such thing as good or bad luck. It is all in God's hands!

Do you want some perspective; I love this, read the first few chapters of Job? Does that not say that God is in control at all times? Satan can do NOTHING, but that God allows it. Do you think God knew what Job's reaction would be? Of course, He did. Does God know what will happen in your life three years from now? Of course.

I knew this person who was just devastated when, a company she had worked for over seventeen years, "downsized," and she was let go. She was in tears. I keep encouraging her, praying for her to be patient, God is up to something. She had a few short-term jobs. Now she works for the Federal Reserve in what she calls the best Job she has ever had. Point made!

That is what is going on in your life! You wonder if God even knows what you are going through. I had a period of "questioning". A year later God chose to reveal to me that He just wanted to see if I would remain faithful. God is trying to "grow" us as Christians. He is trying to "stretch" our faith to greater strengths. The more we learn to trust God (Proverbs 3:5-6), the more God can use us to accomplish His will and plan for our lives.

Are you willing to step out of that "comfort zone," and trust God next time He asks you to do something you are afraid to do? You will be amazed at what God will show you if you step out!

46. On what island did the apostle John write the book of Revelation?
    a. Patmos   b. Crete   c. Cyprus   d. Cuba

> Better is the one who is slighted but has a servant, then he who honors himself but lacks bread. A righteous man regards the life of his animal, but the tender mercies of the wicked are cruel. (Proverbs 12:9-10)

One of my favorite old Hallmark movies is called, "The Lost Child." There is a scene, where this city guy is walking in the desert with an Indian chief. The city guy asks the chief, "How can you survive in this wilderness?" The chief replies: "A man once hired a servant to walk beside him every day; to remind him, to praise his God. A place can be like that servant." That struck me. What is it, around you, that "reminds you" to praise God?

I heard it said that you can tell the "character" of a person by how they treat animals, interesting thought. You could really examine how they treat anything, - their car, their home, their friends, etc.; their priorities can reflect the content of their heart.

When I began this project, I wondered if there was enough to inspire a deeper walk with God in these Proverbs. I have never been a fan of the Proverbs; they didn't make sense to me. It was a "collection" of sayings, no plot, no storyline, etc. As I have worked through the first twelve chapters it is apparent that there is a "storyline". Obedience brings blessing, rebellion brings punishment, - A truly biblical principle.

The contrasts? The "righteous" versus the "wicked" or some variation of those two words; Do this, don't do that. Maybe we could start another page in our notebooks. "Do" - "Don't do" then after a couple of chapters read through the "Do" list. Just focusing on the things, we are to do. It might make more sense. Just a thought.

It is interesting, as I said before, Solomon's focus on animals. In the Bible, Solomon is said to have had over four-thousand horses (2 Chronicles 9:25). You might say he loved horses. Just as an a-side you might want to read Deuteronomy 17. Solomon broke all three of these commands.

Sometimes it is not hard to see what is in a man's heart. His speech, his priorities, his treatment of animals and children!

> He who tills his land will be satisfied with bread, but he who follows frivolity is devoid of understanding. The wicked covet the catch of evil men, but the root of the righteous yields fruit. (Proverbs 12:11-12)

Now, what might Solomon's point be here? Hard work produces fruit. Doesn't it frustrate you when you look around and see laziness rewarded? Don't even talk about the "unfairness" of it. It wasn't fair that we all need to suffer because of what Adam did in the Garden. If you want to complain, take it up with God.

The thing is, as a Christian, we trust God to work out everything. I mentioned it before if you want "unfairness" read the book of Job. The funny thing is, he had all these friends (four) that came to console him and ended up condemning him. It wasn't until he took the issue up with God that he got some answers. Don't forget to check out the conclusion.

Here is something to always keep in mind. God has His ways, His methods, and His time table. We want everything done right now. A good practice is to be patient and "watch God work." I have seen it so many times. I used to get so frustrated that God didn't deal with something right now. That's where a journal comes in. After this storm has passed you can look through that journal and see how God worked everything out. It will amaze you and strengthen your faith!

It is a tough lesson to learn. First, you MUST take your hands off the situation. Remove yourself from the "drama". Turn it over "completely" to God. Then watch Him work, until you are out of the picture, God won't touch it. Pray, turn it over to God and His timetable. You will be amazed. It was a tough lesson for me to learn.

It will also strengthen your faith. As a Christian of thirty years, I have seen God do some amazing things. I have also learned many lessons the hard way. Usually, the best lessons we learn are from mistakes. The consequences are such great "teachable" moments, usually, when I have said something I wish I hadn't.

I think these two verses might deal with our "work ethic", are we diligent in our work that God has called us to do? Or are slothful and lazy and expect others to do it for us? Think about it.

> The wicked is ensnared by the transgression of his lips, but the righteous will come through trouble. A man will be satisfied with good by the fruit of his mouth, and the recompense of a man's hands will be rendered to him. (Proverbs 12:13-14)

Usually when I begin typing the verses above a thought comes to mind, things I have heard or read; that will happen to you the more you read the Bible. You might read a verse in the New Testament and think you've have read that before; usually in a passage in the Old Testament or a principle will remind you of a story illustrated in the Old Testament? It is so important you read the whole Bible several times; the more you read the more the connections will jump out at you.

The funny thing is, the beginning of verse 13 reminds me of a "truth" from Dr. Charles Stanley. I know I have shared this before but it is so important you get this; someone once said (probably Dr. Stanley) you are either headed into a storm, in a storm, or coming out of a storm. That is so true.

Here is the principle I am referring to: Because God is Omniscience (all-knowing) He knows where you are at in a storm. Because God is Omnipresent (everywhere) He is with you in this storm. Finally, because God is Omnipotent (all-powerful) He will bring you out of the storm. Please, meditate on this truth. I can testify to this truth!

The righteous will come through trouble. Did you notice Solomon did NOT say the righteous will avoid trouble? I saw this great plaque in Branson, Missouri once. It said: "If God brings you to a storm, He will bring you through the storm", something like that. It might be a short version of Stanley's message.

This is a fantastic truth to grasp as a Christian. Just because you have asked Jesus into your heart, you have the Holy Spirit living within you, doesn't mean you will not have problems. Just a test. Do me a favor. Read the story of Moses freeing Israel from bondage in Egypt. Notice how many times it says, "God hardened Pharaoh's heart." The freedom of Israel was not God's only purpose for these plagues. Their main purpose was to discredit all the Egyptian gods. Check it out!

47. Who was the first king of Israel?
    a. David   b. Saul   c. Moses   d. Solomon

The way of a fool is right in his own eyes, but he who heeds counsel is wise. A fool's wrath is known at once, but a prudent man covers shame. (Proverbs 12:15-16)

Now there is a word worth creating a page in your notebook: "fool".

It is used twice here. Notice a characteristic of a "fool," he refuses to listen to counsel. Have you met someone like that? I think we all have. It is very frustrating, isn't it? You know what is right, you present your evidence, and still they refuse to admit your counsel. Yet, today we are not allowed to call them "fools". "Misguided" "stubborn" I am sure you know some words. BUT, we can't call them fools. Solomon does!

I wonder where this "proverb" is. "A fool and his money are soon parted." Isn't it funny how many "proverbs" we pick up growing up? I would venture to say most of them are based on the Bible. Here is another characteristic: wrath!

There is something God has blessed me with after Jesus came into my heart. I don't get upset nearly as much as I used to. Sure, I see things that get me very angry. My remedy is to turn it over to God. He takes care of my "light work." You won't believe the peace I get when I use that concept. God knows what is going on. He knows what is right, He will deal with it. I just move on. That is peace that passes all understanding.

I used to get so disappointed when things didn't happen the way I wanted, or expected them to. The closer I get, walking with God, the less I fret over these, and just give it to God and move on. If it is God's plan He will bring it to pass. If it is not God's plan, I don't have any business worrying about it in the first place. I love this verse in Matthew:

Therefore, do not worry about tomorrow, for tomorrow will worry about its own things. Sufficient for the day is its own trouble. (Matthew 6:34)

If God's people could grasp that concept, just think of the grey hairs that it would save. You might even live longer. The key? "Give it to God". Then leave it there. Take your hands off completely. You might want to check sometime and see the miracle God worked.

He who speaks truth declares righteousness, but a false
witness, deceit. There is one who speaks like the piercing
of a sword, but the tongue of the wise promotes health.
(Proverbs 12:17-18)

I learned so much in my two and a half years as a pastor. I visited with a church member in the hospital; he was there for minor, out-patient, surgery. I remarked that it wasn't serious because it was "minor," I was soon corrected that "No surgery is minor to the one having the surgery."

Most of the time we don't stop to think of the impact of our words; I have learned, by running what I am about to say, through a sort of "delay" that a lot of times I don't say what is on my mind. By learning that discipline, I have found that when I do speak it is more receptive.
I am appalled at how easy it is to lie today. It has become an art form. The sad part is that the one telling the lie is not held accountable, even after the lie is uncovered! That is scary!

We used to care about the impact of our words. Today, it doesn't matter if it is true or false, as long as it accomplishes the talebearer's goal. I have quoted this passage in James before: James 3:1-6.

It is disgusting the way a lie can turn into truth just by it's being repeated, over and over, it becomes a truth. No matter the facts. That is where we have come to in our culture. Even when it has been refuted the repetition becomes the truth, not the fact!

Do you remember, in the life of David, Solomon's father, what was David's response when Nathan confronted David about Bathsheba?

So, David said to Nathan, "I have sinned against the Lord." (2 Samuel 12:13a)

Of course, what would be the use to lie to God, right? We do it all the time. We think God will wink at our "transgressions". Don't forget that God's wrath was not brought to David's attention until over nine months after the deed. During that time of silence, David had Uriah, Bathsheba's husband killed. God will not wink at our lies. There will come a time of judgment, you can bank on it.

> No grave trouble will overtake the righteous, but the wicked shall be filled with evil. Lying lips are an abomination to the Lord, but those who deal truthfully are his delight. (Proverbs 12:21-22)

I don't remember the Ten Commandments dealing with lying.

Look at this:

You shall not bear false witness against your neighbor. (Exodus 20:16)

You're right, it doesn't "say" lying. Come on, you know exactly what God is saying. A cross reference to "lying lips" is in Revelation. Note who these, lying lips, are associated with:

Blessed are those who do His commandments, that they may have the right to the tree of life, and may enter through the gates into the city. But outside are dogs and sorcerers and sexually immoral and murderers and idolaters, and whoever loves and practices a lie. (Revelation 22:14-15)

My concordance lists six references to the word "abomination" just in the book of Proverbs. I think it is one of God's "strongest" proclamations against something. When God uses that word in reference to "laying lips" it is worth paying attention to; he also uses the word "abomination" in reference to idols.

Lying lips and idols, - God hates anything that is not TRUE. Lying lips, idols, deceit, and wickedness! God back the Garden of Eden. What was Satan's trick on Eve, "Hath God said?" To begin to question God's commands is Satan's first lie.

You are of your father the devil, and the desires of your father you want to do. He is a murderer from the beginning, and does not stand in the truth, because there is no truth in him. When he speaks a lie, he speaks from his own resources, for he is a liar and the father of it. (John 8:44)

48. What weapon did David use to kill Goliath?
    a. spear   b. stone   c. arrow   d. lightning

> A prudent man conceals knowledge, but the heart of fools proclaims foolishness. The hand of the diligent will rule, but the lazy man will be put to forced labor. (Proverbs 12:23-24)

I love the story of the founding of our country; exploring an unknown wilderness heading west. I often think sometimes when I drive through the Ozarks, for example, what it might have been like, when it was first discovered, - The point? The hard work and dedication it took to tame a wilderness.

The hand of the diligent will prevail. I would love to work with wood. My dad made so many nice things in his basement workshop. The problem is, I don't have the patience to work with wood. The sanding, gluing, painting and staining, varnishing. I just don't have the patience. It is a special gift.

The same can be said for walking with God. God knows the future; He knows what is up ahead. He is in no hurry to get where He is going. He desires that we "wait" patiently for His plan to play out. It is when we get impatient, run ahead of God, try to do it our way, we get into so much trouble. I struggle with this a lot.

God has been working on my impatience for years. I am getting there, but it has been a struggle.

Look at this verse in James:

*My brethren, count it all joy when you fall into various trials, knowing that the **testing** of your faith produces patience. But let patience have its perfect work, that you may be perfect and complete lacking nothing.* (James 1:2-4)

It is a process, it doesn't happen overnight. Notice how this patience is perfected through trials, testing. God is always trying to "stretch" our faith. It is like any muscle, the more you use it the stronger it gets. When was the last time God "tested" your faith? How did you do? Did you doubt because you couldn't "see" how God could do it? - That is sad, that is putting God in a box of restraint that hampers His doing great things in your life. Trust Him! Give it to God and watch Him work. Get out of that "comfort zone" and watch God work.

> The righteous should choose his friends carefully, for the way of the wicked leads them astray. The lazy man does not roast what he took in hunting, but diligence is man's precious possession. The way of righteousness is life, and in its pathway there is no death. (Proverbs 12:26-28)

Solomon should have heeded his own advice.

Look at these verses:

And he had seven hundred wives, princesses, and three hundred concubines; and his wives turned away his heart. For it was so, when Solomon was old, that his wives turned his heart after other gods; and his heart was not loyal to the Lord his God, as was the heart of his father David. (1 Kings 11:3-4)

I mentioned yesterday about the early pioneers of our country. When they went hunting they didn't have a fridge to store their meat; it had to be consumed quickly. I think about hunters today; when they go deer hunting after the deer is killed, they immediately "dress" it. I have never been, just heard stories. The sooner this is done the better, I am told; that is the picture I get from this proverb. Just killing meat is only part of it; you need to "finish the job."

There is that word "diligence" again; that is what I am talking about. A commitment to a process that is not "complete" until all are addressed. Every step is complete.

Wow! I just thought, that might apply to salvation also. If you think walking the aisle and getting baptized is all there is to salvation, you are sadly mistaken. When you ask Jesus into your heart, at that point, receive the power of the Holy Spirit, as a child of God; that same Holy Spirit has with Him a gift, - a "spiritual" gift that you are to use in the service of God. You have a place in God's work, in His church, to serve your community, and be a part of God's mission for His church. It is NOT to occupy a pew. There are so many ways to serve in God's work, through His church. Praying is vital. Giving can be a gift from God; teaching, assisting, cleaning up after events can be a gift (helps). You were not saved to sit, but to serve.

A wise son heeds his father's instruction, but a scoffer does not listen to rebuke. A man shall eat well by the fruit of his mouth, but the soul of the unfaithful feeds on violence. (Proverbs 13:1-2)

Interesting verse listed in my margin:

"If one man sins against another, God will judge him. But if a man sins against the Lord, who will intercede for him?" Nevertheless, they did not heed the voice of their father, because the Lord desired to kill them. (1 Samuel 2:25)

Why is that so difficult? It is a generational thing. When we reach a certain age, we believe we know more than our parents. Granted, I will say our grandchildren know a lot more about "electronics" than we do. I knew a lot more about certain things than my parents. Sure, but the basics? Nothing changes; it is the "life lessons" that seem to pass by the next generation until they learn for themselves. That is sad.

I so envy families that pass down their commitment to God through active participation in the church. That is so essential. The problem is, it is rare today, I think, that that commitment is passed on. We have one or two families in our church. For the most part, the next generation can't wait to get away from God. What a concept.

I know the argument. You "don't" have to go to church to have fellowship with God. - Really? Show me someone who does not attend church regularly and I will show you a "worldly" Christian. We need accountability, the commitment, and the fellowship of fellow believers to keep the world from creeping into our Christian walk. Remember Solomon from yesterday's devotion?

Solomon was a man God used greatly. The Queen of Sheba "marveled" at all that God had done in his life and for Israel (1 Kings 10). So, what happened to Solomon? Think about it.
You might want to "chew" on that verse from 1 Samuel again; think about what it says. Also, don't just take each proverb separately but consider the author and his testimony!

49. How long did Israel wander in the desert after refusing to enter the Promised Land?
    a. 7 years   b. 1 year   c. 40 years   d. 3 years

> He who guards his mouth preserves his life, but he who
> opens wide his lips shall have destruction. The soul of a lazy
> man desires, and has nothing; but the soul of the diligent
> shall be made rich. (Proverbs 13:3-4)

You wonder how many different ways can Solomon say the same thing? Now, why do you suppose God thought it was important enough to repeat these truths over and over; the same truth, in twelve different ways, - Why? Maybe one of them will click! One of them will get your attention.

Have you read through the Bible? I always like to read Genesis to Revelation. If I get passed Leviticus, it is downhill from there. So, why do I struggle with Leviticus anyway? One day, I will read through there, God will open a verse to my heart and it will change my life; I don't know how many times I have read Jeremiah. One day I saw this sign in some bathroom, Jeremiah 29:11. It blew me away; I looked it up, read 29:11-13, I kept reading it over and over. The more I read it the more it fed my soul.

It can happen to you; God's Word is so alive with basic truths that will change your life. It is funny how God took me on a journey through my Christian walk. When I was first saved I fell in love with Galatians 2:20. As I grew in my walk, I found Isaiah 40:31. A time in my life I needed to learn about waiting on God. Then finally, Jeremiah 29:11-13. The verses changed as I grew in my Christian walk. How much time do you spend "prospecting" in God's Word? Has God got your attention yet?

I have always had trouble with Proverbs; there is no story-line, no plot, and no consistency. It reminds me a lot of a bottle of vitamins; you take one a day for years. You may not "see" any tangible results but it contributes to the needs of your body; they are important to your health. The same is true with Proverbs and the whole Bible. The more you ingest these powerful truths your "spiritual" health gets stronger and stronger. You can go to places you never dreamed of in your Christian walk. You learn to recognize God's hand in your life, where God wants to take you, most important to trust His guidance.

A righteous man hates lying, but a wicked man is loathsome and comes to shame. Righteousness guards him whose way is blameless, but wickedness overthrows the sinner. (Proverbs 13:5-6)

Maybe we could take a different look at this word righteousness:

And he believed in the Lord, and He accounted it to him for righteousness. (Genesis 15:6)

We are talking about Abraham here; Abraham is interesting. God went to great lengths to assure Abraham that God would provide an heir for him.

Look at the previous verse:

The He brought him outside and said, "Look now toward heaven, and count the stars if you are able to number them." And He said to him, "So shall your descendants be." (Genesis 15:5)

Did God keep His promise? When Jacob and his sons joined with Joseph in Egypt at the end of Genesis there were about 70 in Jacob's family; now look at this verse as Israel is freed from bondage to Egypt:

Then the children of Israel journeyed from Rameses to Succoth, about six hundred thousand men on foot, besides children. (Exodus 12:37)

Some have estimated a million and half "people" left Egypt. Would you say God kept His promise? Because Abraham "believed" God and followed Him, God blessed him. Sure, Abraham made some mistakes; Abraham also believed in God enough to take his only son up on Mt. Moriah to sacrifice him, as God commanded. God tested Abraham's commitment. Is God testing you right now? What will it take for you to "question" God's will? Are you committed to following God, but on your terms?

Our "righteousness" can be measured in our commitment to God's plan for our life; just like Abraham.

> There is one who makes himself rich, yet has nothing; and one who makes himself poor, yet has great riches. The ransom of a man's life is his riches, but the poor does not hear rebuke. (Proverbs 13:7-8)

How would you seriously "measure" your worth? Do you begin with the balance in your checkbook? How about your "net" worth? - Stocks, investments, real estate, etc. Money was never meant to measure our life or our life's work; money is simply a unit of currency. Life cannot be measured in money; your worth cannot be measured in dollars and cents.

Have you ever heard the phrase, "invested in someone else's life?" That is what parents do with their children. You can't begin to measure the "investment" that a parent puts into their children's lives. It can't be measured. How about a "return" on that investment? How would you measure that return? You can't. Oh, you hope they "make" something of themselves; they make you "proud". Then again, how do you "measure" that?

Like in verse 7, what is Solomon talking about? Remember Solomon? - The richest man in history.

Look at this:

The weight of gold that came to Solomon yearly was six hundred and sixty-six talents of gold, besides that from the traveling merchants, from the income of traders, from all the kings of Arabia, and from the governors of the country. And King Solomon made two hundred shields of hammered gold: six hundred shekels of gold went into each shield. (1 Kings 10:14-16)

Funny thing, I would bet if you asked Solomon how much of that gold would he give to restore his relationship with God, he would say, ALL. A relationship with Almighty God is "priceless". I think that is what he is getting at in the seventh verse. When we begin putting a price tag on things, we begin a downward spiral, to emptiness. What exactly is "priceless"? How would you put a price tag on where you spend eternity? Oh, that price has already been paid; - the blood of the very Son of God has bought you eternity in heaven. Think about it.

50. How many spies did Moses send into the Promised Land the first time?
    a. 6   b. 40   c. 10   d. 12

                    Lonny E. Young

> The light of the righteous rejoices, but the lamp of the wicked will be put out. By pride comes nothing but strife, but with the well-advised is wisdom. (Proverbs 13:9-10)

If you have spent any time in Psalm 119, this may be a familiar verse:

Your word is a lamp to my feet and a light to my path. (Psalm 119:105)

A "light", a "lamp", two references to helping us determines the direction of our feet, where we are headed, what is in front of us. The "path", if you will, of life. I have talked about this before. What do you use, or who, do you consult with, to make your daily decisions? Do you trust your "instincts"? Where did those come from? What do you usually do? A lot of people rely on "habit".

As a Christian, we have the added advantage of the Holy Spirit of God to direct us. That assumes we take the time to listen, or even better still, to obey His prompting. If you haven't asked Jesus into your heart, what or who influences your decision-making process? - A critical question.

You have certain "truths" that were taught to you from your childhood, until now. They will influence your decisions, you have the influence of your peers; assuming you seek their advice. So, their "upbringing" can affect your decisions. What kind of books do you read? Books, believe it or not, can influence your decision-making process.

It is no big deal. I might make a wrong decision, no big deal. It is if it affects the rest of your life! Don't dismiss this decision-making process. That is what Solomon is talking about in the verses above. The "light" and the "lamp" are to help you choose the right path. A "decision" time is a fork in this path of life. How will you determine which fork (decision) will you take?

I don't remember the author, but there is a quote I heard once, that came to my mind: *I chose a road less traveled by.* Notice he made a choice.

Look at these words of Jesus:

"Enter by the narrow gate; for wide is the gate and broad is the way that leads to destruction, and there are many who go in by it. Because narrow is the gate and difficult is the way which leads to life, and there are few who find it. (Matthew 7:13-14)

How do you determine the path to take? Or better still, WHO?

> Wealth gained by dishonesty will be diminished, but he who gathers by labor will increase. Hope deferred makes the heart sick, but when the desire comes, it is a tree of life. (Proverbs 13:11-12)

How do you measure wealth?

Look at this verse in Matthew:

"For what profit is it to a man if he gains the whole world, and loses his own soul? Or what will a man give in exchange for his soul? (Matthew 16:26)

I don't know what your belief is, in the hereafter. Good, go to heaven, the bad, well you know. If you put no stock in such things these verses mean nothing. You probably have no plans for next year, let alone next week. "I just take each day as it comes." Cool! Let me ask you this: Are you willing to bet (think of the stakes) "eternity" in Hades that what the Bible says may not be true? That is what you are doing.

Should the day come that you stand before Almighty God. And you say, "Okay, it is true, I believe." Friend, it is TOO late. You have made your choice. Just a thought, "do you know when you will die?" I thought not. Do you know how you will die? I thought not. So, if you don't know when or how, how can you plan when you accept the Lord? You may not have that chance this side of heaven. Then it is too late.

I love this verse in John:

Jesus said to Him, "Thomas, because you have seen Me, you have believed. Blessed are those who have not seen, and yet have believed." (John 20:29)

What is your "hope" in? Do you think about eternity? "I will deal with that later." - Really? And you think you have a "later?" You can take care of that right now. It is simple. BY FAITH you simply pray and ask God to forgive the sins in your past life. Acknowledge that Jesus died for your sins; ask Jesus to come into your heart and be your Savior. THEN you can look forward to eternity!

     Lonny E. Young

He who despises the word will be destroyed, but he who fears the commandment will be rewarded. The law of the wise is a fountain of life, to turn one away from the snares of death. (Proverbs 13:13-14)

Check this verse in Isaiah:

Therefore, as the fire devours the stubble, and the flame consumes the chaff, so their root will be as rottenness, and their blossom will ascend like dust; because they have rejected the law of the Lord of hosts, and despised the word of the Holy One of Israel. (Isaiah 5:24)

Anything that promotes the "word of the Lord", I pay close attention to. I have been a Christian for over thirty years. The ministry that God has called me to is "teaching"; I have been a Sunday School Director for most of those thirty years. My "passion" is the Word of God. I have no idea how many times I have read through the Bible. Every year I learn something new; a new verse that jumps out and grabs my soul. It is the miracle of God's Holy Word.

In reference to yesterday's devotion, - I can stand before God completely assured of my entry into heaven because of what the Bible says, NOT anything I have done; only my accepting of Jesus as my Savior.

After a few years I asked myself, "Why did Jesus have to die on the cross?" I began looking for answer. I found the Passover in Exodus 1, and then connected that with what John said:

The next day John saw Jesus coming toward him, and said, "Behold! The Lamb of God who takes away the sin of the world!" (John 1:29)

Then it all made sense. God, from the very beginning (Genesis 3:21) required a blood sacrifice to pay for sin. Instead of bulls and goats, He provided the ultimate, end-all, sacrifice, His Son Jesus. Jesus paid for my sins on the cross of Calvary for eternity, past, present and future. That fact and my faith will allow me into the presence of God for all eternity; I have God's Word on it!

51. Who sided with Joshua concerning the conquest of the Promised Land?
     a. Moses   b. Miriam   c. Caleb   d. Jacob

Good understanding gains favor, but the way of the unfaithful is hard. Every prudent man acts with knowledge, but a fool lays open his folly. (Proverbs 13:15-16)

Here is an interesting verse:

"Talk no more so very proudly; let no arrogance come from your mouth, for the Lord is the God of knowledge; and by Him actions are weighed. (1 Samuel 2:3)

The speaker? ; Hannah, the mother of Samuel, the prophet who anointed David and called Saul to be king of Israel. Okay, I must remind you of what James says as well:

If any of you lacks wisdom, let him ask of God, who gives to all liberally and without reproach, and it will be given him. (James 1:5)

The problem is the timing of our request; we, as men especially, don't ask for help (wisdom) until we have exhausted all other options, or made a mess of things, - Our own strength, and our own knowledge, our own determination, on and on.

When I found this verse one day, it has become a "daily" prayer of mine. "Lord, give me the wisdom each day, to serve you." *Every prudent man acts with knowledge.* Did you catch that?

Do you remember your first day of school? Probably not, if you are like me about all you remember is "fear."; strange people, strange surroundings, etc. Today the little ones get conditioned with "pre-school". Kindergarten was my first exposure to "school". My "greatest" exposure to "school" was the night I open my Bible; with the help of God's Holy Spirit, I was given access to the mind of God. The more I read, the more I studied, the closer I got to the "will" of God.

Spend some time in God's word, don't just skim. Let me give you some homework. Begin in 1 Samuel 16 (David is called out of the shepherd's field). Take it slow; follow the life of David through 1 Kings 2.

> A wicked messenger falls into trouble, but a faithful
> ambassador brings health. Poverty and shame will come to
> him who disdains correction, but he who regards a rebuke
> will be honored. (Proverbs 13:17-18)

How much do you know about the "rapture" of the church? You might want to check the concordance of your Bible. You can check, but it is not there. There are many "theories" about the "timing" of this event. The description is usually centered on the idea that the "church" will be taken to heaven, before the beginning of the "Tribulation". I am in that camp.

Some have used the picture of Noah and the ark as an illustration. One of my favorite theories was brought to mind by the word "ambassador" in verse 17, above.

If my "civics" class was correct, it is the custom of every nation, before going to war, that they "recall" their ambassadors from the nation they are going to war with. You don't want any of "your" people in a hostile land when you are fighting them.

Now look at this verse:

*Now then, we are **ambassadors** for Christ, as though God were pleading through us: we implore you on Christ's behalf, be reconciled to God.* (2 Corinthians 5:20)

To me, I love the analogy. God is about to go to "war" with Satan who claims the world as his own. Of course, as Christians, we know that Satan is simply "occupying" until the rightful owner returns, and claims what is His. Before this battle takes place, God will remove His church from the chaos that will take place. If you want a full description read the book of Revelation.

I kind of left you hanging yesterday about David; as you read through 1 & 2 Samuel and the first two chapters of 1 Kings, make some notes, list the characters and write down your thoughts, as you go along. The battle with Goliath, Bathsheba, Abigail, Joab, Jonathan, Saul, etc.; Find out why David was called: A man after God's own heart.

A desire accomplished is sweet to the soul, but it is an abomination to fools to depart from evil. He who walks with wise men will be wise, but the companion of fools will be destroyed. (Proverbs 13: 19-20)

Isn't it strange, the things that stick with us? ; The memories that seem to return from our past at the weirdest times. For some reason, the verses above remind me of a book our grade school teacher read to me, hundreds of years ago.

"Happy Hankey Half-Done", that was the book. It was about a boy who never finished anything he started; you get that from the title, of course, I just thought it was so weird. My father taught me that lesson early on, finish what you start.

The last house we lived in before I left for the United States Air Force was bought by my dad as a "condemnation". He got it really cheap. I'm sure he made it "safe" before we moved in. After we moved in, my brothers and I watched as he redid the walls; the electrical and the plumbing. The biggest project was the basement wall; it was a stone wall that had collapsed. He worked for a month, putting just the right stone in the right place to use the least amount of concrete, to save money. I learned a lot just watching that experience.

The word "diligent" is used a lot in Proverbs. It is an awesome trait if you have mastered it. Every year between Christmas and New Year's I try to take that week for vacation; during that week, I make a special effort to finish up any "loose ends" that are hanging from the past year. I want to begin the New Year with nothing left over. It is a dividing point for me; it is a good trait to think about.

I like the first part of verse 20. *He who walks with wise men will be wise.* I am so thankful when I was saved, I had a church full of godly men to encourage me and put up with my questions and zeal that occasionally got me in trouble; they were patient with me. The thing I loved was to absorb from those godly men a strong desire to study and learn the Bible. I had only been a Christian for six months and was encouraged to teach a Sunday school class. That experience brought the Word of God deep within my heart and soul. I have been hungry ever since.

52. Herod gave the crowd a choice between two people, Jesus or –
     a. Barnabas   b. Barabas   c. Lazarus   d. Judas

                    Lonny E. Young

> Evil pursues sinners, but to the righteous, good shall be repaid. A good man leaves an inheritance to his children's children, but the wealth of the sinner is stored up for the righteous. (Proverbs 13:21-22)

I have had this thought recently, probably influenced too much by Hollywood. I wonder if, after I'm gone, if I could influence events in my children and/or grandchildren's lives after I'm gone? Nice thought maybe, but the influence I need to do it is right now. What can I leave in the way of an "inheritance," that would influence them the rest of their lives?

Have you ever thought about what your "inheritance" would be to the next generation? Of course, I am in my seventies, you may be much younger; think about something, and how will you be remembered by those you come in contact with daily?

Do you realize the number of people who pass through your life? It could be hundreds. I worked for United Parcel Service for twenty-six years. I served in three churches, so far. Sometimes I will see someone in the store or out-and-about and they will say "high" and I say to myself, "Where do I know them from?" "Who are they?" "What is their name?" It is so frustrating sometimes.

The interesting thing to me is that they "recognize" me. That would mean I have left an impression on them. The scary part is "they know my name." How about the people around you? Those you work with, your neighbors, your peers, etc. Do you know what they think of you?

The older I get, the more I think about this "inheritance" thing. Do you want an example? Do you remember the last funeral you went to? What did they "say" about the person who died? Of course, that is not the place for negative comments, but what are they "remembered for?"

Of course, we don't know when our time will come. It might be a good idea to think about your "inheritance" today, no matter what age you are. Your "inheritance" will be what you leave behind in the minds of those who pass through your life. How will they remember you? What might they say at your funeral? Think about it! How about your "eternal" inheritance?

> He who spares his rod hates his son. but he who loves him
> disciplines him promptly. The righteous eats to the satisfying
> of his soul, but the stomach of the wicked shall be in want.
> (Proverbs 13:24-25)

Have you ever been "spanked" by the Lord? It is not pleasant. The challenge is to recognize, one that it is from the Lord, two, the lesson to learn.

Look at this verse:

Now no chastening seems to be joyful for the present, but painful; nevertheless, afterward it yields peaceable fruit of righteousness to those who have been trained by it. (Hebrews 12:11).

There are lessons to be learned when we are corrected. That is the point! To get our attention, and to point us in the right direction! I love this verse:

And you have forgotten the exhortation which speaks to you as to sons: My son, do not despise the chastening of the Lord, nor be discouraged when you are rebuked by Him; for whom the Lord loves He chastens, and scourges every son whom He receives. (Hebrews 12:5-6)

The author of Hebrews is quoting from Proverbs 3:11-12. I love this idea! As a father, I remember those rare times, when I had to correct our girls. It wasn't pleasant but necessary. We correct our children out of love and the desire that they might be obedient; just as God corrects us, for the same reason.

It has long been a habit of mine since reading this passage, that when I go through a trial, I immediately ask God, "Okay, Lord, what is it you are trying to teach me in this?" Usually, He is dealing with my lack of patience, but sometimes it may be my "priorities," it may a bad habit I have fallen into. I want to know what God is doing in my life. I ask Him! If there is a lesson to learn, He will help me learn it. You do know that the best lessons we learn are from "correction"? About that verse in Hebrews, I love how I am referred to as "son". Cool!

The wise woman builds her house, but the foolish pulls it down with her hands. He who walks in his uprightness fears the Lord, but he who is perverse in his ways despises Him. (Proverbs 14:1-2)

An interesting picture in the first few words, a principle to keep in mind when reading the Proverbs. I hope you realize that a woman does not build a house; she may work on the construction, I'll give you that, and she does not build it. BUT! Any man or husband will tell you that the "home" does not function without the contribution of his wife! That is a fact.

So, what do you think Solomon is talking about? Much of what a wife contributes to the functions of a well-run household goes unnoticed. Much of the success of a successful household is due to the work of this "wise" woman. Solomon is emphasizing that importance. As well as pointing out the opposite effect of a foolish woman.

I mentioned that I consider myself a "people-watcher". I will sit in my car outside the department or grocery store, and watch people; I think the thought that comes to my mind most often is, "what do those two see in each other?" I guess the same could be said about my wife and me.

I am reminded of a phrase that used to be used in the marriage ceremony: "What God has joined together, let not man put asunder." (Matthew 19:6). Exactly! It is God (hopefully) who has matched these two individuals together; most of the time they have very little in common. God knows just the right person to be attracted to another; a big case for that all-important prayer before choosing a mate.

Solomon touches on the wife here. Another author, Lemuel, will address this subject in greater detail in chapter 31.

It seems our culture is drifting away from the "husband-wife" concept. Fewer and fewer are getting married; that is the foundation that God established from the very beginning. When we start ignoring God's divine plan, we are looking for trouble. I heard a survey recently that said the "Millennial Generation" is beginning to see the benefits of marriage. I hope that is true. There is something special when two people commit before God to be one!

53. How many stones did David take with him to slay Goliath?
    a. Three   b. one   c. two   d. five

> In the mouth of a fool is a rod of pride, but the lips of the wise will preserve them. Where no oxen are, the trough is clean; but much increase comes by the strength of an ox. (Proverbs 14:3-4)

Have you heard this? "It is foolish to argue with a fool: Listeners can't tell which is which." I think I saw this at a supermarket meat counter once. I'm not sure if that is what Solomon is talking about here, but it makes sense.

Do you know how hard it is to keep your thoughts to yourself when you know someone is making a fool of themselves? It is so hard. Do you know what Solomon is saying here? *But the lips of the wise will preserve them.* He is saying "keep your thoughts to yourself!" Most of the time, a lesser wise person will enlighten them, and thus jump in where you have been wise enough to keep quiet.

It is a shame it took me seventy years to learn that fact. As a young Christian, I was not afraid to speak what was on my mind. After a few rebukes and embarrassing moments, I learned my lesson. How about this one: "It is better to be thought a fool than to speak and remove all doubt?" It is funny how these "proverbs" have stuck in my mind; thank you, Lord, for bringing them to my mind.

The problem is, just like the Bible, we know these truths but rarely act on them. The same is true with the Proverbs. I'll bet, if someone took the time, they could trace many of our "sayings" to verses in Proverbs. Of course, we put a contemporary spin on the truth; they are true just the same. That could be said of his reference to oxen.

What do you suppose Solomon is getting at about the oxen? Does prosperity take work? Close maybe. Speaking of prosperity let me share a favorite verse about prosperity:

*This book of the Law shall not depart from your mouth, but you shall meditate in it day and night, that you may observe to do according to all that is written in it. **For then you will make your way prosperous, and then you will have good success.*** (Joshua 1:8)

Mark this in your Bible. A very basic principle!

A faithful witness does not lie, but a false witness will utter lies.
A scoffer seeks wisdom and does not find it, but knowledge
is easy to him who understands. (Proverbs 14:5-6)

So, what have you learned these past six months? Can you make a list? Probably not; it doesn't work that way, I have used this analogy before. Are you taking a multi-vitamin? How long have you been taking them? I have been taking them for over thirty years. Can I point to a significant difference? No. So why do I take them? I am sure there are nutrients there that I need. I don't know how it works; I just know that they do.

The same is true with God's Word. You could read through the Bible multiple times. You may not notice an effect. Does that mean that the Bible isn't working? No. If you took the time to notice, you might notice a greater peace in your life. You might notice a better and stronger prayer life. The greatest thing you might notice is the calm assurance that God is walking with you on this path called life. It is like a close friendship. You don't notice it until it is not there.

The study of God's Word is not academics, it's much more personal. It is not learning history, or facts, it is a personal "relationship" or "fellowship" with the God of the universe! Think about that a minute!

The more you read and absorb the Word of God, the more intimate you become with your heavenly Father. You know the picture. Your child comes in the living room and climbs up on your lap and says, "Daddy, tell me a story." It is the same picture when you open the Word of God. It is God Himself, telling a story about His plan, for your life. God is sharing His love and desire for you as His child.

Let me close with these fantastic verses:

For as many as are led by the Spirit of God, these are sons of God. For you did not receive the spirit of bondage again to fear, but you received the Spirit of adoption by whom we cry out, "Abba, Father." The Spirit himself bears witness with our spirit that we are children of God. (Romans 8: 14-16)

Do you see it?

> Go from the presence of a foolish man, when you do not perceive in him the lips of knowledge. The wisdom of the prudent is to understand his way, but the folly of fools is deceit. (Proverbs 14:7-8)

I am on a roll, so I want to continue along the lines I started yesterday; I ran out of the room yesterday. There is so much more to this walking with God in His Word. First off, if you're not a child of God, as the verses in Romans talks about, you have no clue what I am talking about. Until you ask Jesus into your heart and are saved, you do not have the power of the Holy Spirit living within you. Until that happens, you have no clue what I am talking about.

When I was inducted into the United States Air Force I was given a pocket New Testament. Later that evening (I had just turned seventeen) I was on a train headed for Lackland AFB, Texas. I was scared to death; I had no idea about God and such things. My parents gave me a "reverence" for God but nothing about a "relationship". In my fear, I finally got around to opening that New Testament.

I opened to Matthew chapter one. If you know your Bible you know what that is, "the be-gats". I had no clue what I was reading; that didn't last long. By contrast, I shared this before, the night I asked Jesus into my heart, I opened my Bible and read Third John, all fourteen verses. I was so excited, that I had read a whole book in the Bible; I fell in love with God's Word then, and have been in love ever since.

The difference was the presence of the Holy Spirit. He opened the Bible in such a way I just couldn't get enough. If you are "lost" and trying to read the Bible it is foolishness.

Look at these verses:

For the message of the cross is foolishness to those who are perishing, but to us who are being saved it is the power of God. (1 Corinthians 1:18)

But the natural man does not receive the things of the Spirit of God, for they are foolishness to him; nor can he know them, because they are spiritually discerned. (1 Corinthians 2:14)

54. What Psalm begins with: "The Lord is my shepherd"?
    a. 119th   b. 1st   c. 23rd   d. 7th

Fools mock at sin, but among the upright there is favor. The heart knows its own bitterness, and a stranger does not share its joy. (Proverbs 14:9-10)

I have shared this frustration before. We have been talking about a "relationship" with God earlier, to have that kind of fellowship with Almighty God is so hard to explain until you are there. That is the point. Like the verse earlier (1 Corinthians), the things of God are "foolishness" to those who don't believe.

That is the key, - Faith! I had no idea what was ahead the night our pastor stopped by our house and led us to the Lord. We had just started going to church, we started by attending a revival; our daughters were riding the church bus on Sundays.

That night, God opened a whole new world for me. Do be honest; I just fell in love with the Lord. The more I read the Bible, the more I got to know God through His Son Jesus, the more excited and the more amazed I became when I saw what God was doing in my life.

You see, until you cross that threshold, enter God's will, receive His Holy Spirit, learn to pray and seek God's will and purpose in your life you can't possibly understand what awaits you on this side; that is the hard part. God makes this offer. It is free! You just open your heart and invite Jesus in. He will do the rest. It must be honest. God knows your heart. You can't fool Him.

I love this picture in Revelation:

Behold, I stand at the door and knock. If anyone hears My voice and opens the door, I will come in to him and dine with him, and he with Me. (Revelation 3:20)

It is that picture of dining with the Lord of the universe that gets me. There is no greater picture of "fellowship" than sitting around a dinner table, with friends, - that is as close as you get. To have that kind of relationship with God is the picture I am trying to draw here, from this side. If you have never opened your heart and asked Jesus to come in, now is the time. Read that verse in Revelation again. Then say your prayer!

> The house of the wicked will be overthrown, but the tent of the upright will flourish. There is a way that seems right to a man, but its end is the way of death. (Proverbs 14:11-12)

Have you ever read the book of Judges? It is the book following Joshua. This verse appears twice in the book:

In those days, there was no king in Israel; **everyone did what was right in his own eyes**. (Judges 21:25)

The verse also appears in 17:6, - what a perfect description of the book of Judges, and today! I pray that our country is in the "seeking God" stage. What does that mean?

The book of Judges consists of a "merry-go-round". First, Israel drifts away from God. Joshua has passed. There is no leadership, no guidance. The people drift away from God. There were no churches to go to and refresh your faith.

God would send a neighboring country usually the Philistines to take Israel into bondage. The people would pray. Then God would rise up a "deliverer" from among the people. He or in one case Deborah would gather the people and free them from bondage. This would last a few years then the people would drift back away from God. The "merry-go-round" would repeat itself. This goes on several times. As our pastor points out, each successive cycle gets worse and worse. Then along comes Samuel.

This attitude is so pervasive today, it is sad. Everyone thinks they are "entitled," that they are right, and everyone else is wrong. It is scary! It just points out the relevance of scripture! There is nothing that is not illustrated in the Bible. The more time you spend it in the more you will see this.

Solomon refers to the house versus a tent in verse 11. How about your house (heart)? What kind of condition is it in? We are a bit past the "spring cleaning" time but it is not too late. How about an inventory of your lifestyle? Are there some things in your life that would benefit you to discard? Some "habits" that might need changing?

          Lonny E. Young

> Even in laughter the heart may sorrow, and the end of mirth
> may be grief. The backslider in heart will be filled with his
> own ways, but a good man will be satisfied from above.
> (Proverbs 14:13-14)

Do you know what it means to be satisfied, truly satisfied? Just what does that word mean to you? Let's try "contentment". Do you think that word will work?

Look at this verse:

Not that I speak in regard to need, **for I have learned in whatever state I am, to be content.** (Philippians 4:11)

Just a note about this letter from Paul; Paul is writing while "in jail", a prisoner of Rome. Can you be "content" in those circumstances? Think about it. Here is another verse in that same chapter:

Be anxious for nothing, but in **everything** *by prayer and supplication, with thanksgiving, let your requests be made known to God; and the* **peace** *of God, which surpasses all understanding, will guard your hearts and minds through Christ Jesus.* (Philippians 4:6-7)

Think about it, just like Paul in jail; he had a "peace" that he was right where God wanted him to be, doing what God wanted him to do. If that isn't a recipe for "peace," I don't know what is. Paul gives us the "formula" in the verses above (6-7). *Be anxious for nothing!* When you have that kind of fellowship with God you can't help but be content.

When you can have that relationship with God that is two-fold: One, you trust God enough to turn EVERYTHING over to His sovereign will, that is peace. Second, when you can "let go" and take your hands off, give it to God, there are such peace and contentment that you will want to do it over and over. Paul did!

How would you define a "backslider"? Let's be clear right off: It is NOT someone who has "lost" their salvation. If they are truly saved it is a "permanent" condition. A "backslider" is someone out of fellowship with God; maybe someone who blames God. How is your "fellowship?"

55. Name one of the two Old Testament books that contain the Ten
    Commandments.
    a. Genesis   b. Exodus   c. Judges   d. Deuteronomy

The simple believes every word, but the prudent considers well his steps. A wise man fears and departs from evil, but a fool rages and is self-confident. (Proverbs 14:15-16)

Check out this verse from the Psalms:

The steps of a good man are ordered by the Lord, and He delights in his way. Though he fall, he shall not be utterly cast down; for the Lord upholds him with His hand. (Psalm 37:23-24)

One of my favorite Psalms; this is something that has challenged me, the deeper I get into God's Word. The fact that God has a plan for our lives (Jeremiah 29:11); when God created us in our mother's womb, God has had a plan for our life! (Jeremiah 1)

But, just like the Garden of Eden, God also gave us a free will, to walk in that plan, or one of our own making; our "steps" or His "steps". It is our choice, our call. Don't miss that promise in Psalm 37: *For the Lord upholds him with His hand.* Whose hand? Gods! It is a "given" we are going to stumble. So, who will lift you up? God or the wisdom of this world? My money is on God!

In the world we live in today, there are very *few* authoritative words, whether it is the newspapers, TV, or the internet. Where do you get your "facts"? How do you know it is "factual"? Do you research it yourself, or just believe what you read or see? What is your "final" authority? How do you determine "truth"?

I can't use the Bible in every circumstance, it is outdated and irrelevant. - Really? More than once I have seen times in our Sunday school class when we have "struggle," to keep from applying the Word of God to today's headlines. It is TOO relevant!

Okay, let's put the Bible aside for now. How else can we determine what is true today? Are you a Christian? If you are, you have the person of the Holy Spirit of God living within you. God, Himself will guide you to ALL truth. Nothing is irrelevant to God; God knows the hearts of men, and God knows what is true. Trust His Spirit!

A quick-tempered man acts foolishly, and a man of wicked intentions is hated. The simple inherit folly, but the prudent are crowned with knowledge. (Proverbs 14:17-18)

I am sure you have never lost your temper and regretted it, right? I know we all have. Have you said anything you wish you hadn't said? Of course, you have. Why is that? Let me ask you this. Do you do it less frequently as a Christian? - Probably. Why is that?
Look what Jesus said in the gospel of Matthew:

But those things which proceed out of the mouth come from the heart, and they defile a man. (Matthew 15:18)

Kind of harsh, are they not? So, what is the answer? A heart transplant! You're kidding! No, I am not. God can change that wicked black heart overnight; if God dwells in your heart in the person of Jesus Christ.

Look at this verse:

Or do you not know that your body is the temple of the Holy Spirit who is in you, whom you have from God, and you are not your own. (1 Corinthians 6:19)

If God's Holy Spirit dwells within you, He will begin "temple cleaning" right away. Those snide remarks and hurtful comments will disappear from your heart and thus your mouth. God has His way of cleaning up His children very quietly; you may not even notice that your speech patterns have changed, better yet your "heart" will have changed.

Solomon has often remarked about the condition of our heart. He may not use that word, but much of his instructions originate from what is in our hearts. If it is black and controlled by Satan we will make hurtful remarks. If God is in control, there will be a whole new change of attitude and love toward others you never realized you had.

Let's do a "heart" inventory right now. Who is living in your heart? It can be one of two people, God or the devil, which one?

> The evil will bow before the good, and the wicked at the gates of the righteous. The poor man is hated even by his own neighbor, but the rich has many friends. (Proverbs 14:19-20)

An interesting conversation in our Sunday school class this morning; how do you "witness" to a lost neighbor?

My approach? You start with prayer. First, you pray that God would change their heart; make them receptive to your approach, a funny thing about praying for your neighbor. When you begin praying, God will work on your heart as well. Make you more understanding, maybe give you some sympathy, a different approach.

The point? By praying God will work on both sides of the fence.

Solomon is big on the "contrast" between good and evil, righteous and wicked. Something else crossed my mind in Sunday school this morning; the conversation talked about the battle between the "flesh" and the Spirit in Galatians 5. David came to mind.

Think about it for a minute. Our teacher talked about the choice made in the Garden of Eden. God said, "Don't touch" they ate anyway. The thing about David is a "great" illustration about this battle between the "flesh" and the Spirit!

We know the story of David and Bathsheba. I want you to think about that night he was out walking on his balcony. He sees this young lady bathing, STOP! Right there, the battle is decided! My Bible notes tell me he had at least eight wives. He had other options. He yielded to the flesh.

In sin, there will always come a turning point, other options; it is your choice what you do next. Some in the class remarked, "We will always be tempted (even Jesus was "tempted" in the wilderness) but it is how you respond to that temptation that will determine your relationship with God. David paid dearly for his decision that night, as we will when we make the wrong "choice."

Maybe that is the theme Solomon is trying to get across to us. There are alternatives, choices, you always have an out. How about some choices you have made lately? Are they godly choices or choices determined by the "flesh"? Have you asked God for guidance?

56. Which Gospel contains the "Great Commission"?
    a. Matthew   b. Mark   c. Luke   d. John

                    Lonny E. Young

Do they not go astray who devise evil? But mercy and truth belong to those who devise good. In all labor there is profit, but idle chatter leads only to poverty. (Proverbs 14: 22-23)

We talked yesterday about choices. So, how do we make the right choices? Evil and good, idle chatter. Solomon is always, I think in almost every verse, giving us options, choices. What might Jesus' approach be?

*He went a little farther and fell on His face, and **prayed**, saying, "O My Father, if it is possible, let this cup pass from Me; nevertheless, **not as I will, but as You will.**"* (Matthew 26:39)

Are you walking so close to God that you can pray that prayer? AND, accept the answer. We might give "lip-service" to the prayer, but are you willing to accept God's answer? Jesus was.

Jesus knew what was coming; He knew when He left heaven what God's plan was. Yet! He still asked God if there were any other way. But see, this principle was long established before Jesus came on the scene. (Genesis 3:21), later Exodus 12. (12:13).

All through the Old Testament, God painted this picture, this principle. The payment that would "satisfy" God would be a "blood" sacrifice. Nothing else would do! Sin required a sacrifice! Look what God said in Isaiah:

"To what purpose is the multitude of your sacrifices to Me?" Says the Lord. I have had enough of burnt offerings and rams and the fat of fed cattle. I do not delight in the blood of bulls, or of lambs or goats." (Isaiah 1:11).

Why would God make that statement when He is the one who established the cost? - Because they came to be meaningless. It was a "ritual" containing nothing of the heart. God "requires" a changed heart, not changed lifestyle. That is why Jesus came as a man and died as a man. To make it "personal"!

> In the fear of the Lord there is strong confidence, and His children will have a place of refuge. The fear of the Lord is a fountain of life, to turn one away from the snares of death. (Proverbs 14:26-27)

Don't misunderstand that phrase, "Fear of the Lord." I believe I have mentioned before that you could replace the word "fear" with "reverence". So, with that in mind, how do you "look" at God? What is your "relationship" with God? Do you think of God every day? Only on Sunday? Rarely at all? Maybe when you get in a bind, you might think to pray. Sadly, the last is the norm.

A great turn of words in verse 26: *In the fear of the Lord there is strong confidence."* Maybe we could think of the word "confidence" as the word "faith". You trust in God because you believe what He says in His word? No. To me, that confidence comes from God doing a work in your life.

When you got saved there was a change in your life, or there should have been. Think back to that moment. Are you walking closer to God today than you did that first moment you asked Jesus in your life? There definitely should be a difference.

You see, your Christian walk is a "growing", "learning" process. You go from a "baby" Christian, steadily toward maturity, at least you should be. Have you taken inventory on your walk with God lately? You might want to stop here and think about it.

Has your prayer life grown? How about the time you spend in your Bible? Oh, here is the unpleasant one, how often do you attend church? If you are uncomfortable in a church you might want to ask yourself why. The highlight of your week should be that time you spend with fellow Christians. If not, you should ask yourself why.

"Strong confidence" and "fountain of life", - great phrases! Does that describe your Christian walk? Why not? How closely are you "walking" with God? What kind of "fellowship" do you have with your heavenly Father?

All this assumes you are a child of God; you have asked Jesus to come into your heart and you have become a child of God, adopted into God's family. Otherwise, this makes no sense!

> A soft answer turns away wrath, but a harsh word stirs up anger. The tongue of the wise uses knowledge rightly, but the mouth of fools pours forth foolishness. (Proverbs 15:1-2)

Allow me to share a story. As a pastor, I was very involved with the Sunday school ministry in our church. We had quarterly teacher's banquets. We discussed ways to improve our Sunday school program and outreach.

One meeting, our youth teachers were on vacation. It was the consensus of those present that we needed to split our youth class into Senior High and Junior High classes. I found a teacher for the Junior High and ordered the material.

When the Youth teachers returned they were VERY upset. I acknowledge I did not handle the process correctly, I apologized. After church, I met with the Youth teacher; we met one on one. I explained our thinking, our motivation, also admitted I was wrong in how it was handled. By the end of the meeting, the Youth teacher was ordering new material.

I think this whole story demonstrates the wisdom of Solomon's words; that teacher could have left the church mad, and never returned. It would have been my fault of course, instead, both parties took some time to sit down and discuss where each was coming from. How each saw the process and results; would that this was the norm, instead of the exception. When two parties have a different view, it is time to talk, not yell, or accuses, but as Solomon puts it: *The tongue of the wise uses knowledge rightly.* Discuss each view, each motivation, and each option. There may be a third option that neither party had thought of. Talk it out!

I am a "major" introvert; I HATE confrontation. If an argument stirs up, I will shut up. I will not argue with someone. It is not worth it. I will usually continue, and let the results speak for themselves, or I will move on to something productive, arguing accomplishes nothing. The wisdom of Solomon.

There are some great verses in the book of James that deal with the tongue. I guess the question might be: Who or what controls what comes out of your mouth? Is it God's Holy Spirit, pride, arrogance, or the devil himself? You ask yourself before you speak.

57. Which of the four Gospels is the shortest?
    a. Matthew   b. Mark   c. Luke   d. John

> The eyes of the Lord are in every place, keeping watch on
> the evil and the good. A wholesome tongue is a tree of life,
> but perverseness in it breaks the spirit. (Proverbs 15:3-4)

Check out this verse in Jeremiah:

You are great in counsel and mighty in work, for Your eyes are open to all the ways of the sons of men, to give everyone according to his ways and according to the fruit of his doings. (Jeremiah 32:19)

I knew a youth pastor once who told his young charges that as Christians, having the Holy Spirit living within them that God was with them always, even in the backseat of a car. I think that got their attention.

That is nice for youth maybe, what about you? Do you ever think that, as a Christian, God knows exactly what you do at all times? Not just Christians. God knows what everyone is doing. I love this analogy.

Do you know how God got Israel's attention and corrected them in the Old Testament? God used the nation of the Philistines to get Israel back on track. They are not His people, yet God used them to bring Israel back in line. God can use anyone or anything to get our attention, and often does.

Think about this as well. Since God knows the future, He may be bringing someone into our lives to take us where God wants us to go. God is years ahead of us, working out details to bless us. We get impatient; we jump ahead of God and mess up these plans that He has for us.

For God to bless us, we need to be where God wants us to be, when He wants us there. He has worked through countless people to bring us right where we are supposed to be. The sad part is we have no clue. God could be working a miracle, right in front of us. If we are not walking with Him, listening to His guidance through His Holy Spirit, we will miss it!

Is God working in your life right now? Are you sure? Think about it.

          Lonny E. Young

> A fool despises his father's instruction. But he who receives correction is prudent. In the house of the righteous there is much treasure, but in the revenue of the wicked is trouble. (Proverbs 15:5-6)

Have you ever been on a treasure hunt? I was involved in a "youth" scavenger hunt once. A very "memorable" occasion.

Solomon uses the word treasure here. I know he is not talking about a "monetary" treasure, of course. Jesus talks about this treasure in the Sermon on the Mount:

*Do not lay up for yourselves treasures on earth, where moth and rust destroy and where thieves break in and steal; but lay up for yourselves treasures in heaven, where neither moth nor rust destroys and where thieves do not break in and steal. **For where your treasure is, there your heart will be also.*** (Matthew 6: 19-21)

I heard this story once, it has stuck with me. A rich widow and poor servant died and went to heaven. An angel was showing them their heavenly abodes. The rich widow was given a shack in bad shape. The servant was shown this luxurious mansion on a hill. The widow asked the angel why was this? The angel replied, "The servant had sent his treasure on ahead of him to heaven; the widow had kept everything for herself on earth". I think you get the picture.

"Where your treasure is, there your heart will be also." God created us to serve Him with our momentary time spent on this earth. We will be spending an eternity in one of two places. That option is up to you. If your "heart" is in the treasures of this world, you will be likewise compensated. If your treasure is serving God and His creation your treasure will be sent on up to heaven.

If you have asked Jesus into your heart, you will naturally wish to serve God, thus sending your "treasure" where your heart is, with God. Think about this.

Anyone who has asked Jesus to come into their heart has a change of "priorities". They are more giving, more caring, more in tune with God's purpose and priorities.

> The lips of the wise disperse knowledge, but the heart of the fool does not do so. The sacrifice of the wicked is an abomination to the Lord, but the prayer of the upright is His delight! (Proverbs 15:7-8)

This has been a challenge. When I began this project, I thought Solomon would have all kinds of insights into God's wisdom. But, I am sure you have noticed that Solomon seems to be repeating the same basic principles over and over in different ways. Isn't that the way God works? - Simple.

Just look at the Garden of Eden, no complicated instructions; God just gave them two instructions:

*Then the Lord God took the man and put him in the garden of Eden to **tend it and keep it**. (Genesis 2:15)*

And the Lord God commanded the man saying, "Of every tree of the garden you may freely eat; but of the tree of the knowledge of good and evil you shall not eat, for in the day that you eat of it you shall surely die." (Genesis 2:16-17)

Two commands, two instructions. Simple, right? You know what happened; disobedience, sin, rebellion, etc. Man has been at odds with God ever since. Just think of man's history from this point throughout the Old Testament.

But, then God makes another offer, another command, another simple instruction; God never makes things complicated. It is man who complicates the simple truths of God.

"For whoever calls on the name of the Lord shall be saved." (Romans 10:13)

Simple, right? I wonder how many people have memorized John 3:16 but have no clue what it means. God simply explains the price HE paid to restore our relationship with Him. It is simple. Why is it so hard for man to grasp the simple? It is right here in black and white!

58. In Pharaoh's dreams that Joseph interpreted, what did the seven represent?
    a. Sabbaths   b. years   c. good luck   d. days

The way of the wicked is an abomination to the Lord, but He loves him who follows righteousness. Harsh discipline is for him who forsakes the way, and he who hates correction will die. (Proverbs 15:9-10)

One of the things that I picked up reading through the Old Testament is how God feels about idols. Here are a couple of verses from Deuteronomy:

*"When you come into the land which the Lord your God is giving you, you shall not learn to follow the **abominations** of those nations.* (Deuteronomy 18:9)

"But the cities of these peoples which the Lord your God gives you as an inheritance, you shall let nothing that breathes remain alive, but you shall utterly destroy them: the Hittite and the Amorite and the Canaanite and the Perizzite and the Hivite and the Jebusite, just as the Lord your God has commanded you, lest they teach you to do according to all their abominations which they have done for their gods, and you sin against the Lord your God. (Deuteronomy 20:16-18)

A warning to God's people from Moses before they entered the Promised Land; now look at a verse about Solomon:

*And he had seven hundred wives, princesses, and three hundred concubines; and his wives **turned away his heart.** For it was so, when Solomon was old, that his wives turned his heart after other gods; and his heart was not loyal to the Lord his God, as was the heart of his father David.* (1 Kings 11:3-4)

Has something or someone come between you and God? That is an idol. Solomon's wives slowly drew him away from the God who blessed him more than any other man. We laugh, that God gave Solomon so much "wisdom," but he was drawn away from God by his wives. Does that not show you the power of idols? "Abominations"

> Hades and Destruction are before the Lord; so how much more the hearts of the sons of men. A scoffer does not love one who corrects him, nor will he go to the wise. (Proverbs 15:11-12)

My editors will not let me use the alternative to Hades. It is clear what Solomon is saying. I hope I have stressed it throughout this narrative. Since the days of the nationwide revivals in our country, the warning has been heralded! "Repent, and turn to God." The message will never change. It was the message of Jesus in the first century; it is the message today.

Just as Solomon has used various ways to teach a few simple principles of obedience to God, I have tried different "approaches" of bringing the same message here. Pastors throughout the centuries scratch their heads, trying to come up with innovative ways of saying:

For whoever calls on the name of the Lord shall be saved". (Romans 10:13)

It is that simple. Do you remember, in the old days when your teacher, to teach you something, would have you write it on the blackboard a hundred times? If that would work I would challenge you to do that right now.

The problem with that exercise is that it would be in your mind, your memory, but not in your heart. That is where it must be. I love the line someone told me once: "Most people will miss heaven by eighteen inches," the distance between the head and the heart. They will know what the Bible says. They will "know" who Jesus is, historically, but have absolutely no personal "relationship" with the God of the Bible.

You CANNOT stand before God at the judgment and say, "Now I believe". That will not fly. That decision must be made here and now. Unless, you have some guarantee of tomorrow, which you don't. Let me close with this verse from the gospel of John.

Jesus said to him, "Thomas, because you have seen Me, you have believed. Blessed are those who have not seen and yet have believed! (John 20:29)

> A merry heart makes a cheerful countenance, but by sorrow
> of the heart the spirit is broken. The heart of him who has
> understanding seeks knowledge, but the mouth of fool's
> feeds on foolishness. (Proverbs 15:13-14)

I think Solomon is talking about the heart? Sorry, couldn't resist! When I see a reference to the heart my thoughts always go to this reference about King David:

*But the Lord said to Samuel, "Do not look at his appearance or at his physical stature, because I have refused him (Eliab). For the Lord does not see as man sees, for man looks at the outward appearance, **but the Lord looks at the heart.**" (1 Samuel 16:7)*

Samuel was sent by God to anoint another king after Saul had failed Him; Samuel went to Jesse's house. Jesse has eight sons. Samuel looks at the first, Eliab, the oldest, and says "this must be the one." God said no, after looking at the remaining seven, God rejected all of them. Samuel asks Jesse, "Do you have any other sons?"
Jesse replied, "Just the youngest, in the fields, tending the sheep."
"Fetch him", said Samuel. It was David.

If you want a fascinating study begin here in 1 Samuel 16 and study the life of King David, Solomon's father. Take your time; notice David's relationship with God. I would like you to notice one more important verse:

*Then Samuel took the horn of oil and anointed him in the midst of his brothers; and **the Spirit of the Lord came upon David from that day forward.** So, Samuel arose and went to Ramah. (1 Samuel 16:13)*

David would later break God's heart with Bathsheba, BUT, the Spirit of God never left David. God removed the Spirit from Saul after his transgressions (16:14). There are so many great lessons to learn from David's walk with God. Along with keeping up with this devotional you would learn about God's personality by studying King David.

59. Name one of the two prophets who appeared with Jesus at His transfiguration.
    a. Moses   b. Elijah   c. Enoch   d. Jacob

> All the days of the afflicted are evil, but he who is of a merry heart has a continual feast. Better is a little with the fear of the Lord, then great treasure with trouble. (Proverbs 15:15-16)

"Time, it goes so fast, and it takes so long." I was told that is a line from a song. When I meditated on that phrase, it makes SO much sense. I am in my seventies; I never thought I would get this far. I have had blood clots in both my lungs; a section of my colon removed because of cancer. A tough bout with pneumonia, a bad wreck, working with U.P.S; I just didn't think I would get here.

My life changed when the pastor of our home church led my wife and me to the Lord. I think Solomon nailed it this time: *"But he who is of a merry heart has a continual feast."* (15:15b)

I have so many fond memories of our family sitting around our dining room table for dinner. We didn't eat together during the day but I loved the evening meal. Dad would show us how to hold our fork, how to use a knife and fork to cut our meat, and not to put our elbows on the table, etc. The evening meal should always be a special time.

Have you invited Jesus to your meal? After we were saved, we won't eat a meal but that we pause and ask God's blessing.

That is such an important "picture". Not by accident. Let me share one of my favorite verses, the words of Jesus:

*"Behold, I stand at the door and knock. If anyone hears My voice and opens the door, I will come in to him and **dine with him**, and he with Me."* (Revelation 3:20)

The door our Lord is referring to, of course, is our heart. If you don't know Jesus as your Savior, He is knocking on the door of your heart right now. It's your choice whether you let Him in or not, but look at the picture; He wishes to DINE with you, to set at your table and talk about the life He has planned for you. He wants to share His powerful love for you, and wants to bless you. All you must do is open that door of your heart and invite Him in. It is just that simple; a simple prayer. Do it now.

Lonny E. Young

> A wrathful man stirs up strife, but he who is slow to anger allays
> contention. The way of the lazy man is like a hedge of thorns,
> but the way of the upright is a highway. (Proverbs 15:18-19)

An interesting term that Solomon uses; "The way" gives the picture of a path, a highway, a direction. Isn't it interesting how hard it is for us to move away from our desired direction? To change our "habits"; my favorite is: "out of your comfort zone." We go through each day in a "routine", especially if you have a job; it is hard to break a routine.

Do you try? Are you "afraid" to try new things? Why? The unknown is always scary, the unexpected. I think those people, the "comfort zone" people, are mentioned in the passage above. *The way of the lazy man.* You see it takes courage, and desire to try new things. The thing about new things is, you always "learn" something! That can be scary as well.

Take reading your Bible for instance, - that assumes you have one. It takes work to open those pages each day. We are not talking about the "once a week" churchgoers. I am talking about a regular "once a day" Bible reader. What happened the first time you read something that touched your heart? You went back. What happened when you read something that "convicted" you? It was a while before you went back.

We hate "correction" or "conviction", don't we? The thing is that is where the learning takes place; that is where your understanding of God's will and purpose for life takes place. You learn God's heart. What God wants and desires for your life. Get back in there, read God's message to you.

We talked earlier about choices. There are only two. It is not like a buffet, there are only two choices. God's way or the world's way, it is your choice. Have you noticed that God doesn't try to "make" you go a certain way? If you're a Christian, He will try to influence your decision through His Holy Spirit. The choice is still yours! The "way" you choose is still yours.

One thing though, when you reap the results of disobeying God, don't blame Him. You can't blame the messenger.

A wise son makes a father glad, but a foolish man despises his mother. Folly is joy to him who is destitute of discernment, but a man of understanding walks uprightly. (Proverbs 15:20-21)

This goes along with what we talked about yesterday. *Destitute of discernment.* Today they would say, "He has no clue"

I have been amazed, the closer and more frequent my talks with God, how much peace there is; the more I learn about God, through reading His Word, the more amazed I am at the way He works in His children's lives. He is a loving Father, who cares about His children.

I just finished a lengthy study of King David. That night on the balcony he broke God's heart, God didn't kill him right there, He could have. He waited for over nine months, then during that time, David has Uriah killed. Still nothing. God worked through Nathan the prophet, to finally confront David. David paid for that sin the rest of his life. Read for yourself, beginning in 2 Samuel 11. The thing about David's whole life is his gradual restoration in his fellowship with God. Read about it!

God is so much like the father in the parable of the Prodigal Son. His son rebelled and squandered his fortune, yet the father welcomes him back with open arms; that is how God looks at us. We make mistakes, we are "human". It breaks God's heart to see us suffer. The picture God gives us all through the Bible is that God is also a forgiving God, and His grace is more than sufficient for our mistakes.

But did you notice something about the story of the Prodigal?

Look at this verse:

*But **when he came to himself**, he said, "How many of my father's hired servants have bread enough to spare, and I perish with hunger. (Luke 15:17)*

You must realize your condition. You are the one who must turn to God. God is waiting, make no mistake about that, He is waiting, watching at the end of that road for your return. You took the wrong fork in the road. When you realize it, turn and go back to where you left God. Renew that fellowship. God is willing!

60. How much silver was Judas paid to betray Jesus?
      a. 40 pcs   b. 10 pcs   c. 13 pcs   d. 30 pcs

Without counsel, plans go awry, but in the multitude of counselors they are established. A man has joy by the answer of his mouth, and a word spoken in due season, how good it is! (Proverbs 15:22-23)

We make a joke and are criticized sometimes as Baptist, about our "committee" mentality; for we have committees for everything. The funniest thing I've seen in our church constitution was the phrase "Committee on Committees". They do serve a unique function. It is their job to fill vacancies on other committees. Don't laugh!

As a Sunday School Director, I try to meet once a quarter with our teaching staff to examine our progress, our goals and seek ways to improve our ministry. It is essential, we are all working together. That is the point as teachers and leaders.

In these meetings, I am seeking the "counsel" of others who serve as teachers. Solomon doesn't use the word here, but his father used it quite often. After King David was anointed king he met with God in prayer. In 2 Samuel 7, David has a lengthy prayer, thanking God for His hand on David's life. I encourage you to read that chapter. In my Bible, I underlined the word "servant" in David's prayer. Ten times David refers to himself as "servant".

Why is that significant? This is the KING of Israel. God's chosen people. Just his calling from God, you would think, would elevate him above a servant. That is NOT how David saw himself. That is NOT how we should see ourselves. We are ALL servants of God, no matter our "title." Here is a great description of David's attitude:

Then King David went in and sat before the Lord; and he said: "Who am I, O Lord God? And what is my house that you have brought me this far? (2 Samuel 7:18).

When we seek God's counsel, what is the attitude of our heart? Do we recognize our status before God as "servant"? Do we recognize our status among God's people as "servant"? Do we recognize our status in this world as "servant"? God has put us here for one reason; to serve each other and our neighbors, to glorify God!

> The heart of the righteous studies how to answer, but the mouth of the wicked pours forth evil. The Lord is far from the wicked, but He hears the prayer of the righteous. (Proverbs 15:28-29)

A couple of things, because we pray, as Christians, does God automatically grant our petition?

Check these verses:

*Now this is the confidence that we have in Him, that if we ask anything **according to His will**, He hears us, and if we know that He hears us, whatever we ask, we know that we have the petitions that we have asked of Him.* (1 John 5:14-15)

Did you catch that? God is not "Santa Claus"; God is not there to grant our "wishes". Don't miss this *according to His will*. We can ask; God encourages us to ask (Matthew 7:7-8), but, God has a specific plan for our lives. We may ask for something that is not good for us, or it will derail His plan for us. Aren't you glad that our Father, who knows the future, will not grant our every wish?

Look at the first few words here, *the heart of the righteous studies how to answer, -* That is a unique gift that God gives His children, that is the power of the Holy Spirit to filter our speech through God's will; it takes time and practice. As a young Christian, I often put my foot in my mouth. It is a learning process, to listen to the promptings of His Spirit!

You would think from verse 29 that God doesn't hear the prayers of the lost. That is not true. Wait a minute, don't misunderstand! The ONLY prayer of a sinner, that God hears and answers, is "Lord, save me!" Until that happens God is not interested in the "requests" of those who are not His children. If God answered all the prayers of a lost person, why get saved? Again, don't misunderstand; that is not to say that God doesn't "care" about the lost. He loves them and wants them into His family. It is their choice.

I hope you are being challenged by this study in Proverbs. Solomon is amazing. He can say the same thing ten different ways. One of them will catch your attention. Speak to your heart.

                    Lonny E. Young

The preparations of the heart belong to man, but the answer of the tongue is from the Lord. All the ways of a man are pure in his own eyes, but the Lord weights the spirits. (Proverbs 16:1-2)

I have often wondered what takes place on Saturday evening. Is there any thought to The Lord's Day? I like to use this phrase I found in the gospel of John:

Now it was the Preparation Day of the Passover, and about the sixth hour. And he said to the Jews, "Behold, your King?" (John 19:14)

Pilate's comment to the Jews, who wanted Jesus crucified. That phrase stuck with me. I wonder if any Christians "prepare" for worship on the Lord's Day. In this passage, they wanted to get Jesus crucified before the Passover, ritual reasons. But think about this:

"And you shall take a bunch of hyssop, dip it in the blood that is in the basin, and strike the lintel and the doorposts with the blood that is in the basin. And none of you shall go out of his house until morning. (Exodus 12:22)

There were specific tasks that needed to be completed, before God would send His death angel into Egypt. They were to "prepare" themselves for the Passover. I encourage you to read the whole 12th chapter of Exodus; the choosing of the lamb, detailed preparation, getting prepared for God's salvation. How much "preparation" do you put into your visit to God's house on the Lord's Day?

You can prepare your clothes (12:11). You can prepare your heart. You can read your Bible. You can pray for the pastor and your Sunday school teacher, and others in leadership.

I think Saturday evening should be a time of "preparation" for God's blessing on the Lord's Day. Then, on Sunday watch for God's Spirit moving in your worship experience. Think about the consequences for the Jews, had they "not" prepared for that night of deliverance.

61. Who did God commission to talk for Moses?
    a. Aaron   b. Joshua   c. Elijah   d. Isaac

> Commit your works to the Lord, and your thoughts will be
> established. The Lord has made all for Himself, yes, even the
> wicked for the day of doom. (Proverbs 16:3-4)

Do you see it? Guess who is in charge? I love those first few words; it all boils down to where our heart is, but, he doesn't say heart he says thoughts.

I love these words of Jesus in Matthew:

But those things which proceed out of the mouth come from the heart, and they defile a man. For out of the heart proceed evil thoughts, murders, adulteries, fornications, thefts, false witnesses, blasphemies. (Matthew 15:18-19)

You see, it begins with the heart. So, if the heart is wicked how do we change it? Check this out:

*If you confess with your mouth the Lord Jesus and believe in your **heart** that God raised Him from the dead, you will be saved.* (Romans 10:9)

It is the heart; it begins and ends with the heart. You can be the smartest man in the world (Solomon was). If your heart has turned from God or devoid of God's presence it will reflect in your words and deeds. I love the promise in the latter part of verse 3: *and your thoughts will be established.* Once you have opened your heart and invited Jesus in, God will begin working on you, through His Holy Spirit.

He will clean up your speech, turn the light on in your blackened heart, and renew a right spirit within you. If I may, two more verses:

The Spirit Himself bears witness with our spirit that we are children of God, and if children, then heirs—heirs of God and joint heirs with Christ, if indeed we suffer with Him, that we may also be glorified together. (Romans 8:16-17)

          Lonny E. Young

> Everyone proud in heart is an abomination to the Lord;
> though they join forces, none will go unpunished. In mercy
> and truth atonement is provided for iniquity; but by the fear
> of the Lord one departs from evil. (Proverbs 16:5-6)

I pointed out earlier the message in 2 Samuel 7; David's prayer that uses the word "servant" ten times. That was King David's attitude toward God.

We spoke yesterday about the heart. Do you remember how David was referred to by the apostle Paul?

*And when he had removed him (King Saul), He raised up for them David as king, to whom also He gave testimony and said, "I have found David the son of Jesse, **a man after My own heart**, who will do all My will." (Acts 13:22)*

David is also given this description in 1 Samuel 13:14. That can't be right. Look at what David did with Bathsheba and Uriah. Yes, he did. He also paid a dear price for that sin. David also admitted and confessed his sin. God knew David's heart; just as He knows your heart.

You can walk the aisle of the church fifteen times. Be baptized fifteen times. Until it becomes real in your heart, those are just actions with no meaning. Don't think you can fool God. May I quote one more verse?

*But the Lord said to Samuel, "Do not look at his appearance or at his physical stature, because I have refused him (Eliab). For the Lord does not see as man sees; for man looks at the outward appearance, but **the Lord looks at the heart."** (1 Samuel 16:7)*

You cannot fool God with actions. He knows your heart! *In mercy and truth.* (v. 6); that must be our approach to God, as a "servant" with a servant's heart. Take a minute and look at Revelation 3:20. God is standing at the door of your heart. He is knocking. It is YOUR heart. You must open that door and invite Him in.

When a man's ways please the Lord, he makes even his enemies to be at peace with him. Better is a little with righteousness, then vast revenues without justice. (Proverbs 16:7-8)

It is simple!

Look at the words of Jesus:

"If you love Me, keep My commandments." (John 14:15)

"He who has My commandments and keeps them, it is he who loves Me. And he who loves Me will be loved by My Father, and I will love him and manifest Myself to him." (John 15:21)

So. What "commandments" are Jesus talking about?

Jesus said to him, "You shall love the Lord your Go with all your heart, with all your soul, and with all your mind. And the second is like it: You shall love your neighbor as yourself. On these two commandments hang all the Law and the Prophets." (Matthew 22:37-40)

That is what Jesus is talking about. That is what Solomon is talking about. That is what God was talking about in the Garden of Eden. Obedience! That has been God's message from day one! Of course, God could have "programmed" us to be obedient. He could "arrange" our paths to go only where He wants us to go. God is not like that. He created us to "want" to be obedient. It must be OUR choice, not His will.

It is like this. God created us with a plan and a purpose (Jeremiah 29:11). He also gave us the ability to "go our own way." That choice is up to us. Much of what Solomon talks about in the Proverbs are the options we face every day, - Righteousness or wickedness, wisdom or rebellion; Solomon points out all these "options." It still boils down to our choice.

The world versus God, through God's grace He left the choice to us. We choose to follow God or the world's way. We even have the option to choose where we will spend eternity; one of two options. I hope you have made the right choice! If not, you need to right now!

62. Who met Jesus, while walking on the water?
    a. John   b. Thomas   c. James   d. Peter

     Lonny E. Young

A man's heart plans his way, but the Lord directs his steps.
(Proverbs 16:9)

I haven't quoted this verse yet in this study. When I found these three verses it gave me a whole new perspective on God's working in my life. Take a few minutes and meditate on these verses:

"For I know the thoughts (plans) that I think toward you," says the Lord, "thoughts (plans) of peace and not of evil, to give you a future and a hope. Then you will call upon Me and go and pray to Me, and I will listen to you. And you will seek Me and find Me, when you search for Me with all your heart." (Jeremiah 29:11-13)

I bracketed the word "plans" because that is the word used in the NIV, and I prefer it better. The point is the same. If God's children ever grasped the meat that is in these three verses, God could change your life. God has a PLAN! Here is another way I describe it.

We are on a path called life. The main goal should be to put God in the lead and follow close behind Him. We will come to many forks in this path as we grow up. We have two options. We can take the path that God travels, or we can choose to take the alternate path. We might travel down that alternate path for a while then realize we made the wrong choice. Sometimes it comes quickly; sometimes we may travel it for years.

Once we realize we have chosen the wrong path, what do we do? We go back to where we left God at the fork in the path. We repent, say we're sorry, and get back on the right path. We lose valuable time, we miss some blessings. But we make a new commitment to stay with God, and follow His leading.

When we are not sure where God is leading, we stop, we pray, we wait for God's direction. When we head off in our own wisdom, our own desires, we miss God's blessing. We need daily, to ask God for His will and direction for the coming day. I hope these devotions in Proverbs have caused you to seek God's wisdom, not yours. Be led by God's Spirit not the flesh. Stay right behind God's leading!

> Divination is on the lips of the king; his mouth must not transgress in judgment. Honest weights and scales are the Lord's; all the weights in the bag are His work. (Proverbs 16:10-11)

Do you see the contrast? Divination is seeking advice from a source other than God. King Saul is a great example. When God had removed His Spirit from Saul, because of his disobedience, Saul sought advice from a witch.

Then Saul said to his servants, "Find me a woman who is a medium, that I may go to her and inquire of her." And his servants said to him, "In fact, there is a woman who is a medium in En Dor." (1 Samuel 28:7).

At first, God used Saul, so long as Saul walked with God. Soon Saul began to disobey God. To do things as he saw fit, not God. Saul was instructed to destroy the Amalekites (1 Samuel 15).

Look at this verse:

"I greatly regret that I have set up Saul as king, for he has turned back from following Me, and has not performed My commands." And it grieved Samuel, and he cried out to the Lord all night. (1 Samuel 15:11).

The point is clear throughout the Proverbs. Where do you seek your guidance? How do you determine your path in life? Are you seeking God's guidance, wisdom, and leadership or the worlds? When God turned His back on Saul, Saul went looking for divination, a witch, a medium. How do you determine the path, the fork in the road, to take? Toss a coin? Do you have the Holy Spirit within you to guide you?

One more verse if I may:

But the Spirit of the Lord departed from Saul, and a distressing spirit from the Lord troubled him. (1 Samuel 16:14).

          Lonny E. Young

July 6   187-178   Proverbs 16

It is an abomination for kings to commit wickedness, for a throne is established by righteousness. Righteous lips are the delight of kings, and they love him who speaks what is right. (Proverbs 16:12-13)

I hope I didn't give the wrong impression yesterday. In New Testament time's we will not have to happen to us, what happened to Saul? Once we have asked Jesus into our hearts, we receive the Holy Spirit that is a promise from God. The Holy Spirit is the "seal" of our redemption and a seal of our adoption into the family of God. It is permanent! (2 Corinthians 1:22)

In the Old Testament God used the Spirit to accomplish His will and purpose through those He chose to use. Samson is another example.

Every election cycle in our country I use as a "gauge" to see where our country is going. I think it is interesting that the Bible promises that it is God who raises and sets down those in authority. If we are supposed to be a "godly" nation; you would think God's people would make the right choices. Not necessarily so!

Think about that the next time you vote.

There is that word "abomination" again. Can you think of any stronger word to use? I think Solomon is making his point quite clear. The reason God turned His back on Saul? The first fifteen chapters of First Samuel tell the story of Saul's fall from God's blessing to pure disobedience.

We need to seek God's guidance when it comes time to vote. As a "godly" country, God uses His children to accomplish His will and purpose. The further our country drifts from God, the more "ungodly" we become and this is reflected in the leaders we choose. We get what we ask for. Many time's God will allow us to go down a road to teach us the importance of the choices we make.

Solomon is focused on kings in these verses; an important aspect of our lives as Christians. Who do we follow? Jesus is first of course. But, we also have a responsibility to choose wisely those we appoint above us, in leadership positions. They must be godly leaders, we must pray for them, encourage them, and support them. I guess one of the greatest responsibilities we have in this area would be our choice of a pastor. Godly leadership is the key to walking in God's will!

63. In which Gospel can you find the Be-attitudes?
    a. Matthew   b. Mark   c. Luke   d. John

> As messengers of death is the king's wrath, but a wise man
> will appease it. In the light of the king's face is life, and his
> favor is like a cloud of the latter rain. (Proverbs 16:14-15)

I wonder how much of David's life he shared with his son, Solomon. These verses remind me of when David was running from King Saul. Twice David had an opportunity to be rid of his enemy; in a cave (1 Samuel 24) and later in an encampment (1 Samuel 26). Both times, David chose the high road; David was willing to wait on God's will and God's time.

Are you waiting for something? Are you willing to wait on God's time? Let me tell you from experience, don't get ahead of God! You will never win.

Let's suppose we capitalize the word "king". Making it refer to God or Jesus.

Look at this verse in the gospel of John:

In Him was life, and the life was the light of men. And the light shines in the darkness, and the darkness did not comprehend it. (John 1:4-5)

We are living in a dark world. It seems to be getting darker by the minute. I used to challenge myself, by moving around in our home without a light, late at night. I would walk down the stairs, into the kitchen for a drink of water. In the dark, you search for two things. A light, just the slightest light gives you a focal point. The second is sure footing. When I came down the steps, I would search out each step with my foot.

Jesus is the guide, the light, the point of reference in the dark. God will also guide our footsteps, one step at a time, toward the goal, the Light. I have often thought that our country, right now, could use an old-fashioned revival. Then, there is a "revival" happening EVERY Sunday in your local church. The same message is preached, as there would be in a revival. Accept the Lord Jesus as your Savior; ask God to come into your heart, through the power of the Holy Spirit. Shine a light in the darkness of your heart. It is the same message with the same result—repentance. When was the last time you followed the light of the gospel and attended your local church?

          Lonny E. Young

> How much better to get wisdom than gold! And to get understanding is to be chosen rather than silver. The highway of the upright is to depart from evil; he who keeps his way preserves his soul. (Proverbs 16:16-17)

I never really understood this, - how a person can ask Jesus into their heart, walk down the aisle, make a profession of that faith, be baptized, and never set foot in a church again. I love a phrase I heard recently: There is C.E.O. Christians, "Christmas and Easter Only". That is sad to me.

There are those two famous words that Solomon uses over and over. No, not silver and gold but "wisdom and understanding". I guess the ones I described earlier after they are baptized, know all there is to know about God; they have their ticket, what else is there?

I marvel most of the time, I can't begin to guess how many sermons, Sunday school lessons, Wednesday night and Sunday night devotions I have heard; I have delivered a few, myself. Yet, there always seems to be something each time that "enhances" my walk with God. Something in the text I hadn't noticed. The teacher brings out something I hadn't thought about. Even the Holy Spirit gets in the act and reveals something I hadn't noticed; that is the "wisdom" and "understanding" that Solomon is talking about.

I think I have marked up my current Bible more than any other Bible I have owned. It is a grand adventure every time I enter our church. Sometimes, I may be wrestling with something in my life. I can't tell you how many times God has blessed me with a direction, or a piece of wisdom in the worship service. It doesn't have to be "spiritual" it just must be consistent. CEO's are missing so much!

Bible teaching and understanding was never meant to be hit and miss; it must be consistent, it must be regular. It is a commitment between you and God. "I don't have to go to church to have "fellowship" with God". - Really? Then why did Jesus make such a point of telling Peter that Jesus was sent to establish His church, "And the gates of Hades will not prevail against it." (Matthew 16:18). The devil may not have prevailed but, it seems, apathy has!

> Pride goes before destruction and a haughty spirit before a
> fall. Better to be a humble spirit with the lowly, then to divide
> the spoil with the proud. (Proverbs 16:18-19)

An interesting verse; I'm sure you have heard a version of verse 18 quoted before. "Pride goes before a fall" right? It is usually said when someone starts "bragging" on an accomplishment, or from a jealous competitor. We need to look at this idea.

Are you not supposed to be proud of your accomplishments? Are you not supposed to be proud of your children's accomplishments? Today we don't have "winners," today EVERYBODY gets a trophy.

I remember when I used to bowl regularly in a league; most of the time our team won the "I Tried" trophies. We don't even get those anymore. Does everybody get first place?

Don't miss the first words of verse 19: *Better to be a humble spirit.* We can have a "humble spirit" and still be proud of our accomplishments. Don't confuse the two. Do you know what I have learned? If the deed is worth committing on, "someone else" will do it.

I learned very early in ministry not to "request" to speak. You can do it in such "subtle" ways. I refuse to ask to speak. If the Lord wants me to say something, He will lay it on someone's heart to ask me. Then I know that God is in it, and not my "pride". I don't know how many times the Lord will give me a "sermon," and I just wait. If God gave me the words, someone will ask me to speak. It is God's way of telling me in advance He has a message for me.

That is what Solomon is talking about, *"a haughty spirit"* not the "spirit" God wants in His messengers. He wants a "humble" spirit! The message is God's, you are simply the messenger. Any praise belongs to God. The minute you begin thinking you are something God will show you the door. The glory belongs to God and Him alone!

It is the attitude of the heart. Don't fool yourself; God knows your heart, your motive, and your attitude. I learned this the hard way as well.

64. Who sold his birthright for a bowl of stew?
    a. Jacob   b. Isaac   c. Esau   d. Ishmael

July 10   191-174   Proverbs 16

He who heeds the word wisely will find good, and whoever trusts in the Lord, happy is he. The wise in heart will be called prudent, and sweetness of the lips increases learning. (Proverbs 16:20-21)

Heeds the word, trusts in the Lord. - That is what this whole treatise is about; reading God's word, but not just reading it, obeying it, heeding it. There is a big difference. We have a guy in our church that is working hard at memorizing scripture. He leads the singing on Wednesday nights sometimes. He will try to quote some verses between songs. I applaud his efforts! More power to him. The thing is, the word must be "lived" as well as memorized. He is a godly man and I applaud his desire!

When I, on rare occasions, buy a new Bible, the first thing I do is go through the New Testament and underline (I mark in my Bible) the word "faith." That word means SO much to me. Let me give you a trivia question: Which book in the New Testament has the word "faith" the most? (Only appears twice in the Old Testament, KJV). Would you guess Hebrews? The eleventh chapter of Hebrews? "The Hall of Faith" chapter? Maybe James?

The book with the most appearances of the word "faith" is Romans. Now I have been wanting to compare the number of times by the size of the book. Both Hebrews and James could be contenders. As far as the "number" of times, it is Romans.

Why is that word so important to me? I guess one way to explain it would be to think of a Christian as an automobile. That vehicle goes NOWHERE without gas. It looks good; it has plenty of power under the hood, etc. If it doesn't have gas, it is a huge paperweight! It serves no function. Faith is the gas that makes that car useful. It goes nowhere; it does nothing, without the gas. Really, if you think about it, it's the gas that "makes" it a car.

Look at this verse:

But without faith it is impossible to please Him, for he who comes to God must believe that He is, and that He is a rewarder of those who diligently seek Him. (Hebrews 11:6)

> He who is slow to anger is better than the mighty, and
> he who rules his spirit than he who takes a city. The lot is
> cast into the lap, but it's every decision is from the Lord.
> (Proverbs 16:32-33)

When do you have your devotions? Do you have a "quiet time" with the Lord? - A time spent in reading God's Word and prayer. Do you set aside a time each day? That is the point of this book; a slow walk through the book of Proverbs, a time to meditate on the words of Solomon which are the words of God through the son of David.

Do you have your time with God in the morning? That is my preference, - starting the day asking for God's blessing; lifting those who have physical and/or spiritual needs, in prayer. Whatever Bible reading schedule you may be using; I want to always challenge and encourage you to read through the whole Bible at least once. Even if it is a chapter a day; read the "entire" Bible at least once.

If your devotions are in the evening, do you take time to reflect on what God has done through your day? This is a great time to have a journal. Record those events in the day that you felt God's presence saw His working in your life; saw His hand on you or someone around you. Maybe God taught you a lesson today—WRITE IT DOWN! I am a big believer in journals.

However, or whenever, you have a "quiet time" you need to do it daily! Not hit-and-miss, a regular time "set aside" to meet with God. It is so important. If you do this every day for a couple of weeks you will surely miss it when you neglect it. It becomes part of your life. Which it should! A time to fellowship with your Creator, your heavenly Father, the one who loves you so much He was willing to send His Son to the cross that you and He might have this relationship! Don't you think that deserves a few minutes each day to sit and talk?

But it's every decision is from the Lord. Can you say that? That is key to a "quiet time". Asking God for direction, His hand on your life DAILY! Lifting in prayer, those decisions you can't seem to get a handle on. Lift them God, and then WAIT for His direction, His guidance, and His peace about that decision. That would be a great entry in your journal, wouldn't it?

          Lonny E. Young

> Better is a dry morsel with quietness, then a house full of feasting with strife. A wise servant will rule over a son who causes shame, and will share an inheritance among the brothers. (Proverbs 17:1-2)

I know, I had to skip some verses in chapter 16. When I began this project, I figured twelve verses from each chapter would cover the book. Then I found two verses from each chapter and then I had to skip some. This isn't a "commentary"; it is meant to challenge you, and encourage you, to read God's Word. If I have done that by these few words each day, I have accomplished my goal.

Have you ever been to a "noisy" restaurant? It distracts from the meal, doesn't it? It does for me. Yet when we have family get-togethers it seems they are just as noisy, until the eating begins.

There is something about the fellowship around the dinner table, isn't there? Boy does this bring some verses to mind:

Now it came to pass, as He (Jesus) sat at the table with them, that He took bread, blessed and broke it, and gave it to them. Then their eyes were opened and they knew Him; and He vanished from their sight. And they said to one another, "Did not our heart burn within us while He talked with us on the road, and while He opened the Scriptures to us?" (Luke 24:30-32)

"Behold, I stand at the door and knock, if anyone hears My voice and opens the door; I will come in to him and dine with him, and he with Me. (Revelation 3:20)

This kind of goes with the devotion yesterday; both verses give the picture of "intimate" fellowship with God around the dinner table. I heard, just the other day, that people are encouraged to have at least one meal together, as a family, around the dinner table, - at least one meal. Put away the phones, turn off the TV, gather together and visit about the day. What a great "stress" reliever. You might even talk about what God is doing or has done in your life; an interesting topic.

65. Who was Jacob's first wife?
    a. Rebekah   b. Sarah   c. Leah   d. Rachel

The refining pot is for silver and the furnace for gold, but the Lord tests the hearts. An evildoer gives heed to false lips; a liar listens eagerly to a spiteful tongue. (Proverbs 17:3-4)

James is such an interesting book; so many often choose it for Bible studies. The principle that Solomon talks about here is talked about in James:

But the Lord tests the hearts. (Proverbs 17:3)

My brethren, count it all joy when you fall into various trial (tests), knowing that the testing of your faith produces patience. But let patience have its perfect work, that you may be perfect and complete, lacking nothing. (James 1:2-4)

God is in the process of "growing" us as His children. Once we have opened our heart and received Christ as our Savior, we become children of God (Romans 8:15). As children, God must use different means to strengthen our growth; just as parents try to teach their children.

The method that God uses is trials or tests. Think about it, when you were growing up the best lessons you learned were from the "mistakes" you made; they seem to stick better. God puts trials in our life to teach us to trust in Him. The hardest lesson for me was "waiting" on God. And how does He teach that? - By making us wait.

God brought a special verse into my life, just as I was trying to learn this lesson:

*But those who **wait on the Lord** shall renew their strength; they shall mount up with wings like eagles, they shall run and not be weary, they shall walk and not faint.* (Isaiah 40:31)

God brought that verse to me through a chorus we used to sing to kick off our worship service. It became such an encouragement to me when I needed it; lessons learned to grow our faith.

          Lonny E. Young

He who mocks the poor reproaches his Maker; he who is glad at calamity will not go unpunished. Children's children are the crown of old men, and the glory of children is their father. (Proverbs 17:5-6)

Grandchildren, - when our first grandson was born, I was at the hospital with my daughter; I remember thinking, "No big deal, it is another child born in our family." Then Kenny was born. The only way you can know this feeling is to be a grandparent. It totally blew me away; my daughter had "infection" problems, and it was touch and go for Kenny for some time.

As we were praying for Kenny, I attended Wednesday Night prayer at church. The second verse to the Gaither's hymn, "Because He lives," just blew me away: "How to hold a newborn baby." I was in tears, still, do. It is funny that most song leaders "skip" the second verse. No matter, that verse will always remind me of the "trial" our grandson, and my daughter went through then; today Kenny has finished a stint in United States Marines in Iraq. He is healthy and big as a house. God is so good!

I sometimes think we forget just who God is; I have long contended that most Christians tend to put God in a box. If we can't "conceive" of how something could be done, or if it could be done; then God can't do it. Don't bother to pray, that is beyond God's ability! Really? - The same God that brought you into this world, the same God who "spoke" the world into existence, really? Think about your limitations on God.

You do know what that is? It is "faith" plain and simple. Let me lay this verse on you to meditate on:

Then He touched their eyes, saying, **"According to your faith** *let it be to you."* (Matthew 9:29).

Meditate on that a bit; God will work in your life just as far as your "faith" will allow Him. Read through the gospels; look to see how many times Jesus chastised His disciples because of their lack of faith, yet commended a Gentile for their "great faith." It is amazing to me. Is God working in your life? Why not? *"According to your faith!"*

Excellent speech is not becoming to a fool, much less lying lips to a prince. A present is a precious stone in the eyes of its possessor; wherever he turns he prosperous. (Proverbs 17:7-8)

Isn't it interesting how keywords trigger passages or verses or stories in the Bible? Assuming you're that familiar with your Bible, that word prosperous really triggers a couple of verses:

He shall be like a tree planted by the rivers of water, that brings forth its fruit in due season, whose leaf also shall not wither; **and whatever he does shall prosper.** (Psalm 1:3)

This Book of the Law shall not depart from your mouth, but you shall meditate in it day and night, that you may observe to do according to all that is written in it. For then you shall make your way **prosperous,** *and then you will have good success.* (Joshua 1:8)

What a picture! Don't misunderstand! God never promises "prosperity" in the way the world looks at prosperity. There are many ways to measure prosperity. Notice in Solomon's verse here (v. 8). It is a "present" as a precious stone. That gift? - Salvation through Jesus Christ, the Chief Cornerstone! (Isaiah 28:16 and Matthew 21:42). You will never know how precious it is until you stand before God.

I think there is another interesting picture here; notice Solomon's contrast between how and what we say to our status.

When I started writing these books (this is my third), I was afraid to even try; I had not finished high school, I dropped out in the tenth grade. I got my G.E.D. in the United States Air Force, as you can probably tell. What business do I have writing a book? I had this same conversation with the Lord.

Through a set of circumstances, God challenged me to write my first devotional (THE PATH). When I began, I thought, "365 pages?" - Really? I started; when I would write a page or two, I would shut the computer down and go into my living room and as I am leaving my desk I think, "What did God just do?" I sat down, and God takes over.

66. Into what city did Jesus make His "Triumphal Entry"?
    a. Nazareth   b. Jericho   c. Capernaum   d. Jerusalem

July 16   197-168   Proverbs 17

> He who covers a transgression seeks love, but he who repeats a matter separates friends. Rebuke is more effective for a wise man than a hundred blows on a fool. (Proverbs 17:9-10)

Have you heard the definition of insanity? - It is doing something wrong and repeating it hoping for a different result, or something like that. I think that is what Solomon is referring to, when he says, *"Rebuke is more effective for a wise man."* A wise man will correct what is wrong; a fool continues doing the wrong thing, hoping for a different result.

I have a sister that comes to mind with those last few words. She is not a fool, don't misunderstand. Before I went into the military, I watched over my siblings; my sister, no matter how many times you correct her, continued to turn right around, and does the same thing. It was so frustrating. Do you know people like that? No matter how much you show them they are wrong they still continue on their merry way.

Do you have a "love" relationship with God? If you have one, you know what I am talking about. If not, you don't. There are two kinds of "Christians" today. Those who have their ticket, yet continue to live in the world. Then some have a "working" fellowship with God the Father. I use the words "fellowship" and "relationship" interchangeably. To me, these two have different meanings.

A "relationship" with God means you have been saved. You have asked Jesus into your heart and are now a "child of God." (Romans 8:15)

A "fellowship" with God is different. You are still saved. It is that walk with God that I am talking about here. Do you have daily devotions? Are you listening and responding to God's Spirit speaking to you? Are you in God's will and plan for your life? (Jeremiah 29:11-13).

They are two different "walks" with God; there are far too many "Christians" that have a "relationship" with God but not the "fellowship". As I said, they have their ticket to heaven but are missing out on so much that God wants to offer. He wants that "intimate" walk with you. He wants to be a part of your everyday life. Then there are those who only "visit" God on Sunday.

> An evil man seeks only rebellion; therefore, a cruel messenger will be sent against him. Let a man meet a bear robbed of her cubs, rather than a fool in his folly. (Proverbs 17:11-12)

I have told this story several times; I have had my mustache for almost 50 years. Why do I have a mustache? When I worked for United Parcel Service we were told by the company we could not have facial hair. Our union stepped in, and we were "permitted" to have a mustache, 90% of the drivers grew mustaches. Why? - "Rebellion", it is in our nature.

It might be interesting to look at the heart of most who do not attend church. My guess is rebellion against God for something they think God did to them; this is their way of "punishing" God. - Really?

Rebellion can be a dangerous thing. Solomon talks a lot about it. It is your way of "striking back" at authority. When that authority is God, you are looking for trouble.

Are you a parent? You know what rebellion is. They don't have to be teenagers either. The first time your child says "NO". Or even worse, "I hate you!" - Rebellion.

Sometimes we rebel against something we know is wrong. We refuse to admit that we might be wrong. Our rebellion doesn't change the facts; our rebellion simply makes the inevitable consequences that much worse. I think that is part of the reason people don't spend a lot of time in the Bible. The stories, especially in the Old Testament, make the consequences of rebellion, clear, - Adam and Eve in the garden.

Solomon seems to spend a lot of time talking about fools. That might be an interesting "word study" for Proverbs. I count fifteen references in this chart I have that refers to "fools". They seem, to Solomon, to be the opposite of knowledge. Of course, but fools tend to act out their ignorance.

I just finished watching Dr. Charles Stanley. More Bible wisdom! He made this statement: "Decisions have consequences." - Really? In the context of a "fool" is that not true? Of course, it is. The wisdom of a godly person, through prayer, can give guidance.

     Lonny E. Young

Whoever rewards evil for good, evil will not depart from his house. The beginning of strife is like releasing water; therefore, stop contention before a quarrel starts. (Proverbs 17:13-14)

Look at this verse from 1 Samuel:

Then all the assembly shall know that the Lord does not save with sword or spear; **for the battle is the Lord's,** *and he will give you into our hands.* (1 Samuel 17:47)

David is about to face Goliath. Throughout this whole confrontation, David acknowledged God's power. ANY confrontation can be given to the Lord; I learned this the hard way. I used to "debate" my cause. Now, if I don't get my way, I just turn it over to God. Sounds easy, but it isn't. If it is what God wants He will bring it to pass; if it isn't, I have saved the embarrassment of being wrong. Let God do the fighting.

Have you ever had a pipe burst in your house? What happens? - PANIC! You scramble to find the shutoff valve, the damage is done. The same is true with strife, by the time you find the "shut-up valve," the damage is done. Strife never solves anything; fighting, bickering, snide remarks, hurtful comments, each a nail in the coffin of common sense, each an arrow that can't be taken back.

So, how do I eliminate strife? You might try praying. I think the key is to trust God, just refuse to engage, turn it over to God. He knows the circumstances and the best outcome. Think of the "peace" from just giving it to someone wiser and stronger than you.

You do know it takes TWO to fight. If you refuse to be drawn in, you have gone a long way toward putting out the fire, stopping the water flow. - I don't know exactly when I learned this. I guess I saw too many "fights" growing up. Almost every weekend my parents would get into it with my aunt and uncle; fighting was "expected". Today, the madder I get the quieter I get. I REFUSE to fight. As a Christian, I have learned to turn it over to God; if it is His will, He will bring it to pass. If it is not His will, I have lost nothing.

67. According to the Gospel of Matthew how many generations are there between Abraham and David?
    a. 7   b. 14   c. 10   d. 16

> He who justifies the wicked, and he who condemns the just,
> both of them alike are an abomination to the Lord. Why is
> there in the hand of a fool the purchase price of wisdom,
> since he has no heart for it? (Proverbs 17:15-16)

Is this not a picture of our world today? With all the news outlets, social media, etc., it is so hard to know what is right and true. But then Solomon touches on an interesting thought: *a fool the purchase price of wisdom.* What would that be? How much does the average Bible cost? A good Bible can cost upwards of $60.00. Is that the "purchase price" of wisdom?

How much time do you spend in the Word of God? The time you spend in the Bible corresponds to how much you know God. It is proven. Think about this; God through thousands of years through 40+ authors spoke to mankind ALL of God's perfect will.

I have sat in countless Sunday school classes and the question always comes up, "Why didn't God give us the answers to our questions." Usually irrelevant questions about situations and circumstances that is not important. If God gave us ALL the answers there is no way we could carry that book.

God completely revealed ALL that is necessary for an intimate relationship with Him. We can know the "mind of God," if we spend enough time in His word. The problem is we want all our answers in one chapter or less. Let me give you one of my favorite verses:

*But without faith it is impossible to please Him, for he who comes to God must believe that He is, and that He is a rewarder of those who **diligently seek Him.*** (Hebrews 11:6)

How would God reward those who seek Him? He reveals Himself, His character, His personality, His love toward us; if we would simply spend time in His word. I am not talking five or ten minutes a day, I am talking about a commitment to read His entire book, from the beginning (Genesis) to the end (Revelation). It doesn't matter when you start, it matters that you finish this challenge. Read, and learn of God.

Lonny E. Young

A friend loves at all times, and a brother is born for adversity.
A man devoid of understanding shakes hands in a pledge,
and becomes surety for his friend. (Proverbs 17:17-18)

How many times have you made a commitment you wish you had never made? - Many times, I suspect. Why is that? As Solomon states here, "devoid of understanding"; you don't "consider the consequence", the many alternatives in making your decision.

Check out these verses in Haggai:

Now therefore, thus says the Lord of hosts: **"Consider your ways."** *You have sown much, and bring in little; you eat, but do not have enough; you drink, but you are not filled with drink; you clothe yourselves, but no one is warm; and he who earns wages, earns wages to put into a bag with holes.* (Haggai 1:5-6)

An interesting book, - Haggai. It is toward the end of the Old Testament. The prophet is chastising Israel for focusing on themselves and their needs, instead of God's house. Twice in this short book, Haggai says, "Consider your ways." Think about your priorities, - Things done for self seldom prosper, things done for God will multiply a thousand-fold.

Commitment, - I hadn't been saved but less than a month. I was on my way to Wednesday Prayer Meeting. I asked my family if any wanted to go with me. They were all too busy. On the way to church, I had a conversation with the Lord. At first, I said, "Lord if this is the attitude of my family I might as well stay home." Then, after the Holy Spirit spoke to my heart, I said, "Lord, I commit right now, when the doors are open I will be there, if physically possible." God has blessed that commitment I made over thirty years ago. Many time's I have gone by myself. I am the one blessed!

Have you made any commitment to God lately? What about God's commitment to you about your salvation? When you stand before God and trust His commitment to let you in heaven, I know His commitment is firmer than yours. "Consider your ways?"

> He who has a deceitful heart finds no good, and he who has a perverse tongue falls into evil. He who begets a scoffer does so to his sorrow, and the father of a fool has no joy. (Proverbs 17:20-21)

James is a great book. Check this verse:

But no man can tame the tongue. It is an unruly evil, full of deadly poison. (James 3:8)

James has more to say, in many verses, in his epistle.

Look at this verse:

For we all stumble in many things. If anyone does not stumble in word, he is a perfect man, able also to bridle the whole body. (James 3: 2)

The third chapter would be a good study when Solomon refers to the tongue, which he does often. The Word of God warns against the tongue! Wait a minute. God created the tongue, didn't He? Yes, and just like everything else God has created; leave it to man to corrupt it. Just like the Garden of Eden. Even the very Word of God is often corrupted by uneducated teachers and preachers.

There is another element that Solomon talks about often. *The deceitful heart.* It all comes back to the heart. look what Jesus said in the gospel of Matthew:

"But those things which proceed out of the mouth come from the heart, and defile a man. (Matthew 15:18)

Most of the time the mouth will betray what is in the heart. That is sad. So, your speech begins with a clean heart; a heart focused on God and God's leadership through His Holy Spirit. Is the Spirit in control of your tongue? If the Spirit isn't, who is? Meditate on these verses and the verses of Solomon. It is clear. Our speech and the intent of the heart are similar. As a Christian, I think, the first thing God wants to "clean up" is what proceeds from our mouths.

68. How many times did Jesus speak from the cross?
    a. 3   b. 7   c. 5   d. 2

> A merry heart does good, like medicine, but a broken spirit dries the bones. A wicked man accepts a bribe behind the back to pervert the ways of justice. (Proverbs 17:22-23)

I think if you have spent much time in the Bible, you might know this passage. Ezekiel 37, - The "Valley of Dry Bones".

*Again, He said to me, "Prophesy to these bones, and say to them, 'O dry bones, **hear the word of the Lord.**'"* (Ezekiel 37:4)

Ezekiel is led to a valley full of dry bones. God tells Ezekiel to "preach" to these bones. Preach what? - "The word of the Lord." Now check this verse:

*"Then you shall know that I am the Lord, when I have opened your graves, O My people, and brought you up from your graves. I will put My Spirit in you, **and you shall live**, and I will place you in your own land. Then you shall know that I, the Lord, have spoken it and performed it," says the Lord.* (Ezekiel 37:14)

A great chapter, - A valley full of dead men's bones; it is the Spirit and the spoken Word that brings these bones to life. The same is so true today. As bad as things are, I still believe that God could and would bring another great revival in our land, like the revivals of Moody and Graham and Wesley and others who stirred our country back to God. A nation of dry bones; God's Spirit can accomplish anything God deems needed!

Do you have a "merry heart"? What might that consist of? How about faith in God's mighty hand working in your life? Your family's lives, your church's life, your city's life, even your nation's life? God is at work all around us. Do you want a "merry heart"? Just look around you at what God is doing. Is He alive in your church? Why not?

A merry heart means your focus, your faith; your trust is in God's working in your life. You get up each morning excited to see what God is going to do today. That is a "merry heart"!

> He who has knowledge spares his words, and a man of understanding is of a calm spirit. Even a fool is counted wise when he holds his peace; when he shuts his lips, he is considered perceptive. (Proverbs 17:27-28)

To me, this is one of the greatest gifts of being a Christian. There is nothing to prove. You don't have to "out-talk" someone. In fact, it is amazing what God does with your silence. One thing I love to do, in a crowd, is to just listen; you would be surprised what you can learn by listening to others ramble on.

I used to "jump" into a conversation whenever possible. I have my "two-cents" and I wanted everyone to know I had something to say. It has taken years to learn what Solomon is saying here. The less you speak the more "curious" you become to those around you, - Interesting.

I have heard of a trick that a pastor has pulled on his congregation. Think about this. In fact, it almost happened on Sunday. The computer guy was supposed to play a video on the screen, it malfunctioned. Everyone was waiting for the pastor to begin his message. - The trick? The pastor would get up, and stand there, and not say anything. You would be amazed at how quickly people get "uneasy" "uncomfortable" that nothing is being said. It really bothers people, - Silence!

I am sure you have met people that just won't stop talking. When I used to teach a Sunday school class there always seemed to be someone in the class who dominated the conversation; that is one of the toughest jobs of a teacher is to maintain "control" of a class.

I had a high school teacher like that. The students knew that if you asked her a question totally unrelated to the lesson that she would take off and talk for twenty minutes about that subject and forget the lesson to teach.

I learned early on how to obtain sympathy, to obtain a compliment, or lead others to do things; I also learned that it was not right. The key is to realize that you are doing that, manipulating those around you to say or do what you want them to. I learned that God's Spirit can do a much better job of directing the will of others than I could!

     Lonny E. Young

> A man who isolates himself seeks his own desire; he rages against all wise judgment. A fool has no delight in understanding, but in expressing his own heart. (Proverbs 18:1-2)

How are you doing in this walk-through Proverbs? I have noticed that Solomon repeats a lot of wisdom, maybe in different terms, but the lesson is the same; it seems to all stem from the heart. What is in your heart?

If you're married, your wife is there in your heart, if children I'm sure they are there. A lot of things can "occupy" your heart. How about God? Is He there? I haven't talked about this that much; I have touched on it now and then.

I just finished a book about King David. *David's Walk with God.* I learned a lot about David. I learned about his sin, of course, his punishment. I also learned a lot about God's heart. You know that twice in the Bible David is called: "A man after God's own heart." (1 Samuel 13:14 and Acts 13:12). Using this premise, I asked myself, "If I knew why God referred to David that way, maybe I could learn what touched God's heart." It is a great study. Take some time and read and meditate on David's life from 1 Samuel 16 to 1 Kings 2. See what made David "A man after God's own heart."

You see, it is the heart. Over and over Solomon refers to the heart in Proverbs. It is the condition of the heart that God is most concerned about:

*If you confess with your mouth the Lord Jesus and believe **in your heart** that God raised Him from the dead, you will be saved. For **with the heart** one believes unto righteousness, and with the mouth confession is made unto salvation.* (Romans 10:9-10)

Don't miss this! It isn't WHAT you say; it is what is in your heart. You can say "anything," but God knows your heart. You may fool those around you. You may walk the aisle, get dunked in the river and come up just as lost as you were when you went in. It's the heart that makes the difference, not your words!

69. Who refused to let Jesus wash his feet in the upper room?
    a. John   b. Thomas   c. Judas   d. Peter

> When the wicked comes, contempt comes also; and with dishonor comes reproach. The words of a man's mouth are deep waters; the wellspring of wisdom is a flowing brook. (Proverbs 18:3-4)

It was easy when I was growing up. The good guys wore white hats the bad guys wore black. Do you remember those days? If you're as old as I am. The thing is, today it is tough to discern what is right and wrong. I guess it depends on your source of measurement. What is your "standard"? How do you determine right or wrong?

That is one of the reasons for this study in Proverbs. The thing is Solomon never talks about "political correctness" "social media" "peer pressure" etc. So how are we to know? Again, what is the standard?

Of course, the "standard" is Jesus Christ. And we will all agree that we could never achieve that standard. But, let me ask this, WHAT IS YOUR STANDARD? What your parents taught you? What you learned in church, assuming you even went to church. The same refrain! What is your "standard"?

In verse three above, Solomon talks of evil, of wicked, dishonor. All negative standards. I am sorry I just keep coming back to this question: What is your standard? What do you use to determine right or wrong? That may be easy to an extent, but what about those "gray" areas? You MUST have a standard to guide you.

Let me offer a suggestion. If you're like me, you hate "instructions". I usually use the pictures and some common sense to put things together. How about life? You could use the same principle. How much time do you spend in the Old Testament? Not much I'll bet. But, you see, the Old Testament is stories about New Testament principles.

The New Testament, through the wisdom of Paul, led by God's Holy Spirit, gave us the instructions. The Old Testament, Adam, Abraham, Jacob, the Judges, Samson, Moses, Elijah, and others teach us through "example". If you think I'm crazy, read the book of Judges. Let me quote a verse:

In those days, there was no king in Israel; everyone did what was right in his own eyes. (Judges 17:6, 21:25)

Check it out!

It is not good to show partiality to the wicked, or to overthrow
the righteous in judgment. A fool's lips enter into contention,
and his mouth calls for blows. (Proverbs 18:5-6)

Have you ever been in that situation? You're not a violent person, but this guy just won't quit, until you come to blows. Violence is his goal, and you are the target. Oh, we hear the "turn the other cheek" thing, especially as a Christian. "Well, I would do this." - Really? You never know until you are in that situation.

Many friends and relatives are buying and learning to use guns. All will have to buy insurance, so if they must use it they won't be sued, - that is sad. I am sure you have heard of "road rage", people lose control. That is the key, isn't it? And now they have guns. The sad part is they never come to grips with their rage until someone gets hurt or killed.

If that is you, you need to get some help. How often and how easily do you lose your temper? Too often? Too easily? - You need to get some help. I know this is going to sound crazy but you need to get Jesus in your heart.

You would be surprised how much the power of the Holy Spirit can help you gain and maintain control in those situations when cooler heads need to prevail. When that happens, when you "lose it" who is in control? You certainly are not, or you wouldn't be in that condition.

God wants to be in control of your life. Those people that Solomon is talking about do not have God in control of their life, just as he talked earlier about the tongue. It is all about control. Are you in control ALL the time, or do you "lose it?" Do some series reflection and meditation. What do you do when you begin to get "hot under the collar"? What is your reaction?
Let me leave you with this verse:

*And let the **peace of God** rule in your hearts, to which also you were called in one body; and be thankful. Let the word of Christ dwell in you richly in all wisdom.* (Colossians 3:15-16a)

A fool's mouth is his destruction, and his lips are the snare
of the soul. The words of a talebearer are like tasty trifles,
and they go down into the inmost body. (Proverbs 18:7-8)

I wonder if you noticed, through the Bible, how our "diet" changes? In the garden, we were vegetarians. Later, with Moses, God gave the Israelites specific dietary restrictions. Then, in the New Testament, along comes Peter and God changes the diet again.

Look:

And a voice came to him, "Rise, Peter; kill and eat." But Peter said, "Not so, Lord! For I have never eaten anything common or unclean." And a voice spoke to him again the second time, "What God has cleansed you must not call common." This was done three times. And the object was taken up into heaven. (Acts 10:13-16)

Peter was keeping the Law of Moses, but God was using food as an example of the Gentiles and salvation through Jesus Christ. Up until then, only Jews were permitted to be "Christians." There was a big "discussion" in Jerusalem with the leaders of the church (Acts 15). Should Gentiles be allowed in the church?

Paul's argument: There should be NO restrictions put on Gentiles. Kind of like baptism being "required" for salvation. Paul's argument: Salvation is through Christ alone PERIOD. Dietary restrictions were for the Jews, any additional conditions become "works" and that adds to Christ's work on the cross. Contrary to the Gospel!

That is an interesting thought, tell me something. Can you see what is in someone's heart? We talked early that it is the "heart" that determines our salvation. We must believe in our "heart" that Christ was raised from the dead. So, if we are to determine someone's salvation we would, of course, need to look in their heart. Be careful.

Many discussions between Paul and James about "works"; read the book of James and see. James does not "contradict" Paul; he simply takes a different approach. The principle is the same. Our "works" demonstrate our faith, not get us to heaven. Jesus also condemns judging one another on our works. It is God who judges the heart!

70. Which Commandment concerns our parents?
    a. third   b. sixth   c. fifth   d. tenth

          Lonny E. Young

> He who is slothful in his work is a brother to him who is a
> great destroyer. The name of the Lord is a strong tower; the
> righteous run to it and are safe. (Proverbs 18:9-10)

Each day I sit and write these words; I never know where God is going to take me. When I finish and close my laptop and leave the room, I just shake my head and say, "Lord, what have you done?" I am always amazed at His words.

"The name of the Lord." When I was first saved, I had a hard time saying God. My parents taught me a "reverence" for God but not a "relationship." Don't get me wrong. God is "Almighty God" the Creator, and we approach Him as such. BUT, as a Christian He is also our "Heavenly Father." (Romans 8:15) It can be confusing. Anyway, the more I grew as a Christian, the closer I became to my Father in heaven, the easier it became to say God.

Not so, with Jesus. Don't get theological! I know they are both the same. The point is that, I guess because of Christmas and the gospels, I knew Jesus better, more intimate than God the Father. I could "talk to Jesus". Later, as I became more familiar with the Old Testament, I could combine the two and they became one God. Does that make sense?

Through our "fellowship" with Jesus, we get to know God in a deeper more intimate way. I often thought that when I get to heaven I would get this picture of sitting on a park bench and getting my "fifteen" minute to talk to Jesus; I would never think of talking to God that way.

God? - I picture walking down this huge Roman corridor with columns on each side, approaching God's throne; bowing, humble, praising God, prostrate at the throne in awe. Do you see the contrast? YET, He is the same God. Can you be "intimate" with God on the throne? Not likely. Can you have an intimate conversation with Jesus? Of course, His disciples had many such conversations. He is the same God!

The God, whose Son died on the cross for my sins, is the same God who will judge me at His appointed time. And He will ask me, "What think ye of Jesus?" That decision has already been made in my heart!

> The rich man's wealth is his strong city. And like a high wall in his own esteem. Before destruction the heart of a man is haughty, and before honor is humility. (Proverbs 18:11-12)

Ever dream of being wealthy? - I think we all have at one time or another. We tend to think of all the things we will do; even the "security" it will bring. Don't miss the subtlety, where will your "faith," your confidence be? - That is the consequence of being wealthy. Solomon is trying to bring this out. In a sense, your faith then is in you, and not God. What you can accomplish, what YOUR will is. Ask Solomon, he knows.

I think it is ironic that long before Solomon, God cautioned Israel about three dangers.

Look here:

*"But he shall **not multiply horses** for himself (king), nor cause the people to return to Egypt to multiply horses, for the Lord has said to you, 'you shall not return that way again.' Neither shall he **multiply wives** for himself, lest his heart turn away; nor shall he **greatly multiply silver and gold** for himself.* (Deuteronomy 17:16-17)

Notice at what point God tells Moses of these three things. This is before Joshua, and Israel entering the Promised Land, before the "Judges" stage, before Saul and David's reign; a LONG time before Solomon. This is in the "Books of the Law," which Solomon had access to.

Now check out 1 Kings 11. Solomon disobeyed all three of these cautions, rules, warnings whatever you wish to call them. I guess you could put these three into the warnings God gave John in 1 John 2:

For all that is in the world—the lust of the flesh (wives), the lust of the eyes (horses), and the pride of life (gold & silver) - is not of the Father but is of the world. (1 John 2:16)

Anything that comes between us and our worship of God is an abomination, as Solomon puts it, and he should know.

          Lonny E. Young

> He who answers a matter before he hears it, it is folly and
> shame to him. The spirit of a man will sustain him in sickness,
> but who can bear a broken spirit? (Proverbs 18:13-14)

I am thinking it was Roy Smalley, maybe Dr. James Dobson, who talked extensively of a child's spirit. In correcting that child you don't want to break his spirit. - An interesting approach. You want to correct them, break their "self-will," yet not destroy their "spirit"; that is so true.

How about a child of God? The Bible talks of two things that affect our "Spirit". We can "grieve" (Ephesians 4:30) the Holy Spirit, and we can "quench" (1 Thessalonians 5:19) God's Spirit. I heard the difference once; it is not important. Neither one is helpful in our "fellowship" with God. God gave us His Holy Spirit when we asked Jesus into our heart. He is there to guide, instruct and convict us (John 14).

This "quenching and grieving" occurs when we fail to listen, or completely disobey God's prompting. They deal with attitude and motive. Either way, we refuse to listen and obey God's Spirit.

It is much the same as a father correcting his children. You want to point them in the right direction, encourage and support them, at the same time, correct their rebellion. You try to do it in such a way as to maintain their relationship with you. God deals with us in much the same way. He wants to guide, direct, and correct without causing us to fully turn our backs on Him.

The sad part is that is exactly what we do. If God's efforts at correcting us are not received properly, we will rebel; we will turn our backs to the very one trying to get our attention and trying to put us on the right path. We will "grieve/quench" God's Spirit. Parents don't like being ignored and neither does God.

I mentioned earlier that the three things that Solomon disobeyed God were written down in the Law, the books of Moses. Solomon had those, his priest and/or prophets had them. Yet, he ignored them or never knew them.

You might want to read 1 Kings 11:11. God removed the kingdom from Solomon's rule. His heart was turned away from God.

71. In which New Testament book do we find the "Armor of God"?
    a. Galatians   b. Ephesians   c. Philippians   d. Colossians

> The heart of the prudent acquires knowledge, and the ear
> of the wise seeks knowledge. A man's gift makes room for
> him, and brings him before great men. (Proverbs 18:15-16)

Ever wish you could do something like someone else? When I was a young preacher, I wished I could preach like Dr. Charles Stanley or Charles Swindoll. One day it dawned on me; there already is a Dr. Stanley or Chuck Swindoll. God created me just the way I am for a "purpose". Someone once said that if there were two people just like one of them would be "unnecessary".

I wonder why Solomon stresses knowledge and wisdom. Remember Solomon's prayer?

At Gibeon, the Lord appeared to Solomon in a dream by night; and God said, "Ask! What shall I give you?" "Therefore, give to **Your servant** *an understanding heart to judge Your people, that I may discern between good and evil. For who is able to judge this great people of Yours?"* (1 Kings 3:5, 9)

Does Solomon say anything about wisdom and knowledge? - No! Yet that was the reputation he had. His "wisdom" was known throughout the world, ask the Queen of Sheba (1 Kings 10). I hope you will read: *"David's Walk with God"*. I was fascinated by the life of David and wrote a book about his relationship with God.

What is your gift? We could start with your "spiritual" gift, but what is your gift in general. God has created you with a "talent," a gift, a personality, that is unique to you. Do you know what it is? Why not? Have you asked God? Have you tried to learn what that gift is? If you know what it is, are you using it? God created you for a purpose. He gave you this special gift to be used to glorify Him. Are you? Ask God!

Again, Solomon references to the heart. Do you have a "heart for God"? Do you sense His presence? Do you feel Him working in your life? Why not? How is your fellowship with God? Are you on speaking terms? If not, why?

                    Lonny E. Young

The first one to plead his cause seems right, until his neighbor comes and examines him. Casting lots causes contentions to cease, and keeps the mighty apart. (Proverbs 18:17-18)

For most of my childhood, I had two brothers, I was the eldest. Later mom and dad decided to add five more. Anyway, have you seen this? You and the siblings are confronted with a "wrong". What happens? Everyone wants to be the first to make their excuses. They think if they get in first they will be believed first. Parents are quick to learn. You might say the "parents" are the neighbor here.

Fighting, contentions, disputes, arguments, - How do you resolve them? In the verses of Solomon here, he suggests casting lots. If I remember right that is what they did at the foot of the cross for Jesus' clothes (Mark 15:24). It is also what the sailors did to find out that Jonah was the cause of their "storm" (Jonah 1:7). So how do you settle disputes?

How about you and God? If you're a Christian I am sure you and God have not seen eye-to-eye on some things. How do you settle that? I heard a fellow once, he said, "If you pray about something, and it doesn't seem to be answered, it may be that God is changing your heart, not your circumstances." Think about that.

Disputes with God can be very costly. If you don't get your way, or it doesn't work out the way you want it to, what happens? Do you get mad at God? Surely not! Do you blame God? I have talked about this before; it just really upsets me, because I see it a lot. People refuse to have anything to do with God because they "blame" Him for something that happened in their life. Do you think you are "hurting" God? Seriously!

God is not going to try to "change your mind"; God will wait patiently until you realize who was at fault and ask God's forgiveness. Sometimes God must wait years, watching His children suffer and grieve, and their relationship with their heavenly Father, rather than admit it was them all along.

You hurt no one but yourself when you turn your back on God, when you blame Him, for your mistakes; God desires an intimate relationship with His children, but they must want it too.

> A brother offended is harder to win than a strong city, and contentions are like the bars of a castle. A man's stomach shall be satisfied from the fruit of his mouth; from the produce of his lips he shall be filled. (Proverbs 18:19-20)

How many "Witnessing" seminars and conferences have you been to? My guess is not many; most of the time we don't want to talk about that. It is so hard. I think, just speaking from experience, we tend to put the "results" on our shoulders. That is NOT how it works!

Look what John says in his gospel:

*"And when He (Holy Spirit) has come, **He** will convict the world of sin, and of righteousness, and of judgment: of sin, because they do not believe in Me.* (John 16:8-9)

Let's stop there; there is more but this is the point I want to make. Who does the convicting? The Holy Spirit must be at work in this process. I think that is what Solomon is talking about here in Proverbs. When you go "convicting" your neighbor of his relationship with God, you are trying to do the work of God's Spirit.

Your job, calling, responsibility is to simply "share" or "sow" the word of God. Tell them what God said. Let God's Spirit germinate that seed. If we ever found a way to do that germinating process on our own farmers would be flocking for the process; THAT is in God's hands. We are simply called to sow!

Of course, we have a burden for those we "witness" to. God has laid them on our heart. God wants us to share, tell them about Jesus, but the rest is up to God. God meant for it to be that way (John 16). BUT, if we don't tell them, who will? That is our job. And what do we tell them? - Simply, what God has done in our life; how God has changed us. Just share that you might throw in your favorite verse or two. They may dispute the Bible but they cannot argue against what God has done in your life!

That's why Jesus, in Matthew's gospel, gives us the parable of the "sower". A fantastic illustration!

72. In which New Testament book is the "Fruit of the Spirit" listed?
    a. Galatians b. Ephesians   c. Philippians   d. Colossians

Death and life are in the power of the tongue, and those who love it will eat its fruit. He who finds a wife finds a good thing, and obtains favor from the Lord. (Proverbs 18:21-22)

When I was a teenager, one afternoon I prayed that God would give me a wife to love, and a family to provide for; this was in 1962. Soon after that, I went into the United States Air Force, served four years, with one year in Vietnam.

When I returned from Nam, I had 10 months to go in my enlistment. I was stationed at Forbes Air Force Base in Topeka, Kansas, about 60 miles from my home in Kansas City. During those ten months, I met Mary; we were married eight months after we met.

Today, we have celebrated 51 years of marriage. I often think of that prayer I made as a teenager; God came through in spades. We have two wonderful daughters, six grandchildren, and two great-grandchildren; God has blessed beyond my dreams. When you find God's choice for your mate you can claim the promise of Solomon here.

I was engaged while in Vietnam. That broke off. The interesting thing is, I wasn't "saved" until we were married for fourteen years. Was God watching over us? - Of course. Even before we came to know the Lord, when God created us in the womb, He had a plan for His creation. He sees our whole life in front of Him. It boils down to the choices we make; simple choices at first, - right or wrong, good or bad.

Those choices can lead us down two separate paths. As Jesus talks about in Matthew 7:

Enter by the narrow gate; for wide is the gate and broad is the way that leads to destruction, and there are many who go by it. Because narrow is the gate and difficult is the way which leads to life, and there are few who find it. (Matthew 7:13-14)

It is the choices we make in life that determine the path we travel. If it is God's path it will lead to blessings (Psalm 16:11).

> The poor man uses entreaties, but the rich answers roughly.
> A man who has friends must himself be friendly, and there is
> a friend who sticks closer than a brother. (Proverbs 18:23-24)

I am not sure of the exact date, or time. I have been a Sunday school Director for most of my "Christian" life; one year I got a hold of this promotional package called, "Friend Day."

On the first week of this five-week promotion, our pastor and I posted in the front of the church, (on stickers) the "friend" that we had signed up to commit to being there on "Friend Day". The next week, all our deacons would do the same. One the third Sunday our teachers would post their invites. Finally, on the fourth week, the congregation would come up and post who they invited for Friend Day.

During the week before the actual Friend Day, we went out and rented one-hundred folding chairs to handle the crowd. At the time, we were averaging 85 to 100 in Sunday school; our goal was "200".

That Sunday, Friend Day, we hit 198. Did we fail? You tell me. We were "averaging" just fewer than 100. One Sunday we had 198. I don't think we failed. Two points: One, the theme of this promotion was Proverbs 18:24b *But, there is a friend who sticks closer than a brother.* That friend?-Jesus, of course! Second, we had enough faith in our prayers and the seed we sowed to go out and "rent" 100 folding chairs. We believed God would honor our efforts. I think that is called "faith."

One year I thought I would post on Facebook, a verse a day from my Bible reading schedule; the problem, as I came to realize was I began "measuring" the impact by the number of "likes" I received. I had put a number to the response of my posts. When I realized that, I quit checking; those posts led to my first book: THE PATH.

You can't measure your "friends" by the number of "likes" you receive on Facebook. I have come to learn that you can't "number" your friends. Here today, gone tomorrow. The only friend, who will never leave you or forsake you, is Jesus; that is assuming you have a "relationship" with the Son of God. How close are you to your friend? Do you have an intimate relationship with the God of the universe?

                    Lonny E. Young

> Better is the poor who walks in his integrity than one who is
> perverse in his lips, and is a fool. Also, it is not good for a
> soul to be without knowledge, and he sins who hastens with
> his feet. (Proverbs 19:1-2)

How would you define "integrity"? Someone once said, "It is what you do when no one is watching." Have you ever watched a baseball game on TV? Have you noticed that once in a while they will show camera shots of fans in the stands? These are the shots they want you to see. How many are filmed that doesn't show up on the screen. How about on the stadium screen? The point is that you never know when or who is watching today.

We know, as Christians, that God is very aware of our deeds. As a Christian, you have God living within you; there is nothing hidden from God. Look:

Or do you not know that your body is the temple of the Holy Spirit who is in you, whom you have from God, and you are not your own? For you were bought at a price; therefore, glorify God in your body and in your spirit, which are God's. (1 Corinthians 6:19-20)

Allow me to point something out about this verse. Here, Paul is sharing that God's Holy Spirit lives within us, okay. That means we also have the "power" of that same Holy Spirit. The same Spirit that can bring to our minds Bible passages that we need when we need them; the power that energizes our prayer life.

Look at this verse:

Likewise, the Spirit also helps in our weaknesses. For we do not know what we should pray for as we ought, **but the Spirit Himself makes intercession for us** *with groanings which cannot be uttered.* (Romans 8:26)

If we, as Christians, ever grasp the power that lies within us, through God's Holy Spirit, we could accomplish miracles. I am not talking about turning water to wine, I am talking about a life that glorifies God and touches all those around us.

73. Which of the twelve tribes of Israel did not receive an inheritance in the Promised Land?
    a. Judah   b. Levi   c. Dan   d. Ephraim

> The foolishness of a man twists his way, and his heart frets
> against the Lord. Wealth makes many friends, but the poor
> is separated from his friend. (Proverbs 19:3-4)

This is my third book. I started with a devotional called "The Path". Next, I wrote a devotional of the life of David called, "David's Walk with God." In each effort, it has been my goal to encourage you, in whatever way I could, to consider your "walk" with God; in David's case, using him as a guide of sorts.

I think there are two camps. One believes that God sits up in heaven on His throne and doesn't care about the small things going on here. Of course, He wants us all to come to know His Son as our Savior. But, other than that, He pretty much is not interested in our daily lives. We like it that way! The second camp is the one I am in. I believe, through God's Spirit that dwells within us, that God is not only "interested" in our daily lives He "participates" in our daily walk.

Take tonight for instance. A few days ago, I mentioned a hymn that was special to me. They don't sing it very often. Tonight, they sang "Because He Lives" by Gloria and Bill Gaither. Coincidence? Okay, if you want, - Providence, maybe. It spoke to me and tells me God is listening. God wanted to bless me tonight.

Sometimes someone will comment on my book, those who bought it. Just to take the time to comment is such a blessing. Such things are no big deal to the one who thinks God sits on His throne and is not interested in the goings-on here. To me, they encourage me and let me know God is near and wants to bless me. Which "camp" are you in?

It boils down to "walking with God" or, you are alone in this world walking in your own strength and wisdom. I much prefer seeking God's guidance, God's wisdom and strength. There isn't a day goes by that I don't pray, usually for meals, that I don't ask God for wisdom and guidance in all things. When you know God is walking this "path" along with you it gives you comfort and peace. I much prefer my camp. How about you?

          Lonny E. Young

> A false witness will not go unpunished, and he who speaks lies will not escape. Many entreat the favor of the nobility, and every man is a friend to one who gives gifts. (Proverbs 19:5-6)

Wow! Where has this summer gone? It is back to school soon. Vacation time is fast coming to a close; Thanksgiving, Christmas, just around the corner. Where does time go?

Are these verses not a commentary on today's world? - Lying, greed, seeking favor with whoever is in control, etc. It is a sad commentary on this world we live in. The thing is "social media" makes it all possible. It is interesting. Now instead of just quoting what someone said, you can show a video of them saying it. Do you know what I have noticed? No one is denying it; they simply ignore that they were caught in a lie.

Here is another phrase of today, "Double standard." What was good then is not good now, now that the shoe is on the other foot. - Okay, you've gone to meddling. Not really.

Think about it. What is Solomon talking about in these verses written over two thousand years ago? "I don't care for the Old Testament, it is so outdated, and I prefer the New Testament". - Really? How current can Solomon get?

Much of these proverbs we have been looking at are such a picture of our society today. Are they not? Think about it. You could read similar comments in our newspapers today if you read such outdated modes of communication. How about "Facebook" feed? The same problems exist today that Solomon talked about in his day.

Wait a minute. Solomon says these "false witnesses" will not go unpunished, - Really? They sure seem to get away with it now. I don't think Solomon is talking about punished right now. Don't you think God, as we talked about yesterday, knows what is going on? - Of course, He does. Will He punish evildoers right now? - You know God doesn't operate like that.

I have learned to "watch" these individuals who think they are putting something over. God has a "unique" way of dealing with sin. If they are "professed" Christians they are soiling God's name. God could very well take them home soon. If they are "lost" God will deal with them in due time, in His time, in His way.

All the brothers of the poor hate him; how much more do his friends go far from him! He may pursue them with words, yet they abandon him. He who gets wisdom loves his own soul; he who keeps understanding will find good. (Proverbs 19:7-8)

This may not make sense. Verse seven is referring to the previous verse 6, "A man of nobility"; People who try to buy "friendship," Solomon points out the danger of being attracted to them. You follow what you think you can gain, but in the end, you are disappointed.

I am the eldest of my family; I grew up with two brothers, one and two years younger than me. Therefore, I was always looked at as the "leader, bigger, older, etc. We were very close; we did everything together, including fighting. Later, with nine years between number three and number four, my parents decided to have five more children, three boys, and two girls. Eventually, I became the "babysitter".

Really, in a sense, two different families, - I left for the United States Air Force before the last two were born; I watched three of the last five. Why am I telling you all this? I grew up with brothers, - that word jumped out at me. "Brothers" in this context, I am sure Solomon is not talking about siblings, but those are close. How they, as a group, follow after "nobility". It is so much easier to do things as a group, isn't it?

Wisdom and understanding, - they are paired up in Solomon's teaching; they go hand-in-hand. Have you ever said, "If I had only known then, what I know now."? I think we all might have said that at some point. Why is that? Of course, we know so much more today than when we made all those mistakes growing up, and how did we become so "educated", from the mistakes, we made growing up. I think there was a country song once entitled "Lessons Learned."; that is life, is it not?

I used to be frustrated as a young parent that our children did not listen to our "sage" advice. Today, I have learned to allow them to make mistakes to learn by; to be there when they need some help. Not to say, "I told you so" but to reinforce the lesson, and help them back on track. Sometimes, all we can do is pray; allow them the room to "learn for themselves" then encouraged them once they learn.

74. In what Old Testament book is Saul anointed king?
    a. 1 Samuel   b. 2 Samuel   c. 1 Kings   d. 2 Kings

A false witness will not go unpunished, and he who speaks lies will perish. Luxury is not fitting for a fool, much less for a servant to rule over princes. (Proverbs 19:9-10)

Ever heard of "Publishers Clearing House"? How about "Reader's Digest"? That was my lottery when I was younger, and before I became a Christian. I used to buy the books, the record sets, etc. to enter to win all this money. After I became a Christian, I realized that if God wanted me to have that money, He would have given it to me; so, I stopped.

I even dabbled in the "Lottery" a time or two. Again, after my car broke down both times, I realized God will supply my needs (Philippians 4:19), not the state. If you would back up and take an overall look at this scheme you will realize the fallacy of it.

Solomon, again, is talking about lying. I thought it was interesting the term he uses, "False witness" that is the same term used in the Ten Commandments:

You shall not bear false witness against your neighbor. (Exodus 20:16)

That is all it says, we think "false witness" is testifying in court; it is much more than that, it is simply lying.

I think the funny thing about lying is that soon you get all tangled up, not knowing what lie you told when, and it comes back to bite you! We talked earlier about the "recording" that we leave around. It always seems to come back to bite you. The simplest remedy is DON'T LIE.

We have lost today the value of our word, I said before, our handshake is only as good as the number of "lawyers" behind it; that is sad. Take a day and watch the news. I prefer Fox of course. Anyway, just imagine how different it would be if EVERYONE spoke the truth and stood behind their words, Washington D.C., of course, is the worst.

Let me get to it. How does your word stack up today? Do people "trust" you when you say something? Why not?

> The discretion of a man makes him slow to anger, and his glory is to overlook a transgression. The king's wrath is like the roaring of a lion, but his favor is like dew on the grass. (Proverbs 19:11-12)

Immediately this verse brings a passage in James to mind:

So, then, my beloved brethren, let every man be swift to hear, slow to speak, slow to wrath. (James 1:19)

There is so much good stuff in James; someone once called the book of James the "Proverbs" of the New Testament. I can see why. It is often chosen for a verse by verse Bible study.

Can you "overlook a transgression"? Do you know how hard that is? Only by God's Spirit can we hold our tongue, let alone wanting to get even.

Speaking of the king's wrath, I reflect on King David. Look at an episode in 2 Samuel 13. The scene: David had a son named Amnon; he "lusted" after his cousin Tamar. If you read the chapter you will know why I said "lusted." Anyway, Amnon had his way with Tamar. The news got back to David that one of his sons did this thing.

Look at David's response:

But when King David heard of all these things, he was very angry. (2 Samuel 13:21)

Later it was his son Absalom, who took revenge. So, think about this (after you read the chapter) WHAT WOULD YOU DO? How would you have dealt with this? - Interesting question.

I finished a study of King David; fascinating walk with a man who was called, "A man after God's own heart." You would do well to walk with David through 1 Samuel 16 to 1 Kings 2. Keep asking yourself, WHY was David called a man after God's own heart? (1 Samuel 13:14 and Acts 13:22). That quote began my search for an answer.

Something I realize in my search. If David was after God's own heart, maybe this would shed some light on God's heart; how God felt about certain things. You might ask the same question.

A foolish son is the ruin of his father; and the contentions of a wife are a continual dripping. Houses and riches are an inheritance from fathers, but a prudent wife is from the Lord. (Proverbs 19:13-14)

They say "opposites attract"; that is true in our marriage, to the extent of how we deal with anger. My wife came from a family with a demonstrative mother to the extent of throwing things. My parents fought but not with each other, mainly relatives. Anyway, I will not show my anger. Early in our marriage when her "anger" boils up, she had no one to fight with; I simply would not fight, I shut up. Soon her anger subsides; there are a lot fewer disagreements. I guess the point is: It takes two to fight.

I have come to learn that men and women look at marriage differently. Don't laugh. The sooner we learn this, the better. While men, like Solomon, seek riches and inheritance, women want security and love. So, you have opposites again. How do you deal with that? My wife and I had been married fourteen years when God came into our lives. We were both saved about the same time, in 1981, we were married in 1967; it has made such a difference in our marriage.

Here, Solomon is talking about marriage. We will get into more detail in the 31st chapter of Proverbs. Not written by Solomon but addressing a godly wife. We touched on this earlier.

Let me ask you this, Solomon, here, talks about a "foolish son" just how much do parents have to do with the way their children turn out? Let me illustrate: Both of my parents smoked. I don't smoke because I saw what it did to my parents. I have brothers and sister who smoke, is it because their parents did? Do you see the paradox?

To continue my line of thinking, - How much influence do their peers have, their fellow students? How about a church? If they attend regularly, will that affect? How about what they read, their intake of outside influences? Just how much "influence" do parents have in the direction their children take? Maybe it would depend on what they thought of their parents. Are they good role models? Do they portray the characteristics that can be transferred to their children? Do you "influence" your children? - Interesting questions.

75. Where did Moses spend the first forty years of his life?
    a. Canaan   b. the desert   c. Mt. Sinai   d. Egypt

> Laziness casts one into a deep sleep, and an idle person will suffer hunger. He who keeps the commandment keeps his soul, but he who is careless of his ways will die. (Proverbs 19:15-16)

I have a friend that encourages me to claim disability; I have a minor back problem. He says, "It's free money." It is sad to say that today that is the norm, instead of the exception. We look from the "government" to supply our needs. Is that what Solomon is talking about? - To an extent.

I do collect Social Security; I have paid into that for over forty years. There is a difference, Laziness is the point. This isn't the first time Solomon addressed this, (6:6-11, 10:4-5, 12:27, 13:4, 15:19 and on and on).

Why would Solomon think this subject needed so much attention? It must have been prevalent in his day. Many people lying around seeking a "hand-out" instead of trying to better themselves. Sound familiar? Have you seen people with signs by the highway? LOOK OUT! Don't start judging; we don't know their circumstances. God does.

I have a friend, a while back, that thought, as a gag, he would pan-handle one night. He ended up being disgusted. He was amazed at how much he raised, more than he made in his job; it broke his heart. You say that just shows the generosity of the people, - it shows their gullibility. We can't and shouldn't judge those in need. Our church and many others will not give "cash" anymore. We can buy food, clothing, gas, whatever the need, but no cash; that is what it has come to.

I know I am focusing on the negative. Solomon is too. There are needs all around us that need addressing. Solomon is speaking to those who take advantage of the "system".

I wonder what "commandment" Solomon is talking about. He used the singular "commandment", there are ten in the Old Testament and Jesus condensed it to two. Maybe the second one:

"And the second is like it: You shall love your neighbor as yourself. One these two commandments hang all the Law and the Prophets." (Matthew 22:39-40)

Lonny E. Young

He who has pity on the poor lends to the Lord, and He will pay back what he has given. Chasten your son while there is hope, and do not set your heart on his destruction. (Proverbs 19:17-18)

I talked yesterday about how our church helps those in need. Where do you suppose that money comes from? Don't miss the promise in that last part of verse 17. How about this promise from God?

*"Bring all the tithes into **the storehouse**, that there may be food in My house, **and try Me now in this,** "says the Lord of Hosts. "If I will not open the windows of heaven and pour out for you such a blessing that there will not be room enough to receive it."* (Malachi 3:10)

That is a promise from God. I had to learn this lesson the hard way. I have an issue with Solomon's use of the word "lend". We don't "lend" anything to God; it all belongs to Him in the first place. When we give back that portion that belongs to Him, God will not only bless us, but He will bless others through His church (storehouse). I think it is interesting that Malachi uses the term "food".

I must repeat one of my favorite verses about chastening. I love the thought in this verse, it is SO true!

And you have forgotten the exhortation which speaks to you as to sons: "My son, do not despise the chastening of the Lord, nor be discouraged when you are rebuked by Him; for whom the Lord loves He chastens, and scourges every son whom He receives. (Hebrews 12:5-6).

This is the author of Hebrews, quoting Solomon in Proverbs 3:11-12. So, it is used in both the Old and New Testaments; that nails it. Don't miss the key point, - *For whom He loves He chastens.* That is the very same concept when a parent "corrects" his children. It is because they love them, they correct them. It depends on what it takes to get their attention. The same is true with God. What does God have to do to get your "attention"?

> A man of great wrath will suffer punishment; but if you rescue him, you will have to do it again. Listen to counsel and receive instruction, that you may be wise in your latter days. (Proverbs 19:19-20)

I think, what Solomon is talking about in these first few words are, today, called "stubborn." I am sure you have met these people. You can put the facts right in their face, and they will deny the truth continually! It is so frustrating; it is like the Bible.

Have you approached someone about their salvation and you quote the Bible, and their response is, "I don't believe the Bible." How crazy is that? Okay, why should they believe God's Word? Can you give them an answer?

You can tell them why you believe it; you can tell them all sorts of "facts" about the Bible. How do you convince them that it IS the Word of God? Let me give you a hint. Tell them what God has done in your life; there is no way they can argue your personal testimony. That is assuming God has come into your life by way of His Son Jesus. If the Holy Spirit lives within you, you have a testimony.

Isn't it interesting that you can read John 3:16 to someone over and over? Even the Romans Road: Romans 3:23, 6:23, 5:8, 10:9-10 and they look at you with this "so what" look. The "truth" is right there, why don't you believe?

Then, you tell them about the day you asked Jesus in your heart. The peace, the prayer, and the personal relationship you have with the Creator of the Universe. How can they argue with that? "That is okay for you, but not me." You might want to ask one more question: "Are you willing to bet eternity in hades that this book may not be true?" That is what they are doing; when they stand before God it is too late to accept the truth.

Remember, the words of "Solomon" are the words of God, inspired by His Holy Spirit for Solomon to write down. Don't miss the warning in verse 20:

Listen to counsel and receive instruction, that you may be wise in your latter days. (Proverbs 19:20)

76. Which two disciples did Jesus call, "Sons of Thunder"?
    a. Peter & John   b. John & James   c. Peter & James   d. John & Judas

> There are many plans in a man's heart, nevertheless the Lord's counsel—that will stand. What is desired in a man is kindness, and a poor man is better than a liar. (Proverbs 19:21-22)

One of my favorite parables by Jesus, it says so much:

Then He spoke a parable to them, saying: "The ground of a certain rich man yielded plentifully. And he thought within himself, saying, 'What shall I do, since I have no room to store my crops?' So, he said, 'I will do this: I will pull down my barns and build greater, and there I will store all my crops and my goods. And I will say to my soul, Soul, you have many goods laid up for many years; take your ease; eat, drink, and be merry.' But God said to him, 'Fool! This night your soul will be required of you; then where will those things be which you have provided?' "So is he who lays up treasure for himself, and is not rich toward God". (Luke 12:16-21)

Don't misunderstand God here. He is NOT saying we should not plan for the future, He is saying that plan must involve God; the motive behind this planning, the ultimate goal of this plan.

Check this verse:

*"Do not lay up for yourselves treasures on earth, where moth and rust destroy and where thieves break in and steal; but lay up for yourselves treasures in heaven, where neither moth nor rust destroys and where thieves do not break in and steal. **For where your treasure is, there your heart will be also.** (Matthew 6:19-21)*

I might have known this is in the Sermon on the Mount. There is the story. Have you ever heard "Thank You" by Ray Bolts? Do you want treasure in heaven? Picture this: You have taught Sunday school for many years, you die and leave this earth. Standing in heaven, one of your former classmates comes up to you and thanks to you for sharing the gospel in your class, because you told him about Jesus, he is now in heaven for eternity, - THAT is the treasure in heaven!

> The fear of the Lord leads to life, and he who has it will abide in satisfaction; he will not be visited by evil. A lazy man buries his hand in the bowl, and will not so much as bring it to his mouth. (Proverbs 19:23-24)

I guess it depends on your definition of life. I can tell you as someone who wasn't saved until he was thirty-five; it can make a world of difference, having a relationship with the Lord Jesus Christ. I have been a Christian long enough, not to remember too many things before my salvation. I can say this; there is a world of difference.

There is the word Solomon uses here: "Satisfaction", - The peace that comes from settling where you will spend eternity. Your relationship with God is settled. Don't fall for the lie that you can 'lose" your salvation. There are far too many verses that refute that notion. Let me share my favorite:

For as many as are led by the Spirit of God, these are sons of God. For you did not receive the spirit of bondage again to fear, but you received the Spirit of adoption by whom we cry out, "Abba, Father." The Spirit Himself bears witness with our spirit that we are children of God, and if children, then heirs—heirs of God and joint heirs with Christ, if indeed we suffer with Him, that we may also be glorified together. (Romans 8:14-17).

If you have "doubts" about your salvation, not sure, you need to check with God. It says His Spirit will bear witness with our spirit. We can have peace within our soul that we belong to God. If it is not there you need to get with God and get that secured.

Did you notice that Paul talks about "fear" when we are lost? That is one of the things that vanish when we ask Jesus into our heart; it doesn't mean we are not afraid of anything, it means our destiny is sealed. One day we will be welcomed into God's kingdom because of the suffering Christ did on the cross of Calvary. I think that is the suffering referred to here. Christ has endured our suffering that we might be spared that agony; it has all been taken care of.

> Wine is a mocker, strong drink is a brawler, and whoever is led astray by it is not wise. The wrath of the king is like the roaring of a lion; whoever provokes him to anger sins against his own life. (Proverbs 20:1-2)

My parents drank, my wife's father drank; I drank for years before I was saved. I know whereof I speak. We had a New Year's Eve party at our house once, drinking of course. The next morning, I got a phone call from someone who was at the party: "Could you look out on your front lawn, I think my dentures are out there." Seriously!

Something I realized early on as a Christian, "Anything that distracted me from hearing God's voice, and took self-control away from me, I would not permit! Just think of the stories you have heard of people who had done things they regretted, were ashamed of, or would NOT have done if they were sober. Ask yourself, why would I turn over control of my will to outside influences?

One more thing; Do you remember how you felt the next morning? Why would you deliberately put yourself through that, knowing the results? It just doesn't make sense to me.

We are in a unique position in our country, and contrary to the Bible. Throughout the Bible the kings assumed their role; they always fascinated me in the book of Kings. You could have a godly king followed by an ungodly son who becomes king, and the opposite occurs. Why is that? The point is, people have no "say" in who is over them; even in 1 Samuel, when the people wanted a king, God appointed Saul.

In our country, the people choose their king (president); unique to most of the world. Did you know that they offered George Washington the "opportunity" to become king? He turned it down. They put an eight-year limit on the presidency. George said that the war we just fought was to rid of us a monarchy.

I often think, after the election, I will see who the "people" choose to be their king; their choice demonstrates to me the moral "condition" of our country. Who we choose to lead us, to represent us to the world, is a reflection on what we are as a country!

77. Who said, "I have fought a good fight"?
    a. John   b. Paul   c. David   d. Joshua

> It is honorable for a man to stop striving, since any fool
> can start a quarrel. The lazy man will not plow because
> of winter; he will beg during harvest and have nothing.
> (Proverbs 20:3-4)

Dr. Charles Stanley has taught about the "Law of the Harvest." The application can be made in several ways. Here are the verses he uses:

Do not be deceived, God is not mocked; **for whatever a man sows, that will he also reap.** *For he who sows to his flesh will of the flesh reap corruption, but who sows to the Spirit will of the Spirit reap life everlasting.* (Galatians 6:7-8)

Through the book of Galatians Paul talks a lot about the battle between the "flesh" and the Spirit. A battle we constantly face. Solomon alludes to it in verse 4.

Dr. Stanley's Laws of the Harvest:
>You will reap **what** you sow,
>**more** than you sow,
>and **later** than you sow.

You could use this verse in Galatians in connection with Solomon's first words above: *It is honorable to stop striving, since any fool can start a quarrel.* Do you "sow" strife? When an argument breaks out do you "contribute" your two-cent worth? Or, do you try to resolve the problem and move on? Do you add fuel to fire or cold water? - Something to think about.

Interestingly, Solomon has no problem calling people "fools"; today that is politically incorrect. Fool is a "bad" word, it is not polite. Also, another word that is "incorrect" is "stupid", that is just not nice. Meanwhile, that person continues to think about what they are doing or saying is okay. So, which is worse? Being corrected "nicely" or getting their attention with some harsh words? Interesting question!

How are you doing with some of these proverbs? Do they touch a nerve? They are meant to do just that; that is the power of God's Word and the Holy Spirit. If you are a child of God you have the benefit of God's Spirit "teaching" you great truths.

     Lonny E. Young

Counsel in the heart of man is like deep water, but a man of understanding will draw it out. Most men will proclaim each his own goodness, but who can find a faithful man? (Proverbs 20:5-6)

Ever gaze into a deep pond? You "strain" your eyes trying to see the bottom; a deep stream or lake. You want to know what is beyond your eye-sight. "A man of understanding", - what do you think Solomon is talking about? Understanding what? Has your "curiosity" ever got the best of you? So, how do you find out the answer? Of course, you "step" into the unknown. Is that smart? Why do you need to know?

I have talked about this so much, "The counsel in the heart of man" - what or who do you rely on for wisdom and direction. Solomon has approached this so many ways. It is what might determine the path in life we take; what has been "programmed" into our hearts and minds. We "instinctively" travel the road we are most "comfortable" with, don't we? Why? It is what we have been taught.

Do you question that direction, that "wisdom"? Why do you trust that knowledge? Has it "proven" itself true? All good questions, - The point is, what or who determines your life path? It is such a critical question.

I have made two critical decisions in my life; I wish I could take back. One was dropping out of school; the second was leaving a church I was pastoring. I would love to have those decisions back. I can't. In one, the church, if I had listened to God instead of my own desires, I wouldn't have made that mistake.

There! It is who or what influences your decisions. Like Solomon says, "The counsel of the heart." I listened to my "flesh" not my heart. Are you about to make a decision? Are you praying about it? What is God telling you? The toughest response is "wait". Today we want instant action, instant results; God is NOT instant anything. God is patient; God wants His children to be patient, wait on Him, trust Him, God knows where this path leads, you don't. Trust His wisdom, listen to your heart. If you have given your heart to God, that is. If not, about all I can say is good luck!

> The righteous man walks in his integrity; his children are blessed after him. A king who sits on the throne of judgment scatters all evil with his eyes. (Proverbs 20:7-8)

We acknowledge that Solomon is the author of Proverbs (except in the last two chapters). Solomon also wrote Ecclesiastes and Song of Solomon. Look what Solomon wrote in Ecclesiastes:

For there is not a just man on earth who does good and does not sin. (Ecclesiastes 7:20)

How about this verse in the New Testament?

For all have sinned and come short of the glory of God. (Romans 3:23)

So, what is Solomon talking about? Basically, the Bible condemns any "righteousness" of our own. Righteousness, being "works" that are supposed to get us to heaven. There was a guy who got to heaven without dying:

*So, all the days of Enoch were three hundred and sixty-five years. And Enoch **walked with God;** and he was not, for God took him.* (Genesis 5:23-24)

Would that be considered "righteousness"? Do you see how it is worded? "Walked with God" Enoch was walking close enough to God, as one preacher put it, God said, "Your closer to Me than there, just come on home." - Interesting.

I heard this Christian song once. The chorus spoke to me:
One day Jesus will call my name.
As Days go by I hope I don't stay the same.
I want to get so close to Him, there is no big change.
On that day that Jesus calls my name. (Paraphrased)

Does that sound like Enoch?

78. Which city was called, "The City of David"?
    a. Bethel   b. Nazareth   c. Bethlehem   d. Jerusalem

Who can say, "I have made my heart clean, I am pure from sin"? Diverse weights and diverse measures, they are both alike, an abomination to the Lord. (Proverbs 20:9-10)

Do you remember when our government was going to convert the United States to the metric system? It was an all-out effort. It didn't last, did it? Some dogs you just can't teach new tricks. Think about the "measuring system" in the Old Testament, a "cubit"; I was told it was about eighteen inches. A span was the length of a hand, or breath, not sure. Anyway, not exactly EXACT, are they? God said a cheater in measuring is an "abomination". Solomon doesn't mince words.

I remember my grandmother telling me about butchers who used to put their hand, hidden of course, on the scale to not give an accurate weight. Same thing, an abomination!

Did you catch the wording of verse 9? "**I** have made my heart clean." "**I** am pure from sin." According to whom? Who determines the condition of our hearts? It certainly isn't us. Maybe that's why Solomon put these two verses together. I love this verse in 1 Samuel:

But the Lord said to Samuel, "Do not look at his appearance or at his physical stature, because I have refused him (Eliab). For the Lord does not see as man sees; for man looks at the outward appearance, but the Lord looks at the heart. (1 Samuel 16:7)

Can you make your heart pure, pure enough to suit God? Not hardly. That is why Jesus had to give His life on the cross of Calvary. It is HIS blood, "applied" to our hearts, that what makes it pure enough to suit God's requirements. NOTHING we can do. I can be a "saint" my whole life but I will fall woefully short of God's perfect standards. It is only what God has done on my behalf that allows me access into His presence.

Only a child of God can claim what Solomon has written, "I am pure from sin." The condition is ONLY because God allowed His Son to pay for our sins on the cross, - That is the love that God desires from His children.

> Even a child is known by his deeds, whether what he does is
> pure and right. The hearing ear and the seeing eye, the Lord
> has made them both. (Proverbs 20:11-12)

Is that not the challenge of every parent? I remember praying as I left for the military, "Lord, please don't let me embarrass my parents"; we often forget that our actions reflect on our family. I don't think that is a priority today, not as much as in my generation. Sad!

Have you noticed this phrase in the Bible, "He that hath an ear, let him hear."? - A plain statement just makes sense, right? How often do people listen? A lot of times, in a time of grief, people just want someone to "listen"; they don't need someone to tell them of a "similar" thing that happened to them. Just listen.

I like the fact that Solomon says, *the Lord has made them both.* If you take note of that, also consider that He gave us TWO ears and only one mouth. Sadly, that is not in proportion to their use.

This brings up a good point about our prayer life. Sadly, I am just as guilty as the rest of us. How many times, when we pray, we say "In Jesus name, amen." and we go our merry way? Have you ever thought of waiting a couple of minutes AFTER you pray? Maybe God wants to respond to your prayer. Think about it.

That brings me to one of the reasons for this book. All my books are meant for one purpose: More time in the Bible! This is my second daily devotional; a daily time of opening God's Word. If you do not do it daily you are passing up a great opportunity for God to speak to you; this Bible is His letter, if you will, to us.

Do you have any old letters you keep, for remembrance? Why do you keep them? God has spent thousands of years and over forty authors to bring us His heart. You read that right; God put down His plans and purpose for mankind. The more time we spend in God's Word the more we come to know God and His heart for us.

I just finished a devotional study of the life of David; there are so many "neglected" episodes in David's life that helped me to understand his relationship with God, and thus mine, as well. God's heart is revealed through His relationship with David.

> Do not love sleep, lest you come to poverty; Open your eyes, and you will be satisfied with bread. "It is good for nothing" cries the buyer; but when he has gone his way, then he boasts. (Proverbs 20:13-14)

I am sure you have had those mornings far too many to think about. "I don't want to get up!" - I remember those days when I was working a regular job. I was controlled by the clock; I hated it when that alarm went off. Thank God for the weekends. Ever think that on Sunday morning? It is time to go to church. Think about what you are saying.

Suppose God heard you and said, "Okay, if it is sleep you want, don't open your eyes, and just come home." He could do that, you know. The body says sleep but your soul should be excited to wake and work. See, with anticipation what God is going to do today. That should be our attitude, especially on Sunday!

Now that I am retired it can be hard. The first thing I did when I retired was taking my wristwatch off. It is "rebellion" of course; I am still controlled by the clock, but not near as much. It seems I am as busy now as before I retired. There always seems to be things to do. - The difference? These are things I want to do, not someone else's demands on my time.

Do you wake each day with "anticipation"? If you have ever noticed God doing something in and through you, you will be excited with each new day, to see what God is going to do. I start the day in God's Word. I read Sarah Young, then my devotional, my normal three chapters in God's Word, and then I have a long prayer list, - that is my "quiet time" with the Lord. Sometimes during the day, it is hard; I shut everything off, sit in my chair and listen to my heart that is where Jesus is. I listen to His prompting, His encouragement, and relax in His peace.

That is "fellowship" with God; taking some time each day to listen to God. Don't just say your prayers, say, "Amen" then on your merry way. Take a minute or two and listen, see if God has a response.

I used to hate the Proverbs; they didn't make much sense until I began this study and meditate on each verse or two. Digest them, - That is what Solomon intended, don't hurry, meditate!

79. Which of Jesus' disciples was a "tax collector"?
    a. Peter   b. Matthew   c. Phillip   d. James

> There is gold and a multitude of rubies, but the lips of
> knowledge are a precious jewel. Take the garment of one
> who is surety for a stranger, and hold it as a pledge when it
> is for a seductress. (Proverbs 20:15-16)

There goes one of those triggers. Verse 15 reminds me of a favorite passage in 1 Corinthians:

*For no other **foundation** can anyone lay than that which is laid, which is Jesus Christ. Now if anyone build on this foundation with gold, silver, precious stones, wood, hay, straw, each one's work will become clear; for the day will declare it, because it is revealed by fire; and the fire will test each one's work, of what sort it is.* (1 Corinthians 3:11-13)

I love this third chapter of 1 Corinthians. Of course, you noticed the six "works" listed? You didn't see any works? That is interesting. Both Paul and James talk about "works". What is funny is that there is no "list" of these works. That is because THERE ARE NONE! Here, check out this verse:

*For by **grace** you have been saved through faith, and that not of yourselves; it is a gift of God, **not of works**, lest anyone should boast.* (Ephesians 2:8-9)

Do you see that? *"Lest anyone should boast"* it is all done by Christ on the cross. The only thing God wants from us is "faith", the rest has been accomplished on the cross.

Look at these words: *It is a gift of God.* You don't "earn" a gift. It is free.

The "foundation" in verse 11 of 1 Corinthians is the "grace" of God, nothing more, nothing less. It is God's plan to restore the relationship with a fallen world because of Adam's sin of disobedience in the Garden of Eden. Man has been in rebellion ever since, just read the Old Testament, even the Scribes and Pharisees in the New Testament ADDED to God's simple instructions, - a form of rebellion.

> Bread gained by deceit is sweet to a man, but afterward his mouth will be filled with gravel. Plans are established by counsel; by wise counsel wage war. (Proverbs 20:17-18)

In the "old days" I remember traveling with my parents and stopping beside a cornfield at night; I'm sure you know the rest. We didn't understand, when our parents would, suddenly, say, "Be still, be quiet, for a while." Later we had this bushel of corn in the back of our car. By the time my brothers and I had realized what was going on; farmers had started planting feed corn on the outside rows.

We didn't taste the difference because we didn't know what was going on. Think on this proverb a minute. ANYTHING gotten by deceit has a "taint" to it you can't erase. If anything, it robs you of peace.

When I see this word "war", I don't think of it in the context of country versus country, been there, done that, I think about the war I fight every day.

We talked earlier about how hard it is to get out of bed, - that is the war of the flesh versus the Spirit. Who wins? There are many, many other such battles, how about obesity? Ooops, I am meddling; it is a daily battle, war if you will.

Look at this verse in Galatians:

For the flesh lusts (wars) against the Spirit, and the Spirit against the flesh; and these are contrary to one another, so that you do not do the things that you wish. (Galatians 5:17)

In other places, Paul speaks about his struggle with this battle in his own life. It is such a struggle today. The world pulls you this way and that; it is hard to win a battle. The closer you can walk with God; it becomes easier, not perfect, but easier. The closer you walk with God, the harder Satan will work to break that bond. If he can get you to stumble, to be discouraged, to drift from walking with God, Satan has succeeded. It is a daily "battle!"

By wise counsel wage war - Who is your "counsel"? Where do you go when this battle is raging? If it is anyplace other than the Lord and His Holy Spirit, you lose!

> He who goes about as a talebearer reveals secrets; therefore, do not associate with one who flatters with his lips. Whoever curses his father or his mother, his lamp will be put out in deep darkness. (Proverbs 20:19-20)

It is sad to say but the worst place for this is the church, I have been in church life way too long not to see this. Usually, the best way to accomplish this is to say, "We need to pray about. . . "That makes it sound holy, doesn't it? I love what someone told me once about curing "gossip". Just simply ask that person if you could "quote" them, - that puts a damper on gossip quickly!

Of course, Solomon's verse on the father and mother are strait out of the Ten Commandments:

Honor your father and your mother, that your days may be long upon the land which the Lord your God is giving you. (Exodus 20:12)

Someone once pointed out that this is the only commandment with a promised blessing, - maybe so. Did you notice how Solomon words it?

His lamp will be put out in deep darkness, - Interesting. Could he be talking about death? I wonder. If you have spent any time in the Japanese culture, they have this commandment down pat. I just know what I have seen in movies and TV. They have no idea who Moses was or the Ten Commandments.

Did you notice Solomon's solution for "talebearers"? Do not associate with them. The best way to put out a fire is to "smother" it, deprive it of oxygen. If the "tale" goes no further than your ears it will die out.

I won't go into the musings of the tongue. We have been there. Solomon recognizes the dangers and warns us several times.

Just a note, - In my study of David, I often wondered how, being born in a family, like David's, of at least eight wives, how David could have two sons who threatened to kill David for the throne; thinking they were next in line. God made it clear to David and Bathsheba, Solomon would be next in line for the throne. Surely there must have been "word" around the castle that Solomon was the next king, - Interesting.

80. In which New Testament book is found God's "Hall of Faith"?
    a. Romans   b. Revelation   c. Hebrews   d. James

> An inheritance gained hastily at the beginning will not be blessed at the end. Do not say, "I will recompense evil"; wait for the Lord, and He will save you. (Proverbs 20:21-22)

Have you bought your "Lottery" or "Power Ball" ticket yet? It is up to a BILLION dollars. You might have the winning ticket. - Seriously?

One of my favorite shows growing up was called: The Millionaire. This multi-millionaire each week, the premise of the show, would give away one million dollars to a stranger, tax-free! There was one catch, they could not tell anyone how much or how they got it; it made for some very interesting episodes. I think in the two or three years it ran, only two people returned the money. - Instant inheritance?

What do you do when you receive an "extra" amount of money? Some people have extra taxes taken out so they can get a "refund" each year. How many hours do you spend thinking about how you're going to spend that money? Lose any sleep?

At the risk of being redundant let me explain an often misinterpreted verse:

*For the **love** of money is a root of all kinds of evil, for which some have strayed from the faith in their greediness, and pierced themselves through with many sorrows.* (1Timothy 6:10)

It is not the money that is the sin; it is the LOVE of the same. Paul is very clear here. In fact, most people don't even notice or ignore the context of this verse. Paul is talking about money becoming a "god," replacing the one true God. It becomes their god. Again, it is the "love" of the money, not the money itself.

I wonder if they showed the "Millionaire" today, even a remake if it would be popular. You hear on the news all the time about the "billionaires" we have today. It would not hurt them to try this. Just as an experiment. What would you do? Oh, don't forget those individuals that promise God to give Him a portion if He would allow them to win. I wonder if they would consider ALL of it. How about keeping 10% and giving God the rest? - That won't fly either!

> The king's heart is in the hand of the Lord, like the rivers of water; He turns it wherever He wishes. Every way of a man is right in his own eyes, but the Lord weighs the hearts. (Proverbs 21:1-2)

So, how important is the heart? Aside from the physical aspects, let's think "spiritually".

Check these verses:

The heart is deceitful above all things, and desperately wicked; who can know it? I, the Lord, search the heart, I test the mind, even to give every man according to his ways, according to the fruit of his doings. (Jeremiah 17:9-10)

God says there is no hope for the heart, yet, God rewards according to the heart, - Interesting. Our mind might be able to fool out heart, but God knows the intent of the heart. We cannot fool God. The "heart" is the focal point of God's working in us. The mind can be deceived. But the heart is wiser than the mind. Think about that. Do you think I am kidding?

Look here:

*If you confess with your mouth the Lord Jesus and **believe in your heart** that God has raised Him from the dead, you will be saved. For with the **heart** one believes unto righteousness, and with the mouth confession is made unto salvation.* (Romans 10:9-10)

You see? - Raising someone from the dead is not "logical," faith is, believing what your heart reveals to you. You will never be saved "logically". One Man dying on the cross to pay for your sins, past, present, and future is not logical; that He should have to die is not logical. It is what the heart reveals due to the work of God's Holy Spirit within you. The Holy Spirit was sent by Jesus to "convict" the world of sin. It is the Holy Spirit's work that draws you to the cross. God never meant for it to be "logical!" That is where faith comes in. You "trust the Word of God."

Jesus said to him, "Thomas, because you have seen Me, you have believed. Blessed are those who have not seen yet believe!" (John 20:29)

        Lonny E. Young

> To do righteousness and justice is more acceptable to the
> Lord than sacrifice. A haughty look, a proud heart, and the
> plowing of the wicked are sin. (Proverbs 21:3-4)

Look what God told Isaiah:

"To what purpose is the multitude of your sacrifices to Me? Says the Lord. I have had enough of burnt offerings of rams and the fat of cattle. I do not delight in the blood of bulls, or of lambs or goats. (Isaiah 1:11)

Why? That was the "sacrificial" system that God set up at Mt. Sinai. Why is He saying it means nothing? - Exactly for that reason.

In the beginning, it represented "repentance". In Isaiah's day, it meant nothing to the people. God knew their hearts. Look in verse 4 in Proverbs 21: *A proud heart.* Their hearts were turned from God. The killing of bulls and goats meant nothing to the people. It became a "ritual only".

See what he says in verse three? It is the "act" of righteousness that gets God's attention not the rituals. It is how we treat each other, not the "prayers". God searches the heart, He doesn't note the deeds. Let me back up a bit to Proverbs 21:2, - *Every way of a man is right in his own eyes.* Does that sound familiar? It is if you have read the book of Judges:

In those days, there was no king in Israel; **everyone did what was right in their own eyes.** (Judges 17:6, 21:25).

The criteria for "righteousness" is God's domain, not ours. It is God who searches the heart, not a list of dos and don'ts. Let me offer one more verse, if I may, just how important is obedience to God?

If you love Me, keep My commandments. And I will pray the Father, and He will give you another Helper, that He may abide with you forever. (John 14:15-16)

81. Who was the oldest man in the Bible?
    a. Enoch   b. Methusalah   c. Moses   d. Adam

> The plans of the diligent lead surely to plenty; but those of everyone who is hasty, surely to poverty. Getting treasures by a lying tongue is the fleeting fantasy of those who seek death. (Proverbs 21:5-6)

Diligent, diligent? Let's see, I remember that word from somewhere:

*But without faith it is impossible to please Him, for he who comes to God must believe that He is, and that He is a rewarder of those who **diligently** seek Him.* (Hebrews 11:6) - One of my favorite verses.

What might be your definition of "diligent"? - Committed? Faithful? Steadfast? What word comes to your mind? Don't miss the point, God will reward those who are committed to seeking God's guidance.

One stipulation about Solomon's verse 5; those plans that Solomon talks about MUST be "approved" by God. If your plans conflict with God's, you surely will not be blessed or rewarded. Take a minute and check Jeremiah 29:11. God has His plans for us. If we think we can go our merry way and God will bless our "rebellion," we are sadly mistaken.

I learned this lesson of Solomon's, the hard way. I used to think that it didn't matter what something cost; the cheaper the better. After you replace something three or four times you realize, cheap doesn't always work, - short cuts, hasty work, cutting corners is not God's way; just look at the cross.

Remember when Jesus prayed, "If there is any other way, let this cup pass." (Matthew 26:39). Think about it. What other way could God "justify" our sin, than by the blood of His Only Son? There was absolutely nothing sufficient to pay the price that would satisfy God, - that is how much God loves us!

How are you doing in Proverbs? Has it made you "rethink" some things in your life? Solomon is simply pointing out basic biblical truths that God wants us to incorporate into our daily living. Some lifestyle changes that will improve our "fellowship" with God!

> The violence of the wicked will destroy them, because they refuse to do justice. The way of the guilty man is perverse; but as for the pure, his work is right. (Proverbs 21:7-8)

I never thought I would see my country in such turmoil. The "rule of law" has become "mob" rule. No respect for law enforcement. No civility. It is scary. I want to claim God's promise. There is no telling when you might read this. The "principle" is the same. It used to be called "anarchy" now they call it "mob rule." That is not how things are done in a representative democracy.

God condemns it, and God will judge it. This kind of chaos should only be seen in third-world countries, not ours! A couple of verses please:

God is not the author of confusion but of peace, as in all the churches of the saints. (1 Corinthians 14:33)

Let all things be done decently and in order. (1 Corinthians 14:40)

Remember who Paul is writing to? One of the most "corrupt," misguided and corrupt churches in Asia.

Okay, how about your life? Is their confusion in your daily living? Are you not sure which way to go or what to do? Remember, "God is not the author of confusion" If God is not the author then where is it coming from? I will give you one guess! Satan doesn't want you "focused", let alone focused on God. The devil wants you distracted, confused, unsure, just enough to distract you from God's leading in your life. I mentioned Jeremiah 29 before; you would do well to put these verses in your mind and heart:

*For I know the thoughts that I think toward you, says the Lord, thoughts of **peace** and not of evil, to give you a future and a hope. Then you will call upon Me and go and pray to Me, and I will listen to you. And you will seek Me and find Me, when you search for Me with all your heart!* (Jeremiah 29:11-13)

> Better to dwell in a corner of a housetop, then in a house shared with a contentious woman. The soul of the wicked desires evil; his neighbor finds no favor in his eyes. (Proverbs 21:9-10)

My cross-reference says, James 2:16. Here is what it says:

If a brother or sister is naked and destitute of daily food, and one of you says to them, "Depart in peace, be warmed and filled." but you do not give them the things which are needed for the body, what does it profit? (James 2:15-16)

I can understand James completely. "Words are cheap." It seems that today all we get are words. Do you see what James is getting at? He sums it up in the next verse:

Thus, also faith by itself, if it does not have works, is dead. (2:17)

But someone will say, "You have faith and I have works." Show me your faith without your works, and I will show you my faith by my works. (James 2:18)

Here is the argument between James and Paul; they are NOT contrary. James is not talking about salvation. James is speaking of the "results" of salvation. - BECAUSE you have asked Jesus into your heart, no strings attached, you will serve the Lord with "works". It is not the deeds, works, or whatever, that gets you saved. It is simply the work of Christ on the cross.

Solomon is pointing out that the wicked, the "lost", do not care about their neighbor, about doing "good"; their desire is toward themselves, their gain, not helping anyone else. That is the cross-reference to James.

I have been avoiding the previous verse (9). A "contentious" woman in Bible days was an "excuse" for divorce. Anything was an excuse for divorce. Today, we just simply don't get married. There is no longer a "commitment" to each other. A marriage is a commitment!

82. Besides Levi, which of Jacob's twelve sons did not receive an inheritance in the Promised Land?
    a. Dan   b. Gad   c. Joseph   d. Benjamin

> When the scoffer is punished, the simple is made wise;
> but when the wise is instructed, he receives knowledge.
> The righteous God wisely considers the house of the
> wicked, overthrowing the wicked for their wickedness.
> (Proverbs 21:11-12)

It is a paradox, isn't it? It just seems the wicked are prospering and we who live for the Lord are getting the short end. It is easy to say, "We win in the end" but that doesn't help right now. I guess I could pray that you might look into their (wicked) heart. If you could see the hurt, fear, unrest, tension, - you would not think so highly of them, would you? You look in the heart of a child of God; you see peace, joy, respect, compassion, etc. Which would you prefer?

That is a great point that Solomon is trying to bring out in these proverbs, - the contrast in the heart of the wicked and the child of God. I ran across this verse this weekend in a sermon. Here is David's counsel to his son Solomon:

"As for you, my son Solomon, know the God of your father, and serve Him with a loyal heart and with a willing mind; for the Lord searches all hearts and understands all the intents and thoughts. If you seek Him, He will be found by you; but if you forsake Him, He will cast you off forever. (1 Chronicles 28:9)

It almost has the theme of Jeremiah 29:11-13, both talk about seeking after God, - Obeying God. It also points out to Solomon that God knows our heart. Solomon's heart was drawn away from God by his many wives.

I love the first part, *"know the God of your father* (David)." There is only one way to know God; you must spend time in His Word. The more you read, both the Old and the New Testament, the more you know God's heart. He already knows yours. You need to get to know His.

My deeper walk began when I asked myself, "Why did Jesus have to die on the cross?" When I found Exodus 12 and understood the "Passover," I realized how much God loves me.

> Whoever shuts their ears to the cry of the poor, will also cry
> himself and not be heard. A gift in secret pacifies anger, and
> a bribe behind the back, strong wrath. (Proverbs 21:13-14)

Do you suppose this is a principle that God has programmed into each of his creations? Let's see if this verse rings a bell:

Do not be deceived, God is not mocked; **for whatever a man sows, that will he also reap.** (Galatians 6:7)

Is it any wonder? God makes it so simple. He asks only two things from us, His children:

Jesus said to him, "You shall love the Lord your God with all your heart, with all your soul, and with all your mind. This is the first and great commandment. And the second is like it: **you shall love your neighbor as yourself.** *On these two commandments hang all the Law and the Prophets."* (Matthew 22:37-40)

These two commandments encapsulate the Ten Commandments. The first four commandments speak of our relationship with God. The following six refer to our relationship with our fellow man. It is that simple. That is what Solomon is talking about in verse 13.

I love giving in secret; I love to frustrate the receiver. It will drive them crazy trying to figure out who gave them something. I have often dreamed of asking my waitress how many tickets she had, pay them all off, and then watch the faces of those around me when the waitress says, "Your bill has been paid." It is priceless.

That is the true test of giving, - When you can give with no one knowing.

Look at Matthew:

But when you do a charitable deed, do not let your left hand know what your right hand is doing, that your charitable deed may be in secret; and your Father who sees in secret will Himself reward you openly. (Matthew 6:3-4)

> It is a joy for the just to do justice, but destruction will come to the workers of iniquity. A man who wanders from the way of understanding will rest in the assembly of the dead. (Proverbs 21:15-16)

This is a picture I have developed recently. It speaks of our "walk" with God, which seems so prevalent in the Bible.

I have this picture of walking a path (life) with God. (Psalm 16:11) Of course, He should always be in the lead. I made the mistake once of taking the lead and it cost me! As God leads He will, if we follow close, guide us on the path of blessings! It is when we decide to take a separate, different path, we run into trouble.

I have this picture of us wandering off, deceived by lies from Satan, on this alternate path. It could take days or years before we realized we have made a grave mistake. We should have never have left God's side. So, now what do we do?

It is simple; you go back to where you parted from God's guidance. You confess, repent, and commit to God's guidance. God is right there, where you left Him. For most of us, it is in the church.

One problem with this alternate path, - we will pick up "consequences" from that alternate path. We will make mistakes that God could have avoided, but we will now have to pay for those mistakes. We can re-join God where we left Him. The consequences will remain. Just ask David. David made things right with God after his affair with Bathsheba, and his murder of Uriah. When Nathan confronted him, he repented and found God's forgiveness. BUT, there were "consequences" for the rest of his life. It took David a while but he restored the "fellowship" he once had with God.

Let me encourage you to make a study of David's life, 1 Samuel 16 through 1 Kings 2. Take your time; notice how God works in David's life. David, the man God said was, "A man after God's own heart." (1 Samuel 13:14 and Acts 13:22). There is so much to learn about our walk with God in the life of David. I wrote a devotional book on David in my study, it is called "David's Walk with God." It gave me a whole new insight into our relationship with God; our disobedience has consequences, nothing God can't forgive.

83. Which one of Jacob's four wives had six of the twelve sons?
  a. Rachel b. Bilhah c. Leah d. Gilpah

> He who loves pleasure will be a poor man; he who loves wine and oil will not be rich. The wicked shall be a ransom for the righteous, and the unfaithful for the upright. (Proverbs 21:17-18)

Now, what would Solomon mean by loving pleasure, wine, and oil? If you were to make a list of your "pleasures" what might be on that list? - Material things, people, recreational, hobbies. I wonder where the Lord would fit on that list if you think to add Him. God gives us an idea in His Word:

"But seek first the kingdom of God and His righteousness, and all these things shall be added to you. (Matthew 6:33)

There is God's priority. Again, where does God fit on your priority list? How about three hours once a week? Is that a priority? God gives us 168 hours a week. Don't neglect the fact that God could "end" those 168 hours whenever He desires. He simply asks that you give him three of those hours.

Wait a minute. Church only lasts about 90 minutes. Where are the other 90 minutes? You must include Sunday school in those hours you are giving God. For most, that is the closest thing to Bible study you will get. Three hours out of 168, that's not even 10%; just three short hours. Dedicated to worship and study of the Creator of this universe, and YOU!

Solomon even talks about the "unfaithful" here. That reminds me of another verse. I like this verse so much I wrote it on the bookmark I keep in my Bible. Check this out.

Then He touched their eyes, saying, "According to your faith be it unto you." (Matthew 9:29)

Think about that a minute. Is God saying, "According to the amount of faith you have, will determine the amount of "blessing" you receive?" I wonder what He means here. Jesus often chastises His disciples for their "lack" of faith, - His own disciples. How about you?

     Lonny E. Young

September 6   249-116   Proverbs 21

> Better to dwell in the wilderness, then with a contentious and angry woman. There is desirable treasure and oil in the dwelling of the wise, but a foolish man squanders it. (Proverbs 21:19-20)

Have you had your "wilderness" experience yet? - That might be an interesting question to ask Christians. I think every child of God has had a wilderness experience; a time when God tests them to evaluate their faithfulness. Of course, Jesus' wilderness experience was for a different reason. You might want to do some research into different characters in the Bible. See how many had a "wilderness experience" in their walk with the Lord. Has God "tried" you and found you faithful?

Have you noticed how much Solomon talks about "contentious" women? I guess, if anyone would know, Solomon would:

*And he had **seven hundred wives, princesses, and three hundred concubines;** and his wives turned away his heart.* (1 Kings 11:3)

His father, David, at one point that I know of, had eight wives, before Bathsheba. God only gave Adam one; you see how that turned out. It is so important that the wife you choose to spend the rest of your life with is the one God chooses. It is the second greatest choice you will ever make in your life, - the first, of course, is to ask Jesus into your heart.

Once you and God have made that decision there must be a commitment between the two of you; a commitment for a lifetime. No matter the "contentions" or the blessings. You are committed to the one God has blessed you with, for eternity! It must be prayed about and you must have a feeling of peace between you and God that this person is the one God has chosen for you.

People, in the beginning, including my mother thought we were moving too fast. We met in November of 1966 and married in June of 1967. We have been married fifty-one years; neither of us was saved at the time. God was watching over us, God has richly blessed us with two wonderful daughters and six grandchildren and two great-grandchildren. We are truly blessed!

> He who follows righteousness and mercy finds life, righteousness, and honor. A wise man scales the city of the mighty, and brings down the trusted stronghold. (Proverbs 21:21-22)

What are you looking for in life? Solomon says, *"He who follows righteousness and mercy finds life."* So, if you're looking for life, where do you start looking? Here is an idea:

"The thief does not come except to steal, and to kill, and to destroy. **I have come that they may have life, and that they may have it more abundantly.** (John 10:10)

How would you describe "abundant life"? Pay attention now! I am NOT talking about "things". I am talking about "life!" What would make your life "abundant"? Here's one, how about "peace". Do you have peace? - A peace that passes all understanding?

How about this verse:

"Peace I leave with you, My peace I give to you; not as the world gives do I give to you. Let not your heart be troubled, neither let it be afraid". (John 14:27)

The problem with your abundant life in the context of "things" is that they are "temporary"; just as your abundant life would be temporary if it was based on things. Don't measure your "happiness" by your bank account or 401K; those riches will never bring you peace OR security. You know the parable of the farmer and his barns (Luke 12:16-21). He had all these plans but God decided to bring him home.

Let me close with this verse. Do you want abundant life? Have you thought of asking God?

Here is one of my favorites:

"Ask, and it will be given to you; seek, and you will find; knock and it will opened to you. For everyone who asks receives, and he who seeks finds, and to him who knocks it will be opened. (Matthew 7:7-8)

84. What nation was Goliath from?
    a. Midians   b. Canaanites   c. Moabites   d. Philistines

September 8   251– 114   Proverbs 21

Whoever guards his mouth and tongue keeps his soul from
troubles. A proud and haughty man—"Scoffer" is his name;
he acts with arrogant pride. (Proverbs 21:23-24)

Does this guarding come easy? Not hardly. It takes practice. Sometimes it takes offending a friend or co-worker; something that gets your attention about the words you flippantly throw out of your mouth. I learned this the hard way.

We have these two-way radios at work, several on the same line. I got caught up on "slamming" this co-worker. I put in my two-cent worth. Oh, did I mention I was a young Christian? Anyway, he drove over to my truck, got in my face and said, "So, you're a Christian, you sure don't act like one!" - That got my attention.

Sometimes we are not aware of the damage we do with our "loose lips." It has been a tough lesson, but I am still learning to THINK before I speak. Do I "really" need to comment here? Just a couple of seconds can save some problems later. Like Solomon says, *"keeps your soul from troubles."*

Solomon speaks a lot about the tongue, so, does James; James is only four chapters but there is so much wisdom there. Spend some time there. I have heard James called the "Proverbs" of the New Testament. It is worth a study!

I hope this walk, through Proverbs, has stirred some thought, some meditation. God gave Solomon this wisdom; Solomon took the time to write down God's wisdom. The more we can incorporate these truths into our lives, the better.

How do you deal with these "scoffers"? Do you argue with them? Debate them? Ignore them? If you're a Christian it will not be hard to find scoffers. They will find you. Can you "defend" what you believe? Do you know what you believe? If you're not sure, how can you be sure you are saved? Your salvation is based on your "faith" in Jesus Christ. Do you know who your faith is in?
Someone once said, "Jesus is either a lunatic, a liar, or Lord." Could you defend your relationship with the Lord to a "scoffer"? How would you do that? Has He changed your life? Tell the "scoffer".

> The desire of the lazy man kills him, for his hands refuse to labor. He covets greedily all day long, but the righteous gives and does not spare. (Proverbs 21:25-26)

Someone once said, "It is your **attitude**, not your **aptitude** that determines your **altitude**." That is the point of the guy Solomon is talking about. I love this. Maybe you need an "attitude adjustment", I am sure you have heard that; this is so important in life. A "lazy" attitude will get you nowhere and accomplish nothing.

Each year, when I was employed, I tried to take the week between Christmas and New Years as a vacation; I would try to finish up any loose ends from the year, so I could "focus" on the coming New Year. Then, here is the key; - I would approach the New Year with "anticipation". Excited about what God was going to do in the New Year.

I kept a daily journal for years (20) and recorded what God was doing in those days and years. Now, I can look back and see where God took me from one place, one project to another and make the connection; see how God worked to bring me to where I am now. Just this journey to writing, now my third book, is amazing to me. He brought several pieces together to lead me on this point.

Is God working in your life right now? Would you know if He was? Are their circumstances going on that you just don't understand (Proverbs 3:5) why they are happening? Stop right now, get some paper, and think back to when these circumstances began. Now, try to write down what has happened from then till now. It might be hard but try. The key is, look where God may have had a hand in the events up to now. Pray about this journey. Ask God to reveal His plan, His direction, to open your eyes.

One of the things about the fellow Solomon is talking about in the verses above is his focus. The "desire" is where his focus was. Not on God, not on what God's plan was, but on his own "comfort," his own desires and plans. When your focus is inward you cannot see God working around you; working in your circumstances, your friends, the people you meet at church. Don't let me get started on the church. You need to be there every Sunday for God's perspective!

     Lonny E. Young

September 10   253-112   Proverbs 22

> A good name is to be chosen rather than great riches, loving favor rather than silver and gold. The rich and the poor have this in common, the Lord is the maker of them all. (Proverbs 22:1-2)

Wait a minute, there are several more verses left in chapter 21. Yes, and I hope you will read them, meditate on them. Due to space restraints, I need to move on.

Don't miss a point Solomon is making here, with one simple word: *A good name is to be **chosen** rather than great riches.* Life is a series of choices; some are more obvious than others. I have mentioned several times some ways we can make the right choices. That can be the main purpose of Proverbs, to help you make the right choices.

The picture of walking this path of life with God, - that is a choice. You can choose to walk your own way, God will not stop you. Just remember, when you run into a "problem," that God is not there to help you. He is there but will allow you to continue your merry way until you return to His guidance and direction. He does not force Himself on anyone. It is your **choice.**

I have shared this before; it is a lesson that took me some time to learn. When I was a pastor I wished I could preach like Dr. Charles Stanley, Dr. Chuck Swindoll, etc. One day, I realized that God made me "just the way I am". If he created another like Charles Stanley, one of us would be unnecessary. Granted, God may not have led me on this particular path early in my life; He did create me with this heart.

The last part of verse two: *The Lord is the maker of them all.* That is something we need to come to grips with. God created us just the way we are, for a "specific" purpose; a certain role to play on this earth, at this time. The challenge for all of us is to discern that role, seek God's guidance, walk the footsteps He has prepared for us, - to bless us! I love the story of "Footprints", if you haven't read it you need to Google it, - it is so true.

The picture is that God is always walking beside us on this path of life (Psalm 16:11). If you're a lost person you have no idea what I am talking about. The trick is to learn to discern His direction, His will, and not your own. When we learn to trust His guidance, the path becomes so much easier.

85. In what New Testament book is found "The Seven Sealed Book"?
    a. James   b. Matthew   c. Revelation   d. Jude

> A prudent man foresees evil and hides himself, but the simple
> pass on and are punished. By humility and the fear of the
> Lord are riches and honor and life. (Proverbs 22:3-4)

I wouldn't exactly call King David "simple," but a very interesting point in David's life turned his life upside down.

Then it happened one evening that David arose from his bed and walked on the roof of the king's house. And from the roof he saw a woman bathing, and the woman was very beautiful to behold. (2 Samuel 11:2)

This is such a critical point in David's life. You may have had such a moment. There is a fork in your road of life. Which way to go? Where to turn? One note, at this point David already had eight wives. Which makes the choice he made all the more ridiculous!

Well if David had the Holy Spirit he would have made the right choice, - Really?

Then Samuel took the horn of oil and anointed him in the midst of his brothers; ***and the Spirit of the Lord came upon David from that day forward.*** *So, Samuel arose and went to Ramah.* (1 Samuel 16:13)

David HAD the Holy Spirit, he just refused to listen. Do you think the Spirit warned him? Of course, He did. It is the same in our life. How many times has God's Spirit told us or warned us of a serious mistake, but we refused to listen? We know better than God what the right thing to do is.
By humility and the fear of the Lord are riches and honor and life. Solomon learned this lesson as well, later on. He listened to his peers instead of the older men around him. - The council?

Gee, even Christians make mistakes. Of course, we do. Usually, it is of our own making; we refused to follow the guidance of Scripture or the prompting of God's Holy Spirit. Choices - we are faced with them every day. How do you determine your course of action?

> Thorns and snares are the way of the perverse; he who guards his soul will be far from them. Train up a child in the way he should go, and when he is old he will not depart from it. (Proverbs 22:5-6)

How often have you heard that verse (6) quoted? As a young parent, I am sure many times, especially in church. I have my theories which I will share in a moment.

Do you know the hardest Sunday school classes to get started, and harder still to maintain? - The "College and Career", "Young Adults Class" that age group. They have left high school, they are on their own; they probably are not married yet, or just newly married, no children. It is next to impossible to get a consistent class attendance in this age group.

When they begin to have children, starting a home environment, then they gravitate to the church, usually, because of roots established early in life, which brings me to my theory.

You, as parents, have laid a foundation (hopefully) that will be built on later. I guess, as a parent, you have to hope nothing happens between leaving high school and beginning a family that will turn them away from your early teachings. That is the "train up a child" part of Solomon's proverb; laying that groundwork early in life.

It is hard to say when that teaching will take root, and begin showing fruit. I guess if a parent ever needed patience it is now; it can be so frustrating at times. You know they know better, they just must find their way. That is the work of the Holy Spirit. Now if your children have never asked Jesus into their heart, you are working from scratch. Prayer is your first tool; consistent testimony maybe another.

He who guards his soul, - an interesting phrase. I wonder what Solomon was talking about, of course, in the Old Testament you could lose the presence of the Holy Spirit (1 Samuel 16:14). In the New Testament, once we have asked Jesus into your heart you are sealed through the presence of God's Spirit that remains with you forever.

Look at this verse from Psalm 51:

Do not take your Holy Spirit from me. (Psalm 51:11b)

> The rich rules over the poor, and the borrower is servant to the lender. He who sows iniquity will reap sorrow, and the rod of his anger will fall. (Proverbs 22:7-8)

You can read these words over and over, but until they hit home, you will ignore them, which is true for most of the Bible; "These don't apply to me," not until they impact your life.

For years, every cent I made on payday had somewhere that it MUST go; nothing really "belonged" to me. I would work hard for a week to get this paycheck. When I got home I started giving this creditor his share, then another, and another. Of course, in the end, there was nothing left. So, what do you do till next payday? You borrow to make it to next payday, - a terrible cycle!

One day, the Lord got my attention. I said, "Lord if you will tell me who NOT to pay so I can tithe, I will commit to tithing!" Within a month or two, by rearranging some debt and paying off some, I had "exactly" the amount of my tithe "extra" that month. I couldn't believe it. No more, no less, exactly that amount. I didn't need a building to fall on me. I started tithing. The funny thing is I was right back to NO EXTRA MONEY, I continued to tithe. In a couple of months, I had the same amount of my tithe "EXTRA". Spending money, I didn't know what to do. I am a believer now; it will work for you too! It is a promise from God.

When you meditate on verse 7 you will realize the ancient words of Solomon are so true today. We are "slaves" to our creditors. They have priority to the money we work hard for each week. After them, you come first. That is sad! Take a minute. Dream a little. What if, every penny you brought home, aside from the Lord's, belonged to you? To do with as you see fit. It would be like winning the lottery, we won't go there!

Need I remind you of God's promise?

*"Bring all the tithes into the storehouse, that there may be food in My house, **and try me now in this,**" says the Lord of hosts, If I will not open for you the windows of heaven and pour out for you such a blessing that there will not be room enough to receive it.* (Malachi 3:10)

86. Name one of the four Major Prophets in the Old Testament.
    a. Joel   b. Isaiah   c. Joshua   d. Zechariah

He who has a generous eye will be blessed, for he gives of his bread to the poor. Cast out the scoffer, and contention will leave; yes, strife and reproach will cease. (Proverbs 22:9-10)

One of the more interesting chapters in the Sermon on the Mount (Matthew 5-7) right in the heart of this awesome sermon in chapter 6; Jesus gives three areas with this promise:

"and your Father who sees in secret will Himself reward you openly." (Matthew 6:4b)

Three areas, Jesus makes this promise: giving, praying and fasting. Look at the "promise" again. When we do these things in "secret," God knows our heart. By faith in secret, we give, pray and fast and God promises to reward us openly.

Have you ever made fun of someone for doing something you have never tried yourself? That is the "scoffer." They will say it doesn't work. They will laugh at your testimony, "That's fine for you" they say. "It won't work for me", - Really? Have you tried it? - Of course not.

Many outside of God's family scoff at the Christian walk. I told someone once that my wife and I have been saved. We are in the Baptist church. "I couldn't punish myself that much" was their response. Is that how the world looks at Christians? - Because they are on the "outside" looking in. They see what they want to see.

Until you have given your heart to Christ, asked Jesus to come into your heart and save you; you can't possibly know what it is like on THIS side. There are the "scoffers", they make fun or ridicule those who know better. That is where faith comes in. I must share these verses:

And Thomas answered and said to Him, "My Lord and my God." Jesus said to him, "Thomas, because you have seen Me, you have believed. Blessed are those who have not seen and yet have believed." (John 20:28-29)

> He who loves purity of heart and has grace on his lips.
> the king will be his friend. The eyes of the Lord preserve
> knowledge, and He overthrows the words of the faithless.
> (Proverbs 22:11-12)

Do you ever wonder why God didn't "preserve" the original Ten Commandments, or the five books of Moses, the writings of Paul, etc.? Let me share some verses that might help you understand:

Then the Lord said to Moses, "Make a fiery serpent, and set it on a pole; and it shall be that everyone who is bitten, when he looks at it shall live. (Numbers 21:8)

Israel was "complaining again", God didn't provide enough, etc. So, God brought a plague of fiery serpents on the people as punishment. Again, they came crawling to Moses for respite; and God tells Moses to make this stick with a bronze serpent on it. When they look on the stick, after being bitten, they will live. Thus, the plague was averted. So, what became of this stick?

Look:

*He (Hezekiah) removed the high places and broke the sacred pillars, cut down the wooden image and broke in pieces the bronze serpent that Moses had made; for until those days the children of Israel burned incense to it, and called it **Nehushtan.**"* (2 Kings 18:4)

You see, they had turned something God created for their healing into an idol. Hezekiah was going through the land destroying all idols bringing a revival to the people of Israel. The people had turned it into an idol.

What do you suppose the Christian community would do if someone discovered the Ark of the Covenant? Every once in a while, we get stories of sightings of Noah's ark in Turkey; they haven't found it yet. Thank heaven!

How easily man can take the things of God and make "idols" of them; if you want to know what God thinks of idols check out Psalms 115 and 135. Any "idols" in your life?

> The lazy man says, "There is a lion outside! I shall be slain in the streets!" The mouth of an immoral woman is a deep pit; he who is abhorred by the Lord will fall there. (Proverbs 22:13-14)

This has always been a problem for me. I guess it is true everywhere. Ten percent of the people do ninety percent of the work. I forget the exact numbers but it is close: the top ten percent of the tax payers pay 75 percent of the taxes. It may be higher than that.

This has always been a problem for me; I guess it is true everywhere. Ten percent of the people do ninety percent of the work. I forget the exact numbers but it is close: the top ten percent of the taxpayers pay 75 percent of the taxes; it may be higher than that.

This "lazy man" is in trouble and looking for someone to bail him out. Meanwhile, the person who needs help will rarely "ask" for help. Isn't that human nature? It is also a "pride" thing.

One of my favorite subjects in school was early American history, the founding of our country. If you study it any length of time you will realize it was "impossible"; farmers fighting against the greatest army of the day. I read some books on Columbus' journey here from England, the perils and hardships he suffered; Columbus always thought that God directed him to this land.

If you read about our Founding Fathers, all were men of God; different "denominations", sure, but all believers in God. If you want some interesting reading, try if you can find a copy of the Mayflower Compact; that document ruled our country until a constitution could be written. It started with state constitutions, and when we won our freedom from England, we wrote a national constitution.

From the very beginning, the odds were against us. It was the determination to be free that spurred godly men to rise up. Where are those godly men today? Do you remember our churches, the Sunday after September 11? They were full; it didn't take long to drift back to "normal".

I have been praying for a revival in our country. The revivals of Moody, Whitfield, even Billy Graham; godly men who stirred our country with the truth of God's word. Have you ever listened to a Billy Graham sermon? It is so simple, but it is the Word of God! How about you? Where does God fit into your busy life?

Are you "afraid" of what is outside? Why? If you're a child of God, you can trust God for security, 1 Samuel 16.

87. In what Old Testament book is found "The Valley of Dry Bones"?
　　　a. Ezekiel　　　b. Hezekiah　　　c. Jeremiah　　　d. Joel

> Foolishness is bound up in the heart of a child; the rod of correction will drive it far from him. He who oppresses the poor to increase his riches, and he who gives to the rich, will surely come to poverty. (Proverbs 22:15-16)

Okay, before you get all upset about this "rod" business, let me remind you of this verse:

*And you have forgotten the exhortation which speaks to you as to sons: "My son, do not despise the chastening of the Lord, nor be discouraged when you are rebuked by Him; for whom the Lord **loves** He chastens, and scourges every son whom He receives."* (Hebrews 12:5-6)

Granted, and I am not overlooking the obvious, this does not imply or condone "abuse!", - interesting that the quotes in Hebrews are also from Proverbs 3:11-12.

Parents think about this process, the greatest responsibility we have as parents is to "instruct" our children; from the day of their birth, we are to train, instruct, encourage, and if need be chastised (I like the word better than "spank") our children. We are their primary teachers until they venture out into this world, even superseding that of the school teacher. It is OUR responsibility. If that entails correction, so be it.

Don't overlook that word I put in bold type. We do all this teaching and correcting out of, and because, we love our children. The same way our heavenly Father loves us, and sometimes must correct us because He loves us.

Think about the alternative. If there were no love, children would grow up, selfish, greedy, lying, and ungrateful. Without the loving guidance of godly parents, you cannot imagine the type of children who will be your "offspring!"

The same is true as a child of God; without God's hand and direction in our life, we would not even know there was a God in heaven that loves us and cares about the path we are taking. He would not care if we fall into sin, and death, eternally separated from God.

    Lonny E. Young

September 18   261-104   Proverbs 22

> Incline your ear and hear the words of the wise, apply your heart to my knowledge; for it is a pleasant thing if you keep them within you; let them all be fixed upon your lips. (Proverbs 22:17-18)

I think it is fascinating that Solomon presents the destination of all of this knowledge as the heart. You would think he would suggest it be the mind; his "seat" of knowledge is the heart, not the brain. What do you think?

How many "decisions" we make are based on our heart, instead of our head? Let's take the one we will be spending the rest of our life with, - head or heart? Aside from the obvious, we will determine where we spend eternity based on our heart, not our head:

*If you confess with your mouth the Lord Jesus and believe **in your heart** that God raised Him from the dead, you will be saved. For with the **heart** one believes unto righteousness, and with the mouth confession is made unto salvation.* (Romans 10:9-10)

Cool. Look how Solomon words this: *apply your heart to my knowledge,* - That is interesting. You have the "facts" but if your heart is "not in it", you will doubt. Salvation is not "logical"; it is a 'FREE' gift from God. God has done everything necessary to restore your relationship with the holy God. All you must do is believe and accept that gift, BUT, that is against our nature. We MUST reciprocate in some way. We just cannot accept something for free.

It was NEVER free. It cost God the life of his only Son (John 3:16); that is why it is illogical. If you try to "reason" it out, it won't work. You simply accept God's gift by faith and trust God for eternity.

I mentioned this before; let me ask you this question: "Are you willing to bet eternity in Hades that what I am telling you what the Bible tells you, might be wrong"? - That is what you are doing. When you stand before God and say, "Okay, God I believe now", it is TOO late! God will say, "You had your chance on earth. You rejected My Son then, I reject you now." - Is that what you want to hear? But then, this may all be a myth, are you willing to take that chance?

> So that your trust may be in the Lord; I have instructed you today, even you. Have I not written to you, excellent things of counsels and knowledge? That I may make you know the certainty of the words of truth, that you may answer words of truth to those who send you. (Proverbs 22:19-21)

Someone commented on our Sunday School Class, "Why didn't God give us more details?" If God had written everything we wanted to know, there is no way we could carry that book; God gave us just enough to bring us to His throne in repentance and salvation.

God revealed the "judgment" side of His character, the "obedience" side throughout the Old Testament. The Ten Commandments, the book of Judges, the life of David, the numerous prophets, all pointing to salvation through the sacrifice of a blood offering; even the Old Testament prophets chastised Israel for "idol worship", all pointing to the New Testament.

In the New Testament, God came to visit, to show a different side of His character, - the loving, caring, and compassionate side. The religious leaders had taken God's Old Testament commands and had stretched them so far beyond God's plan. God also had a "sacrifice" problem. They had come to be meaningless. God needed to "satisfy" His requirements once and for ALL.

The Bible and teaching the Bible has always been my passion, from the night, I was saved I have had a hunger for God's Word. It started as a quest for knowledge, the more I read, the more I became aware of God, personally; I think that is why Jeremiah 29:11-13 means so much to me. It is a perfect picture of the Old Testament God's goal in the New Testament Christ Jesus. "*When you seek Me.*" That has always been God's goal.

That's why I wanted to focus on these Proverbs; they "interrupt" the storyline. It is a collection of "one-liners" if you will. They can be difficult to follow for that reason. It is full of basic truths that God wants to incorporate into our daily lives, - our thinking process. It is like a bottle of vitamins, they must be taken regularly and consistently to be effective. I hope this devotion will encourage you to do just that.

88. What prophet was swallowed by a great fish?
    a. Job   b. Peter   c. Jonah   d. Jacob

> Do not rob the poor because he is poor, nor oppress the afflicted at the gate; for the Lord will plead their cause, and plunder the soul of those who plunder them. (Proverbs 22:22-23)

I love the picture of David going to face Goliath; (1 Samuel 17) King Saul had offered David his armor to wear. It was clumsy, awkward, hard to maneuver, etc. David discarded it in favor of his slingshot, something he was familiar with, but David had something else in his arsenal.

"Then all this assembly shall know that the Lord does not save with sword or spear; **for the battle is the Lord's***; and He will give you into our hands."* (1 Samuel 17:47).

I think that is what Solomon is talking about in Proverbs. When we try to rely on our own strength, wisdom, expertise, we will fail. As a child of God, we have a resource far beyond the "world's" knowledge. God will watch over and supply His children with whatever is necessary to accomplish God's will and purpose. I think, too often, we forget whose child we are.

I love these verses:

For you did not receive the spirit of bondage again to fear, but you received the Spirit of adoption by whom we cry out, "Abba, Father." The Spirit Himself bears witness with our spirit that we are **children of God***.* (Romans 8:15-16)

Feeling "afflicted" lately? -Remember whose child you are. God has a plan (Jeremiah 29:11). Are you walking with God? If you're out of God's will, walking your own path, don't expect God's help. God is waiting, right where you left Him. If He is not walking with you or you with Him, how can you expect His help?

Many times as parents we need to allow our children to travel their own path, to teach them the folly of not walking with God. It is a tough lesson. The only way for them to learn is to allow them this "path" and hope they will return soon.

> Make no friendship with an angry man, and with a furious man do not go, lest you learn his ways and set a snare for your soul. (Proverbs 22:24-25)

I have noticed this concept "profoundly," Christians tend to hang around with Christians. We just naturally gravitate together. I have heard it said, if a Christian walks into a room full of people, they, very quickly, will find other Christians. There is a verse in 2 Corinthians that warns against this very thing Solomon is talking about:

Do not be unequally yoked together with unbelievers. For what fellowship has righteousness with lawlessness? And what communion has light with darkness? (2 Corinthians 6:14)

We think that is a warning against marrying an unbeliever, so it is, it is also a warning against any "partnership" with unbelievers; their priorities, their goals, and many times their methods are contrary to ours.

There is a great scene in the movie "Courageous". The boss calls an employee in and promises him a raise if he will be complicit in "cooking" the numbers. He goes home, talks with his wife. They really could use the raise. He decides to be honest. He can't accept the job. Then his boss gives him the job because it was a "test" of his honesty. I love the comment by the boss as the employee was leaving, "You are the sixth person we asked, we were beginning to lose hope."

I love the contrast in 2 Corinthians: *light versus darkness*. That is perfect. The problem is that most of the time when given the choice, we trend to the darkness. That is why the warning against joining with darkness. If anyone should know, Solomon should:

And he had seven hundred wives, princesses, and three hundred concubines; and his wives turned away his heart. (1 Kings 11:3)

Solomon, knowing all that God had done for him, was still slowly turned away from God to idols, - it can happen to you.

      Lonny E. Young

> When you sit down to eat with a ruler, consider carefully what
> is before you; and put a knife to your throat if you are a man
> given to appetite. (Proverbs 23:1-2)

For a few years, I had the opportunity to be a "secretary" for local disc jockey. At one point, we were invited to his home for dinner. It was such an awesome experience. I had to keep telling myself, "He is no different than I am." He is a friend, not the "king". We can be so influenced by "titles" than the actual person.

I think the point Solomon is making is not to be "misled" by the appearance, by the wealth, the power, the image, and do something you will regret. We can be "blinded" by power, opulence, majesty, if you will, and forget who we are, or our morals and conscience. How many times are we led to do something against our better judgment, because of the way it is presented or WHO is presenting it?

We come back to an argument I stressed earlier, - On what do you determine your decisions? What influences the path you take? You come to a fork in the road. The "trick" play is "You need to decide now!" That always gets us. If you must decide now, say a quick prayer, and go with God. Your Spirit will guide you if you listen. Of course, if you're lost, you only have your conscience, - that is only as good as the foundation it is built on.

Solomon is warning about being "tricked" by the opulence. Ask yourself what the "motive' might be. Why am I here, for what purpose? One precept I learned early on was not to "ask" for positions, or opportunities, etc. I don't trust my "flesh". If God wants me to do something He will lay it on someone else's heart to ask me. Maybe that is wrong but I don't trust my "pride" or the desire of the "flesh" to rely on something I "want". I was fooled before and it cost me.

The "world" is always trying to bring God's people "inline" with its priorities, its values, and its goals. The question we need to ask, apart from the influence of the "world", what does God want? What is His plan for me, not MY plan but God's plan?

It is about focus. Is our focus to be a servant of God or a servant of this world? The world will pass away, but God is eternal.

89. Which of the 66 books in the Bible is the shortest?
    a. Jude   b. Nahum   c. 2 John   d. 3 John

Do not overwork to be rich; because of your own understanding, cease! Will you set your eyes on that which is not? For riches certainly make themselves wings; they fly away like an eagle toward heaven. (Proverbs 23: 4-5)

Look at these words from Haggai:

Now therefore, thus says the Lord of hosts: **Consider your ways:**

"You have sown much, and bring in little; you eat, but do not have enough; you drink, but are not filled with drink; you clothe yourselves, but no one is warm; and he who earns wages, earns wages to put into a bag with holes." Thus, says the Lord of hosts: **"Consider your ways!"** (Haggai 1:5-7)

Let me put it this way: Consider your priorities. Like the Lord points out above, "How much is enough?" Isn't it interesting that the more you have the more you want? Again, how much is enough?

"Not that I speak in regard to need, **for I have learned in whatever state I am, to be content.** (Philippians 4:11)

Did you notice a keyword there? "Learned", - it is a "learned" state of mind. We just had a winner in the largest lottery ever, 1.6 billion I believe, after taxes, maybe 800 million. Everyone "dreams" of having all the money they need. Again, "How much is enough?" When can you say, "I have enough, I don't need any more"?

Let me refresh your memory of Adam and Eve. They had "everything" they could want. God said He would supply their every need. What did they do? They picked the one thing God said they couldn't have.

We keep talking about money. Money isn't the point, is it? We think we can buy "peace," if we have enough money. It doesn't work that way. Money buys just the opposite! Where do you get this "priceless" peace? - An intimate fellowship with your heavenly Father. When you are walking with God, you have the peace that passes all understanding.

Do not eat the bread of a miser, nor desire his delicacies; for
as he thinks in his heart, so is he. "Eat and drink" he says to
you, but his heart is not with you. (Proverbs 23:6-7)

We were talking yesterday about enough money to bring peace. There was a guy in the New Testament who thought this:

And I will say to my soul, "Soul, you have many goods laid up for many years; take your ease; eat, drink, and be merry." But the Lord said to him, "Fool! This night your soul will be required of you; then who's will those things be which, you have provided?" So is he who lays up treasure for himself, and is not rich toward God. (Luke 12:19-21)

He thought he had it all planned out. Such is life. Does this mean we should not "plan" for the future? - Of course not! That would not be good stewardship, BUT, they must be according to God's plans. In there lies the "peace" we talked about yesterday. If your "faith" is in your finances you have failed to understand God's plan and purpose for your life.

Before I became a Christian, I used to do the Reader's Digest and the Publisher's Clearing House contests. One day I realized, "If God wanted me to be rich He would provide. He knew I couldn't handle that money, it could not bring peace." Instead, God leads me to His Word and I have been so blessed ever since.

Money does NOT bring peace, quite the opposite. We think it would, "no more worries", right? Not hardly. True peace, as I said before, comes from an intimate relationship with Jesus Christ, walking with God daily, learning His plan for your life, and following it. Believe me, I know.

When you can go to bed at night and know without a doubt you are where God wants you to be, doing what He wants you to do, that is genuine peace, - the peace that passes all understanding (Philippians 4:7). Where is peace? Check out John 16:33 also, that is where a real peace comes from.

> Do not speak in the hearing of a fool, for he will despise the wisdom of your words. Do not remove the ancient landmark, nor enter the fields of the fatherless. (Proverbs 23:9-10)

Has this ever happened to you? You give counsel, you speak what is on your heart, well-meaning, from the heart, and you are condemned for speaking the truth. It has happened to me several times, even in a sermon. I spoke to someone afterward, "It is the truth, but you're not supposed to say it." It has caused me, more and more, just to keep my mouth shut, especially today with all the "Political Correctness."

Speaking the truth is not accepted anymore, just like speaking of sin from the pulpit. It is not acceptable!

The interesting problem here with Solomon's words. How do you know a "fool" is listening? I guess we must assume all those around us are fools. The easiest way is to just keep your mouth shut. I gave my insights the other day to someone who "asked" for my input; it seemed to offend him. People don't want the truth, they want strokes today.

I wonder what Solomon is talking about "ancient landmarks"? I think about the time Joshua and Israel finally entered the Promised Land (Joshua 4).

"Take for yourselves twelve men from the people, one man from every tribe, and command them, saying 'Take for yourselves twelve stones from here, out of the midst of the Jordan, from the place where the priests' feet stood firm. You shall carry them over with you and leave them in the lodging place where you lodge tonight.'" (Joshua 4:3)

It was to be a "memorial" to the people of what God had done by parting the river so they could cross (Joshua 4:6-7).

Do you have any "mementos" of what God has done in your life? Any "landmarks" of how and when God changed your life? How about just a "reminder" of what God has done for you? Simple things, yes, but very necessary.

How long did it take Israel to forget what God had done for them after He freed them from Egyptian bondage? How quickly they were willing to return to Egypt.

90. In which book of the Bible is the shortest verse found?
    a. Exodus   b. John   c. Judges   d. 2 Chronicles

  Lonny E. Young

September 26   269-96   Proverbs 23

> For their Redeemer is mighty; He will plead their cause,
> against you. Apply your heart to instruction, and your ears
> to words of knowledge. (Proverbs 23:11-12)

Identical twins can go through college, each with the same classes, even seated under the same teachers in the same classes; each will come out with two totally different perspectives and truths. Isn't that strange? - No, God created each of us differently. We each receive "knowledge" differently, we each process it differently. The funny thing is that the WORD never changes; it is how we process and "apply" it that makes it different.

When I say the word "Redeemer" what comes to your mind? Since it is capitalized it is referring to Jesus. That is simple. Jesus took our place on the cross, died FOR US, for our sins, that we may have access to the presence of God; He Redeemed our sin payment for us.

In the Old Testament, God provided a sacrifice, in bulls and goats, to help us understand that a payment was required for our sin. They soon became "ritualistic," and had no meaning to His people. So, God sent His Son Jesus to replace what had become these "meaningless" sacrifices, with the blood of His Own Son.

The sad part is it has become just as the Old Testament, - meaningless. Until we fully grasp what God was willing to do, to allow us to enter His holy presence, we will continue to miss out on a very special intimate relationship that God desires for His children.

As a child of God, Jesus is today, standing before God the Father pleading our cause. Every time we sin, we make a mistake, Jesus as our Advocate (Lawyer) (1 John 2:1) is standing before God, by His authority, pleading for mercy on our behalf. I like the odds of our chances since our Advocate is the Judges' Son, and He is also the one who purchased that mercy from God the Father.

I think it is interesting that Solomon says, "Apply" this knowledge. It is our choice whether we listen and obey; we can have all the knowledge we need. - Remember the twins earlier? It is what we do with that knowledge, that wisdom, especially coming from the very Word of God. Read His Word, - apply it, learn it, and use it!

> Do not withhold correction from a child, for if you beat him with a rod, he will not die. You shall beat him with a rod, and deliver his soul from Hades. (Proverbs 23:13-14)

Okay, the Bible condones abuse. - Seriously? One of the key principles of interpretation is to consider the culture. In the Old Testament times, it was different. Let me caution the "literalists" crowd. I have had my disagreements with them. I guess it is like most if it suits your beliefs you believe it if not, it doesn't apply. It is called "context".

Okay, answer this, how do you "train a child in the way he should go" (Proverbs 22:6)? - There must be a correction! Granted, we have moved past a "rod" type of correction. I have no problem with pain administered to the set of your pants. Nothing else is necessary. You must make your point. Take my word for it; most of the time "stern words" have little or no effect.

I can hear the critics now. Just look at our society today, there is little or no respect for authority. It begins in the home. If there is no respect for the parent's authority, why should there be any respect for authorities outside the home? Again, I, in no way advocate "abuse" that is what rear-end is for, that is why there is so much padding there!

How important is "correction"? Do you see what Solomon says? It will "deliver his soul from Hades!" A child must be corrected early on. The longer you wait the harder the correction. If God must do the correction it will not be pretty. How does God feel about "correction?"

Look at these verses in Proverbs:

*My son, do not despise the chastening of the Lord, nor detest His correction; **for whom the Lord loves he corrects**, just as a father the son in whom he delights.* (Proverbs 3:11-12)

I usually quote the same verses in the New Testament in Hebrews 12:5-6. The writer of Hebrews simply quotes Proverbs. Don't miss this important fact that I noted in BOLD type. We and God correct out of love. - Never forget that!

My son, if your heart is wise, my heart will rejoice—indeed, I myself. Yes, my inmost being will rejoice when your lips speak right things. (Proverbs 23:15-16)

I am sorry; I keep being overwhelmed at Solomon's continual reference to the heart being the source of our speaking. Most, I'm sure, think our mouth is connected to our brain. Not according to Solomon and thus God, through His Holy Spirit. The words we speak spring from our heart. One of my favorite quotes is: "Consider the source!"

Let's try these verses first. The words of Jesus:

*Do you not understand that whatever enters the mouth goes into the stomach and is eliminated? But those things which proceed out of the mouth **come from the heart**, and they defile a man.* (Matthew 15:17)

Here is my favorite from the Old Testament:

For the Lord does not see as man sees; for man looks at the outward appearance, but the Lord looks at the heart. (1 Samuel 16:7b)

All through the Bible, you find God is much more interested in what is in our heart, than our head. Solomon talks a lot about wisdom and knowledge, but if it is not "controlled by the heart" it is simply a collection of facts. It is the heart that determines how those "tools" are put to use. I must share one more verse to prove my point:

*If you confess with your mouth the Lord Jesus and believe in your **heart** that God raised Him from the dead, you will be saved. For with the **heart** one believes unto righteousness, and with the mouth confession is made unto salvation.* (Romans 10:9-10)

How important is the heart? Someone once said that many people will miss heaven by eighteen inches: the distance between the heart and the head. Think about this in your life.

91. In which Old Testament book do we find the villain, Haman?
    a. Ruth   b. Joel   c. Amos   d. Esther

> Do not let your heart envy sinners, but be zealous for the fear
> of the Lord all the day. For surely there is a hereafter, and
> your hope will not be cut off. (Proverbs 23:17-18)

What does HOPE mean to you? I think one of the greatest illustrations of this concept, believe it or not, to me, was demonstrated in the movie, "Hunger Games." At one point, the President asked his aide, "Why do we have a winner? We could just gather twenty-four people and execute them and be done with it. Why do we have a winner?" The aide didn't know. The President responded, "To give them hope. Without hope you have nothing."

What is your "hope" in? There are so many things we can hope in. How many people put their "hope" in winning last week's "Power Ball"? How about the Stock Market? It has been going crazy this month. Up 600, down 300, up 200, if your future, or your hope, is tied up in the Market you must be going crazy. How about Social Security? I am on Social Security. How much "hope" do you have there? I have another pension that is running out of money soon. They have warned us it could stop.

My "hope" is in a God who loves me and will see to my every need. He has promised never to leave me or forsake me (Hebrews 13:5). My assurance of this "hope" is the presence of God's Holy Spirit within me, the promise of His Word in the Bible. If I may, I would like to ask a question I have posed before.

Are you willing to **bet** eternity in Hades, that the Bible may not be true? Think about this bet now. If you refuse the gift of salvation, offered to you in the Bible by faith in Jesus Christ, you are betting the words of this book are not true.

When you stand before God, which you will one day, and you proclaim, "It is true okay I accept your gift of Jesus." Friend, it is too late. God made the rules; if you refuse to believe in this life, it will be too late in the next!

So, what or who is your "hope" in? Maybe you think because your parents were saved, you are too. That doesn't work like that either. You are your only "hope". It is your decision!

September 30   273-92   Proverbs 23

> Hear, my son, and be wise; and guide your heart in the way. Do not mix with winebibbers, or with gluttonous eaters of meat; for the drunkard and the glutton will come to poverty, and drowsiness will clothe a man with rags. (Proverbs 23:19-21)

I would love to talk about the heart some more, but, like most preachers, I won't ignore the rest of these verses.

We have a guy in our church who refuses to eat pork. He gets kidded sometimes. Health-wise he is probably right. I remember, not too many years ago, that coffee was a nail in your coffin; eggs would lead to heart attacks, etc. There always seems to be something that will lead to an early grave. We are all going to die someday; they haven't come up with a cure for that.

Speaking of which, - Did you know that we will ALL live forever? That is a promise from God, - Eternal life. The question we must decide, during our brief visit on this planet is, "Where are we going to spend that eternity?" Whether we live five years or one hundred five, the choice must be made before we leave. We talked about this yesterday.

I think the point that Solomon is trying to make if you look at his wording, is moderation. Both of the words he uses, Winebibber and Glutton refer to overuse, do they not? Both give the picture of the excess of wine and food. If you want a promise from God, look at a vision Peter had on the roof of a Gentile's house:

And a voice spoke to him again the second time, "What God has cleansed you must not call common." This was done **three** *times. And the object was taken up into heaven again.* (Acts 10:15)

God created it, God blessed it, and we are free to eat it. Just remember this critical word "moderation". That would be where that word "glutton" comes in. You can be a "glutton" for many things. It doesn't have to be food, - things, clothes, shoes, money, cars, house; anything can be taken to excess. The only thing we cannot be a glutton about is our prayer life and our walk with God. Our relationship with God can never be "gluttonous!" Think about that a minute.

> Listen to your father who begot you, and do not despise your mother when she is old. Buy the truth, and do not sell it, also wisdom and instruction and understanding. (Proverbs 23:22-23)

I never was one for "study"; I had a hard time in high school. I must read something several times to absorb the content. I guess that is why I enjoy reading my Bible over and over. If you have spent any significant time reading your Bible, you realize the "miracle" of the Bible.

You can read, let's say, the gospel of John five times. Each time you read it you will find something new. You may read the same passage five times and God's Holy Spirit will reveal something new each time; I can never get tired of reading.

Not just your own private reading but sermons, there is the Sunday morning worship message. The Sunday school class lesson, the Sunday night sermon, and finally the Wednesday night prayer lesson, - teaching, listening, growing in the knowledge and wisdom of the Bible. It is awesome! A kid in a candy store!

Contrary to Mr. Solomon's words above "It is all free!" When you begin to establish a "foundation" of the truth of the Bible you will be amazed at how much it will impact your life. Your thought patterns will change. You will be more aware of the working of God's Spirit in your life. You will make better decisions.

I think the thing that has slowly impacted my life more than anything else is the "peace" that comes from a closer walk with God. You finally realize you don't have to do it all. You begin to see God at work around you, noticing what He is doing in those around you, excited to watch His working out this plan that is changing your life as well.

This is a commercial for reading your Bible, and it is free! Do you have a Bible? Do you know the Author? Let me tell you right now unless you know the Author, it will make no sense. When you open your heart and receive Jesus as your Savior you also receive the Holy Spirit, the third person of the Trinity. He will help you in so many ways to understand God's word and His working in your life.

92. How many plagues were brought upon Egypt by God, through Moses?
    a. 9   b. 5   c. 7   d. 10

                    Lonny E. Young

> The father of the righteous will greatly rejoice, and he who begets a wise child will delight in him. Let your father and your mother be glad, and let her who bore you rejoice. (Proverbs 23:24-25)

Interesting wisdom, - Do you think your children are "born" smart? They were born with the capacity of course; it is the parents that begin instilling in them the godly wisdom that will point them to God later on.

Here is a verse that comes to mind:

*"And these words which I command you today shall be in your **heart**. You shall teach them diligently to your children, and shall talk of them when you sit in your house, when you walk by the way, when you lie down, and when you rise up. You shall bind them as a sign on your hand, and they shall be as frontlets between your eyes. You shall write them on the doorposts of your house and on your gates.* (Deuteronomy 6:6-9)

That is pretty clear, is it not? It is our responsibility as parents to pass down to our children the words of God; to instruct them, encourage them, and lead them. But, there is one thing a parent cannot do, - save their children. That must be done by the child. You can show them the truth but THEY must make that decision for themselves. You can "point" them to God, but it is their choice that they will follow, who they will believe.

It can be very frustrating at times. You want your children to someday join you in heaven, but, again, it must be their choice. One thing we can do is be a testimony to them. You can see that in the Deuteronomy passage; you display God's word in your home, they see you praying, trusting God, that will go a long way to bringing them to the Lord.

Father, I pray for all the parents who are reading this passage, I pray that you will lay on their hearts the need for their children to walk in Your ways, to come to a personal relationship with Jesus Christ. Encourage them; give them the words to speak. I pray that one day their whole family will be united together in heaven. In Jesus' name.

> My son, give me your heart, and let your eyes observe my ways. For a harlot is a deep pit, and a seductress is a narrow well. She also lies in wait as for a victim, and increases the unfaithful among men. (Proverbs 23:26-28)

My son, give me your heart. Let me share the proper prospective for those few words:

For as many as are led by the Spirit of God, these are sons of God. For you did not receive the spirit of bondage again to fear, but you received the Spirit of adoption by whom we cry out, ***"Abba, Father."*** *The Spirit Himself bears witness with our spirit that we are children of God.* (Romans 8:14-15)

The spirit of bondage and fear comes from verses 27-28 of Proverbs. That is exactly the picture of not having a bond with your heavenly Father. "A deep pit, a narrow well, victim, unfaithful," -all these words describe that person who is NOT adopted into God's family, there is nothing out there for you but misery.

That is why I love these verses in Romans. It gives us that picture of an intimate (Abba) relationship with our Heavenly Father. When we ask Jesus into our hearts we become children of God by "adoption." Someone once said, in Bible days, adoption was even stronger than a birth relationship; it is a bond that cannot be broken.

Notice these words: *The Spirit Himself bears witness with our spirit* (Romans 8). We have this "special" peace within us that we are now God's children; too many times we are the ones to disrupt this peace. We get angry with God, we sin, God may not answer a prayer the way we think He should, any number of reasons; it is us who break that "peace", NOT the "relationship". We are still His children if we have truly asked Jesus into our hearts. It is the "fellowship" that has been broken.

Just read Jesus' parable of the Prodigal Son in Luke 15:11-24. What a great picture of a restored "fellowship". He is still his son, always was, their relationship is intact. It is their "fellowship" that was broken!

Lonny E. Young

October 4   277-88   Proverbs 24

> Do not be envious of evil men, nor desire to be with them; for their heart devises violence, and their lips talk of troublemaking. (Proverbs 24:1-2)

Ever been in that situation? - You know it just isn't right and you want out. Do you have the courage to walk away? God will give you that courage. You said I shouldn't have been in that situation in the first place. As a "baby" Christian, it is easy to be there. You have not yet "purged" those bad influences. It is funny, after we become a child of God, how our eyes can be opened to something we would not have noticed before.

The closer we grow with God, the more we learn to listen to God's Spirit within us, the easier it is to avoid those situations. It is a "walk" it doesn't happen overnight. The more we allow God to influence our life the greater the blessings.

It is funny, too. The verses that Solomon wrote also help us to not envy the things of the wicked. We become content with the blessings God gives us. We have no "need" for lottery tickets or wealth as such. We can dream, you can't erase that, but, it does not become an obsession, a desire, envious, etc. We acknowledge God's wisdom and God's control in our life.

You will be surprised how your environment, your peers, your priorities change when you become a child of God. Someone once said, "Your want-to's change" yours become God's. You see and hear things around you that you hadn't noticed before. You become more aware of the snares and traps Satan puts out to trick us.

We are in the last quarter of the year, three more months. Summer is over and we are headed into the holiday season. The stress is beginning to build or soon will. You will be tempted to revert to your old ways, your old friends. You must fight those urges. The key is not to get "stressed". Trust God. Let Him take the lead.

First is Halloween this month, then Thanksgiving, and very shortly after that, is Christmas. You have parties, shopping; your life can get turned upside-down. Don't let it. Commit to begin each day with God. Have a "quiet time" with God each morning. Ask God's will and direction.

93. What river was turned to blood by Moses?
    a. Euphrates   b. Gihon   c. Jordan   d. Nile

> Through wisdom a house is built, and by understanding it
> is established; by knowledge the rooms are filled with all
> precious and pleasant riches. (Proverbs 24:3-4)

Isn't that a wonderful picture? - A household in harmony. The problem is that is rarely the case, isn't it? It is a nice thought, a great "picture," but not reality. I like the word used today: "Drama". Everyone has their issues, not collectively, but individually. It is MY needs that are not met. It is my wants that are not addressed. That is not a "home."

Have you ever pondered the difference between a 'house" and a "home"? Maybe we could get a clue from Solomon. Of course, Solomon grew up in a household with at least eight "mothers" (wives of David). I wonder what the "authority" structure was like then. Of course, the same could be said today, as far as "authority structure". I am not talking about husband versus wife; I am talking about the "place" God holds in this house or home. That can make a huge difference in whether it is called a "house" or a "home".

Here is an interesting verse:

Except the Lord builds the house, they labor in vain who build it; unless the Lord guards the city, the watchman stays awake in vain. (Psalm 127:1)

Great chapter to do some meditating on, most of the time I have heard this verse, at least the first part, refer to some new construction at the church but think about it. It can also apply to two people committed to a life together, looking to build a "home" together. If God's not in it, there are struggles and mountains to climb that need not be.

Look over Solomon's words again, - "Wisdom", "Understanding", "Knowledge". And where are these essential "building blocks" found? The Word of God of course, and if I may be so bold, the house of God. An important bond with your neighbors and support for a young couple is found in God's house. The "right" God's house, where the Word of God is preached, taught, and lived!

                    Lonny E. Young

> A wise man is strong, yes, a man of knowledge increases strength; for by wise counsel you will wage your own war, and in a multitude of counselors there is safety. (Proverbs 24:5-6)

I have long been a huge supporter of the local church. Oh, I have had my problems, as everyone has; I have learned some very valuable lessons from my brothers and sisters in the faith, some good, some not so good. If you spend any real-time in a church you begin to pick up that churches' "personality". The critical thing is how much they preach or teach the Word of God.

I think that is what Solomon is talking about here, - Knowledge, the knowledge of the Word of God. Man's wisdom is just that! It is God's wisdom we seek. "I can get all that from reading my Bible", - Really? And how do you know how to "apply" that wisdom?

Our Sunday school teacher will tend to "breeze" through the Bible commentary and get to the "questions" throughout the lesson. Why? They spur conversation, - testimonies, life experiences that illustrate the truth of the Bible lesson. If you do that on any regular basis you will discover just how "relevant" this ancient book really is.

We try to avoid "politics" if possible. Sometimes that is just "impossible" because the Bible is so relevant for today, even in politics!

Who would you put in this category of "wise counsel?" - Friends, peers, co-workers, how about brothers and sisters in the Lord? The fascinating thing about Sunday school is that no two people are on the same "level" of spiritual growth. Most are hungry to learn, those with godly "experience" must share with others the lessons they have learned.

I was in a meeting the other day; we were talking about our older men sharing testimonies with the younger men. One of the men spoke about a testimony I had given on learning the lesson about tithing, my experience. He said it really blessed him. That is what I am talking about. We share our struggles, those who have won victories, share with them how to get a victory, - "A multitude of counselors", that is just part of the ministry of the church.

> Wisdom is too lofty for a fool; he does not open his mouth in the gate. He who plots to do evil will be called a schemer. The devising of foolishness is sin, and the scoffer is an abomination to me. (Proverbs 24:7-9)

Do you have any self-discipline? Do you know what that is?

I love Tetris. I had it on my computer; I would play it for hours. I would go in to do some work on my computer. I would say, "Just a couple of games", three hours later my hand hurt and I got absolutely nothing done. - Solution? I had to delete the game. I could not leave it alone; as much as I love the game I knew my addiction. Do you?

Is there something in your life you "can't do without"? Does it replace things you know you should be doing? Where is it on your "priority list"? Self-discipline? Here is a tougher question: "What is your priority list?" Do you stick with it? Ah! Self-discipline.

There, Solomon goes using that word "abomination" again. You might be "scoffing" at my reference to a "priority list". We all have them. They may not be written down or even consciously followed, but we have them. That is part of this decision-making process. You have choices all the time. Your decision is based on your "priorities," is it not? What are your priorities?

Okay, you wondered when I was going to get to it. Where does God fit on this "priority list"? Here is a tough one. What comes before going to church on Sunday? Stepping on toes, I know. It is a serious question.

If the church was not a "priority" for God why did His Son make it a point to establish it? The whole book of Acts is about the Apostle Paul establishing "churches" in Asia. We will skip over Bible reading and prayer. So many think these exercises can replace the church. "I have my time with God, my quiet time." I guess we don't need the book of Acts? Jesus made such a point of "establishing" His church (Matthew 16), yet we just kind of put it off, like it is no big thing. It is with God!

Priorities, - We make our daily decisions based on our unconscious priority list. Sit down some time. Write out the top five things on your priority list. Where is God on that list? Don't fake it, God knows.

94. In which book of the Bible do we NOT find the word "God"? (King James Version)

    a. Numbers   b. Ruth   c. Esther   d. Joel

          Lonny E. Young

If you faint in the day of adversity, your strength is small.
(Proverbs 24:10)

I love this principle from Dr. Charles Stanley:

Because God is:

Omniscient—All-knowing
        He knows where you are at in this trial.
Omni-present—everywhere
        He is with you IN this trial.
Omnipotent—All-powerful
        He will bring you through this trial.

Is that not awesome? It is also true. There is a small problem. We think we must do It Instead of letting God handle it. Until we take our hands "off the wheel", God cannot or will not act. As long as we are in control, God will not step in.

I don't know who said this, probably Dr. Stanley, - You are either headed into a trial, are in a trial, or just coming out of a trial. That is a good description of life. We face these every day, some worse than others. It is how you "deal" with them demonstrates your faith in God. Is He your "last resort?"

That is what Solomon is talking about in this proverb. *Strength* in the day of adversity is determined by your faith, your faith (trust) in God.

Mark this verse in your Bible:

Then he touched their eyes, saying, "According to your faith let it be to you." (Matthew 9:29)

I love this so much I have the "address" written on my bookmark, I keep a bookmark by each day of Bible reading, reading through the Bible in one year. There is a great schedule in the book entitled THE PATH. It will help you read through the Bible in one year. Just spending time in the Bible every day will help "grow" your faith, to learn to trust God through these daily trials.

> Deliver those who are drawn toward death, and hold back those stumbling to the slaughter. If you say, "Surely, we did not know this," does not He who weighs the hearts consider it? He who keeps your soul, does He not know it? And will He not render to each man according to his deeds? (Proverbs 24:11-12)

Is this the "age-old question?" What about life after death? That is assuming you believe there **is** life after death. I am sure you have seen Hollywood's version of heaven, the afterlife, what happens after you die. How about, "Here Comes, Mr. Jordan"? We all have our "fantasies" of what happens. So, what is the truth?

Do you believe the Bible? Why not? That is the key, isn't it? If you have no "point-of-reference" how do you know what or who to believe? Would you believe a source that has lasted "thousands" of years, through so many attempts to destroy or discredit it, yet it is as powerful now as ever? Would you believe something that has consistently proven its authority in daily living? Understand the "credibility" of this source. You must start there. Let me ask you this; - is there any other authoritative source?

I have asked this question before, it bears repeating: "Are you willing to BET eternity in Hades, that this book (the Bible) might NOT be true?" That is what you are doing.

If we have established some credibility, let me give you this verse:

As it is appointed for men to die once, but after this the judgment. (Hebrews 9:27)

Isn't it interesting that God doesn't tell us a whole lot about heaven? We get a small glimpse in the book of Revelation, but just a peak and that during the Tribulation period.

Here is my favorite:

But as it is written: "Eye has not seen, nor ear heard, nor have entered into the heart of man the things which God has prepared for those who love Him." (1 Corinthians 2:9)

        Lonny E. Young

> My son, eat honey because it is good, and the honeycomb which is sweet to your taste; so shall the knowledge of wisdom be to your soul; if you have found it, there is a prospect, and your hope will not be cut off. (Proverbs 24:13-14)

Wisdom! I ran across these verses last night in our evening worship service, the pastor was teaching on the Holy Spirit:

And my speech and my preaching were not with persuasive words of human wisdom, but in demonstration of the Spirit and of power, that your faith should not be in the wisdom of men but in the power of God. However, we speak wisdom among those who are mature, yet not the wisdom of this age, nor the rulers of this age, who are coming to nothing. But we speak the wisdom of God in a mystery, the wisdom which God ordained before the ages for our glory. (1 Corinthians 2:4-7)

Please read that again, remember when it was written. Paul wrote this in the first century. Isn't it just as applicable today? Is not Satan busy today trying to water down and discredit the power and authority of God's word? It is really simple; Wisdom comes from the Word of God! The more time you spend absorbing God's Word into your life, the more you come to know God personally, and the better off you will be.

Does that mean if you "memorize" the Bible nothing bad will happen? - Of course not, it does mean that when God allows certain things in your life (Job 1 and 2) that you will seek God's purpose in those trials, rather than blaming God (as Job's wife) you will seek God's purpose for those trials.

There are, of course, two types of "wisdom", - The world's wisdom and God's wisdom. Which do you suppose is the best? It is not a trick question. Where do you get God's wisdom? - In His Word, of course. You need a regular, consistent Bible reading plan. If you have never read through the Bible, Genesis to Revelation you are missing out on one of life's greatest blessings. You get to know God more intimately; you find the heart of God!

95. How many books of the Bible did the physician Luke write?
    a. two   b. one   c. three   d. five

> Do not lie in wait, O wicked man, against the dwelling of the
> righteous; do not plunder his resting place; for a righteous
> man may fall seven times and rise again, but the wicked shall
> fall by calamity. (Proverbs 24:15-16)

Indulge me a minute, if you will. From Solomon's wording, we immediately think a house, a dwelling place, if I may let's think of it as the "heart".

How often and how thorough is Satan's attack on our heart? - I'm not talking about heart attack, come on. I am talking Satan attacks where it hurts, - our children, our spouse, our relationship with others. He attacks our heart.

A person's "resting place" is their heart. When they are at peace, especially with God, there is no better place to be. So, of course, Satan will attack our most vulnerable spot, - our heart. Now, of course, if we have Jesus in our heart, Satan won't get to first base. He may throw a curveball once in a while, but if we have a strong fellowship with God, walking with God daily, Satan won't get to first base! (No pun intended).

The righteous man may fall seven times. Of course, we will have our "days," relentless attacks will take its toll. That is where a strong "fellowship" with our heavenly Father is so vital. I use the word "fellowship", meaning we are already saved and thus have a "relationship". I am talking about our daily "walk" with God, maintaining a personal intimate "fellowship" with the God of our salvation.

You see the picture Solomon is painting? - The "wicked" lie in wait to get a foot-hold on the righteous; just waiting for that one lapse in our testimony. A bad word said in anger, a lack of courtesy, some slip up that will be an opening for attack from the wicked. Remember what Solomon said? *A righteous man may fall seven times.* - Most of the time it is the devil sticking his foot in the path, to trip us up. Oh, I forgot the rest of that, *and rise again.* You see, the Lord is always there to pick us up, dust us off, put us back on the right path, walking in God's will and God's way. No matter how many times we fall, God is always there to pick His children up and encourage them.

Don't forget who inhabits that "dwelling place" (heart). The King of Kings and Lord of Lords reside in that dwelling place, or should!

        Lonny E. Young

Do not rejoice when your enemy falls, and do not let your heart be glad when he stumbles; lest the Lord see it, and it displeases Him, and He turn away His wrath from him. (Proverbs 24:17-18)

This reminds me of an interesting verse:

"You have heard that it was said, 'You shall love your neighbors and hate your enemy.' But I say to you, love your enemies, bless those who hate you, and pray for those who spitefully use you and persecute you." (Matthew 5:43-44)

Paul also addresses this concept in Romans:

Beloved, do not avenge yourselves, but rather give place to wrath; for it is written, "Vengeance is Mine, I will repay, "says the Lord. Therefore, "If your enemy is hungry, feed him; if he is thirsty, give him a drink; for is so doing you will heap coals of fire on his head." (Romans 12:19-20).

Paul is quoting from Proverbs 25, - interesting. The point is, "let God handle it." Did you notice this admonition from Solomon? *Do not let your heart be glad when he stumbles.* I wonder, is that possible? It is if Jesus lives there. Jesus ALWAYS had compassion on others. That same compassion should be in our hearts if Jesus is there.

It is sad to say, but my favorite part is "vengeance is mine, I will repay, says the Lord." That means I seek vengeance. We all do at some point. If we can come to the point where we just turn it over to God you will be surprised at the peace you will attain!

It seems I remember doing this once or I saw it in a movie. Anyway, the other person responded, "I know what you're doing, you are heaping coals of fire on me," - interesting they should know that passage.

I'll tell you what the real blessing is and reward when you treat someone the way God wants us to, - It is the look on their face when they realize what you are doing; utter surprise and bewilderment!

> Do not fret because of evildoers, nor be envious of the wicked; for there will be no prospect for the evil man; the lamp of the wicked will be put out. (Proverbs 24:19-20)

What are your buttons? You know, those things that other people push to get you upset, agitated, irritable, confrontational, etc. Those buttons you can't seem to control. The sad part is, once people know what they are they love to "push" them, don't they?

That is what Solomon is talking about. Oh, Christians have them too, especially young Christians. We all must constantly deal with the battle of the "flesh".

Isn't it interesting how much Solomon deals with this? Glance back at how many times Solomon cautions about "fretting", allowing the "wicked" to control our lives. It usually involves envy, doesn't it?

Fretting can be the opposite of "peace". If we have God's peace, living within us, we can defeat this "fretting". It is interesting too when that wicked person realizes that "button" doesn't work anymore, he will quit pushing it. When you allow someone to control your emotions, you are no longer in charge, they are!

Look at these verses in Galatians:

But if you bite and devour one another, beware lest you be consumed by one another! I say then: "Walk in the Spirit, and you shall not fulfill the lust of the flesh. For the flesh lusts against the Spirit, and the Spirit against the flesh; and these are contrary to one another, so that you do not do the things you wish. (Galatians 5:15-17)

When you allow the Holy Spirit to disconnect those "buttons," your adversary will find out they don't work anymore. There is always a battle, as Paul points out, going on in our soul; - the battle of the "flesh" versus the "Spirit", and the victory goes to the one you allow to have control. Who you yield to, or listen to? - It is your choice.

Does God have control, or your desires, or, as Solomon says, the wicked? It takes practice, it doesn't happen overnight; the more "victories" you have the easier it becomes.

96. How many people in the Bible reached heaven "without" dying?
     a. One   b. two   c. three   d. none

     Lonny E. Young

> My son, fear the Lord and the king; do not associate with those given to change; for their calamity will rise suddenly, and who knows the ruin those two can bring? (Proverbs 24:21-22)

There is calamity in change; we all hate change. It depends on the type of change, but sometimes it is good to get outside our "comfort zone." It depends on the "change". Satan loves to disrupt our lives, keep us in confusion, disoriented, etc.

Here are a couple of verses in 1 Corinthians:

For God is not the author of confusion but of peace, as in all the churches of the saints. Let all things be done decently and in order. (1 Corinthians 14:33, 40)

If there is chaos in your life it is not from God. You have taken your eyes off God, and focused on the world, much like Peter did when he trusted God (Jesus) enough to step out of the boat:

So, he said, "Come." And when Peter had come out of the boat, he walked on the water to go to Jesus. But when he saw that the wind was boisterous, he was afraid; and beginning to sink he cried out, saying, "Lord, save me!" And immediately Jesus stretched out His hand, and said to him, "O you of little faith, why did you doubt?" (Matthew 14:29-31)

This story always fascinates me, both for the circumstances and the lesson here. Just to have the faith to step out of that boat, Peter's "comfort zone," and trust Jesus is amazing to me. Then Peter looks around at the world around him. Isn't that the way we are?

When I took the pastor's position in Freeman, I was willing to step out of my "comfort zone." I saw God do some amazing things, but I begin to look at my home church, I took my eyes off Jesus. I made a bad mistake.

If God has led you to take a step of faith, keep your eyes on Jesus, continue to be obedient to HIS calling, trust God for the results!

> I went by the field of the lazy man, and by the vineyard of the man devoid of understanding; and there it was, all overgrown with thorns; its surface covered with nettles; its stone wall was broken down. (Proverbs 24:30-31)

Have you noticed? Life takes work, through the Proverbs Solomon contrasts the "diligent" with the lazy; those who sit around and wait for things to happen. Maybe they think that is what heaven will be like. Would you say that the Garden of Eden would be as close to heaven on earth?

Let's take a look:

*Then the Lord God took the man and put him in the garden of Eden to **tend and keep it**. (Genesis 2:15)

This was before he created Eve. God created men and women for a purpose. Do you know what your purpose is? I have heard some say that God created us to have fellowship with Him. Nice thought. I prefer this reason: God created mankind to "glorify" God! God has millions of angels if He wants "fellowship". We were created to "glorify our Creator." Of course, God wants us to "fellowship" with Him, - that must be our choice. His "purpose" was to glorify Him.

We glorify God by being and doing what He created us to do. Our testimony on this earth should reflect God, our lifestyle, our work ethic, our accomplishments should glorify God.

When we are lazy as in Solomon's scenario, it does not reflect God's glory. As we saw in the garden, God created us to accomplish something, His will, and purpose. A great example is the picture Paul paints in 1 Corinthians:

I (Paul) planted, Apollos watered, but God gave the increase. (1 Corinthians 3:6)

There was much discussion in the Corinthian church about who "baptized" who. Who gets the "credit", Paul said it doesn't matter, God gives the increase. We all have a job to do, God gets the glory!

   Lonny E. Young

October 16   289-76   Proverbs 25

> It is the glory of God to conceal a matter, but the glory of kings is to search out a matter. As the heavens for height and the earth for depth, so the heart of kings is unsearchable. (Proverbs 25:2-3)

I started my second book, DAVID'S WALK WITH GOD, to discover why David was called in the Bible, "a man after God's own heart" (1 Samuel 13:14, Acts 13:22). I found in my search a better understanding of God's heart, by studying David's life, finding out why God said this of David it revealed God's heart.

I have heard numerous teachers and others put down the Old Testament, they much prefer the study of the New Testament. The New Testament is simply the "application" of the Old Testament truths. If you want to "understand" why Jesus had to die on the cross you simply read the narrative of the Passover in the book of Exodus 12. Don't miss this picture in Genesis 3:21.

Principles that God illustrates in the Old Testament are taught in the New Testament. We get a pencil drawing of godly concepts in the New Testament, but the "color" is filled in in the Old Testament. If you want a "commentary" on today, just read the book of Judges:

In those days, there was no king in Israel; everyone did what was right in his own eyes. (Judges 17:6, 21:25)

If that isn't a "picture" of today's philosophy, I don't know what is. God has been slowly and systematically removed from the marketplace. In Deuteronomy, we are instructed to pass these truths on to the next generations (Deuteronomy 6). We have failed! Each generation seems to get farther and farther from the precepts of God's Word.

I don't mean to be a downer; I just noticed how Solomon worded the beginning of verse 2: *It is the glory of God to conceal a matter.* God works in the heart. I just don't see a lot of evidence in the lives around me. That doesn't mean He is not at work. I pray for my family, my church and my country every day. I would love to see a great "nationwide" revival in our country. The days of George Whitfield and even Billy Graham sweep across our country. Pray!

97. How did God stop the building of the Tower of Babel?
    a. destroyed it b. by rain   c. confused language   d. war

Take away the dross from silver, and it will go to the silversmith for jewelry. Take away the wicked from before the king, and his throne will be established in righteousness. (Proverbs 25:4-5)

Have you heard this illustration used concerning a Christians walk with God? It is almost the same picture that the writer of Hebrews uses:

Therefore, we also, since we are surrounded by so great a cloud of witnesses, **let us lay aside every weight, and the sin which so easily ensnares us,** *and let us run with endurance the race that is set before us.* (Hebrews 12:1)

Those weights that hinder us are the dross that Solomon is talking about; anything that "hinders" your walk (race) with God. God has a plan for your life (Jeremiah 29:11). When we get bogged down with sin, disobedience, we can't run the race that God wants us to run. It is like running with a twenty-pound sack on our back; we tire easily, don't run as fast, and not as effective as we should be.

Just as Solomon says, *"Take away the dross."* I think one the great hindrance to our race is the focus. If you're trying to run a race, and thinking about everything except the race, (will of God) you are missing the commitment to win.

Have you ever melted silver or even a chunk of lead? When it turns to liquid there is a "film" that appears on the top. That is the dross, - interesting that it always floats to the surface when the heat is applied. The same is true with our sin. When God applies some heat (trials) to our lives the sin floats to the top. God has an interesting way of getting our attention.

Interesting comparisons Solomon makes, - Dross in our life, the wicked before a king. Where do you suppose a king's "focus" is with the wicked in front of him? It is the same with us. When our "focus" is away from God, things in our life that ought not to be there, we can't run our race.

Is there any "dross" in your life? Ask God in prayer.

        Lonny E. Young

> Do not exalt yourself in the presence of the king, and do not
> stand in the place of the great; for it is better that he say to
> you, "Come up here," Than that you should be put lower
> in the presence of the prince, whom your eyes have seen.
> (Proverbs 25:6-7)

This, in a way, is the fleece I put out to find out if God called me to ministry; I wrestled for some time with that call, I could not believe that God wanted me to be a minister. One night, on the way to church I prayed, "Lord if you want me to preach, have the pastor ask me to preach soon." When I got to church and headed for my pew, the pastor stopped me and asked if I would preach next Sunday night. Can you imagine the shock that went through my mind? I was stuck.

To this day, I don't know why God chose me. I was a pastor for two and a half years in a small church in Missouri; it was the greatest experience of my life. Then I took my eyes off God and focused on my desires. God put me on the shelf! It became MY will, and not God's.

To this day, I will always remember those 30 months in that loving, fantastic church! I left "humbled," led by God's Spirit, and started thinking I was going to do what I wanted.

David did the same thing, in a way, that night on the balcony when he threw away God's best for a desire of the flesh. He took his eyes off God and turned to his own desires. If God is using you in some fantastic way, always keep your eyes on God. He must be your first priority!

Today, it is interesting, more than once God will give me the text of a message. I will write up my sermon and then wait. It is really scary! Soon, someone will ask me to speak. A men's breakfast, fill-in sermon, somehow that sermon gets "used." God always seems to give me one in advance. That is the application to the verses Solomon is talking about. You let God do the asking, not your ego.

Then, you must have the courage to act on what God has given you. God will always give you the words to speak. He simply wants you to trust Him. Trust His Holy Spirit to lead you in the things to say. There God is leading again. It is not you but God that gets the glory!

> Do not go hastily to court; for what will you do in the end, when your neighbor has put you to shame? Debate your case with your neighbor, and do not disclose the secret to another; lest he who hears it expose your shame, and your reputation be ruined. (Proverbs 25:8-10

Our youngest grandson has gotten involved in the "Youth Court" program. What a fantastic program. It goes a long way in relieving the courts of minor cases. It also teaches our justice system to young people, - Restitution and justice. It is an awesome program.

Did you know that Paul argues that Christians should bring their grievances to the church for resolution? We should not be "judged" by the world.

Jesus addresses the "proper" procedures in Matthew 18:15-17. The less the world influences our lives the better. Why let the "world" pass judgment on God's people. We should be able to handle our own judgments according to God's will.

Even Solomon, in his day, argued against taking things to the courts. Of course, today, that is the first thing we think of. "Instant riches" just sue somebody. If you don't get your way, "sue" somebody. The problem is these frivolous suits degrade and hurt the true causes.

Interesting that God approaches this same scenario. God, of course, is the Judge, always will be. And, we have a "lawyer" and Advocate to argue our case before the Judge:

My little children, these things I write to you, so that you may not sin, And, if anyone sins, we have an Advocate with the Father, Jesus Christ the righteous. (1 John 2:1)

Interesting that John is writing to "Christians" (little children), - Meaning, as Christians, when we sin, as Christians, Jesus is pleading our case before the righteous Judge, God. Do you know what Jesus argument might be? "Father, I bought this child with My own blood on the cross of Calvary. I took his place to pay for his sin. I ask Your forgiveness on his behalf." What a wonderful picture of "grace!"

98. Who saw Jesus first after His resurrection?
    a. His mother   b. Martha   c. Peter   d. Mary Magdalene

A word fitly spoken is like apples of gold in settings of silver. Like an earring of gold and an ornament of fine gold is a wise rebuker to an obedient ear. (Proverbs 25:11-12)

We were talking in our Sunday school class about comfort and encouragement. I mentioned that when I went to visit church members in the hospital that I simply introduced myself, asked how they are, and the patient carries on from there. They don't want my platitudes, clichés, or MY stories. They want to talk. It is a wise minister that allows that.

How do you "receive" rebuke? How do you take criticism? Solomon is addressing this here, - both the "rebuker" and the one being rebuked. It is a delicate time. Where is the Holy Spirit in this scenario? Hopefully, He is both. The rebuker for just the right words to convey the message, the one receiving the rebuke, in receiving it properly.

I had a supervisor once who called me into his office. I had done something wrong (rebellious) and I knew it. He confronted me about it. When I left his office, I stopped, thought a minute, and realized I had just been "rebuked". That is "exactly" what Solomon is talking about, - the proper words, the proper tone, hits the heart every time. It is all in the "spirit" of the rebuke!

It is not unusual for Solomon to dress up the importance of this exchange. The "flowery" words I think add to the importance of this approach. I have heard it is being taught that you begin a session of rebuke with "praise" for the person before you address the problem. I guess that works today, much like Solomon talks about here.

How does God get your attention? He must get your attention, before imparting His "rebuke", does He not? Let's put it this way. How hard does God have to work "to get your attention"? Are you listening, or does God have to try drastic measures?

I have had those moments when after the fact I realize that God had been trying to get my attention. He has usually accomplished His will, and then I look back and see my folly. Then I realize that God was in it all along, I just wasn't paying attention. He accomplishes His purpose despite my ignorance. That is so embarrassing!

> Like the cold of snow in time of harvest is a faithful messenger
> to those who send him, for he refreshes the soul of his
> masters. Whoever falsely boasts of giving is like clouds and
> wind without rain. (Proverbs 25:13-14)

Here is a chapter to make a note of, in the front of your Bible. Matthew 6, part of the Sermon on the Mount, the words of Jesus. Jesus speaks of three things in chapter six. Giving, praying, and fasting.

Look at these verses:

Take heed that you do not do your charitable deeds before men, to be seen by them. Otherwise you have no reward from your Father in heaven. But when you do a charitable deed, do not let your left hand know what your right hand is doing, that your charitable deed may be in secret; and your Father who sees in secret will Himself reward you openly. (Matthew 6:1, 3-4)

The same as Matthew says for praying and fasting; it is the same principle for all three. The thing I like about this concept is the frustration on the receiver's face when they can't figure out where the gift came from.

In Solomon's proverb, he is talking about a person who "falsely" boasts of his giving, totally opposite of what Jesus is talking about. He not only doesn't give but brags about it as if he did. That is dangerous!

We are entering the Fall Season, that first morning with a touch of frost on the ground, that first day of freezing temps. It can be refreshing. I am not a "cold weather" person, neither is my wife. Some look forward to winter. That is the picture here with Solomon's proverb. The "refreshing" that a faithful messenger gives.

Do you send any mail? I am NOT talking about "text" or "e-mail" or the like. I am talking about a real note to someone who has blessed you lately. I received one of those notes once, years ago. I am still in remembrance of that special blessing when I opened Don's note and the encouragement that was in it. I will never forget that.

Lonny E. Young

> By long forbearance a ruler is persuaded, and a gentle
> tongue breaks a bone. Have you found honey? Eat only as
> much as you need, lest you be filled with it and you vomit.
> (Proverbs 25:15-16)

Immediately this story from the Old Testament comes to mind:

Then the Lord said to Moses, "Behold, I will rain bread from heaven for you. And the people shall go out and gather a certain quota every day, that I may test them, whether they will walk in My law or not. (Exodus 15:4)

Does this sound familiar? How about the Garden of Eden? God is always "testing" our obedience. When we are obedient He will bless that obedience. When we are not. . .

So, when they measured it by omers, he who gathered much had nothing left over, and he who gathered little had no lack. Every man had gathered according to each one's need. (Exodus 16:18)

God gave them specific instructions about when and how much to gather; one omer per person per household. And, of course, some took much more than the prescribed amount. Do you see what happened? God also told them to gather two omers per person on the day before the Sabbath. That they would NOT gather on the Sabbath. Guess what?

Now it happened that some of the people went out on the seventh day to gather, but they found none. And the Lord said to Moses, "How long do you refuse to keep My commandments and My laws?" (Exodus 16:27)

Do you think that God does not see our disobedience? - Really? How many tests of God's laws do you ignore, thinking God won't notice or care? God dealt with Israel throughout the Old Testament, dealt with their disobedience. It is no different today.

99. Who spoke to Mary and Elizabeth about them having a child?
    a. Angel Michael   b. Jesus   c. Angel Gabriel   d. Beelsebub

> Seldom set foot in your neighbor's house, lest he become weary of you and hate you. A man who bears false witness against his neighbor is like a club, a sword, and a sharp arrow. (Proverbs 25:17-18)

I know you have heard the caution, "Don't wear out your welcome." I heard someone say once that the good "cue" to let your neighbor know it was time for them to leave is to scoot up on the edge of your seat. That is supposed to let them know it was time to leave. Some, sadly, don't get the message. Why do you suppose Solomon thinks this is important enough to include in his proverbs?

It is called "rude". Have you noticed how this concept has been getting far less important today? People can be rude and think nothing of it. My wife and others think it goes back to upbringing. Of course, it does. If parents don't teach etiquette, who will? - one of the key responsibilities of parents. Of course, if you don't teach your children, they won't be able to teach their children, and so on.

"Please" and "thank you" seem to have been lost in the culture. If you hear anyone say it they are over forty! Seriously, when did this go out of style? Just common courtesy is rare today. Okay, I'll get off my soapbox. Maybe that is why Solomon thought it was important to mention.

Bearing false witness against your neighbor; lying, plain and simple. "False witness" is how the Ten Commandments word it. It is just plain lying! It has become an art form today. I am sorry if I seem to have gotten on my soapbox again. I think it is interesting; it seems Solomon, in his day, was just as frustrated as I seem to be. It is the simple things sometimes that irritate us the most.

When was the last time you took a minute and "observed" your world around you? Taken notice of how people are acting, their priorities, their goals, and plans. How much do you notice about those around you? Maybe you could make a prayer list of those you know who might need an "attitude adjustment". Pray for them. God is a great "attitude adjuster". Maybe you could put your name on that list. How is your "attitude?"

  Lonny E. Young

> Confidence in an unfaithful man in time of trouble is like a
> bad tooth and a foot out of joint. Like one who takes away
> a garment in cold weather, and like vinegar on soda, is one
> who sings songs to a heavy heart. (Proverbs 25:19-20)

Okay, I will be honest; I have no clue what Solomon is talking about here. I tried some "cross-references," still nothing. So, I will speak of what grabbed my eye.

Have you ever really noticed how "music" affects you? I am sure you have some "favorite" songs. Why are they your favorite? Because they "move" you don't they. You could listen to them over and over.

One of my favorite movies is "Secretariat." There is a scene; two actually. First, is when they are washing the horse, they have been thwarted in efforts to raise money and the star walks out to see them washing the horse (Secretariat) and she joins in the washing. The song is on the radio. The second is the race for the "Triple Crown" the horse is running the final leg, the Belmont Stakes. She is rounding the final turn with a huge lead. That just "stirs" my soul to my boots! Like Solomon says, *"sings songs to a weary heart."*

Do you have a song that just lifts you to heaven? Our family has been all about music. When I got married, I liked country and western; my wife loves the "oldies" (50's & 60's). I love them both now. Say what you want about Elvis Presley but he had such a gift from God. I put him in a category with Patsy Cline and Jim Reeves, "velvet voices", truly "gifts from God". Take it from someone who can't carry a tune in a bucket. Music is a gift from God. Your appreciation of music is so important. Ah! A verse comes to mind:

Do not be drunk with wine, in which is dissipation; but be filled with the Spirit, speaking to one another in psalms and hymns and spiritual songs, singing and making melody in your heart to the Lord. (Ephesians 5:18-19)

I love the hymns in our church hymn book. I can't read a note of music but I can follow along with the best of them. I love God's music!

> If your enemy is hungry, give him bread to eat; and if he
> is thirsty, give him water to drink; for so you will heap
> coals of fire on his head, and the Lord will reward you.
> (Proverbs 25:21-22)

We have looked at this verse before, it is quoted in the New Testament (Romans 12:20).

I mentioned yesterday that I didn't understand yesterday's verses. That is a funny thing about the Bible. You can read the same verses three or four or many times, and then one day, God uses it to speak to your heart. Don't despair if something doesn't make sense. In God's time and God's way, He will open that passage to you.

There is no mistaking what these verses mean. Understand God is not just talking about an enemy on the battlefield. God means "anyone" who is mistreating you. Anyone who is "pushing" those buttons we talked about. Upsetting you, getting under your skin, any of the clichés you know.

This is something I have worked hard on, me and God's Spirit. When someone begins pushing those "buttons" I just grin and be nice. I learned this while I was in the military.

This guy I knew was from St. Louis, the year was 1963. St. Louis had a great baseball team then. At the time, we had the Kansas City Athletics. He would raze me all the time, contrasting St. Louis and Kansas City. One day I had enough. At lunch, I began "agreeing" with everything he said. He kept trying to push those buttons. I kept agreeing. He got so mad; he got up and left the dining hall. That is about the best definition of those verses above, as I can think of.

Don't miss the end of verse 22, *the Lord will reward you*. You know, it is a funny thing about that guy. He never teased me again and we became "best friends". God works in mysterious ways.

How do you deal with someone that "pushes your buttons"? Ignore them, usually. Let me offer this, - If you let them "get to you, they "win". They have achieved their goal. If you keep an arm around the Lord, listen to God's Spirit encouraging you, you can do as the verse in Proverbs says. Notice that it is God who heaps the coals of fire, not you! Give it to God!

100. How many elders are seated around the throne of God in the book of Revelation?

    a. 12   b. 16   c. 7   d. 24

          Lonny E. Young

> The north wind brings rain, and a backbiting tongue an angry countenance. It is better to dwell in a corner of a housetop, than in a house shared with a contentious woman. (Proverbs 25:23-24)

North to me is always associated with cold. When the wind turns out of the north you know winter, or at least colder temps are coming. What a word, "contentious". Here is another way of saying "pushing those buttons" we have talked about. Did you know that it takes two to argue? I saw this sign in a butcher shop once: "It is folly to argue with a fool. Listeners can't tell which is which."

I don't know why, but God built in me a total aversion to arguing. If someone wants to argue, I shut down. I won't speak. I won't "engage". I refuse. I don't even like to watch "confrontations" on TV. I can't stand wrestling matches, it tears me up inside.

I don't see any benefit from "arguing", - Debate, sure, calm discussion, great. When people talk over each other nothing is accomplished. You watch a debate on TV. Usually, the loser will talk over his opponent to keep him from making his point. It doesn't fly with me, I turn it off.

This is probably one of the biggest arguments for not going to church. "Backbiting", gossip, etc. Of course, that doesn't happen outside the church, only in the church. Ever had a job? -Seriously?

I heard someone offer this advice about gossip: All you must say is, "Can I quote you?" That pretty much stops it there. The "backbiter" prefers anonymity. If you quote them does that make it NOT gossip? Not likely. I have found that a juicy piece of information will never help anyone. It is intended to hurt, by spreading that information, you are contributing to that hurt!

It is interesting what verses in Proverbs can provoke. That is God's intention. To open up your heart, reveal things you thought you had hidden, to provoke your conscious and maybe convict you of some things that need to be addressed, between you and God first, then God's Spirit will urge you to change your ways.

Conviction - A powerful word! Before we open our heart and ask Jesus to be our Savior we need conviction we are sinners! - Right?

> As cold water to a weary soul, so is good news from a far
> country. A righteous man who falters before the wicked is
> like a murky spring and a polluted well. (Proverbs 25:25-26)

Have you ever heard the Sons of the Pioneers sing "Cool Water"? - One of my favorite old western songs. When you hear it, you just automatically get thirsty! Jesus talks about this in Mark:

"For whoever gives you a cup of water to drink in My name, because you belong to Christ, assuredly, I say to you, he will by no means lose his reward. (Mark 9:41)

It is such a simple act, isn't it? Just a cup of water, nothing we do go unnoticed to the Lord. A great cross-reference to a verse in Hebrews:

For God is not unjust to forget your work and labor of love which you have shown toward His name, in that you have ministered to the saints, and do minister. (Hebrews 6:10)

As a former pastor, I know all that goes on behind the scenes just to make a Sunday worship service enjoyable, so many people involved, all serving faithfully every Sunday. No pay, no recognition, why? - They just want to serve the Lord. It is that simple. I hope you are serving in your local church. It is such a blessing!

I noticed also some interesting words from Solomon. *"Is like a murky stream."* I don't know about you but I spent a lot of time, as a child, playing in streams. I have never seen a "murky" stream. A stream gives the idea of "moving" water. "Murky" is stagnant, still water. Much as the well he talks about in this same verse.

There is an interesting concept I ran across once. The idea that God's people are to be "rivers" or streams where the blessings of God flow from God through us to others. We are NOT to be like lakes, or wells, where God's blessings simply sit and stagnate. What are you doing with the Blessings God has given you?

                    Lonny E. Young

As snow in summer and rain in harvest, so honor is not flitting for a fool. Like a flitting sparrow, like a flying swallow, so a curse without cause shall not alight. (Proverbs 26:1-2)

I had a farmer friend once who helped answer a question I had. I had driven the back roads and noticed that not all the corn had been harvested. I asked him why they had left some to be harvested. He said, "It has been raining, they can't harvest in the mud." I would have never figured it out.

The weather plays such a vital part in our activities, especially a farmer. I heard this story once. Two farmers were praying for rain, one farmer just sat around and prayed and prayed, the second farmer went out and prepared his field for the rain. Which had more faith?

Have you ever watched a hummingbird? Fascinating to watch the way their wings are going a mile-a-minute and he is stationary. All that work and doesn't move an inch.

Speaking of harvest, did you notice in Jesus' parable of the "seed and the sower" (Matthew 13) that there is no mention of rain? What are we commanded to do? SOW! There is no soil preparation, nothing about rain or the weather. We are simply instructed, "Sow the seed!" Of course, the seed is the Word of God. We are not expected to have anything to do with the harvest, or its growth, or anything else, just sow the seed. Tell others about Jesus!

This lesson I learned early on. I knew God had called me to ministry. Nothing was happening. I had retired from United Parcel Service, I was ready, and the problem was that I had not done what God required of me. I was to make a resume. I finally got my daughter to help me with my resume. I turned it into the association. Not long after I was called to pastor a church. Could God have led me to a church without this resume? Of course!

There are things God asks us to do. Then there are things God does. Until we are obedient to God, follow His instructions, God will not move. Our obedience shows our faith. Demonstrates we are willing to do what God asks us to do. Once we finish, we THEN put it in God's hands and He works His miracles! First, our obedience!

> A whip for the horse, a bridle for the donkey, a rod for the fool's back. Do not answer a fool according to his folly, lest you also be like him. Answer a fool according to his folly, lest he be wise in his own eyes. (Proverbs 26:3-5)

I guess it depends on your definition of a "fool." How do you determine a fool? Some might say, "No common sense". That makes sense. I wonder what the Bible's definition of a fool might be. How about someone who is confronted with "facts" yet still denies what is before his eyes? Would you call them fools?

Have you ever heard of a guy named Josh McDowell? Josh was a college student, I understand. He was witnessed by several of his classmates. It got so frustrating for him that he decided, one day, he was going to prove them wrong. He was going to put an end to this "Jesus" myth. He began his research, hours of digging through historical documents, etc. In the end, Josh has now written several books. The most famous, I think, is entitled: "Evidence That Demands a Verdict", - A book "proving" who Jesus is.

Josh is not the only one, there are countless stories of professors, and theologians, determined to disprove the Bible. I know of NO successful effort. It can't be done.

As a Southern Baptist, our convention was divided for several years about the inerrancy of Scripture. The infallible Word of God. I have a simple question about that. WHO determines what is right and what is not? - A man? - Seriously? Now, where is the fool?

When confronted with "facts," what is your response? Okay, I believe the Bible. - Really? Do you believe it enough to obey it? Do you know enough about it to make your way to heaven? Do you know what it takes to get to heaven? Why not? You would think that might be important. Of course, a fool doesn't worry or care about where they will spend eternity.

Why do you think Solomon writes so many proverbs about "fools"? Maybe he is trying to point out their ignorance in hopes that some might see the truth and begin a search, in their own heart, for the TRUTH! How about you? Can you accept "facts" or turn your head?

> He who sends a message by the hand of a fool cuts off his own
> feet and drinks violence. Like the legs of the lame that hang
> limp is a proverb in the mouth of fools. (Proverbs 26:6-7)

I wonder where Solomon gets his reference about fools, his illustrations. I must remind myself that Solomon also wrote Ecclesiastes. Have you read that book? - An interesting premise.

Solomon has all the resources at his disposal. All the money he could ever want, etc. Anything he doesn't have he sees that it is imported. Look at this comment from the Queen of Sheba:

However, I did not believe the words until I came and saw with my own eyes; and indeed, the half was not told me. Your wisdom and prosperity exceed the fame of which I heard. (1 Kings 10:7)

She had heard, and could not believe what she heard, so she came to see for herself. And it was twice what she was told. Again, in Ecclesiastes, Solomon begins this quest to find, peace maybe? When he began he said:

The words of the Preacher, the son of David, king in Jerusalem. "Vanity of vanities, all is vanity." What profit has a man from all his labor in which he toils under the sun? One generation passes away, and another generation comes; but the earth abides forever. (Ecclesiastes 1:1-4)

Sounds kind of "depressed" doesn't he? He has all these riches and talks like this. Solomon spends 12 chapters searching for, what I think is peace. Here is his conclusion:

Let us hear the conclusion of the whole matter: Fear God and keep His commandments, for this is man's all. For God will bring every work into judgment, including every secret thing, whether good or evil. (Ecclesiastes 12:13-14)

> Like one who binds a stone in a sling is he who gives honor
> to a fool. Like a thorn that goes into the hand of a drunkard
> is a proverb in the mouth of fools. (Proverbs 26:8-9)

What do you do with the resources God has given you? I, as a young preacher, often wished I could preach like Dr. Charles Stanley or Dr. Chuck Swindoll. One day, I realized that God had already given us those two great preachers; God created me just the way I am "for a purpose." It is up to me to determine that purpose, and use the talents God gave me to serve Him.

I am not a preacher; I learned that the hard way. I do like to teach, I like to tell others what the Bible says, maybe help them better understand God's message for their life.

Maybe I am off, but I get the impression that Solomon is encouraging us not to waste our talents and resources on fools. Now, understand, that is not to say we should not try to teach and witness. Have you ever run across someone who refuses to listen, to even consider your arguments? Those are the fools Solomon is referring to.

It is one thing to be "open" to persuasion, quite another to not even try to understand another point of view. The biggest "weapon" if you will, a Christian has is their testimony. Why? There is no counter-argument. You can't "argue" what God has done in your life! That is your resource. Are you using it?

I have not mentioned the power of the Holy Spirit that is within each believer. Why? - Because most Christians refuse to use THAT resource. When or if you come to grips with the power that is within you, as a child of God, you would be amazed at what God can do through you. I saw that in the one church I pastored. God used my feeble efforts to work miracles in that small church.

After the service, I would be so disappointed in "my" efforts. I know I had not done very well. As the people were leaving they would shake my hand and say, "Great sermon pastor," "That moved me this morning," "Just what I needed, thank you, Pastor!" I was dumbfounded. I realized, I used the resource God gave me (His Spirit) and I did what God asked me to, and He blessed it!

The great God who formed everything gives the fool his hire and the transgressor his wages. As a dog returns to his own vomit, so a fool repeats his folly. (Proverbs 26:10-11)

The older I get the easier it is to repeat things every day; I learned early at United Parcel Service when pre-tripping (checking out) my truck that I was to do the "same" routine each time. By doing it that way you are less likely to "forget" something. I do that each morning, so I don't forget my pills.

Repetition can be a good thing. There is a problem with repetition; you seldom if ever get out of your "comfort" zone. That is the problem with the "fool" above. He repeats everything because he knows no better. How about you? Are you in a "comfort zone"? Someone once said that a "rut" is simply a coffin with the ends kicked out. Are you in a "rut"?

Are you afraid to try new things? How about new foods? – Really? Why is that? There is "safety" in this rut. You know what will happen, usually.

As a young United Parcel Service driver, I had this route in Grandview. After several years, I was wondering if this was all there was, I was in a rut. There appeared an opportunity to move up to an over-the-road driver. I thought "I can't drive those "big" trucks; I stepped out of my "comfort zone" and applied for the training. I passed and finally moved out of "package delivery", - more money, and easier work. If I hadn't taken that step out of my "comfort zone", I would never have known.

Has God lain on your heart to try something? Of course, your first response is, "I can't do that!" Are you willing to trust God? God is always "testing" us, trying to stretch our "faith", trying to see just how much we are willing to trust Him. Tithing is a "super" example of this testing. That is for another time. Let me give one of my favorite verses in Matthew:

Then He touched their eyes, saying, **"According to your faith let it be to you."** (Matthew 9:29)

Just meditate on that verse a minute. Will you "trust" God?

Do you see a man wise in his own eyes? There is more hope for a fool than for him. (Proverbs 26:12)

Being a man I have noticed something, not sure if it applies to women, probably. The last thing you want to admit is that you need a doctor, or you need to see a doctor.

After an Easter service, one year I wasn't feeling well. I was a little dizzy in church but thought nothing of it. We were headed to our daughter's for Easter celebration. I told my wife that I just wanted to go home and rest. I was out-voted by my wife and two daughters.

We went to the Emergency Room; I was diagnosed with "blood clots" in both of my lungs. We were joking around in the waiting room and the nurse came in and said, "Lie very still, quit laughing, those clots could break apart and enter your heart, or your brain." I was in there three or four days, given blood thinners, etc. What if I was allowed to go home?

- The point? Until you recognize you are sick, you can't be treated; unless it is too late. Why did I share this story? Think about it.

Until you recognize that you are lost and going to Hades, you cannot be saved. That is the guy that Solomon is talking about. Until you acknowledge your need of a Savior, God cannot do anything for you. Isn't that what this verse says?

If you confess with your mouth the Lord Jesus and believe in your heart that God raised Him from the dead, you will be saved. For with the heart one believes unto righteousness, and with the mouth confession is made unto salvation. (Romans 10:9-10)

Until you admit that you NEED a Savior, you cannot be saved. The arrogance of the man in Solomon's proverb will prevent him from going to heaven. I know of no place in the Bible where someone "earned" his way to heaven. If left to our own devises, we are destined for Hades! Until we admit our sin, come to God in repentance, we will continue in rebellion to God and suffer the consequences. It is that simple. You are risking eternity in Hades, admit you need saving.

> The lazy man says, "There is a lion in the road! A fierce lion is in the streets!" As a door turns on its hinges, so does the lazy man on his bed. The lazy man buries his hand in the bowl; it wearies him to bring it back to his mouth. The lazy man is wiser in his own eyes than seven men who can answer sensibly. (Proverbs 26:13-16)

Have you ever seen this list? Someone, years ago, came out with a list of seven cultural things that destroyed the Roman Empire. Laziness was one of them. Dependent on government was another. Do you see any of this today? It is interesting how little we learn from the past. Of course, that can be said for the Bible too. We pay so little attention to the truths of the Bible, and then wonder why we are in such trouble. Solomon talks of this in Ecclesiastes:

Because of laziness the building decays, and through idleness of hands the house leaks. A feast is made for laughter, and wine makes merry; but money answers everything. (Ecclesiastes 10:18-19)

Have you noticed how much Solomon abhors laziness?
I learned an interesting lesson when I studied the life of King David.
Look at 2 Samuel:

It happened in the spring of the year, at the time when kings go out to battle, that David sent Joab and his servants with him, and all Israel; and they destroyed the people of Ammon and besieged Rannah. **But David remained in Jerusalem.** (2 Samuel 11:1)

David was NOT where he was supposed to be. In this same chapter, David has his affair with Bathsheba. It cost him peace for the rest of his life. He broke God's heart; it took years to restore that "fellowship."

When we are LAZY we are not doing what God has called us to do. When we are not where God wants us to be, we are not in a position to be used by God. When we are out of God's will, not doing what God wants us to do, we are in danger of the influence of the world, the flesh, and Satan himself. We are in danger!

> He who passes by and meddles in a quarrel not his own is like one who takes a dog by the ears. Like a madman who throws firebrands, arrows and death, is the man who deceives his neighbor, and says, "I was only joking." (Proverbs 26:17-19)

Have you seen the videos? You know, where this person is beaten to death and numerous bystanders just stand there. It is tough anymore to know when to get "involved" and when not to.

My wife has gotten on me for picking up "hitchhikers." I have this theory. First, I am not a quick re-actor. I see them, I pass them. If I am led, I will exit, crossover and drive back. If they are still there then I might pick them up. Rarely are they still there. - So far, so good.

It is so hard today. I remember stories my dad told me, of hitchhiking all the time "in uniform". Does that make it okay? It is still dangerous anymore? This is such a "key" time to let God's Spirit take the lead. If you don't have peace about it, don't do it.

Has anyone ever said to you, "I was only joking"? Does that make it any more palatable? Not likely. There is a place for joking and it is NOT at someone else's expense. That is usually when you hear these words. When they see it has upset you, they pull out the "joking" card. It is easy to offend someone and very hard to take it back.

I think it is hilarious that Solomon uses this phrase. It shows the "relevance" of the Bible. You would be surprised at just HOW relevant it is! After I was saved, I was teaching a Sunday school class in six months. Not that I knew anything. I didn't know Genesis from Revelation. They needed a teacher and I volunteered. Being a teacher encourages study! In two years I became Sunday School Director and my passion has been the Bible ever since.

I have read through my Bible several times, each time finding out new and exciting things about God. If you want to know God's "heart" you MUST spend time in His Word. There, God has revealed His heart, His desire for YOUR life, His desired relationship with His creation and, above all, His love for His creation.

I also disagree with those who focus on the New Testament. If you want to "understand" the New you must read the Old!

> Where there is no wood, the fire goes out; and where there is no talebearer, strife ceases. As charcoal is to burning coals, and wood is to fire, so is a contentious man to kindle strife. The words of a talebearer are like tasty trifles, and they go down into the inmost body. (Proverbs 26:20-22)

And Solomon says, "You have the ability to put out that fire!" If it goes no further than you, it stops, doesn't it? There is nothing that can destroy a church as quickly as gossip. The problem, as usual, is that no one bothers to find out the "truth" do they? That is not as "juicy".

I don't want to spend a lot of time here. You know exactly what I am talking about. If not, I am sure the Holy Spirit will speak to your heart about it!

I do like this picture as concerning the church in another aspect. A lot of Christians think they can do without the church. And a lot of people disdain it for the reason stated above (gossip). That is not the function of a church. Can you imagine where the early Christians would have been without the church body?

The reason this reminds me of the church is the idea of a fireplace. I heard this very early as a Christian and I love it, if you have a fireplace, try putting one log in the fireplace and starting a fire. It is almost impossible. Now put several logs and try it. Not only that, but several logs will burn much longer and better than just one log. So, what does that have to do with Christians?

How is your "fellowship" with God? If you are a Christian you already have a "relationship" bought by the blood of Jesus Christ. This "relationship" is sealed by God's Holy Spirit. I am asking about your "fellowship", how close are you to God? Do you talk to Him daily? Do you trust Him daily in the decisions in your life? Maybe it is a "once-a-week" thing. How is your "fellowship"?

That is where His church comes in. You fellowship with fellow believers, they inspire, encourage, support, and teach you about God, through their own experiences. A Sunday School class is great for that. My wife and I, for years, sat with these three couples in the pews around us. Great friends! I call them our "Pew Pals". Try it!

> Fervent lips with a wicked heart are like earthenware covered
> with silver dross. He who hates, disguises it with his lips, and
> lays up deceit within himself. (Proverbs 26:23-24)

Interestingly, the "heart" is not on this reference list in my Bible. "Topics in Proverbs" has 18 topics that it says are covered in Proverbs. I wonder why the heart is not listed. - Maybe because so MANY have to do with the heart.

I did a "word search" when I had a functioning Bible program. I searched for "*heart". The "wicked" heart only appeared twice, this being one of them. Some fascinating results with the "word search" ability. What do you suppose would constitute a "wicked" heart?

You would think that a "wicked" heart would show up more than twice. "Your" heart appeared the most with 35 references, followed by "whole" heart with 13 references, this from the King James Version. I guess you could surmise that God is very interested in YOUR heart.

Do you remember what "dross" is? It is the scum that surfaces when silver is melted. Not a pretty picture. Wouldn't it be interesting if we could see the hearts of other people? Of course, then they would be able to see ours. - Interesting.

Do you get a "picture" of the New Testament heart? That picture, though a New Testament concept, is best pictured in the Old Testament. Bear with me a minute.

Look here:

*"Now the blood shall be a sign for you on the houses where you are. **And when I see the blood, I will pass over you;** and the plague shall not be on you to destroy you when I strike the land of Egypt.* (Exodus 12:13)

Do you see it? When God looks at our heart, He needs to see the blood of Christ. Just like John's Gospel says in:

The next day John saw Jesus coming toward him, and said, "Behold! The Lamb of God who takes away the sin of the world! (John 1:29)

When God looks at our heart, He needs to see Jesus' blood.

                    Lonny E. Young

> When he speaks kindly, do not believe him, for there are seven abominations in his heart; though his hatred is covered by deceit, his wickedness will be revealed before the assembly. (Proverbs 26:25-26)

One of my favorite verses in the life of King David:

For the Lord does not see as man sees; for man looks at the outward appearance, but the Lord looks at the heart. (1 Samuel 16:7b)

We might fool others with our "slick" words and our mannerisms, but there is no fooling God! He knows what is in our hearts, just like when we stand before God; we can try all kinds of excuses, alibi's, deceptions, etc. Nothing will fool God. He will simply look into our heart. If He doesn't find the blood of Jesus, the Lamb of God, our sentenced is doomed.

When we ask Jesus into our heart, He is accompanied by the third Person of the Trinity, the Holy Spirit. Let me illustrate.

Look at this verse:

And they said to one another, "Did not our heart burn within us on the road, and while He opened the Scriptures to us?" (Luke 24:32)

This is the testimony of the two disciples on the Emmaus road. After the resurrection, they were walking and the resurrected Christ joined them. They didn't recognize Him until they sat down to eat and He blessed the food. *"Their heart burned within them."* I love that. That is what happens when you ask Jesus to be a part of your life. He turns your life upside-down.

He begins by cleaning the house, slowly taking each room in your heart and removing those things not pleasing to God. It may be language, bad habits, relationships, prejudices, temper, priorities, etc. He goes to work, slowly, He doesn't do it all at once. We couldn't handle that, such radical changes. He begins with each room, cleaning and arranging things to help you have a closer "fellowship" with your Heavenly Father; the more "cleaning" He does the closer your walk with God!

> Whosoever digs a pit will fall into it, and he who rolls a stone will have it roll back on him. A lying tongue hates those who are crushed by it, and a flattering mouth works ruin. (Proverbs 26:27-28)

Pictures, - Solomon deals in pictures, so many of his proverbs draw a "picture", using the culture of the day to illustrate his truth. We do the same, in trying to describe something we can use "metaphors" to illustrate our point. Solomon, in a sense, is using the same method as Jesus, when Jesus spoke in "parables".

Have you noticed how often the word "like" is used in a sentence? It has become TOO used. It is a safety valve when you are thinking of the next thing to say, or don't know exactly what to say. It is a "crutch". It is almost like profanity, it is simply a lack of vocabulary.

Solomon and Jesus use "word pictures" to help us better understand the point they are trying to make. And, if you notice, they use the things familiar to the culture of the day. Look how many times Jesus uses, fishing, farming, vineyards, familiar things of the day. Solomon does the same thing.

Just a note, when you are reading Ezekiel and Daniel and their "visions", they are trying to describe things of our day or the future in terms of things in "their" day. Keep that in mind.

Solomon, again, addressing lying; the results, and the consequences of telling lie. I think the funniest thing about lying is that, pretty soon, it comes around and you can't remember what truth is and what a lie is. Today, we are coming up on an election. Some news stations have recordings of politicians that contradict what they are saying now; they said one thing last year and something different this year. Caught on tape!

When you speak the truth, there is no contradiction. You don't have to worry if it is the same thing you said last year. You take a stand and you STAND on it. It is just Solomon's first "picture" here. *Whoever digs a pit will fall into it.* Lie upon a lie is digging a pit you will someday fall into. You need to stop digging.

Sometimes those "metaphors" are far too real. They are so clear anyone can understand them. Do you see what Solomon is talking about?

        Lonny E. Young

> Do not boast about tomorrow, for you do not know what
> a day may bring forth. Let another man praise you, and
> not your own mouth; a stranger, and not your own lips.
> (Proverbs 27:1-2)

Do you like to make plans? I do. I am always thinking about the next hour, the next day, and the next week; I usually don't go much further than that. Most of the time I have certain "things" I want to get done in a day. Sometimes I get them done, sometimes not. That is one thing I have learned, (the hard way) God is in control. If I don't accomplish what I want, it is because God had other plans. I have learned to accept that.

I am sure you know the parable of the "barns" in Luke.

Let's look at the key verse:

But God said to him, "Fool! This night your soul will be required of you; then who's will those things be which you have provided?" (Luke 12:20)

Here is a "proverb" for today: *The best laid plans of mice and men, often go astray."* I don't know who said that, it could well be a modern translation of the verse above.

We have no idea what the next hour will bring. If you're a Christian you know who does. There is a lot of "peace" in knowing that fact. I am in my seventies. God has his timetable. The future belongs to Him and I have learned to accept that. I make my plans, sure, but they are "always" subject to God's will.

Verse two is also a lesson I learned shortly after becoming a Christian. God raises up, and God sets down, those whom He will. We simply serve; the rest is up to God. I was privileged to serve as a pastor for 30 months in a small church; I saw God do some amazing things. When I took my eyes off God and started thinking I was something, God put me in my place. Thank you, Lord!

When God raises you up it is for His glory. One of my favorite chapters in the Old Testament is 2 Samuel 7. Take a look. That is the attitude God wants from us, - King David's attitude.

> A stone is heavy and sand is weighty, but a fool's wrath is
> heavier than both of them. Wrath is cruel and anger a torrent,
> but who is able to stand before jealousy? (Proverbs 27:3-4)

Here is a trick I learned years back, - find someone who is strong, and then dare them to lift you. No problem, right? When they go to lift you, GO LIMP, your weight seems to double. They may lift you but not nearly as easily as they thought.

That is what Solomon is talking about, "dead weight". He says, *"A fool's wrath"* but any wrath is cruel. If you have ever been that angry before you know one thing, "You have lost control". That is NOT the place to be. We all get upset at times. It is when we "lose control" that it becomes dangerous.

Notice how Solomon describes it: *"Wrath is cruel and anger a torrent"*. We saw the destruction in Florida recently when a hurricane passed through, there was NO stopping it. That is anger. That is the effect anger can have on your life. It can very well destroy you and everything you love. It must be "controlled".

You made your point. So, how do you control it? - You replace it with the Lord. When God's Holy Spirit lives within you, He gives you a whole new perspective, you see things differently. What motivates your anger is replaced with God's perspective, usually, a "long term" perspective that says, "This is not that important!"

Another good point, the cause of most "wrath"? - Jealousy. For whatever reason people know the "buttons" to push. We talked about this before. Do you know what happens when you get angry? You lose "control" don't you? That is exactly what Satan wants, especially if you are a "Christian". You say and do things you would never do if you were "in control" better yet if God were in control.

That is such an important thing to remember when you think you are about to "lose it!" Just remember that you are turning control of your "emotions" to Satan. Listen to the Spirit within you. Focus on the things of God, your "fellowship" with God, not what Satan is trying to do. Write these verses in the front of your Bible: Romans 12:19-20. Read what God says and trust Him.

     Lonny E. Young

> Open rebuke is better than love carefully concealed. Faithful
> are the wounds of a friend, but the kisses of an enemy are
> deceitful. (Proverbs 27:5-6)

Do you have someone like that in your life? If you're married it might be your spouse, or a close friend; someone who will tell you you're wrong when you need it. That is a friend. There is also someone we don't pay near enough attention to, - God's Holy Spirit. He is too easy to turn off or ignore.

The problem both with this friend and with God's Spirit is that when they do "rebuke" us, we get mad and refuse to see them very much. We don't want to be told we are wrong, or we have made a mistake. Then the Holy Spirit becomes less and less vocal, faint to hear, to the point we ignore Him altogether. That is sad.

The Spirit is God's way of communicating with us, directing us, encouraging us, speaking to our hearts. It is our choice, whether we listen and/or obey Him.

None of us like a rebuke. Be honest! What is your first response to "rebuke"? - A simple word, "rebellion", similar to Adam and Eve in the Garden of Eden.

Try this experiment with your children, any children. Put them in a room, and then tell them, they cannot cross the threshold into the adjoining room. Watch what they do. It won't be long before they will come right up to the line and maybe put a foot over the line to see what you will do, - "Rebellion".

We are the same way. I believe that that is why so many people refuse to spend much time in God's word. It is convicting. It was meant to be. It is God's way of "rebuking" you and pointing out some things that need to be addressed. We don't want that so we stay away from it, just like this book of Proverbs.

You can read the book of Proverbs in one month. Try this schedule: The first day of the month read five chapters in the Psalms and one chapter in Proverbs. By the end of the month, you would have read two of the most significant books in the Bible; it will change your life. If you want a REAL challenge, do this for a year, and get familiar with God!

> A satisfied soul loathes the honeycomb, but to a hungry soul
> every bitter thing is sweet. Like a bird that wanders from its
> nest is a man who wanders from his place. (Proverbs 27:7-8)

What would it take to give you peace? - Contentment. A satisfied soul? Eternity doesn't matter to you right now. Maybe you are in your late 20's, late 30's, middle age. That is a funny term, "middle-age". If you died at forty, then twenty would be "middle age." Who determines what "middle-age" is? Does it matter? - Only if you KNOW when you're going to die, and you don't.

Again, what would bring you peace, contentment? How about, if you "knew" when you were going to die? Would that bring you peace? Not hardly! You would be more stressed out the closer the date. What is "supposed" to bring peace and contentment today? - Having enough "money" for retirement, being "secure" for the future? A lot of people think that might bring peace.

Can you "secure" the future? Can you have enough money to "secure" your future? What is the future? Being able to retire at 50, - would that be a "secure" future? I don't know why these verses made me think of the future. What are we working for? - To "secure" a future, a retirement, really?

What is the future compared to eternity? One of my favorite lines in an old gospel hymn; the fourth verse of Amazing Grace:

When we've been there ten thousand years,
Bright shining as the sun.
We've no less days, to sing God's praise
Than when we first begun.

Think about that premise. THAT is eternity. That is a promise from God when God breathed life into our mortal bodies, God promised us eternity. And God has granted us just so many years, or days, on this earth to make one decision. Where will you spend that eternity? You will live for eternity, will you spend it in God's presence, or Hades, tormented for eternity. It is YOUR choice. That is peace!

> Ointment and perfume delight the heart, and the sweetness of a man's friend gives delight by hearty counsel. Do not forsake your own friend or your father's friend, nor go to your brother's house in the day of your calamity; better is a neighbor nearby than a brother far away. (Proverbs 27:9-10)

I shared this story before but it fits here. When the early settlers of our country began to move west they received large parcels of land. The first settlers would build their homes in the middle of their property. Thereby, their neighbors were always far away. It didn't take them long to realize that they needed to build their homes in the corners of their land, so they would have neighbors close by. A lesson learned.

Solomon often talks about neighbors. Today it is rare if people know their neighbors. They might know their names but not much else; a far cry from my parents and especially my grandparents.

Maybe we can thank "social media" for that. Our world, now, is those on our phones or laptops. Those people know more about your life than your own family members. We have lost touch with human interaction.

That is why the church is so important today. It is the one weekly opportunity to meet and converse with your neighbors, your community. I shared a little of this before.

For a long time, Mary and I sat in the same pew every Sunday. There were two couples behind us and two couples in front of us that we visited every Sunday. We had about ten minutes before the service started and a few minutes after the service. We became so close to those four couples. By sharing a need I had in fixing up our house, I found the right person to fill the need we had. I call them our "Pew Pals." We are still close today.

They are our "neighbors" as Solomon likes to call them. People we see regularly every week. We share our lives with them and them with us; more of neighbors than those who live next to us. Do you have any "Pew Pals"? If you attend church regularly you do. You get to know those around you, you share common time, a time of worship, and special time of fellowship with God's people.

> My son, be wise, and make my heart glad, that I may answer him who reproaches me. A prudent man foresees evil and hides himself; the simple pass on and are punished. (Proverbs 27:11-12)

There is so much here, I might pick a few words and focus on them. You may see something else that jumps out at you. Don't let my words distract from what God is speaking to you. Let me encourage you to start your own notebook. Maybe, follow me through these verses in Proverbs; maybe take the 5 Psalms and 1 Proverb route. It doesn't matter. I encourage you to begin a journal on your journey with God. You will be amazed at what God will do in your life.

I guess it has always been the "wish" of parents that their children would have children just like they were. It is a form of "retribution". Interesting question, - If we are concerned about how our children grow up, why do we not teach them the things of God? I often wonder today, what are parents teaching their children?

Are parents "proud" to see their children marching in the streets causing havoc? Hearing of them "arrested" for disturbing the peace? Is that something to be proud of in a child? I am confused.

When I left home at seventeen, I had joined the United States Air Force, the day after my seventeenth birthday (the Vietnam era). Right away I asked God not to let me "dishonor" my parents; I was proud of my name, and my family. It seems today that is not so important anymore.

How would you describe a "prudent" man? Careful maybe? Aware? Notice the contrast that Solomon presents. You know the "saying" of today: *Hindsight is twenty-twenty.* Have you ever looked back and wished you had done something differently? Of course, you have. So, why didn't you make the right choice then? Can we blame "ignorance"? And whose fault is that? Here is another "saying:" *Ignorance is no excuse!*

You sure can't use it standing before God; God has given us all we will need in these 66 books. The claim, "I didn't know" will not fly!

     Lonny E. Young

> Take the garment of him who is surety for a stranger, and hold it in pledge when he is surety for a seductress. He who blesses his friend with a loud voice, rising early in the morning, it will be counted a curse to him. (Proverbs 27:13-14)

Here is where it is so important to understand the culture of the day. We can go into any Wal-Mart or J.C. Penny and buy clothes at will. The clothing then was very precious. A person may own one change of clothes, those he is wearing, the "cloak" or the outer garment was all he had for warmth, and comfort; to offer it for "surety" was quite a big deal, especially for a "pledge".

Your word needed to be of great value to offer such a vital piece of clothing. The point I am trying to make, and God makes in several places regarding "garments", the "value" of the pledge. We don't see it because our clothing is not that precious, we have a closet full of clothes, they didn't!

The importance of a person's word, in this proverb (v. 13); it seems the surety is for NOT a worthwhile thing. It is "frivolous" to say the least. How many times have you bought something on "time" and come to realize it wasn't worth near what you paid. You borrowed money to buy this fancy car. It breaks down (blown engine) you are still making payments for something you can't drive. Get the picture.

"Surety" a "pledge" is so important. Your word is behind that pledge. How "valuable" to you is your word? It should mean something. To use it "frivolously" is dangerous. It is far too easy to get in debt today.

When I was young and stupid, I used to think that if they "approved" my loan they thought I could afford it. Is that "dumb" or what? Now we have all these plastic cards. Do you pay attention to the "interest"? That is money for "rent" on your money. Okay, I will get off my soapbox. It is a lesson I learned far too late in life, a lesson nevertheless.

That is what Solomon's proverbs are, - "Lessons" that he learned and is passing on to us for our benefit. The trick is to learn from these wise words and apply them to our life!

> A continual dripping on a very rainy day and a contentious woman are alike; whoever restrains her restrains the wind, and grasps oil with his right hand. (Proverbs 27:15-16)

Let's see, how Solomon would know about a "contentious" woman:

*And he had seven hundred wives, princesses, and three hundred concubines; **and his wives turned away his heart.** For it was so. When he was old, that his wives turned his heart after other gods; and his heart was not loyal to the Lord his God, as was the heart of his father David.* (1 Kings 11:3-4)

This is happening today, not necessarily wives, but the "world" is turning God's people away from following God. I hate to be such a "downer". It is true. It is funny that the "world" is using the same technique as Solomon describes above in Proverbs; the "drip, drip" of the message of the world. "You don't need God! You are capable of making your own decisions". Do you hear the drip, drip of this subtle message?

I think the church is the biggest indicator. The attendance continues to drop, more and more people shun the fellowship and support from fellow Christians, oh, I forgot to mention "accountability". Satan says, "If I can get you away from the church we have won". You "cannot" sustain a "fellowship" with God apart from regular worship; Jesus made it a point to "establish" His church while He was here.

I think it is interesting that Jesus talked about it, but it wasn't "established" until after His resurrection, and into the book of Acts; Jesus chose a "Pharisee" to begin His missionary tours. Paul described himself as a "Pharisee of Pharisees" (Philippians 3:5)

Drip—drip—drip so goes the message of the world. "You don't need God!" You may have made a decision in the past, that doesn't matter. God understands. You just go on and become part of the world. God doesn't care about you. - Really? He cared enough about you to send His Only Son to the cross so that you may have a "relationship" with the Creator of the universe! -Really?

> As iron sharpens iron, so a man sharpens the countenance of his friend. Whoever keeps the fig tree will eat its fruit; so, he who waits on his master will be honored. (Proverbs 27:17-18)

We talked yesterday about this "drip, drip, drip". Have you ever seen the Grand Canyon? That huge canyon was carved out of the rock by running water. It slowly ate away for centuries, eating away until it formed that canyon. Drip, drip, drip.

In a sense that is what Solomon is talking about here. The continual counsel, encouragement, instruction of a friend "sharpens" his friend.

Pardon me, but I must continue to speak of God's church. That is exactly what happens on the Lord's Day. The message of the pastor, the lesson of the Sunday school teacher, the input from fellow Christians continues to "sharpen" or strengthen your walk with the Lord.

I know I am strange; I have a weird perspective on the Lord's Day. The morning worship service and Sunday school are the beginning of a new week, starting with worship and instruction to encourage me for the coming week's challenges. It just reminds me that God is on my side, and contributes to my knowledge of God and His heart and love for me.

Ah, the evening service. Now here is where I am weird. I look at the evening service as the conclusion of the week. I know that is not "scriptural" but I just sense that. What a fantastic way to conclude the week. In God's house, singing His hymns, praising God and a little Bible study to bring the week to a close. I go home that night with such a peace that God has blessed this past week, looking forward to what He is going to do in the coming week.

"As iron sharpens iron" I know Solomon's context is in a relation of man to man, but I see this as God working on me. The more I get into His word, both Old and New Testament God is revealing His heart to me. We know John 3:16, but what does the *"loved the world"* mean to you? I want it personal; the last few Bibles I have bought I have crossed out "world" and written my name there.

The more time you spend in God's word, the better you get to know the heart of God. Take a minute and read Jeremiah 29:11-13.

> As in water face reflects face, so a man's heart reveals the man. Hell, and Destruction are never full; so, the eyes of man are never satisfied. (Proverbs 27:19-20)

Just a note about the eyes, - When I found out what "covet" meant I used to tease my wife and say, "Let's go to the Plaza and 'covet 'a while", the meaning, of course, to "window shop"; I thought it was funny.

There are so many descriptions of the heart in the Bible. I did a word search using * heart. Here are some results: Broken, contrite, foolish, glad, good, heavy, perverse, rebellious, stout, trembling, willing. Each of these had only one reference (King James Version). The most used was "Your" (35), "Whole" (13), and "Mans" (10). It is clear whose heart God is concerned about.

Why is this so important? It never hurts to reflect on some key verses:

For the Lord does not see as man sees, for man looks at the outward appearance, but the Lord looks at the heart. (1 Samuel 16:7b)

*If you confess with your mouth the Lord Jesus and believe in your **heart** that God has raised Him from the dead, you will be saved. For with the **heart** one believes unto righteousness, and with the mouth confession is made unto salvation.* (Romans 10:9-10)

You see, God sees and knows our hearts. We can "say" anything but we can't fool God, we can walk down the aisle fifteen times, be baptized a dozen times, until it penetrates our heart it is simply for show; God knows.

Did you catch the interesting thing about Solomon's words: *So, a man's heart reveals the man?* That is interesting. We not only can't fool God but eventually, we will reveal ourselves to others; we cannot hide what is in our hearts.

The neat thing about this is that God has given His children the Holy Spirit, if you are a child of God, to discern the heart. That Spirit helps to detect hypocrisy, one of the works of the Spirit.

> The refining pot is for silver and the furnace for gold, and a man is valued by what others say of him. Though you grind a fool in a mortar with a pestle along with crushed grain, yet his foolishness will not depart from him. (Proverbs 27:21-22)

Do you feel "tortured", "punished" going through a tough time you don't "deserve?" "Why is this happening to me?" Is that your thought? If you are a child of God, it is very simple. God is trying to get your attention. I have been there so many times.

Sometimes He is trying to alert you to a mistake you are about to make. He is trying to get you to your knees to seek His guidance, sometimes a "fire" is the only thing that will get your attention. Sometimes He is testing you, NOT tempting you, but testing you. God has a purpose for you. Are you willing to be obedient enough to God's leadership to trust Him to accomplish what God wants to accomplish in your life? He is running you through this crucible to see if you will trust Him. Will you?

God is always working on His children, either correcting, or "growing" us to His likeness, to His standards, not the world's, but God's. So, how do you respond? You blame God and turn your back on Him? Then God will pass you by, and find someone who WILL trust Him and obey Him. You have missed a blessing.

This is a lesson I learned many years ago. When I sense I am entering one of these "testing" periods, I pray, "Okay, Lord, what is it that I need to learn?" "Is there something in my life I need to be rid of?" "Is there a direction I am going, or should be going, that I am not?" It is God's call; He has allowed this in my life for a reason. Read the first two chapters of Job.

I know sometimes we feel like that grain that is being "crushed" in the mill but remember what that is about until that "grain" is crushed and sifted it cannot be used for bread. It must be "prepared" before it can be used.

The exciting thing about God using us, are the miracles He performs. Because once we surrender, allows God to work in our lives, we will be totally amazed at what God can do. Watch!

> Be diligent to know the state of your flocks, and attend to your herds; for riches are not forever, nor does a crown endure to all generations. (Proverbs 27:23-24)

Family. Do you think that is Solomon's point? Of course, he lives in a culture that deals with flocks and herds. There is a danger of "reading" more into the text than what is there. We also know that God intended a "spiritual" context in His message. So, where do you think "God" is going with this?

It is so easy to get "out-of-touch" with "family", isn't it? Kids grow up and move away and we lose track. Of course, with today's "social media" it is easier, but still.

We are nearing the Thanksgiving time of the year. Isn't it interesting that we need a "special" day set aside to remind us to be thankful? Why is that? I think we tend too often to take things for granted, like family. Maybe Thanksgiving is a great time to be "reminded" of family. That is my interpretation of the context of Solomon's verse here.

"To all generations". I mentioned before that I am in my seventies. The younger ones can't "relate". I am looking back a whole lot more than I am looking forward to.

I caught myself recently telling the stories of my "growing up," to our grandchildren. They enjoyed them so much that I sat down and began chronicling my memories. I used the various places we lived, as timelines. By the time I finished, I had 300+ pages full of "my stories". I made three copies, one for each of our two daughters and one for myself; a way of passing my generation on to the next.

I have tried to encourage others to do the same; "I can't write" is usually the excuse I get. You don't have to be "Shakespeare" just write down what you remember. Today I have so many questions I wish I could ask my parents, they are both gone now. Too late!

I lived, what I think, was an interesting life. I wanted to pass those stories on to the next generations. I hope the main thing I can pass on is my love for the Lord. What God has done in my life, the miracle of God allowing me to pastor for 30 months. God has been good and I hope to tell our next generation of God's goodness!

> The wicked flee when no one pursues, but the righteous
> are bold as a lion. Because of the transgression of a land,
> many are its princes; but by a man of understanding and
> knowledge right will be prolonged. (Proverbs 28:1-2)

It is really sad how few participate in choosing the leaders of our great nation. Tonight is the eve of our "mid-term" election. Every four years we elect a President, those who serve in the Senate are elected for six years and those in the House of Representatives for a two-year term. We choose those who will govern us.

The Bible says that God raises up and sets down, those in authority over us. I believe that. That does NOT mean that we should not be involved in the process. God may very well use His people to raise up or set down. If we fail to take a stand we leave the door wide open for Satan to have his way.

God, I believe, established this country for His glory. God led in the finding and the victory over England, to establish a very unique nation. God will preserve it as long as we keep our eyes on God. Just like Peter when he stepped out of the boat. (Matthew 14:28-33) As long as he focused on Jesus he was alright; the same is true for our country!

Every four years I watch to see who "the people" elect to be our leader. I use that as a "spiritual" barometer of our nation's soul. Are we praying and listening to God or the "world" around us? The flesh or the Spirit?

In Solomon's day, it was the "king" who ruled, either a king by birthright or might. I am not one who agrees that God did not want a king, but a theocracy, passing from the "Judges" to the kings. As early as Deuteronomy, the book of Moses, God saw the time of the kings:

"When you come to the land which the Lord your God is giving you, and possess it and dwell in it, and say, 'I will set up a king over me like all the nations that are around me.' 'You shall surely set a king over you whom the Lord your God chooses; you shall set a king over you; you may not set a foreigner over you, who is not your brother." (Exodus 17:14-15)

> A poor man who oppresses the poor is like a driving rain which leaves no food. Those who forsake the law praise the wicked, but such as keep the law contend with them. (Proverbs 28:3-4)

Ever the battle was joined, - good versus evil, right and wrong, wicked and righteous. It is a choice, is it not? We make these choices every day. Our choices are based on the content of our hearts, not our intellectual knowledge.

When I saw the date above one thing popped into my head, I was still seventeen; I had finished Basic Training and had arrived in California for my first duty station, Travis Air Force Base, not long after I had arrived we heard of the assassination. There was a "fog" over the base for several days, not a "natural fog"; everyone seemed dazed, it was surreal.

A turning point in our nation's history; a choice was made by one individual that changed history. Evil, it seemed, had triumphed. We will never know "what if". Do you feel sometimes that you just can't get ahead? You feel these "forces" are against you? You have lost, so what is the use? Have you given up?

If you are a child of God (Romans 8:14-16) you are forgetting the power that dwells within you, - the power to make the "right" decisions, choices; if you listen to God's Spirit of course. Most of us don't. It just takes a minute, do you know how long a "minute" is? It just takes a minute to pray, "Lord, give me the wisdom to make the right choice!" You think I'm crazy? Look:

If any of you lacks wisdom, let him ask of God, who gives to all liberally and without reproach, and it will be given him. (James 1:5)

Now, understand this is a promise God makes to "His children" (Romans 8:15). Then, of course, we must listen and obey. That is another story. The lost only have their own resources to rely on; we have the wisdom of God at our disposal. Oh, one last thing, it helps to read the instructions (Bible). It doesn't mean you must follow them; you can disregard them at your peril. You might start there!

Evil men do not understand justice, but those who seek
the Lord understand all. Better is the poor who walks in his
integrity than one perverse in his ways, though he be rich.
(Proverbs 28:5-6)

It is a fascinating question. Does someone who is doing "wrong" realize they are doing wrong and that it has consequences? If they do, why does that not deter them? Do they think they will get away with it? I wonder.

Here is an interesting example:

Then David sent messengers, and took her; and she came to him, and he lay with her, for she was cleansed from her impurity; and she returned to her home. And the woman conceived; so she sent and told David, and said, **I am with child.** (2 Samuel 11:4-5)

We know the story; I want you to notice something, about nine months later the child is born. During that time David has Bathsheba's husband, Uriah, killed. Then one day Nathan comes to David and tells him a story:

Then Nathan said to David, **"You are the man!** *Thus, says the Lord God of Israel: I anointed you king over Israel, and I delivered you from the hand of Saul.* (2 Samuel 12:7)

This "choice" cost David dearly. He repented, God spared his life, but it cost him. I have always wondered, when David stood on that balcony, he had a choice. He had eight wives; he didn't need to go there. He had a choice.

The thing I want you to look at is this: there were about nine months from the time of the "deed" and God's judgment. God is not a "vengeful" God. He offers repentance. We need to acknowledge our "mistake" and ask for forgiveness. There STILL might be consequences; there are always consequences to disobeying the "rules". Never forget that.

It is so important that we understand the rules that God has set forth in His Word. We all make mistakes. It is those times when we "choose" to disobey that hurt God the most, - understand and obey!

> Whoever keeps the law is a discerning son, but a companion of gluttons shames his father. One who increases his possessions by usury and extortion gathers it for him who will pity the poor. (Proverbs 28:7-8)

I really have a problem with this. Have you ever gotten a Driver's License? What do you have to do? You take two tests, right? A driving test and a written test, right? So, what do you do for the written test? They give you a "booklet" to study, right? Why? To know the rules! So, you can past the test. - Seriously?

So, can you tell me why so many people ignore the Word of God? God has called me to the Sunday school ministry; I have been a Director for over thirty years. Why is this my passion? We need to know the "rules!"

The thing that I have come to realize through writing these books, this is my third, is that, we not only learn the "rules" we learn the heart of God. That heart is finally demonstrated in the Gospels with the sacrifice of God's Son on the cross to pay for our sins. That is love "demonstrated". Yet, we can't spend a few minutes a day reading this love letter.

"Whoever keeps the law!" How can you "keep" a law if you don't know what it is? That is my whole point. How can you know what is "pleasing" to God and what "displeases" Him if you don't know the rules? Just the book of Proverbs is so rich with biblical instruction. I hope these devotionals and this trip through Proverbs this year will open your eyes to the things that "please" God and those that don't!

All through Proverbs Solomon gives us "contrasts". Solomon received these Proverbs through the power of God's Spirit. The same is true with ALL the Old and New Testament. Same "author," different writers. The truth is the same. The application? - That is between you and God.

My second book was on the life of David (David's Walk with God). I have learned so much about God's heart in that study it just gave me a whole new perspective on how God works in each of our lives. Oh, it also showed me, without a doubt, the extraordinary GRACE of God, for David and for us!

> One who turns away his ear from hearing the law, even his prayer is an abomination. Whoever causes the upright to go astray is an evil way, he himself will fall into his own pit; but the blameless will inherit good. (Proverbs 28:9-10)

What is the point? I don't understand half of what Solomon is saying. Do you want to give up? Then you missed the point. Let's try this, if God wanted to call a passage to your mind, could He do it if it is not there?

When we read God's word we are storing on our hard drive if you will, the truth of the Bible. Later, when God needs to teach us, or someone else, those words are there to retrieve. I am not talking about memorizing. That is helpful.

I don't know how many times I have heard someone say, in our Sunday school class, "Doesn't the Bible say something about. . . "They know the Bible says something about a subject. Praise God for our concordance. It can be so helpful. They would not have known it was there if they hadn't read it, would they?

Here, let me share this verse:

For no other foundation can anyone lay than that which is laid, which is Jesus Christ. (1 Corinthians 3:11)

Do you have a "foundation" of Scripture? - The stronger your "foundation" in the Word of God the greater your chances of defeating the lies of this world. It begins with Jesus Christ. My favorite is the Gospel of John, but, read all four; each approaches Christ's life from a different perspective. Four "testimonies" of the same life and message God is sending this lost and dying world.

I am NOT a fan of ignoring the Old Testament, it is as critical as the New Testament. You cannot understand the New without the foundation of the Old Testament. Get on a Bible reading schedule; it will take you a year but it is well worth it. Don't RUSH through your reading allow God to open His Word and allow His Spirit to guide you through the truths of Scripture. The PATH is a great resource!

> The rich man is wise in his own eyes, but the poor who has understanding searches him out. When the righteous rejoice, there is great glory; but when the wicked arise, men hide themselves. (Proverbs 28:11-12)

Isn't it interesting how we tend to measure everything in dollars and cents? Just like Solomon in the first words of these Proverbs, - The "rich" and the "poor"; then in the next verse, the "righteous" and the "wicked." He makes an interesting distinction in the first comparisons. "Understanding", - understanding what?

You see the rich are measured by "his own eyes, while the poor search for the "truth" or understanding. He looks up while the rich looks in. Interesting thought don't you think?

Why does Solomon choose, for the most part, to "contrast" the two situations? We understand contrast. Black & white, up & down, left and right. - Opposites. Oh, I forgot good and evil. Now there, today, we are having a hard time drawing a line, are we not? We want to make this "contrast," into a gray area. Just look at what we have done with "lying". Gray area? Really?

How about sex? Okay, I won't go there; too many "gray" areas in the world today. If you water down the truth, what do you have? - Gray areas. Today, with so many different "translations" of the Bible, maybe we could find one that isn't so "truthful"?

What is your "measuring stick"? What guidelines do you use to determine right and wrong? Your own interpretation of what is right and wrong? Solomon is drawing a contrast here, is he not? The rich and the poor, the righteous and the wicked, pretty drastic opposites are they not? But it is not that simple today. Does that mean the Bible is obsolete? I think not, we just choose to ignore the black and white and settle for gray.

I missed a word in verse 11 above, - "Searches". If we settle for the gray area there is no need to search, we just settle. I guess it is like settling for reading a couple of verses in the Bible and figure you have all you need. You settle for incomplete truth. The Bible is black and white, no gray areas; maybe that is why we spend so little time in it!

      Lonny E. Young

> He who covers his sins will not prosper, but whoever confesses
> and forsakes them will have mercy. Happy is the man who
> is always reverent, but he who hardens his heart will fall into
> calamity. (Proverbs 28:13-14)

What to do with sin? Just so we understand each other, allow me to quote from Romans:

*For **all** have sinned and come short of the glory of God.* (Romans 3:23)

Just so we are clear. And where does this sin come from? - The day that Adam took of the fruit and ate it "contrary" to God's command (Genesis 2:17). Disobedience, - and we have been disobedient ever since. It is our nature if you will. So, you cannot deny your sin. There was only one "perfect" Person, Jesus Christ.

So, what do we do with this sin? We hide it of course. No one knows but us. That's easy. - Really? Do you think God doesn't know? Don't forget our buddy, David. He thought he got away with sin, he didn't, and neither will you.

Again, what do we do with it? The first verse my wife and I memorized as new Christians is found in 1 John:

*If we **confess** our sins, He is faithful and just to forgive us our sins and to cleanse us of all unrighteousness.* (1 John 1:9)

Confess to whom? - God of course. He already knows what I did, why should I "confess" it? God doesn't need to know, He wants YOU to acknowledge your sin. By confessing it, we acknowledge to God what we have done. Have you ever had a Highway Patrolman pull you over? He comes up to your car and says, "Do you know what you did?" He wants to be sure YOU know what you did wrong. The same is true with God until we "acknowledge" what we have done we cannot repent, turn away, from our mistake.

> Like a roaring lion and a charging bear is the wicked ruler over poor people. A ruler who lacks understanding is a great oppressor, but he who hates covetousness will prolong his days. (Proverbs 28:15-16)

We might think a shepherd's job is just to sit around all day and watch the sheep. Did you notice the two animals that Solomon mentions here? The same two that David says he fought off to defend his sheep, before taking on Goliath. (1 Samuel 17:36). A dangerous job!

Both verses pertaining to those who are ruling over us; make no mistake, we have those who are "appointed" over us. I think it is funny that young people can't wait to leave home so they can be "on their own". There is "always" someone in authority over you, in some manner or other.

Lacks understanding. Isn't it interesting how things change once you become "in charge"? We look at leadership and wish we were "in charge" but then, if we get there, it is totally different from that side of the equation.

I wonder if it is the same with a "lost" person versus a Christian. I had someone once after we told them were Christians say, "I can't punish myself that way." That is how the world views Christians. "They would be giving up too much." - Really? You would be giving up the "Lust of the flesh, the lust of the eyes, and the pride of life" (1 John 2:16-17) for what? Peace with God, an inner peace you cannot imagine, not to mention, an eternity in heaven, versus the alternative. Yes, I can see where that would be a tough decision.

Would you consider Solomon a "wicked ruler"? In the beginning, Solomon was walking with God. God blessed him with more wisdom than any other man alive. Then he started listening to those around him, check out 1 Kings 12. It is so sad that we can be drawn away from Godly counsel by those around us; His wives, his peers, until God takes the kingdom from a man whom God blessed so much. How is this possible?

Again, those two words: *lacks understanding.* A walk with God is a "daily" commitment. You pray and you read your Bible; you meditate on your fellowship with a God who wants the best for you. You serve!

     Lonny E. Young

A man burdened with bloodshed will flee into a pit; let no one help him. Whoever walks blamelessly will be saved, but he who is perverse in his ways will suddenly fall. (Proverbs 28:17-18)

That is impossible. Do you know anyone who is "blameless"? I doubt it. If that is the case how can you be saved? Boy, could I fill up this page with the appropriate verses, and rhetoric, would it do any good? Is it something you haven't heard before? Probably not. I pray this whole devotional has challenged your walk with God if you have one. I think if you have gotten this far, you are probably a Christian.

Don't miss that word "walks". All through the Bible, the Word of God portrays our relationship with God as a "walk." We don't sit, we don't lie down, we are walking. Even in the Passover picture in Exodus:

And thus, you shall eat it: with a belt on your waist, your sandals on your feet, and your staff in your hand. So, shall you eat it in haste. It is the Lord's Passover. (Exodus 12:11)

Don't miss this picture. I guess the question would be, who are you "walking" with? Do you have that "fellowship" with God that He is walking next to you? That you are seeking His guidance as to which forks in the road to take? Who is leading who?

Here is an interesting question. Do you know where this road, this journey is headed? In your infinite wisdom? Sorry, I am being sarcastic. We don't know what will happen in the next hour, let alone the path we are about to take. Hopefully, you do know the "destination." It can only be one of two places. The choice of destination is yours.

Now, if you are walking with God, we can assume that the destination has already been established by accepting Jesus as your Savior. Now, if you are walking alone your destination has been established as well. Not good!

Don't despair. God is right behind you, waiting for you to turn around (repent) and ask Jesus to come into your heart. Say yes!

November 30   334-31   Proverbs 28

> He who tills his land will have plenty of bread, but he who
> follows frivolity will have poverty enough! A faithful man will
> abound with blessings, but he who hastens to be rich will not
> go unpunished. (Proverbs 28:19-20)

This coming from the richest man of his time; more gold and silver than he knew what to do with, brought in on barges! (1 Kings 10:22) Do you think Solomon is condemning getting rich? Not hardly! Look at the previous verse. It is two things: work and faithfulness!

We are getting away from that today. You don't need to work hard, just ask the government, they will take care of you. The more people we can get to rely on "government" the more we can trust them to support the "cause".

Do you realize, think about it, the amount of "faith" it takes to be a farmer? You go out and spend hundreds of dollars on the seed. You work hard for several days, sun up to sundown, to get this seed planted. Then you go out every day and you MAKE the seed grow? Not hardly! It is God, and only God, who produces the fruit from your investment, both in labor and money. That is a scary way to live!

Think about it. You do what you are supposed to do. Then you must trust God for the outcome. That is the way life is, is it not? You live your life hopefully walking with God, but the outcome is purely up to God, is it not? Can you "control" what will happen tomorrow, the next day, or the next? Of course not!

A faithful man. How would you describe that adjective? What constitutes a "faithful" man? Faithful to his job, his family, his future, you name it. NO! A faithful man is faithful to his God. He walks with Him, he trusts Him, and he obeys His commands and instructions. That is a "faithful" man. Can you be faithful to all these other things and prosper? I think not. Let me close with this passage from Joshua:

This book of the Law shall not depart from your mouth, but you shall meditate in it day and night, that you may observe to do according to all that is written in it. For then you will make your way prosperous, and then you will have good success. (Joshua 1:8)

      Lonny E. Young

> To show partiality is not good, because for a piece of bread
> a man will transgress. A man with an evil eye hastens after
> riches, and does not consider that poverty will come upon
> him. (Proverbs 28:21-22)

There is one thing about these riches. I hope you have marked Joshua 1:8 in your Bible; a principle straight from the heart of God. What I want you to think about is "focus". To illustrate, I remember this story about a farmer, yesterday we were talking about farmers. Think about this. A farmer is said to have told this story. When you are out in a large field and you want to plow a "strait" line you "focus" on something at the other side of the field and you plow toward it, - it is your focus.

I love this idea, put one finger in front of your eyes about 8 inches away, now, focus on your finger. What do you see behind your finger? It is blurry, isn't it? Now focus on something beyond your finger. Is your finger blurry? Of course, it is.

When we are focused on something today, we can lose focus on tomorrow. And tomorrow takes our attention from the events of today. So, what is the answer? There is nothing we can do about tomorrow; God is in charge of that.

When you are walking along a path following someone, where is your focus? It is on the one in front of you, is it not? That is the way we are to live, instead of the events and circumstances around us that can distract us, we need to focus on the One leading us! If you have that "relationship" with God you want to focus on His direction, not yours.

It can also be related to "priorities" as well. What is important to you? That will, of course, affect your focus. If riches, fame, "the world" is your priority that will also be your focus. They work hand in hand. Have you ever thought of making a "priority list" of your own? List the things in order of importance in your life, and how much time and energy do you spend on each of these. This can be a great indicator of your priorities.

You know where I am going. Where does God fit on this priority list? Where do you suppose you are on God's list?

> He who rebukes a man will find more favor afterward than he who flatters with the tongue. Whoever robs his father or his mother, and says, "It is no transgression," the same is companion to a destroyer. (Proverbs 28:23-24)

Do you feel it? Thanksgiving is over and we are into December. Do you feel the "stress" building? I hope not. I am going to try and help keep you focus on what is important through the coming holiday season. Stick with me. Do your reading, praying and meditating on these verses from Solomon. We talked about "focus"; it is so important to stay focused on the "Reason for the Season."

Have you met either of these "gentlemen" recently? The "flatterer" and the "rebuker"? If you had to choose, which would you prefer to meet? Myself, the one who rebukes me; him I can learn from. The "flatterer" will simply play to my ego and, more likely get me in trouble. We all like the "strokes" but do they really help us? Not likely!

"I would never do that!" Are those your words for verse 24? I am sure most of us would never think of "robbing" our parents. There are many ways of "stealing" from those we love, ignoring them, neglecting them (about the same), talking down to them, taking advantage of them. If I may, let's do some review:

Honor your father and your mother, that your days may be long upon the land which the Lord your God is giving you. (Exodus 20:12)

I like what someone pointed out once. This is the first commandment "with promise". It is the first commandment following the four commandments concerning our relationship with God. - A priority, possibly?

Just a reminder, - Now that I am in my seventies, the holidays are not as hectic as they once were; shopping, dinners, traveling to relatives, etc. It can get very hectic. It tends to distract from the whole purpose of these days that are set aside for us to celebrate the birth of our Savior. Please, take a minute each day and say, "Thank you!"

     Lonny E. Young

December 3   337-28   Proverbs 29

> He who is often rebuked, and hardens his neck, will suddenly be destroyed, and that without remedy. When the righteous are in authority, the people rejoice; but when a wicked man rules, the people groan. (Proverbs 29:1-2)

That is what we will be celebrating in about three weeks, - The birth of a King, the King of kings and the Lord of lords. There is a thought: *When the righteous are in authority.* Is He, In authority?

I know we have talked about this but at this time of year, we need to acknowledge His Lordship. If He is Lord. I heard some preacher, as a young Christian, talking about the Lordship of Jesus. It is one thing to be saved, to ask Jesus into your heart, but quite another to make Him Lord of your life. Later, I realized that should be a "done-deal" You don't get saved one day then later make Jesus the Lord of your life.

Who, or better still, what is lord of your life? What or who controls the decisions you make each day? I say "what" because for most of us it can be "money" that influences our decisions and/or direction in our life. Maybe it is a friend who is always imparting their "wisdom" as to what WE should do, maybe you have read some "self-help" books, or listened to tapes, or watched videos. Eat, Pray, Love, etc. There is always someone or something seeking to direct your life.

Have you considered the Bible? Maybe spending some time meditating on these chapters of Proverb; an interesting book to study as well is Ecclesiastes, written by the same author. If you're into the New Testament you might want to consider the book of James. There is no limit to "advice" to run your life. How about the One who created you in the first place? If anyone knows what you NEED, it would be Him.

It is hard to believe sometimes that little baby in that manger with Joseph and Mary and the shepherds, He loves you so much, that when He is grown up, and He will take your place on the cross of Calvary to pay for your sins so that you have the right to stand before God "forgiven", if you ask this tiny baby to come into your heart and be your Savior.

He is the reason we celebrate each year; that God loved us so much that He took on the form of a man to prove His love for us, to die for our sins, to make us part of His family!

> Whoever loves wisdom makes a father rejoice, but a companion of harlots wastes his wealth. The king establishes the land by justice, but he who receives bribes overthrows it. (Proverbs 29:3-4)

Isn't it interesting how we grow? We begin as little children. I remember in Kindergarten having this huge pile of blocks, sanded smooth and varnished. The possibilities! Have you ever watched children play with "simple" things for hours? The old joke of buying an expensive gift and the child plays with the box. They are learning!

Oh, the famous "leaving home for the first time." What an experience. You can make your own decisions now. The learning process begins again. There is so much "maintenance" to life that young people must learn from experience. It is a learning process.

We never stop learning, especially with today's high-tech world we live in. We get a new "gadget" and we must ask our grandchildren how to work it. It is amazing what they know today, but then again.

I can use a new phone with ease. Could they find Ecclesiastes in their Bible, assuming they have one? Oh, that is "old news" that book is "ancient history". I am sure you have heard the comments. They say that only because there are lessons they are learning the hard way. It is amazing the older they get the more they discover the truth of the Bible if they spend any time checking it out; sometimes they must learn the hard way.

"Wisdom" is written on these pages. If they spent half the time in the Bible that spends on their phones, you would be amazed at the "wisdom" they would acquire. Now we have the "Bible" on our cell phones. Sorry, I can't connect the two. I want to underline, circle, make notes, etc. It is not the same. The Bible is meant to be a "textbook" of wisdom for all who seek wisdom.

Any parent who is a Christian rejoices when their children and grandchildren ask Jesus into their heart, the rejoicing doubles when they see them "growing" in their Christian walk, faithful to church, serving the Lord; much as Solomon speaks of in verse 3.

Did you have your quiet time today? Take a few minutes to talk with the Creator of the universe? Why not?

     Lonny E. Young

A man who flatters his neighbor spreads a net for his feet. By transgression an evil man is snared, but the righteous sings and rejoices. (Proverbs 29:5-6)

Here is a saying maybe you have heard before, - "Flattery will get you anything." Does that sound like something Solomon is dealing with here? Here is an example of "wisdom" for those "young people" that you think might be outdated. The truth is there, we just must learn the hard way.

There is so much talk today about what we eat, what is good for us, what is not. If you're like me you can usually figure on gaining five pounds through the holidays. How about that Thanksgiving dinner? I think it is interesting that the things that were SO bad for us five years ago are now healthy.

Here are some words from Jesus:

"Do you not understand that whatever enters the mouth goes into the stomach and is eliminated? But those things which proceed out of the mouth come from the heart, and they defile a man. (Matthew 15:17-18)

Of course, this is that "out-of-date" book that is not important today in our society. Even still, you can't "argue" with the wisdom, can you?

This is a good verse to keep in mind throughout the holidays. We can get so "stressed" that we will say and do things that might hurt others. We need to practice a little advice that James gives us:

*So then, my beloved brethren, let every man **be swift to hear, slow to speak, slow to wrath.** For the wrath of man does not produce the righteousness of God.* (James 1:19-20)

The "wisdom" of the Bible, - check it out. The five chapters of James contain so much wisdom pertaining to today, that it is scary!

I hope you have made it a "habit" to spend some time with the Lord, leading up to the New Year. Make it a "habit" in your life!

> The righteous considers the cause of the poor, but the wicked does not understand such knowledge. Scoffers set a city aflame, but the wise men turn away wrath. (Proverbs 29:7-8)

Isn't that funny? We are approaching Christmas, we run across a verse that talks about "wise men." "Scoffers" just chalk that up to coincidence. Those who "know" realize the implications.

I don't know how many times I have seen this. Most song leaders don't "consult" with the pastor about what he is going to preach on that Sunday, they make their selections of songs, using their own criteria (Holy Spirit); so often the song selection will perfectly match the message the pastor will preach on. Even the pastors are amazed!

There are countless examples of things that happen in our life that we want to chalk up to "coincidence". Sadly, far too many!

Just like finding a verse on a given day, in your regular reading, that SO speaks to your heart "that day!" It is NOT coincidence; it is God trying to get your attention. Just like reading through these "Proverbs". Most of the time there is nothing there. Then one day, you read a verse that just "grabs" you, - that is my story with Jeremiah 29:11-13. I saw it on a fragrance packet in someone's bathroom. I couldn't wait to look it up myself; I just fell in love with it.

Just a note about verse 7, - Many times, God gives us perspectives on things that the lost have no clue about. We see things differently, as Christians, and then others do. Take Christmas!

As a child and young adult, Christmas was all about family and presents. I really paid little or no attention to the "Christmas story" as such. After I became a Christian, it took on a whole new meaning, - a "personal" meaning. I wonder how many people including Christians connect the Manger Scene with the Cross. We don't want to connect the two. If the "Lamb" had not been born there, it would not have been a Sacrifice!

Are you getting impatient yet? Too early? Not if you're a child. As soon as the calendar moves into December, Thanksgiving is over, you start thinking about Christmas. And, of course, as a child, your "focus" is on the presents. Don't neglect that Baby in the manger!

December 7   341-24   Proverbs 29

> If a wise man contends with a foolish man, whether the fool rages or laughs, there is no peace. The bloodthirsty hate the blameless, but the upright seek his wellbeing. (Proverbs 29:9-10)

Have you ever tried to "convince" someone who would not be convinced? It is a losing battle. You could show them the "proof" in black and white and they would argue the authority. That is where God's Holy Spirit moves in. State your case, then back away. God's Spirit can be much more persuasive than your words; trying to convince someone, who will not listen, is exactly what Solomon is talking about.

I talked yesterday about verses that just jump out at you. I am not a big fan of the book of Job. After the first two or three chapters, I get lost in the rhetoric.

I did run across a verse in chapter 22 that just knocked my socks off:

Now acquaint yourself with Him, and be at peace; thereby good will come to you. Receive, please, instruction from His mouth, and lay up His words in your heart. (Job 22:21-22)

Of course, who is Eliphaz talking about? - God, of course. At least the capitalized words can give you a hint, it did to me. Look at this: *receive instruction from His mouth.* Now, how can that be? When was the last time God "spoke" to you? When was the last time you read your Bible? - Same difference. When you read the Word of God that is God's own heart speaking to your heart. Are you listening?

As a young Christian, being so wise in my own wisdom I asked myself once, I wonder where the "copyright" for the Bible is. That will explain who wrote the Bible. I found it! Not in the front of the Bible but in the end:

For I testify to everyone who hears the words of the prophecy of this book: if anyone adds to these things, God will add to him the plagues that are written in this book; and if anyone takes away from the words of the book of this prophecy, God will take away his part from the Book of Life. (Revelation 22:18-19)

> A fool vents all his feelings, but a wise man holds them back. If a ruler pays attention to lies, all his servants become wicked. The poor man and the oppressor have this in common; The Lord gives light to the eyes of both. (Proverbs 29:11-13)

I don't know how many times this has happened recently, a lot more often, the older I get. I will think of responding to something or "voice" my opinion. One of two things will happen; someone else will say it, in which case, they get the flack, or very shortly it will turn out that I would have made a fool of myself. By holding my tongue, I miss the embarrassment, more often than I care to think, the more I hold my tongue the better off I am.

I also don't care to think about the times I ventured my opinion and truly "regretted" it. Sometimes it is best just to keep your opinions to yourself. Thank you, Solomon.

The Lord gives light to the eyes of both. What do you suppose that means? Let's try this. We all have "access" to the truth (light). We either chooses to ignore it or not accept it, either way, we walk in darkness by choice; one of the major reasons I push reading through the Bible. Truth is not confined to the New Testament. God gave us all 66 books for a reason. I have my doubts about a couple, but that is just me.

There is a lesson in Job I had forgotten; I mentioned yesterday that I was not a fan of Job. I like the first two or three chapters. When his friends begin counseling him, I get lost, too deep for me.

There is a huge lesson at the end:

*And the Lord restored Job's losses **when he prayed for his friends.** Indeed, the Lord gave Job twice as much as he had before.* (Job 42:10)

Philosophical discussions lose me, I am sure many "students" can make more sense of it than I can. His friends were all trying to tell Job where he went wrong with God. Never underestimate the first few chapters. At one point Job's wife told him to "curse God, and die." (Job 2:9) Maybe God just wanted to see if he would be faithful. Job was, and God blessed him!

                Lonny E. Young

> The king who judges the poor with truth, his throne will
> be established forever. The rod and rebuke give wisdom,
> but a child left to himself brings shame to his mother.
> (Proverbs 29:14-15)

Have you heard this "children are NOT born sinners they learn if from their upbringing or their environment"? If that is true, we as parents just need to allow our children to go their merry way and not correct them at all, kind of like most people think God should do for us. - Really?

Have you met any of these children? There is a term used today to describe these children, -"spoiled", like in NO GOOD!

Just spend a few Sundays working in your church nursery; you will observe the first sin. "Selfishness"! It is not "taught" to children by their parents, it is part of their "nature". Next will come, lying, when you confront them with something they have done wrong. Is this not true?

Several times in Proverbs, Solomon exhorts us to "correct" our children. CORRECT not "abuse!" There is a huge difference. I believe that is why God gave everyone extra padding in the posterior, not just for sitting!

Don't miss Solomon's estimation of the benefits of this correction. Wisdom is gained from correction, - a principle Solomon preaches often. When we are "corrected" it is a lesson learned, hopefully; of course, some need correcting more often than others. The lesson is the same, getting the wisdom may take several tries!

Just over two weeks till Christmas, have you made any plans? "It is too far away yet", really? I don't remember who it was; he made fun of those who are caught "off guard" by Christmas, "surprised" that it came so soon. You know what? It comes on the same day every year; just ask your children or any children. Thanksgiving signals the beginning of the Christmas season.

I like to observe people. The funniest thing happens around this time of year. Have you noticed it? The word "giving" all of a sudden becomes popular. It seems this "season" sparks a flame in us that lies dormant, for some, until December. Why is that? Some people around this time talk about Christmas all year round. It is giving!

> When the wicked are multiplied, transgression increases;
> but the righteous will see their fall. Correct your son, and he
> will give you rest; yes, he will give you delight to your soul.
> (Proverbs 29:16-17)

Familiar themes? Why do you suppose Solomon continues these basic themes? Could it be that we tend to tune out "instruction?" I have lived long enough to see the impact of our "educational system" on the young people today; it is rare to see a young person who knows how to count change in the store.

Note the rise of "homeschooling". Our educational system is failing us. The only reason I approach this subject is the drumbeat of Solomon, - the very real need for "instruction" in our homes. From Kindergarten to high school, who has the greatest influence on our children? - The educational system. It is a battle to be joined!

Okay, off my soapbox. I love the fact that Solomon acknowledges that "in the end" the righteous will prevail. I have never seen the devil so active in our country than he is today! No more behind the scenes, no more in the darkness, lurking around. He has made his appearance and is seeking whom he may devour. (1 Peter 5:8)

Another reason for instruction, - If we are not aware of the enemy he will overcome us. So, it is important to spend time in God's Word; put on the whole armor of God (Ephesians 6).

Don't forget our buddy, David. When he took on the giant, Goliath, his only weapon was a slingshot AND the power of God!

Look at this:

"Then all this assembly shall know that the Lord does not save with sword or spear; **for the battle is the Lord's**, *and He will give you into our hands."* (1 Samuel 17:47)

Just what Solomon, David's son, has said, *"But the righteous will see their fall."* - When we turn the "battle" over to the Lord. That is NOT to say we shouldn't engage, David did, but David's strength and power lie in the power of God. We still must stand for what is right; we can make a difference!

> Where there is no revelation, the people cast off restraint;
> but happy is he who keeps the law. A servant will not be
> corrected by mere words; for though he understands, he will
> not respond. (Proverbs 29:18-19)

I often wonder what the prophets and writers of the Old Testament, especially people like Daniel, Ezekiel, Jeremiah, and David were thinking when God chose to reveal the future to them, prophecy. "How can this be?" Like the contrast between Zacharias and Mary in the book of Luke. Here was Zacharias response to the angel telling him they would have a son:

And Zacharias said to the angel, "How shall I know this? For I am old, and my wife is well advanced in years." (Luke 1:17)

Now look at Mary's response when the angel said she would have a child:

Then Mary said to the angel, "How can this be, since I do not know a man?" (Luke 1:34)

Zacharias doubted the "ability" of God to make this happen; Mary doubted her being worthy to receive such an honor. There is a big difference. Do you "doubt" God's ABILITY to accomplish something? - Really? That is not faith. That is the keyword.

One last verse if you will:

But without faith it is impossible to please Him, for he who comes to God must believe that He is, and that He is a rewarder of those who diligently seek Him. (Hebrews 11:6)

Until you can "trust" God to accomplish His will in your life, you will have no power. Just remember that it is that same "faith" that gives you your salvation through Jesus Christ, trust in God; the closer you walk with God the more you will learn to trust Him!

> Do you see a man hasty in his words? There is more hope for a
> fool than for him. He who pampers his servant from childhood
> will have him as a son in the end. (Proverbs 29:20-21)

You're in a group of five or six people. Have you ever tried to make a point? They are either talking over each other, or one person is dominating the conversation. I think I mentioned before that I hate confrontation; I will just sit back and listen. Interesting what you can learn!

I was a Sunday school teacher for several years; I learned an interesting trick to begin the class. Most of you know there is a LOT of visiting when everyone is coming in and being seated. At one point, you must be alert, there will be a lull. Jump in! That is your cue!

I have talked before about listening versus talking. Try it. When I was little, our bedroom was upstairs, my brothers and I would creep down the steps just far enough to hear what the "grownups" were saying. The things you can learn! The point is, if you "listen" every chance you get, you will be that much further ahead. But Solomon makes a great point about *"hasty in words"* sometimes we are in such a hurry to get our opinion out, we miss the "good stuff".

How are God's children referred to often in the Bible? They are called "servants", are they not? Maybe I am stretching Solomon's point here, but think about it.

Do you think of yourself as a "servant" of God? How about a "child" of God? The latter is less likely. We like to think of ourselves more as servants. I have no problem with that.

But, look at the picture in these verses:

For as many as are led by the Spirit of God, these are sons of God. For you did not receive the spirit of bondage again to fear, but you received the Spirit of adoption by whom we cry out, "Abba, Father." The Spirit Himself bears witness with our spirit that we are **children of God.** (Romans 8:14-16)

As a blood-bought child of God, we have a very special relationship with God, not servants any longer but children adopted to be His!

An angry man stirs up strife, and a furious man abounds in transgression. A man's pride will bring him low, but the humble in spirit will retain honor. (Proverbs 29:22-23)

*For all that is in the world—the lust of the flesh, the lust of the eyes, **and the pride of life**—is not of the Father but is of the world.* (1 John 2:16)

This can go back to what we talked about yesterday. We like to refer to ourselves as "servants" to avoid this idea of pride. If we think of ourselves as servants we will have a servant's attitude. - Really? So, being a "child of God" exalts your standing? Tell that to Jesus.

Yes, I can see His arrogance and pride throughout the gospels. Jesus was the humblest person in the Bible, the Son of God. The Bible even goes so far as to call us "joint heirs with Christ" (Romans 8:17). No pride there!

As children of God, we should have the same attitude as our Lord. When Satan tempted Jesus in the wilderness, (Matthew 4) what was Jesus' defense? "Do you know who I am?" No! He simply quoted the "word of God" back to Satan. He claimed no special "authority" only the words of His Father, as we should!

Twelve days till Christmas. Are you ready? - Probably not. Have you got your list? You know those who you MUST buy for. Be it family, friends, those who bought you gifts. Don't forget that last group. Those we must return the favor, respond in kind. - Really?

There was an important event for me, as a young Christian. I had bought a birthday card for one of my Sunday school students. I didn't get a gift so I put five dollars in the card, she would not accept it. Then her father stepped in and told her, "You are depriving Lonny of the blessing by not accepting his gift." That has stuck with me. Before, I would have done the same thing, refused the gift. Someone was thoughtful enough to get you a gift, by refusing to accept that gift you are depriving THEM of the blessing of giving. Think about it.

Of course, God purchased a gift for us, - the gift of salvation through His Son Jesus. It is offered freely. Will you turn it down?

> Whoever is a partner with a thief hates his own life; he
> swears to tell the truth, but reveals nothing. The fear of man
> brings a snare, but whoever trusts in the Lord shall be safe.
> (Proverbs 29: 24-25)

"Fear of man" or *"Fear of the Lord?"* What are you afraid of? What a contrast! We have been talking all through these proverbs how Solomon uses "contrasts" in his verses. Here is a "contrast", FEAR versus FAITH. Now there is a contrast; with that we could measure both of these in our own life.

The He touched their eyes, saying, **"According to your faith be it to you."** (Matthew 9:29)

It seems faith can be measured. At the risk of repeating myself, here is a fantastic verse:

*But **without faith** it is impossible to please Him, for he who comes to God must believe that He is, and that He is a rewarder of those who diligently seek Him.* (Hebrews 11:6)

If you have the "faith" to seek God you believe that He is. That pleases God. It is a start. Okay, one more, please:

*If you confess with your mouth the Lord Jesus and **believe** in your heart that God raised Him from the dead, you will be saved. For with the heart one **believes** unto righteousness, and with the mouth confession is made unto salvation.* (Romans 10:9-10)

The fear of man and faith in God, - an awesome combination; so, do you fear God? If so why? John 3:16 says God loves you. Why would you fear Him? Unless you are not a child of God, but a child of this world, in that case, you should fear God. Just a hint, read the book of Revelation; you will get the point.

Ten days till Christmas Eve. Do you catch yourself thinking more and more about those extra days off? How about the baby Jesus?

> The words of Agur the son of Jakeh, his utterance. This man declared to Ithiel—to Ithiel and Ucal: Surely, I am more stupid than any man, and do not have the understanding of a man. (Proverbs 30:1-2)

Oh, these are not the words of Solomon, so we don't need to take them seriously. Don't miss this! ALL the words in the Bible are written by the same person, - the Holy Spirit of God.

I think that is part of what Agur is wrestling with, as with many other authors of the Old Testament. They were given visions, and prophecy they couldn't possibly understand. What do you think went through Isaiah's mind when the Holy Spirit told Isaiah to write this?

Therefore, the Lord Himself will give you a sign: Behold, the virgin shall conceive and bear a Son, and shall call His name Immanuel. (Isaiah 7:14)

Or this passage:

For unto us a Child is born, unto us a Son is given; and the government will be upon His shoulder. And His name will be called, Wonderful, Counselor, Mighty God, Everlasting Father, Prince of Peace. (Isaiah 9:6)

What do you suppose went through Isaiah's mind and thoughts? I can think of one word, - wonder! What is this I am thinking? Why do I have such words? - Like the words of Agur: *do not have the understanding of a man.* You were not supposed to "understand" just simply write what God has given you to write. The "understanding" will come hundreds of years later.

As we draw even closer to this "special" celebration, many of these verses will be used over and over. Do not let their significance pass you by. This simple birth turned the world upside down. The world would never be the same again. Little did Isaiah know at the time; he was simply told to write these words. Praise God he was willing to listen to God and obey God. Ten days till Christmas Day!

> I neither learned wisdom nor have knowledge of the Holy One. Who has ascended into heaven, or descended? Who has gathered the wind in His fists? Who has bound the waters in a garment? Who has established all the ends of the earth? What is His name? And what is His Son's name? If you know? (Proverbs 30:3-4)

Now, how would Agur know that God had a Son? I spoke about this yesterday. What these writers must have thought when God put these words in their thoughts? Agur, to me, sounds like some of the guys who questioned Job. Flowery!

Interesting comment: *I neither learned wisdom nor have knowledge of the Holy One.* Let's see, all he would have to go on might be the five books of Moses, assuming he had access to them. Notice that a lot of his comments relate to nature. If you took a few minutes and meditated on the wonders of nature you would have to conclude there is a God.

I like what one guy said, "It takes more faith to think this happened by "accident" than to believe in a creator." My wife likes to put this "Hummingbird" feeder out. I had the weirdest thought the other day. I wonder who the predator of the hummingbird is. Every creature has a predator; it is the "circle of life" that God has established.

Ever wake up in the morning and you are just SO content you just wished the clock would stop and you could have ten more minutes? It doesn't work that way, God doesn't stop. God set everything into motion to bring you to this point at this time for a purpose! Maybe that is what Agur is wrestling with. Why me, why now?

Even as a Christian of over thirty years I marvel at how God works. The way He works in people's lives and accomplishes His perfect will. I love watching people, how they respond to events in their life. A lot depends on their "relationship" with the Lord.

Less than two weeks away. Do you see the excitement in your children? It is like they try to will the days to go faster. Do you have your tree up? We usually put ours up around the first of December. Are there any presents under it? Some prefer to wait till Christmas Eve, especially if you have little ones. Got your "plans" in place?

Lonny E. Young

> Every word of God is pure; He is a shield to those who put
> their trust in Him. Do not add to His words, lest He rebuke
> you, and you be found a liar. (Proverbs 30:5-6)

I was privileged to attend First Baptist Church, Dallas, Texas, and the year that the Southern Baptist Convention was held there. On Sunday morning, I got to hear Dr. W.A. Criswell preach on the inerrancy of the Bible. I was blown away; I hadn't been a Sunday School Director for very long. I had found my calling, - The Bible, teaching the Word of God!

I marvel at Agur here. Just think I pointed out earlier how much of God's Word did Agur have access to, - the books of Moses, maybe the life of David, the writings of Samuel the prophet. It is hard to say. The funny thing is that his very words will become part of God's Word. WOW! Think about that. What an awesome feeling to know God is speaking through you

A born-again pastor has that feeling every Sunday morning. I say "born-again" because, sadly to say, not every pastor preaches the Word of God. As for "born-again" that is between them and God. Of course, there are no more "prophets" that speak the "Word of God" we are not adding to the Bible. When you speak the Bible, you are speaking the Word of God. Did I lose you? I am sorry.

Very early on, as a new Christian, I found a schedule to read through my Bible in a year. I even wrote a book, doing just that using that schedule, it is called THE PATH. Anyway, I have probably read through my Bible at least ten times, every year I learn so much, I find NEW verses I hadn't seen before. It is truly a miracle!

We could read through our Bibles a hundred times and God would never cease to speak to us. That is the miracle of the Word of God. The point is, IT IS THE WORD OF GOD! The more time you spend in it, the more you get to understand the "heart" of God. I did a study in the life of David, "David's Walk with God" and the more I studied how God worked in David's life, despite his serious mistake with Bathsheba, the more I could see God's heart. I wanted to know why David was called, "A man after God's own heart" (1 Samuel 13:14).

> Two things I request of You (deprive me not before I die): remove falsehood and lies far from me; give me neither poverty nor riches—feed me with the food allotted to me; lest I be full and deny You, and say, "Who is the Lord?" Or lest I be poor and steal, and profane the name of my God. (Proverbs 30:7-9)

Is that not the heart of a true Christian? "Lord, grant the things I need, to serve You!" What an awesome prayer, BUT, can we be "satisfied" with what God gives us? I am sure you might have said the same thing I have said, "Lord, I could do so much more if You would give me more." - Really? Does God know your heart? Be content with what God has blessed you with:

Not that I speak in regard to need, for I have learned in whatever state I am, to be content: I know how to be abased, and I know how to abound. Everywhere and in all things, I have learned both to be full and to be hungry, both to abound and to suffer need. (Philippians 4:11-12)

This from the apostle Paul, whom by all rights should have been blessed beyond measure but, would have disdained it and welcomed God's presence above all else.

Look at this verse in Hebrews:

Let your conduct be without covetousness; be content with such things as you have. For He Himself has said, "I will never leave you or forsake you." (Hebrews 13:5)

Do you want to enjoy Christmas? Meditate on these verses. Many times my daughters and wife have asked me what I want for Christmas. It frustrates them to no end to tell them, "I don't want or need anything, I have everything I want." Of course, that includes "family time" get-togethers, etc. That is all I need.

I sense that Agur desires a close "fellowship" with his Creator. That should be our desire at this time of year, especially at this time of year; what better time to be reminded of the love God has for us.

     Lonny E. Young

Do not malign a servant to his master, lest he curse you, and you be found guilty. (Proverbs 30:10)

We talked about this before. Let me ask you, - what kind of "relationship" do you have with God?" Let's review: A "relationship" is whether you are a "child of God" or not (Romans 8:14-16). How about your "fellowship" with God? Do you "get along," are you walking with God, attending church, praying, reading your Bible? Is God a "part" of your life? That is the "fellowship" part.

Here is the "servant/master" part. You see you can break "fellowship" with God. You can sin, not repent, and turn your back on God. You have broken that "fellowship". You can NEVER break the "relationship" assuming you have truly asked Jesus to come into your heart and save you.

If you have children you know exactly what I am talking about. Read Romans 8:14-16 again. When you are saved you become a "child of God" by adoption. Now as a parent I am sure there are times when your "fellowship" with your children is strained. At some point, I am sure your child has said, "I hate you!" You have broken "fellowship" but, THEY ARE STILL YOUR CHILDREN! There is nothing that can change that "relationship". It is the same with God.

Now, as a child of God, you also have a "servant/master" relationship. One of my favorite passages is 2 Samuel 7. In this passage, King David is praying to God. David has asked God to build God's temple, God has refused him. Then David offers this prayer; ten times in eleven verses David refers to himself as "servant". That is the heart God is looking for in His children.

I heard a preacher once extol the idea that you must make two decisions when you become a Christian. The first is obvious, accepting Jesus Christ as your Savior, and then you are supposed to acknowledge Him as Lord. I don't think they are exclusive. You can't have one without the other. Of course, so many Christians don't acknowledge that second choice, probably because they haven't learned their true relationship with God, either He is Lord or you are lost. There is no "middle" ground. You may rebel, but God will deal with you like children!

> There is a generation that curses its father, and does not bless
> its mother. There is a generation that is pure in its own eyes,
> yet is not washed from its filthiness. There is a generation—
> oh, how lofty are their eyes! And their eyelids are lifted up.
> There is a generation whose teeth are like swords, and whose
> fangs are like knives, to devour the poor from off the earth,
> and the needy from among men. (Proverbs 30:11-14)

I wonder if Agur is talking about his generation; just think how many generations have passed since the time of David, not to mention since the time of Christ. Some have tried different "numbers" to determine a "generation. Forty years seems to be the consensus, hundreds of generations since David. Why is Agur so condemning of the "next" generation? Haven't we heard this for hundreds of years? That "next" generation is worthless; we will never survive this next generation, etc.

I wonder what the generation just "prior" to the World War Two generation thought of the "young people" coming up then. Yet, when the time came they stood up! They changed the world. How about the generation that came over on the Mayflower? Did they think these kids would help build a whole new nation? God has a way of raising workers and leaders in each generation that can make a difference.

When people find out that I served in Vietnam, depending on their perspective of the war, I tell them I just drove a forklift over there. I may not have carried a gun but I did my part. That is all that God asks of each of us.

You attend church faithfully, you give cheerfully, and you do your part. There arises from your congregation, a "Billy Graham," you have done your part in providing the "support" system that brings men like this, to change our country.

Do you know the story of a Sunday school teacher named Kimball? God laid on his heart to make sure every boy in his Sunday school class was saved. He went to a shoe store, where one of his students worked and led him to the Lord. That boy was D.L. Moody. Through a chain of events, D.L. Moody is in the line that brought Billy Graham to the Lord. One generation passing on to the next the gospel message!

      Lonny E. Young

> The leech has two daughters—give and give! There are three things that are never satisfied, four never says, "Enough!" The grave, the barren womb, the earth that is not satisfied with water—and the fire never says, "Enough!" (Proverbs 30:15-16)

Satisfied? What a terrible word at this time of the year. After all the presents are handed out, do you look for more? After you have opened all your gifts do you think to yourself, "Why didn't I get __?" You are always thinking about more!

One of my favorite themes is that of a "crook". Have you ever heard of a thief, after robbing several stores or banks who says, "Okay, that is enough, I will quit now!" - Really? There is NEVER enough! Have you ever looked at your 401K and said, "Good, that is enough!" Not hardly.

I wonder how many years this "more" thing is robbing us of life, - the stress, the anxiety, etc. We talked earlier about the Apostle Paul's take, - Contentment (Philippians 4:11-12). Think about his life for a minute. He was a chief Pharisee. Prestige, wealth, importance, and then God got a hold of his life. I have never read where Paul regretted what he gave up. He was disappointed that he couldn't do more.

The only "contentment" we have in this world is when we are in the center of God's will. Oh, that triggers one of my favorite verses:

I beseech you therefore, brethren, by the mercies of God, that you present your bodies a living sacrifice, holy, acceptable to God, which is your reasonable service. And do not be conformed to this world, but be transformed by the renewing of your mind, that you may prove what is that good and acceptable and perfect will of God! (Romans 12:1-2)

Written by the apostle Paul; when God got a hold of his life, Paul's only purpose was to serve the Lord. He made three perilous missionary journeys, establishing churches and spreading the gospel message. He suffered so much (2 Corinthians 11:23-28), yet he was content to be in the center of God's will! How about you? Do you know for certain that is where you are?

> The eye that mocks his father, and scorns obedience to his mother, the ravens of the valley will pick it out, and the young eagles will eat it. There are three things which are too wonderful for me, yes, four which I do not understand: The way of an eagle in the air, the way of a serpent on a rock, the way of a ship in the midst of the sea, and the way of a man with a virgin. (Proverbs 30:18-19)

There is so much we don't understand. I am in my seventies and still discovering fantastic things in God's world. Do you know what amazes me the most? - To watch God work. You see, He moves so slow that we tend to miss His plans being carried out.

It is like the parent that prays for their children for years at a time. Just about the time they think God is not going to answer their prayer, God moves. Praying for a lost neighbor or friend, year after year, about the time we want to give up, salvation! We want to give up on God too easily!

I wanted to be sure to mention this. I had a brother, two years younger than I. Lester's birthday was on December 22. He died a few years back from the results of Agent Orange when he served in Vietnam. He rarely if ever got a "birthday" present. Too close to Christmas. I always felt sorry for Les. It never seemed to bother him.

Day after tomorrow is Christmas Eve; because our daughters are grown and have their own families, we celebrate "our" Christmas on Christmas Eve, a great time of family that I look forward to it each year. We gather in the living room after some snacks and I read the "Christmas story" (Luke 2:1-14) then we open gifts. A scene played throughout our country in one form or another.

The Christmas story is about a family gathering, on Christmas, for the birth of a child, the Son of God, - a child who would change history and the world forever. I hope He is the center and focus of your Christmas celebration. The tree, the gifts, the music, Oh, the music! The fellowship with our church family and our family; it is just a great time of year.

It is so appropriate that at this time of year there is such a "sense" of family, and above all, a sense of giving! That is God's message to us!

                    Lonny E. Young

December 23   357-8   Proverbs 30

> This is the way of an adulterous woman: she eats and wipes her mouth, and says, "I have done no wickedness." For three things the earth is perturbed, yes, for four it cannot bear up: for a servant when he reigns, a fool when he is filled with food, a hateful woman when she is married, and a maidservant who succeeds her mistress. (Proverbs 30:20-23)

How many times have you been ill and refused to even think about seeing a doctor? Be honest! It is the same way with our "spiritual" condition. As long as we can ignore it, put it off, don't deal with it, we will be okay! - Really? Do you think if you ignore it, it will go away? It doesn't work that way.

My doctor for years kept "suggesting" I get a colonoscopy. In my mind, I am thinking this is a painful, unnecessary procedure. I kept putting it off and putting it off. One day he explained the procedure, after years of coxing. I had the procedure, they found cancer. I had another procedure where they cut out a section of my colon. They got it all. If I had waited just a little longer it would have been too late.

Sin is the same way. It is cancer, unless it is treated, can lead to an early departure from this earth, and unless you are a child of God it will lead to eternally separated from God. It is cancer with only one cure, asking Jesus to come into your heart and save you!

Agur sounds like Solomon in places. That is because they both have the same author, the Holy Spirit. What do you think "perturbed" means? That is what we are when anyone mentions sin. How is that for a definition? That is a sickness that the world tries to cover up and hide. The sin of lying is so prevalent today. Let's just ignore it!

Tomorrow is Christmas Eve. Are you ready? Of course not! No one is. Don't you just hate these people who shop during the summer and have all their gifts bought by Thanksgiving? That is an exception, not the rule. Most of us are doing "last minute" shopping today or tomorrow. Just do me a favor!

Take thirty minutes in the morning. Recruit God's power through His Holy Spirit to keep your focus through the day. No distractions, nothing taking your Christmas joy from you. Ask God to help you!

> There are four things which are little on the earth, but they are exceedingly wise: the ants are a people not strong, yet they prepare their food in the summer; the rock badgers are a feeble folk, yet they make their homes in the crags; the locusts have no king, yet they all advance in ranks; the spider skillfully grasps with its hands, and it is in king's palaces. (Proverbs 30:24-28)

I doubt that Mr. Agur realizes what he has just done. The more you "study" the creatures that make up our world the more you come to realize that there is NO WAY this was an accident; the perfect design from the very beginning. An all-knowing God had all this created from the beginning.

Speaking of little things, are you participating in "Operation Christmas Child"? We saw a video this morning in church. You cannot "buy" the expressions on those children's faces when they open those boxes. But then I guess you could. A few dollars, worth of trinkets will capture the heart of a child for weeks! We have become so spoiled in our country. We look at these trinkets and think nothing of them. Yet, a child in a third-world country has NEVER seen such things. They are a miracle to them.

We were talking in Sunday school about James chapter three. The instructions in the Bible are SO simple! Yet, that is God's plan. Even our salvation is the simplest thing. Just believe in Jesus. You can't get any simpler than that. God never intended a relationship with Him to be "complicated". It is man who makes everything complicated!

Christmas Eve, after tomorrow it will all be over, presents opened, family fellowship, big meals, exchanging love. I touched on this a while back. What is it about this time of year? Why all-of-a-sudden do we have this "giving" spirit? We must because of Christmas? I don't think so. Other holidays don't affect us like this one. Even Thanksgiving has turned into a "shoppers" delight. Forgetting why we celebrate it in the first place.

Christmas is "special". There is no greater expression of love than what God did for us on that special day. The method He chose to reach His creation with this message shows His heart for us!

> There are three things which are majestic in pace, yes, four which are stately in walk: a lion, which is mighty among beasts and does not turn away from any; a greyhound, a male goat also, and a king whose troops are with him. (Proverbs 30:29-31)

Mr. Agur must have been a scientist. His fascination with nature is interesting. He watches long enough to observe their habits and characteristics. Let me offer a study of your own. Park outside a supermarket or a department store and watch the people for an hour. I think my first reaction might be, "What do those two people see in each other?" Ain't love grand! The thing that gets to me is those who use the "handicapped" parking spaces. I better leave that alone!

I guess the best description of God is "creative!" Do you remember in the book of Genesis that God gave Adam the task of naming all these creatures? (Genesis 2:20). Something that has always fascinated me, I would love to have seen the look the person's face that FIRST discovered bananas were editable. How did he discover that unless he took a bite? The look on his face had to be priceless!

Christmas Day has finally arrived. All the waiting and anticipation is over, those days as a child hardly being able to contain yourself until that "magic" hour of opening presents. I remember a trick we used to play. On Christmas Eve, we would beg our parents, "Can't we open "just one?" If they gave in, we eventually opened them all. How can you expect a child to sleep that night? Especially after you have all these toys to play with.

Weeks of anticipation, guessing, hoping, and excitement, OVER in an hour. As I have gotten much older I am not interested in the gifts, seriously! I like to watch the faces of those receiving the gifts, study their reaction, and see what brings that light to their faces. That unexpected gift from a loved one, hopefully, will bless them for the rest of the year. Every time they look at it or use it they might remember where it came from.

That's church! Every Sunday and Wednesday night I am "reminded" of God's greatest gift to this undeserving soul. The gift of peace and eternal life with my heavenly Father! Amen!

> If you have been foolish in exalting yourself, or if you have devised evil, put your hand on your mouth. For as the churning of milk produces butter, and wringing the nose produces blood, so the forces of wrath produces strife. (Proverbs 30:32-33)

What a verse considering what we have just been through. You can have two different Christmases. One of peace and reflection on the meaning of this special holiday, or you can have one of confusion, strife, contention, and disappointment. It is your choice.

How is it my choice? Circumstances just get out of control. I can't control the chaos around me! Of course, you can. It depends on your "focus". As I have said before. Oh, is anyone pushing your "buttons"? We looked at this before as well. That is what happens. If you "respond" in kind, they have achieved their goal: chaos!

Let God's Spirit take control. Listen to His gentle nudge to the reason for this celebration. It is simple really. Are you looking at Jesus or yourself? That is the "button" that is being pushed. Self-interest, I must defend myself; make sure I don't get pushed around. - Really? This is about the birth of Christ, not you!

Too many times we allow the "slights" of the past two days to linger well into the New Year. They fester, and grow, and ruin what could have been a great time of peace and reflection. Put it away. Think about what you have just celebrated, only that!

This next week has always been an awesome time for me. It is a set time, one week exactly, from the celebration of the birth of our Savior, until the beginning of a whole new year. Use this time wisely!

I have shared it before, use this time to "close out" the old year, clear up any "loose ends" that may need resolving, maybe consider making a list of "unfinished tasks". Make it a goal to begin the New Year "fresh". NO unfinished business.

Usually, when I was working, I tried to take a vacation during this time; time to relax, reflect on the past year. Maybe even read through my journals (more about that later).

Here is a hint. Think about what God has done in these past twelve months. Do you see His hand working? Why not?

    Lonny E. Young

> The words of King Lemuel, the utterance which his mother
> taught him: what, my son? And what, son of my womb? And
> what, son of my vows? Do not give your strength to women,
> nor your ways to that which destroys kings. (Proverbs 31:1-3)

My mother taught me so much. I don't think she knew how much. As a teenager, I became a free babysitter to three of my siblings. One day she brought this old black typewriter home. I wasn't going to school; I had dropped out of High School in the tenth grade. She asked me to type a "report" every day on the happenings of our favorite "soap opera", The Edge of Night.

I never realized it at the time but it was her way of "continuing" at least some education. Later, she showed me the family budget and explained why she was working. I don't know why, but that stuck with me. She was the last one to administer "correction", which I never forgot either.

Our mother impacted our lives in ways we may never understand. I will owe her a lot of apologies when we meet later!

Do you have your "loose ends" cleaned up? Are you "square" for the coming year? Oh, do you realize that we could write a book of "proverbs" for today? I heard our pastor use one Sunday. "It is not the size of the dog in the fight; it is the size of the fight in the dog." I am sure that is probably an old proverb. How many others can you think of Proverbs for today? I would be willing to bet most of them a loose translation of something in the Bible.

We must put "first things first", in that, we first must deal with this past year. If you have never tried keeping a journal, let me stress that right now, - it is a HARD thing. At first, you will not see the need or the importance; it is only at the end of the year, as you reflect, then you will see the benefit.

I use these binders from "Mead", it say's "Five Star" on the front. They are 6x8.5 I think, there is a divider in the middle I use for cards and notes I want to keep, I fill in a page each day. Two notebooks will cover a whole year, six months per notebook. Try it!

> Open your mouth for the speechless, in the cause of all who
> are appointed to die. Open your mouth, judge righteously,
> and plead the cause of the poor and needy. (Proverbs 31:8-9)

Our grandson got his first taste of public speaking recently. He was telling us how "nervous" he was, scared, etc. I remember my first sermon. I had the customary three points and a conclusion. I finished in five minutes.

A friend of mine counseled subtly. "You're repeating yourself". Now when I start doing that I am reminded that I am finished! Public speaking takes "practice," "confidence in your message," and the guidance of God's Holy Spirit!

I learned a valuable lesson in my first church I pastored. I had delivered my message. I was so disappointed that I had not done a very good job, - several mistakes, skipped verses, etc. As I stood at the door and greeted the people as they left I heard these words: "Great sermon pastor!" "Thank you, that was just what I needed." "Your message really moved me, pastor." I am thinking, "Did they hear the same message I heard?"

I have come to realize that God will take our obedient efforts, humble as they may be, and turn them into His message. They will hear what God wants them to hear, not what you voiced! When we preach the Word of God, God will produce the fruit.

Looking forward to the New Year? Do you have any plans for the New Year? I hope they are "subject" to change. God has His plans as well. If you are a child of God, God wants to accomplish certain things in your life. If you are wise, you will be open to God's leadership. It is not that God won't fulfill His will. He will accomplish His will no matter what. The only problem is, if you rebel, you won't be a part of it. Think about that a minute.

At the beginning of next year, put your plans, wants, desires in neutral. "Not my will but Thine be done!" That should be our attitude. Approach the New Year excited about what God is going to do. If you think you might imagine what God is going to do you are woefully inadequate; only God knows what He can do in your life!

Lonny E. Young

> Who can find a virtuous wife? For her worth is far above
> rubies. The heart of her husband safely trusts her; so, he will
> have no lack of gain. (Proverbs 31:10-11)

Lemuel is looking for a "virtuous woman". I wonder if he has ever read the book of Ruth, take a look:

*"And now, my daughter, do not fear. I will do for you all that you request, for all the people of my town know that you are a **virtuous woman**.* (Ruth 3:11)

Naomi instructed Ruth to go and lie at the feet of Boaz, submitting to his authority. Boaz discovered her and sent her back to Naomi with the statement above. There were "procedures" that Boaz had to accomplish before he could marry Ruth.

I have done several marriages as a pastor. One of the things I stressed in a marriage is "commitment". Love is an emotion, subject to change. The biggest thing lacking in marriages today is the sense of commitment between a man and a woman. Commitment will last long after the heated discussions, the disappointments, the frustrations, and disagreements. When you are "committed" to each other, it is a LIFETIME commitment, or should be! Make sure it is right from the beginning.

As we finish up the book of Proverbs with this final chapter, Lemuel speaks a lot about the "virtuous woman", her characteristics, her traits, her "commitment" to her husband. Let me share a verse I quote, along with many other pastors, in their marriage ceremony:

Husbands, love your wives, just as Christ also loved the church and gave Himself for her. (Ephesians 5:25)

Now I skipped the verse about the wives. That is not the point. The "point" is the commitment between the two. We can see that here in Proverbs 31, the "commitment" of the husband is unto death, with Jesus as our example; notice Paul equates it to the church, interesting.

> She does him good and not evil all the days of her life. She seeks wool and flax, and willingly works with her hands. She is like the merchant ships. and brings her food from afar. (Proverbs 31:12-14)

What do these words bring to mind? I remember when I was driving over-the-road and being so far from home. I never worried about what was going on "at home"; when you have a "team", everyone on the same page, the same goals, and the same spirit. I heard a gal in a movie say, "I am looking for a kindred spirit." That is what it is like. Either must care about the other.

I knew when I got home, dinner would be on the table, the kids would be taken care of, and the "home front" was in good hands! It makes it so much easier for the other half of the team.

My wife and I have been married for 51 years. The neat thing is that we knew each other for only 7 months before we were married. It was "right" very early in our courtship. God has blessed us ever since. We didn't become Christians until our fifteenth year of marriage. To this day I don't know how we survived till then. We used to say, "We couldn't afford a divorce." It was because God was working even then, and we didn't know it!

Just like I said yesterday, when we got married it was a "commitment" we made to each other for life. Thick or thin, good or bad, ups and downs we were committed to each other. Even when God called me to the ministry, Mary had her doubts, I can't blame her, but she stuck with me, prayed for me, and God blessed those days!

Tomorrow is the last day of this year. What do you see for the New Year? Of course, you don't know what will happen tomorrow, let alone next week or next year. What I want you to do is look at the coming year with anticipation and excitement. If you're a child of God you will see God do things that will knock your socks off. If you have your "spiritual" eyes open to what God is doing. Of course, if you're not a child of God you will trust the New Year to "providence" or luck. Not a good way to walk into the future.

Take a minute today. Open to Jeremiah 29:11-14. Meditate on the awesome words of these verses. Chew on them a bit. Ask God!

    Lonny E. Young

> She also rises while it is yet night, and provides food for her household, and a portion for her maidservants. She considers a field and buys it; from her profits she plants a vineyard. She girds herself with strength, and strengthens her arms. (Proverbs 31:15-17)

I am not touching these words. The point is every couple brings to the table talents and gifts. It may take years to define their roles, work on it, and find the best solution for YOU! Don't go by your neighbor's suggestions, your parents' example, or some self-help book. Consult the Word of God for direction. The Spirit of God will go a lot further than any secular counsel.

Remember two things: 1. You both made a commitment to each other to work as a team in this thing called marriage. 2. You need to work as a team; both with the same goals, the methods, and the same purpose, to glorify God!

When I did my last few weddings I came across this fantastic analogy. I asked the two participants to imagine there was a string between the two of them, uniting them in wedlock. When the center of that string is raised up, it draws both people closer together. Now, imagine the one lifting up that center is Jesus Christ. The higher Jesus is lifted up the closer He will draw the two parties together. Something to think about!

I hope these studies and our walk through the Proverbs have opened some new perspectives on God's wisdom. I hope our walk together, above all, has opened up God's heart to your heart. The more we can spend time in God's Word the more we get to know God's heart. These Proverbs were written to have a better idea of what God expects from us, to help us have a more blessed life.

Take this challenge. Pray about it of course. I know for a fact you won't be disappointed, begin tomorrow keeping a daily journal, watch for God's hand in your life. You may write something tomorrow that seems disconnected, in a week, you can look back at that entry and see God's plan has brought you to the place you are at now. Don't rely on "memory", write things down; they may seem insignificant at the time but God doesn't do things by accident, He has an awesome plan for your life. With a journal, you will see it unfold! God bless you!

Answer Key:

1. b. Genesis 6	26. d. Revelation 1:20
2. d. Genesis 1:24-31	27. b. Psalm 119 176 verses
3. c. Index	28. c. Acts 9:3
4. c. Genesis 3:20	29. d. Genesis 6:15
5. d. Jonah 1:2	30. a. Daniel 6:16
6. a. Index	31. b. John 11:43-44
7. b. Exodus 19:18-20:17	32. a. Genesis 29:20, 30
8. d. Titles of each	33. c. Genesis 4:8
9. a. Acts 13:9	34. d. John 20:24
10. c. Index	35. b. Acts 9:11
11. c. Malachi 4:6	36. c. 1 Kings 1:28-31
12. c. Index	37. d. Index
13. d. Luke 5	38. a. Zephaniah, Zechariah
14. b. Joshua 6	39. c. Genesis 1:1
15. c. Genesis 19:26	40. b. Exodus 20:11
16. b. Revelation 1:4	41. b & d. Genesis 41:51-52
17. a. Judges 16:18-19	42. c. Genesis 3:21-24
18. d. Acts 13:2	43. c. Genesis 4:25
19. b. Luke 22:48	44. b. Genesis 7:4
20. c. Calvary: Latin Lk 23:23	45. d. Index
Golgatha: Hebrew Matt 27:33	46. a. Revelation 1:9
21. c. Genesis 7:13	47. b. 1 Samuel 10
22. b. Luke 2	48. b. 1 Samuel 17:49
23. c. 1 Kings 1:28-31	49. c. Number 32:13
24. d. Titles of each	50. d. Deuteronomy 1:23-26
25. d. John 19:18	

51. c. Numbers 14:6
52. b. Matthew 27:17
53. d. 1 Samuel 17:40
54. c. Psalm 23
55. b & d. Exodus 20
    Deuteronomy 5
56. a. Matthew 28:19-20
57. b. Mark 16 chapters
58. b. Genesis 41:27
59. a & b. Matthew 17:3
60. d. Matthew 26:15
61. a. Exodus 4:14-15
62. d. Matthew 14:29
63. a. Matthew 5:1-11
64. c. Genesis 25:32-34
65. c. Genesis 29:25
66. d. John 12:12-16
67. b. Matthew 1:17
68. b. Matt. 27:46,
    Luke 23:34, 23:43, 23:46
    John 19:26-27, 19:28, 19:30
69. d. John 13:8
70. c. Exodus 20:12
71. b. Ephesians 6:11
72. a. Galatians 5:22
73. b. Numbers 18:20-21
74. a. 1 Samuel 10
75. d. Exodus 2, Acts 7:23

76. b. Mark 3:17
77. b. 2 Timothy 4:7
78. c & d Luke 2:4
    2 Samuel 5:6-9
79. b. Matthew 9:9
80. c. Hebrews 11
81. b. Genesis 5:27 969 years
82. c. Joshua 14:4
83. c. Genesis 30:19
84. d. 1 Samuel 21:9
85. c. Revelation 5
86. b. custom
87. a. Ezekiel 37:4
88. c. Jonah 1:17
89. d. 3 John 299 words
    2 John 303 words
90. b. John 11:35
91. d. Esther 3:1
92. d. Exodus 7-12

93. d. Exodus 7:14-21
94. c. Esther
95. a. Luke and Acts
96. b. Genesis 5:24
    2 Kings 2:1
97. c. Genesis 11:7
98. d. John 20
99. c. Luke 1:19, 26-27
100. d. Revelation 4:4